TROUBLE IN UTOPIA

SUNY SERIES IN ISRAELI STUDIES
RUSSELL STONE, EDITOR

A publication from the Center for Study and Documentation of Israeli Society, The Hebrew University of Jerusalem

Translated from the Hebrew by Charles Hoffman

TROUBLE *in* UTOPIA

THE OVERBURDENED POLITY OF ISRAEL

Dan Horowitz
Moshe Lissak

State University of New York Press

Published by
State University of New York Press, Albany

Printed in the United States of America

For information, address State University of New York Press, State University Plaza, Albany, N.Y., 12246

Library of Congress Cataloging-in-Publication Data
Horowitz, Dan.
Trouble in Utopia: the overburdened polity of Israel/Dan Horowitz and Moshe Lissak.
p. cm.—(SUNY series in Israel studies)
Bibliography: p.
Includes index.
ISBN 0-7914-0112-X.—ISBN 0-7914-0114-6 (pbk.)
1. Israel—Politics and government. 2. Israel—Ethnic relations. 3. Social conflict—Israel. 4. Jewish-Arab relations—1949- I. Lissak, Moshe, 1928-. II. Title. III. Series.
JQ1825.P3H68 1989 *38-37557*
306′.2′095694—dc19 *CIP*

10 9 8 7 6 5 4 3 2

Contents

Preface

In 1988 Israel celebrated its fortieth anniversary as a sovereign state. A period of four decades seems long enough to provide social scientists with the necessary perspective for a macro-sociological and macro-politological analysis of a functioning polity. Yet, in the case of Israel such an endeavor requires a more cautious approach than in most other cases. Israel is still, in many respects, what it has been for forty years—a society in the making beset by internal and external pressures and haunted by unresolved problems. From the viewpoint of the social scientist, these characteristics of Israeli society are a mixed blessing. On the one hand, multiplicity of problems stimulates research in the social studies. On the other, the volatility of a society in the making renders generalizations concerning its cohesion and stability tentative. Being aware of these limitations, the authors of this book consider it a challenge to attempt a comprehensive reorganization and reinterpretation of much of the available data on Israeli society and politics. We have aimed to place the interpretation within a coherent conceptual framework.

We have already attempted a similar undertaking in our previous study that dealt with the Jewish community in Palestine under the British Mandate and the Jewish community's transition from a community to a state *(Origins of the Israeli Polity: Palestine under the Mandate,* Chicago and London, The University of Chicago Press, 1978). There is, however, a significant difference between the two studies: In the case of the Pre-state Jewish community in Palestine, we dealt with a historical political collectivity which ceased to exist as such with the establishment of the State of Israel; in the case of Israel our analysis relates to a presently existing polity and to ongoing political processes. Consequently, we could not follow the example of our first study. In the present study, we cannot use the social system in its most developed forms as a point of departure for the examination of events and processes. Since we are in the midst of events, we lack a sound retrospective view of the factors which facilitate or hinder the functioning of this system.

In our present study, we had to comply with the absence of a definite point in time that can be considered representative of the system in its "ripe" form and thus serve as a point of departure for analysis. Indeed, the open-ended nature of the developments examined in this book led us to adopt a methodological approach suited to an ongoing, developing system that has not reached the peak of its developments. Therefore, most of our conclusions are tentative and relate to trends that may be considered reversible. The book is written as an interpretive essay. Because of the broad scope of the subject of the book and the large quantity of available data, we avoided presenting these data in detail in the text. We preferred to refer the reader to the variety of sources that are mentioned in the notes.

This book is a translation from the Hebrew. Our work on the Hebrew Manuscript had been completed in December 1987. The following year, 1988, will probably be remembered in Israel as the year of the Intifadah, the Palestinian uprising in the occupied territories of the West Bank and the Gaza strip. The Intifadah shook the foundations of the precarious control system by which the Israeli military and civilian authorities governed these territories from 1967 to 1987. It has become apparent that the measures of control that enabled Israel to maintain her rule in the territories are not effective anymore. The ensuing resort to tougher measures was not more fruitful. Our awareness of the moral, political and economic cost, for Israel, of these developments has almost induced us to extend the scope of the study in order to make it possible to refer to them. We, however, did not yield to such a temptation, mainly because the uprising is an ongoing event whose consequences cannot yet be fully evaluated. Nevertheless, we believe that the information and analysis presented in this book cast light also on the fundamental causes of the 1988 events.

Nineteen eighty-eight was also an election year in Israel. Unlike the Intifadah the elections did not produce a fundamental change in Israeli politics. The only salient change in voters inclinations, the strengthening of the ultra orthodox parties, merely made it more difficult for the two major political blocks to avoid repeating the 1984 pattern and form a broad national coalition.

In the course of our work on this book we were helped by a continuous discourse on Israeli society and politics with colleagues and friends, both at the Hebrew University of Jerusalem and other Israeli Universities. Among them are: Gideon Aran, Gabi Cohen, Shmuel N. Eisenstadt, Emanuel Gutmann, Baruch Knei-Paz, Peter Medding, Nissan Oren and Eli Yoffe. We are particularly thankful to Dr. Baruch Kimmerling with whom we had long and fruitful discussions on issues and ideas related to our work.

We are also thankful to Mr. Charles Hoffman who translated the manuscript from the Hebrew, to Ms. Maya Landau who edited it, to our research assistant Mr. Ofir Bnayahu and to Ms. Morissa Amittai, who patiently typed and retyped the manuscript. Financial aid has been given by the Schanbrun Foundation, the authority for Research and Development of the Hebrew University, and the Leonard Davis Institute for International Relations. We are profoundly grateful to all for their support advice and assistance. Needless to say, full responsibility for any weak points and inaccuracies that had crept into the work falls on the authors alone.

1

Introduction: Israel as a Social Laboratory

The State of Israel: A Threefold Historical Background

The establishment of the State of Israel was a historical turning point for the Jewish People, for the Land of Israel (Eretz Israel), as a territorial entity, and for the Yishuv,—the Jewish community in Mandatory Palestine.

For nearly two millennia the Jews in the Diaspora had lacked a center of political authority and had been vulnerable to discrimination and persecution. Their plight eventually led to a search for a solution to what became known, in both Jewish and European Political discourse, as "the Jewish problem." Various solutions were put forward,[1] among them Zionism—ideologically motivated Jewish immigration to Eretz Israel.[2]

The creation of the State of Israel had a major impact on the Land of Israel as a territorial entity. The partition of Palestine and the exodus of most of the Arabs from what become the State of Israel provided yet another chapter in the turbulent history of this small land, and resulted in a demographic and geographic upheaval that marked out the boundaries of a new "Israeli" collectivity.

It was in this arena of Jewish history that the Jews renewed their connection with the land as the Yishuv emerged in May 1948 as a fully-fledged political community. The social and political character of the Yishuv, a "state in the making" under the Mandate, enabled it to succeed in the armed struggle between Jews and Arabs, and facilitated the transition to statehood.[3]

During the first four decades of Israel's existence, wars and waves of immigration (aliyot) were the major signposts of its development. Apart from the War of Independence, the most important war was the Six Day War of 1967. This war brought about further changes in the state's territorial boundaries and demographic balance, and created a significant gap between Israeli sovereignty and military control.[4]

These three historical entities—the Jewish people, the land of Israel, and the Yishuv—had global significance. Both Zionism and Arab nationalism were stimulated by and modeled on modern European nationalism. The initial intercommunal conflict between Jews and Arabs in Eretz Israel was played out in a region divided into British and French spheres of influence. The emergence of Israel and its neighboring Arab states as autonomous protagonists in their own Middle Eastern conflict resulted from the processes of decolonization after the Second World War. Subsequently, the continuous involvement of the superpowers in the Arab-Israeli conflict derives from the centrality of the Middle East in the global balance of power, stemming from its strategic position and its vast oil reserves. Zionism sought to transform the Jewish people from a passive object of the historical process into an acting subject whose sovereign decisions would influence global developments. This goal has been realized with a vengeance, perhaps more than is warranted for Israel's own good.

These unique historical circumstances have also attracted the attention of social scientists seeking theoretical and comparative lessons from Israel's exceptional social development. Indeed, Israeli society is unique in many respects but its uniqueness is a consequence of a rare combination of features each of which is not necessarily exceptional as such. However, some of these features are more pronounced in Israeli society than in most other societies, thus entailing more significant consequences for its functioning as a collectivity. It is, therefore, the combined effect of marked features that singles out Israel as a case worth studying in macro-sociology and macro-politology. the enumeration of these features provide an appropriate point of departure for the analysis of Israel's social and political system.

Non-Congruence of Territory, Citizenship, and National-Ethnic Identity

Most Jews live outside the State of Israel, while within Israel there is a considerable non-Jewish minority of Palestinian Arabs. For the individual, this creates a problem of identity; for society, that of defining its boundaries. While the establishment of the state resolved some of the issues of collective identity, it retained some of the contradictions of bicommunal Mandatory Palestine. In particular, the identity of the Israeli entity as a state and as an ethno-national community was not fully defined.[5]

"Palestinian citizenship" under the Mandate was described as "nothing but a legal formula devoid of moral meaning."[6] The State of Israel, at least until 1967, was closer than Mandatory Palestine to the model of an integral nation-state insofar as it had a clear-cut Jewish majority (85-90 percent). Still, it had to contend with the problems raised by the symbolic meaning of citizenship as opposed to national-ethnic identity. This problem intensified as a result of the extension of Israeli control after 1967 to territories inhabited by hundreds of thousands of Palestinian Arabs, who in the West Bank were Jordanian citizens, but in the Gaza Strip were stateless. Thus, the problem of collective boundaries and identity links up with the broader Arab-Israeli conflict. Any decision about the ultimate disposition of the territories conquered in 1967 also entails a decision about the definition of an Israeli collective identity and the ethno-political identity of the Palestinian Arabs.

Mandatory Palestine deviated from the ideal type of the nation-state in every conceivable way. First, the country was governed by a foreign power through direct rule, without any representation of the local population. Second, it was in effect a binational entity in which one of the components, the Jewish community, established its own semi-autonomous and legally-recognized network of institutions. third, each of the communities in Mandatory Palestine maintained ethnicnational, religious, and language ties to groups beyond its borders. Each one of these deviations from the model involved problems of identity and definition of boundaries of the collectivity.[7]

The primary loyalty of both the Jewish and the Arab communities was to their own people. But neither of these communities had clearly defined boundaries. For the Jewish community, there was the issue of the degree of involvement of world Jewry in building a national home for the Jewish people in Palestine, a role which was formally recognized by the Mandate given to Britian by the League of Nations.[8]

In the Arab community, the problem of identity was expressed in terms of the concepts of "kawmiya"—pan-Arab nationalist consciousness, as distinct from "wataniya"—particularistic national identity linked to specific Arab countries.[9] In the Arab community under British rule, different groups placed different emphases on the panArab and the Palestinian components of their collective identity.

The partition of Mandatory Palestine and the exodus of most of the Arabs from the area under Jewish rule resulted in a clear-cut Jewish majority in the newly-established State of Israel. The status of the Arab minority remained ambiguous and its connection to the state could at best be expressed through citizenship, but certainly not in national-ethnic terms.

The establishment of the state added a new dimension to the identity of its Arab residents, who, in addition to being Arabs or Palestinians, became Israeli citizens. Israel's Declaration of Independence established the state as a "Jewish state in Eretz Israel," while upholding "full equality of social and political rights to all its citizens irrespective of religion, race or sex."[10] However, for the Arab minority, the ethno-national and citizenship components of Israeli identity were never fully integrated. This is also reflected in their position in the social structure.

The nation-state is a modern concept implying a high degree of congruence and harmony between territory, citizenship and ethno-cultural community.[11] Reality often falls short of this ideal type which is sometimes even further eroded by the existence of ethnic diasporas.[12] Thus, in many cases, ethno-national identity is not coextensive with the legal definition of citizenship. In principle, however, the criteria for citizenship are formally defined and are unrelated to a person's attitudes toward a particular social entity or one's cultural traits. Criteria for ethnic or national membership are vaguer, and are based on primordial factors and/or cultural-historical consciousness.[13] Although the boundaries of ethno-national membership are more difficult to define, in many cases such membership engenders a stronger sense of group solidarity than does citizenship.

In Israel, ethno-national criteria lie at the base of the system of national symbols that express the collectivity's normative commitment to the Jewish people and order the response to the problem of national security anchored in the Arab-Israeli conflict. On its establishment, the State of Israel took over the anthem and the flag from the Zionist movement and adopted the seven-branched candelabrum of Jewish religious tradition as the official symbol of the state,[14] thereby expressing the link to the Jewish people as a historic cultural-national entity. The specific commitment to the Zionist conception that places the immigration and settlement of Jews in Eretz Israel at the center of the Jewish national revival is embodied in the law of Return. This unique law grants privileges to Jews who wish to become Israelis, but confers no privileges on Jewish citizens as against non-Jewish citizens.[15]

At the level of citizenship, the rights of non-Jewish groups to celebrate their holidays and to cease work on their traditional days of rest are guaranteed by law. The adoption of the Arabic language as the second official language of the state is also of symbolic significance.

The most prominent application of ethno-national principles in the sphere of national security is the exemption of all Israeli Arabs (except for the Druze) from compulsory military service.[16] The exemption of Israeli Arabs from the draft is not specified in law, but implemented through the discretionary powers vested in the Minister of Defense.[17]

In contrast, civil rights—the formal equality of all citizens before the law—are defined in terms of citizenship. This fundamental principle of democracy is enunciated in Israel's Declaration of Independence and further elaborated in legislation,[18] as exemplified by universal suffrage in local and national elections even from 1949 to 1966 when most Israeli Arabs lived in areas under military government.

Primordial affiliation has a significant direct impact on public life in Israel through laws governing marriage, divorce, and personal status. These are linked to specific religious communities, but without granting preference to any particular community.[19] As a result, while there is no separation of religion and state, neither is there a state religion.[20]

The territorial component of identity and membership that within the armistice lines of 1949 had been clear-cut became blurred as a result of the Six Day War. After 1967, the population to be included within the territorial boundaries of the collectivity differed according to the criterion used—sovereignty or military control.[21] Moreover, the terms used to define these areas (e.g., "liberated" vs. "occupied" territories) reflected ideological preferences with regard to their ultimate fate: Whether they should remain under ethnonational Jewish control and be formally incorporated into the State of Israel, or whether they should ultimately revert to Arab rule.

The range of affiliations or connections to the Israeli collectivity can be represented by the various patterns created by the elements of citizenship, ethnicity, and territory, some of which reveal only minimal congruence. Maximal congruence is found among Jews who live under Israeli sovereignty and hold only Israeli citizenship. Weaker congruence is found among Israeli emigrants, Diaspora Jews, Arab citizens of Israel, foreign citizens living in Israel, and Jewish permanent residents of Israel who are not citizens.

The post-1967 war events resulted in an extension as well as in an intensification of the problem. The annexation of East Jerusalem and the Golan Heights, and the Israeli settlements in the occupied territories added a new dimension to the problem. There were now in areas under Israeli control several groups whose association with the Israeli collectivity involved legal and political issues: Arab citizens of Jordan and Syria residing in territories where Israeli law applies, such as Jerusalem and the Golan Heights, and Israeli Jewish settlers residing in territories where Israeli law does not apply.

Even the nationality of Jordanian citizens in Judea and Samaria and residents of the Gaza Strip is potentially problematic from the viewpoint of Israeli identity.[22] As long as Judea, Samaria, and the Gaza Strip have the status of occupied territories their populations are not participants in the Israeli identity. However, any change in the existing temporary status of the territories apart from the return to full Arab sovereignty, would raise the problem of the association between their population and Israel.

Lack of congruence between citizenship, ethnicity and territory is not unique to Israel: Very few countries approach the ideal-type of nation-state. However, Israel seems to be unusual in the range of patterns of partial congruence that it presents, involving a multiplicity of communities and diasporas, and vague definitions of religion, ethnicity, and territory.

Ideological Impetus

Prior to independence, the waves of immigration to Palestine were, for the most part, ideologically motivated. Indeed, ideological commitments fueled the separatist tendencies that made the Yishuv a quasi-autonomous society.[23] The revival of Hebrew as a living language which became the cultural common denominator in the Yishuv and in Israel, was inspired by ideology. After the establishment of the State of Israel, Zionist ideology continued to inform some of its fundamental political decisions, the most notable being the decision to facilitate and encourage mass Jewish immigration in the 1950s.[24] Despite the waning influence of ideology in more recent years, its impact is still keenly felt in many important political controversies such as conflict over the ultimate disposition of the territories conquered in the 1967 war.[25]

Overall there remains constant tension between commitment to divergent ideological principles and the possibility of their realization in a rapidly changing social reality. The dominant Zionist ideologies of pre-state colonization in Eretz Israel aspired to a just social order and therefore stressed the goal of social change—the subordination of current needs to future objectives, and preference for collective interests over those of the individual.[26] However, when the bearers of these dynamic ideological tendencies assumed control of the political structures of the state, the preservation of their rule became an end in itself. This, in turn, engendered conservative tendencies inimical to the striving for social change.[27]

Political dominance was a source of material rewards, prestige, and power for members of the ruling elites. Responding to the demands of various groups to meet their immediate needs came at the expense of future-oriented commitments and bred acceptance of the status quo. The gap between ideals and reality was further widened by a political framework that made compromise between parties and movements the prime principle of political alliances.

The erosion of ideological commitment in Israeli society as a whole and within its various political and social movements has several aspects. First, it reflected an incomplete realization of ideology. this is characteristic of attempts to foster revolutionary and utopian ideological commitments under conditions of institutionalization and routinization, and is not peculiar to Zionism or to Israeli society.[28]

In Israel, the absence of a sharp transition from a prerevolutionary to a post-revolutionary situation left a distinctive mark upon the problem of routinization and institutionalization. The social aspect of the Zionist revolution developed gradually with the shaping of a new social order from the waves of immigration. Likewise, the political climax of the Zionist revolution, the conclusion of the British Mandate and the establishment of the State of Israel, was not the beginning of a process of political institutionalization, but the culmination of institution-building that had started earlier.[29]

A second aspect of the erosion of ideology in Israeli society stems from the tension generated by the influence of the general intellectual climate of the "end of ideology." The pragmatic outlook of the new professional and technocratic elites that arose with the state was more compatible with the conception of the "decline of ideology" that marked Western societies in the 1950s and 1960s[30] than with the ideological prescriptions of the veteran movement elites.[31] This gap between them resulted in compromises that at times meant adapting ideology to the need to get things done, or to merely paying lip service to ideology.

rce of the erosion of ideology stems from the fact that sought to provide a broad basis of consensus in Israeli actice offered only a limited common ground on such issues as the shape of the ideal social order, the place of religion in society and the response to the Arab-Jewish conflict. Author Amos Oz clearly grasped this problem when he wrote that "Zionism is a family name, not a proper name," with members of this "family" appearing as Labor Zionism, Religious Zionism, and so forth.[32] Ideology thus became a divisive force in the political system and even a source of polarization, whose disintegrative potential could be blunted only through bargaining that entailed a compromise of principles.

Israeli society therefore provides an excellent example of the dual role of ideology in fostering social mobilization, on the one hand, and triggering political conflict, on the other.

Israel as a New Society

Israel is a "new nation" in terms of its population as well as its institutions. The only common historical connection shared by members of Israeli society is to the cultural and communal traditions of a "people without a land."[33] This clearly sets Israel apart from most, if not all of the new nations that emerged after World War II. Israel does not represent a case of "an old society in a new nation,"[34] but rather of "a new society for an ancient people." The social structure of Israel is therefore not the culmination of historical processes stretching over generations, but the product of recent developments related mainly to the Zionist settlement endeavor. Israel thus differs from most developing countries whose traditional structures served as a source of constraints on modernization.[35]

Nevertheless, Israeli society was not a tabula rasa: It is unique among developing countries in that the diverse social and cultural traditions influencing behavior and values were, for the most part, imported with the immigrants from their countries of origin. Even the common core of Jewish religious observance and belief was overlaid with local or regional variations in lifestyle and behavior.[36]

Many of the immigrants had previously not been exposed to the far-reaching influence of the secularization that accompanied industrialization and political modernization in Europe and the New World. For the most part, Middle Eastern and North African immigrants were not directly affected by secularization, industrialization, and nationalism until they came to Israel.[37] Once there, they had to adapt to a society whose institutions were shaped by elites inspired by these revolutionary processes and who sought to mode Israel as a modern nation-state.

The encounter between the relatively modern institutions and values of the Yishuv and the traditional ways of life of many of the immigrants did not take place on equal terms. The system into which these newcomers were "absorbed," as Israeli terminology put it, was clearly socially and politically dominant.[38] As a result, the immigrants' particularistic traditions had little impact on the development and consolidation of Israeli society that took place rather rapidly in the 1950s and 1960s. Unlike other developing countries in this crucial period, traditional forces hardly restrained modernization in Israel. The institutions of Israeli society could therefore develop synchronically without the troublesome lags that appeared elsewhere in the pace of development of the various spheres such as agriculture, industry, bureaucracy, the military, and the family.

However, when the bearers of traditional ways of life began to break out of their peripheral status in Israeli society and to demand a more central role, their particularistic values began to exert a greater influence on public life.[39] Education was especially influenced by this shift, as ultra-Orthodox approaches gained legitimacy and state financial support and as traditional religious influences penetrated the secular school system.[40] Some manifestations of particularistic religious expressions that were marginal in the 1950s, such as folk medicine and cults of pious religious figures, suddenly became popular.[41]

As in other Western countries, it became apparent in Israel too, that the traditional forces holding back modernization had a higher rate of survival than was thought possible when the foundations were laid for the modern nation-state.[42] Thus Israel, despite the fact that it is a new society, has found that it cannot escape tensions between tradition and modernity, as traditionalist enclaves chip away at the cultural and political patterns that were dominant in the Yishuv and had shaped the emergent institutions of the State of Israel.

A Small Society

Israel is one of the smallest sovereign states in the world. Its population in 1985 came to about four and a quarter million, not including the Arabs in the occupied territories.[43] In area, Israel together with the occupied territories of the West Bank, the Gaza Strip and the Golan Heights comprise 7,391 square miles. The striking disproportion between Israeli's small size and its international prominence is most apparent from the strategic perspective. Militarily, Israel is considered to be the most powerful state in the Middle East,[44] a region of central importance in international affairs, and one fraught with more regional military conflicts than any other since the Second World War.[45] Israel's combat-ready military prowess equals that of certain medium-size powers, and exceeds that of some considerably larger and wealthier states. Moreover, Israel is reported to have either nuclear weapons, or at least real nuclear potential, putting it in an exclusive category of states.[46]

Israel's disproportionate international prominence is also linked to the concern for the Holy Land shared by Jews, Christians, and Moslems. Relations between the latter two faiths and the Jewish people are somewhat problematic. Christianity's ambivalence to the Jews has deep historical and theological roots, while the Moslem world sees Israel as an alien entity in the heart of a predominantly Moslem and Arab region.

The centrality of Israel for diaspora Jewry implicit in Israel's self-definition as a Jewish state, assumes wider significance from the fact that the largest Diaspora communities are located in the United States and the Soviet Union.[47] The prominence of Jews among the elites in Western countries further underlines Israel's importance.

These strategic and cultural factors have also influenced developments within Israel. A major consequence of the disproportion between Israel's size and its international prominence is the great diversity and intensity of its international ties, particularly its economic, political, and security dependence on the United States.[48] Israel's dependence on others has enabled it to mobilize resources for economic development and political support in its conflict with the Arabs.[49] The adaptation of Israel's institutional structure to the country's need for constant exposure to, and ties with, the outside world is manifest in the security and scientific spheres, as well as in culture and entertainment. Israel's disproportionately extensive and highly centralized bureaucracy owes part of its development to its role as an intermediary between Israel's institutions and citizens and various Jewish and other international organizations abroad.

Occasionally, the disproportion between Israel's size and its needs has added to the burdens of an already overburdened system. These burdens have not been borne equally: From the outset some sections of the population have been alienated from Israel's national tasks. For example, the manpower that can be mobilized for security needs does not include Israel's Arab citizens and parts of the orthodox sector. This reduction of effective human resources further increases the disproportion between effective size and of population and overall state's capabilities.

From Diaspora Communities to an Emerging National Center

Israel's existence as a national center alongside Diaspora communities is not the result of migration from the homeland but the reverse. Modern Israel was created by ongoing immigration from the widely scattered Jewish communities of the Diaspora.

Israel perceives the Diaspora as its hinterland, a source of human, economic, political, and moral support. Least problematic is the one-way flow of funds, from the Diaspora to Israel, with the donor enjoying symbolic rewards or political gains in return. These funds have enabled Israel to finance the absorption of mass immigration, economic development, and defense. This capital inflow made it possible for Israel to invest in economic growth, respond to the demands of various pressure groups and at the same time increase the standard of living.[50] It also had a direct political impact in helping to block the emergence of pressures that might have threatened Israel's democratic-pluralistic character.

The political dimension of Israel-Diaspora relations is more problematic and, on occasion, is manifested in conflicts of interest between Israel and Diaspora communities.[51] For example, since the 1970s there have been differences of opinion between Israel and the American Jewish community over the immigration of Jews from the Soviet Union. While Israel has sought to direct all the emigrants to Israel, even to the point of making this a condition of their right to leave the Soviet Union, the American Jewish communal leadership has supported freedom of choice and the provision of aid to all irrespective of their final destination.

Israel's sense of responsibility for Jewish communities living under non-democratic regimes has on occasion come into conflict with its wider diplomatic interests, as was the case with the military regime in Argentina. Likewise, Israel's ties with South Africa, justified in terms of the need to protect the interests of South African Jewry and its ties to Israel, have made it difficult to establish relations with many black African states.[52] On another plane, Israel as a Jewish state was able to represent the Jewish people in claiming reparations from Germany on the legal grounds that it had taken in hundreds of thousands of Holocaust survivors, and brought Nazi war criminals to trial.[53]

The premises of Zionist ideology that negate the Diaspora's status as an autonomous source of Jewish values and its capacity to ensure Jewish existence, and that regard Israel as the national-cultural center of the Jewish people, create problems for the symbolic dimension of Israel-Diaspora relations. However, this issue has waned somewhat over the years with the weakening among Israeli leaders of their advocacy of the doctrine of the "negation of the Diaspora." A feeling of partnership and common destiny between Israel and the Diaspora emerged in the wale of the destruction of the European Jewry in the Holocaust. The course of events expanded the interaction between Israel and the Jewish communities not directly affected by the war, particularly the American Jewry. These ties, formerly maintained mainly by the Zionist organizations, have widened and deepened to encompass organizations previously identified as "non-Zionist." The "negation of the Diaspora" doctrine was further muted by the waning of utopian aspirations and concomitant "normalization," making Israel less attractive to idealistic Western Jewish intellectuals.[54]

The symbolic and demographic dimensions of Israel-Diaspora relations are interrelated. Israel's lack of success in attracting significant immigration from the West has impaired its central symbolic rate. Jews from Western countries who were free to come and live in Israel simply stayed away.[55] To make matters worse, a growing stream of Israeli emigrants began to head for the West, particularly to North America.

Emigration *(yeridah,* literally "going down"—the opposite of *aliyah* or "going up" to Israel) is more problematic for Israeli society than for other societies. Emigration, even more than a lack of immigration, is viewed as undermining the fundamental goals of Zionism, and is striking evidence of its failure.[56] In a besieged Israel, emigration comes close to being regarded as desertion from the front lines. The problem of emigration gained particular prominence in the 1970s and 1980s with the decline in immigration and the rise in the proportion of Israeli-born and educated persons among the emigrants. It peaked in the mid-1980s when the annual number of emigrants exceeded that of immigrants.[57]

Following the drastic decline in the potential for immigration from the countries in Europe and the Middle East where Jewish communities are threatened, Israel began to gather in the remnants of far-flung Jewish communities which had been cut off from the Jewish mainstream for generations. The best-known examples here are those communities whose members have a high degree of physical distinctiveness from other Jews, the Bene Israel from India and the Beta Israel or Falashas from Ethiopia.[58]

Immigration to Israel of Jews from the Diaspora heightened the tensions surrounding the definition and boundaries of individual and collective Jewish identity that derive from attempting to apply traditional Jewish religious law in a non-traditional democratic society. The controversy known as "Who is a Jew?" came into public focus because of the employment, for the purposes of immigrant rights under the Law of Return and in other legislation, of criteria of Jewishness that did not strictly conform to traditional definitions. Amendments to the Law of Return defining Jewishness did not settle the controversy as they raised the question of the validity in Israel of non-Orthodox conversions to Judaism performed abroad.

Israel is not the only society made up of immigrants, nor is it the only country that maintains connections with an ethnically-related Diaspora overseas. Israel's uniqueness is in the interaction between these elements, and in the fact that Israel arose through immigration from its Diaspora communities and not the other way around.

A Party to a Protracted Conflict

Israeli society functions under conditions of protracted external conflict. This conflict has two aspects: The first aspect concerns the national defense posture required in order to meet the strategic threat of all-out war waged by the regular armies of Arab countries and the immediate threats associated with the pursuit of security vis a vis acts of terror and border clashes (defined as "current security"). To meet this dual challenge, Israel has developed various mechanisms requiring the mobilization of considerable resources for national security. To mobilize the manpower necessary to overcome the sharp demographic imbalance between Israel and its potential enemies, Israel has developed a system of military service based on a small professional nucleus, supplemented by men and women doing their three and two years, respectively, of conscript service, and a reserve combat-ready force of men serving until the age of 55.[59] The economic burden imposed by the conflict requires the allocation of a defense budget which is among the highest in the world per capita, (covered partly by taxes and partly by American aid).[60] In addition, Israel has also developed the largest military-industrial complex in the world in relation to population and

GNP.[61] The threats posed by current security problems have made a considerable impact on Israeli society. Israel was induced to introduce restrictions on civil rights such as the military government imposed in Arab areas until 1966 and take measures such as the emergency regulations that permit administrative detention and limitations on freedom of movement within Israel or in leaving the country.

The second aspect of the conflict is rooted in the political-ideological challenge to Israeli society posed by the confrontation between Zionism, the Jewish national movement, and the Palestinian Arab national movement supported by the entire Arab world.

From this challenge stem the problems of delineating the territorial limits on Zionist ideological aspirations, protecting Israel's international legitimacy, and regulating Arab-Jewish relations within the state of Israel proper as well as in the territories occupied in 1967.

With regard to the first aspect of Israel's involvement in a protracted external conflict, there is a firm consensus, at least within the Jewish population, that this conflict poses a potential threat to Israel's very existence. This accounts for the willingness to accept a high level of mobilization of resources for national defense and the acceptance of the burden imposed by the sacrifices demanded by frequent wars. This also accounts for the legitimacy accorded in Israel to limited military actions initiated during periods of "neither war nor peace" such as reprisal raids or the bombings of the Iraqi atomic reactor in Baghdad and the PLO headquarters in Tunis.

On the other hand, the question of Israel's response to the political-ideological challenge posed by the Arab-Israeli conflict has aroused considerable controversy. This controversy has several foci. The first concerns the recognition of Palestinian national rights, and the need to reach a compromise on this issue. Does the Jewish people have an exclusive right to "the Land of Israel," or is this a confrontation between two national movements, each with its own subjective conceptions of rights? Second, what is more important from the perspective of Zionist aspirations, the territorial integrity of Eretz Israel or assuring the overwhelmingly Jewish character of the population of the State of Israel? The positions taken on these two issues lead to differing conceptions of the nature of the Israeli-Arab conflict. Is this primarily a conflict between states, as it was perceived during the period between the signing of the cease-fire agreements in 1949 and the Six Day War of 1967,[62] or is it primarily a conflict between national communities, as it was perceived during the period of the Yishuv and as perceived by the proponents of Greater Israel since 1967? Living with the awareness of an external threat is not unique to Israel, but the sense of acuteness of the threat and its persistence is a characteristic of Israeli society. In these circumstances the conflict is perceived not only as a threat to Israel's existence, but also as a danger that can impinge on everyday life through acts of terror or by the possibility of another round of all-out war that could break out at any time.

Democracy under Pressure

Israel is a democratic society subject to severe pressures due to demographic changes, a protracted external conflict, and deep social and political cleavages. What sets Israel apart from the vast majority of the new states established after World War II is that it has maintained a multi-party democratic regime during its entire existence. Israel also differs from most democratic states in the range and magnitude of the pressures exerted on its political system resulting from a rare combination of rapid demographic expansion through immigration during its early years, a prolonged external conflict marked by several major wars, and a multiplicity of deep social and political cleavages.

The massive defense demands and the needs which arose from mass immigration have required the allocation of extensive resources to collective tasks placing Israel's democratic system under heavy cross-pressures. These collective burdens are augmented by the particularistic demands of groups, a common characteristic of democratic societies. Defense, immigrant absorption, and social welfare thus compete for the same reservoir of resources. Moreover, many of the newcomers who arrived during the mass immigration had no previous experience with democratic society, and were not acquainted with the dominant political culture of the Yishuv that had shaped the institutions and rules of the game in the new state.

Persistent involvement in an external conflict poses dangers to a democracy beyond the need to allocate large amounts of resources to security. Constant awareness of the external threat have helped push the military and defense establishment into a position of centrality, in terms of the share of the population directly and indirectly involved in the defense effort and the special status of the defense establishment in shaping national policy in spheres other than those concerned directly with security. Such a permeation of civilian spheres by defense activity and considerations poses a danger of what Harold Lasswell called a "garrison state," or a government controlled by "experts in violence."[63]

Even if such danger is averted, as it has been in Israel, and such a regime does not emerge, the security sphere may, nevertheless, become preponderantly influential, even without direct control, through manipulation of the civilian decision-making system. To guard against this, the patterns of civilian control of the military characteristic of democratic regimes at peace are insufficient; Israel needed special formal and informal arrangements to balance democracy and national security.[64] Thus is developed a unique model of political-military relationships, that of "a nation in arms." The partial militarization of the civilian sphere—caused by the role-expansion of the military—is balanced by a partial "civilianization" of the defense sphere, arising particularly from its penetration by an extensive system of army reserve duty, and the linking of civilian and military elites in common social networks.[65]

The capacity of Israeli democracy to withstand economic, political, and military pressures has depended, to a large extent, on social solidarity and a broad political consensus, no easy task in a society riven, since its inception, by salient national, ethnic, religious, socio-economic, and ideological cleavages. These five sources of cleavage have weakened social solidarity by generating internal conflicts, some of which are intensified by being mutually reinforcing, as in the cases of the ethnic and socio-economic cleavages, and the religious and ideological cleavages. The fundamental national cleavage between Jew and Arab maintains constant potential for intense conflict.

Social conflicts and the frustrations of marginal groups have impeded the functioning of Israeli democracy to the point of exposing it to the danger of "ungovernability,"[66] making it difficult for the system to mobilize material resources and collective normative commitments. Varied mechanisms have been employed to cope with these conflicts. The conflict arising from the overlap of ethnic resentment and socio-economic inequality has been dealt with by allocating material resources through the public welfare and educational systems. This provided a minimal standard of living for the lowest strata and slowed growth of inequality that would have resulted from the free play of market forces without bringing about any basic change in social stratification.[67]

The severe conflict potential of the secular-religious cleavage has been dealt with by accepting the principle of sub-cultural autonomy for both the modern Orthodox and the ultra-Orthodox camps. Similar to European "consociationalism," the system of "sub-cultural autonomy" granted group access to state resources.[68] This has been utilized in particular to create and maintain a state religious school system for the modern Orthodox, and independent school system for the ultra-Orthodox and other religious educational institutions for children, youths, and adults. The particularistic needs of the religious communities have also been met by the exemption of religious women and yeshiva students from military service.[69]

The ideological cleavages have been handled mainly by bargaining and compromise:[70] cooperation between political parties in government coalitions; deferring the resolution of divisive fundamental questions such as that of the constitution in the 1950s, and of the ultimate status of the administered territories since 1967; and the adoption of ambiguous or vague legal definitions in various laws, as occurred in the case of "Who is a Jew?"

The Jewish-Arab cleavage and conflict has been handled mainly by the development of mechanisms for the control and manipulation of Israeli Arabs, the most direct of which was military government. After its abolition in 1966, control mechanisms became more subtle resting mainly on the internal security services. Mechanisms of direct control were again resorted to after 1967 with the establishment of military government in the West Bank and the Gaza Strip.[71]

The Israeli political system is not the only democratic polity that has encountered difficulties in functioning while having to balance the effects of internal and external pressures. But it may be exceptional among democracies in the variety of sources of conflict in the system and in the intensity of tensions with which the system has had to cope.

The Conceptual Framework and Major Issues

The characteristics of Israeli society and the course of its development from ideological movement to community and from community to state, has attracted the attention of historians and social scientists. This interest accounts, in part, for the large number of studies on Israel—out of all proportion to its physical dimensions and population size. This also explains the use, on occasion, of the term "social laboratory" to describe Israeli society or the society of the Yishuv that preceded it.[72]

This phrase, which appears both in ideological tracts and academic treatises, and which is metaphorical in any case, should nevertheless be subject to certain qualifications. Experiments in a laboratory are controlled and directed while social innovations are regarded as experiments only in retrospect. Nevertheless, this metaphor is apt in several respects. The complexity and intensiveness of Israeli society has turned it into an attractive field of research for social scientists. Moreover, Israel is still characterized by a concentration of varied social phenomena in a small space, and by a large number of events stimulating social change within relatively short spans of time. Israel's small dimensions permit these phenomena to be studied without excessive investment of research efforts or resources. Indeed, the more a society resembles a community, the easier it is, at least from a communications perspective, to study it using a quasi-anthropological approach based upon participant observation. this is especially true for the social networks of the elites which occupy the social and political center. These may be studied with the aid of "tacit knowledge" in addition to the usual kinds of data, whether archival or statistical.

The special characteristics of Israeli society do not only lend themselves to a variety of research methods but also facilitate the formulation of central questions that are relevant to the macro-sociological and macro-political study of society as a distinct collectivity. These characteristics, as we recall, are that Israel is a small and new society; that it arose out of an ideological movement that stimulated migration from a Diaspora to an emerging national center; that it maintains a weak congruence between territory, citizenship, and ethnic-national identity; that its functioning is influenced by its involvement in a protracted external conflict; and that its democracy operates under the pressure of tensions generated by social ideological cleavages and by an imbalance between collective goals and available resources. These characteristics define the major problems of Israeli society, and provide our point of departure for examining the events and processes which have shaped it. A major question worthy of examination in the context of Israeli society is the degree of social cohesion and functional efficacy of a national collectivity whose boundaries are ambiguously defined and whose social and political institutions are overburdened with tasks and crosspressures. A number of topics derive from this question all of which merit thorough attention.

The first topic concerns the integrative and disintegrative processes operating in Israeli society under conditions of social and political pluralism which is rooted in multiple social cleavages laden with tensions. These processes are also related to the structure of elites and their role in shaping the consciousness of both social group affiliations and the national collective identity. This issue is discussed in chapter 2.

The second topic deals with the role of ideology and the characteristics of political culture in Israeli society. Ideology and political culture influence the commitments and loyalties of the various groups in Israeli society. These commitments and loyalties focus on the Israeli collectivity as such and also on particularistic entities such as national or ethnic communities, classes, ideological movements, and political parties. Chapter 3 deals with ideology as a both unifying and dividing factor in a political culture shaped by the genesis of Israeli society as an ideological movement.

The third topic deals with the rules of the game facilitating the fulfillment of the political system's functions of resource mobilization and conflict regulation. The rules of the game determine the extent to which Israel as a democratic polity is governable; or, in other words, the extent to which the over-burdened political institutions can deal with external pressures and internal conflicts without losing their ability to function. These matters are dealt with in chapter 4.

The fourth topic deals with Israel's involvement in a protracted external conflict, its strategic response to this threat to its security and the influence of this response on Israeli society as a democracy. Chapter 5 focuses on these security-related issues.

The impact of the transition from the Yishuv to the state, social and ideological cleavages, political culture, patterns of conflict regulation, and the involvement in a protracted conflict on the social cohesion of the Israeli collectivity and on the functional capacity of its institutions are examined in chapter 6. This chapter, which summarizes the arguments in the book examines not only past developments but also the major trends apparent at the end of Israel's fourth decade. Since the latter developments are still in flux, this chapter also discusses several alternative paths for Israeli society that could emerge from these trends.

These issues and questions may be examined in two ways that are not necessarily mutually exclusive. They may be dealt with in the manner of those historians who examine events and processes as unique phenomena. They may also be dealt with by social scientists who define, describe, and analyze basic structures and processes in the light of theoretical issues. This approach requires analytical concepts to help bridge the gap between the historical treatment of unique phenomena and the generalizing and comparative tendencies of social science. Hence the reliance on conceptual frameworks to introduce order into this type of inquiry. These frameworks do not, as such, constitute comprehensive theories that enable the researcher to predict or even to provide a complete explanation for social phenomena. However, conceptual frameworks are usually anchored in theoretical approaches whose underlying assumptions do not have to be made explicit as long as a particular conceptual framework serves only as a set of coordinates for mapping social phenomena.

Center and Periphery

The selection of a conceptual framework for the purpose of analyzing a particular society is naturally influenced by the unique characteristics of that society. Thus, for example, a conceptual framework that assumes an identity between the boundaries of a collectivity and the boundaries of a sovereign state would not be appropriate for analyzing the transition between the Yishuv and the State of Israel, nor for analyzing the boundary problems of Israeli society after the Six Day War of 1967 which created a gap between the boundaries of political sovereignty and physical control.[73] The approach that views the boundaries of a society as co-extensive with the boundaries of a nationstate, employed in many macro-political studies, would be appropriate for Israel during the period of 1949 to 1967 but, even then, only with serious qualifications. In order to study the changes that have occurred in Israeli society, we require a conceptual framework that permits a flexible definition of the boundaries of a given social system for various analytical purposes. For example, there may be groups with a partial attachment to a society placing them outside society according to one definition of its boundaries and inside it according to another definition.[74] In other words, we require a conceptual framework based not on rigid criteria for societal boundaries such as citizenship or territory, but rather based on the flexible notion of differential attachments of various groups to a society.

The concepts of center and periphery, taken from the model used by Edward Shils to analyze the development of new societies, meet this requirement.[75] These concepts permit the researcher to examine various groups' relations to the collectivity of the Yishuv and to the Israeli collectivity, since the concept of "center" entails political, institutional, and normative-cultural dimensions. The "center of society" is not necessarily co-extensive with the government of a given state since the center's sphere of attraction is not necessarily contained in the formal definition of governmental authority over a given population or territory. Moreover, the concept of center implies that the government is not necessarily viewed as the sole center of legitimate authority. It is clear that a concept of a political and cultural center that is not identical with the formal structure of government is more ambiguous than the formal definitions of political institutions and roles in a sovereign state. Since this concept of center is not grounded in any sort of constitutional framework, it tends to resemble concepts such as the "establishment" or the "elite," which also lack clear-cut definitions. The significance of the center thus entails both institutional and normative dimensions. The center performs inspirational and representative functions, interprets and creates values, and serves as a locus of authority that rests on formal and informal sources of legitimacy among the collectivity that is attached to it and attests its loyalty to that center.

The second component of the center-periphery concept also requires some clarification. The periphery includes those sectors of society that are subject to the authority of the center, whether voluntarily or not, but have no active role in shaping the cultural and political contours of society. The concepts of center and periphery, in their basic sense, are not sufficient for analyzing complex social and political phenomena. This macro-structural concept does not provide an adequate guide to a complex society, particularly one containing many cleavages and subject to intensive processes of social change. The main shortcoming of this concept lies in the assumption that authority and enterprise in society are the exclusive province of a narrow elite identified with "the center," with the rest of society assuming a passive posture. Rejecting this elitist assumption requires us to abandon the simplistic model of center-periphery and to adopt a more sophisticated one in its place. The first modification required is to introduce the concept of sub-centers or secondary centers oriented to a societal center, but partially autonomous.[76] These secondary centers can act as partners in a national coalitionary center, or can act as partial sources of authority for groups emerging in the periphery. It is also possible that a counter-elite may crystallize around a secondary center with the aim of taking control of the national center or seceding from it (for instance, in the case of an ethnic or linguistic minority community seeking to attain sovereignty). Moreover, sectors, groups and individuals can be included in the sphere of influence of several secondary centers that may cooperate with one another. Groups can also maintain attachments to external centers outside the boundaries of their society (for instance, to motherlands exerting an influence on their diaspora communities, transnational centers such as churches, or ideological movements such as Communism.)[77]

The second modification required in the basic center-periphery model relates to the differential attachments of sectors, groups, and individuals to the center. These elements should not be seen as identical in terms of their participation in cultural and political activity or in their acceptance of the authority of the center. Viewed from this perspective, different definitions of membership in society may be distinguished. Certain peripheral groups, therefore, such as diasporas or populations of occupied territories may in certain circumstances be considered part of the social system while in others they could be considered as external to it. The boundary between center and periphery is also ambiguous. Roles and institutions may, for certain purposes, be viewed as part of the center and for others may be viewed as outside the center. For example, the elites that run the system of mass communications may in certain contexts be included in the center, while in other contexts they may serve to articulate the views of the periphery vis a vis the center as representatives of secondary centers.

The third modification in the center-periphery model concerns the distinction between two aspects of the relationship between the center and groups and sectors in the periphery. The first aspect refers to the allocative function of the center, as the entity that determines "the authoritative allocation of values in society."[78] The second aspect refers to the center's function of mobilizing commitment and resources in order to realize society's collective goals.[79] In other words, the first aspect is related to the differential regulation of the needs of groups and individuals while the second aspect concerns what social scientists refer to as social and political participation.[80]

From the foregoing discussion it is clear that the difference between the original model of center-periphery and the revised model is that the latter deals with central and peripheral qualities along a continuum, rather than with center and periphery as dichotomic entities. The revised model which recognizes the vague boundaries of the center and the differential involvement of the periphery, can also be expressed in terms of the concept of "field of authority."[81] This concept refers to a center's sphere of instrumental attraction and/or charismatic inspiration. Subject to such attraction or inspiration are those groups that need its services or feel loyalty toward it to one degree or another. In cases where groups have attachments to more than one center, we may speak of partial overlapping of fields of authority, as in the case of a diaspora community that maintains an attachment to a center outside the society in which it lives. Overlapping fields of authority usually occur as a result of attachments formed to external social and political systems. However, in non-sovereign political systems where a distinction exists between communal authority and sovereign authority, as in a colonial regime, the entire system is located within overlapping authority fields. There are also situations where a national center either delegates authority to secondary centers or permits a high degree of autonomy on their part. In these situations, the central authority field will exist alongside secondary authority fields which comprise social enclaves subject to the prevailing influence of the secondary centers. Such situations occur in deeply divided multi-communal societies in which the primary loyalties of members of a community are focused on the communal secondary center and not on the common center of formal sovereignty. On the other hand, in societies with a consociational structure, subcultures enjoy only limited autonomy and recognize the supremacy of their common center, which is usually coalitionary. Under these conditions, the enclaves or authority fields of the secondary centers will be limited in the scope and nature of their authority.

The concepts which distinguish between sectors and groups on the basis of the extent of their central or peripheral characteristics, are appropriate not only for analyzing the boundaries of the collectivity and the concentration and dispersion of authority within it, but also for studying integrative and disintegrative processes in society. Such an analysis does not focus on mapping the field of authority at any given moment, but rather on the dynamic processes of change in the relation of secondary centers and groups to their common center. In other words, a secondary center may change its position on the center-periphery continuum in relation to other secondary centers. We may thus distinguish between centrifugal movements that weaken the instrumental or normative attachment to the common center, and centripetal movements that strengthen these connections.[82] Since the central or peripheral characteristics of secondary centers are expressed in two dimensions—in relation to either the allocative or commitment mobilizing functions of the center—shifts in a secondary center's position may also occur in several patterns. The secondary center may move either toward the common center or away from it in both dimensions simultaneously. Thus, the demands of the secondary center from the common center may either increase or decrease , and the willingness of the secondary center to respond to the common center's call to identify with and participate in the collective effort may also increase or decrease.

It is also possible for changes in only one of these dimensions to occur. For example, a change in the extent to which the secondary center makes claims on the resources of the common center, may either increase or decrease the overall burden of demands for resources on the common center, depending on the direction of change. On the other hand, a change in a secondary center's commitment to the common center and it willingness to be mobilized for collective goals, will either enhance or detract from the authority of the common center and either increase or decrease its ability to mobilize resources from secondary centers and the periphery, thus affecting the common center's overall capacity for maximum utilization of society's resources. In extreme cases, opposing trends in these two dimensions may occur thereby intensifying the effect on the common center. Changes in orientations to the social and political center on the part of the secondary centers representing groups and sectors thus influence the overall burdens assumed by the common center. If too many demands are imposed on the allocative functions of a center whose mobilizing function has been weakened, it may become over-burdened; while the opposite trend will enhance its capabilities and provide more room for maneuver and open up new options, without having to resort to coercive political measures. The latter situation usually promotes social cohesion, whereas an over-burdened center poses a threat to it. An over-burdened center tends to create problems in the functioning of the social system. These difficulties are reflected in the impaired ability of the center to deal with the consequences of social change or with conflicts between the needs of the entire system and the interests of various sub-systems. An imbalance between the allocative and mobilizing dimensions will thus harm the effectiveness of the political system. In societies afflicted with an extreme degree of instability, this imbalance may even lead to the disintegration of the center, thereby creating a revolutionary situation or widespread anomie.

The Impact of Social Cleavages

The conceptual framework of a common center, secondary centers, and periphery deals with the dispersion of authority and charisma among the various groups and sectors in society. However, it cannot explain the lines of social division that shape these groups and sectors. These social contours or lines of division may be relevant to questions of distance from the center, but they also relate to society's stratification structure and its components such as class and status groups which are not necessarily identical with the center-periphery axis. The strata hierarchy and the center-periphery continuum represent two different points of departure for examining the impact of social cleavages on the functioning of the social system. The mapping of social groups according to their position in the status structure refers to the differential allocation of social rewards: economic rewards (class), prestige awards (status groups), and power rewards (position on the center-periphery axis).[83] There are two aspects to the center-periphery continuum, one which represents the dispersion or concentration of authority and influence in society, and the other which represents the extent of participation and social involvement. These two dimensions of social inequality are only partially related, so that one may not be reduced to the other. In pre-modern societies, with less differentiation between ownership of property, social status, and political power, the relation between these two dimensions is much closer than it is in modern societies. For example, it is possible in modern society for low status groups in respect of property, income, and prestige to have a dominant voice in public affairs as reflected in the concept of populism. Another point of departure for analyzing social divisions, also not necessarily co-extensive with the center-periphery axis, is division according to belief systems and ideologies. It is possible, as in the case of consociational societies, that membership in classes, status groups, religious communities, ethnic or linguistic groups, or ideological movements will be expressed in a dominant attachment to a secondary center such as a trade union, a church, or a political party.

Two sets of concepts deal with the division of society into groups, one related to the concept of social cleavages and the other related to the concept of social pluralism. These two concepts are, to a certain extent, interchangeable. Nevertheless, the usage of each of these terms in different countries to reflect different aspects of social divisions is still justified, since this follows the meaning originally attached to these concepts by certain social scientists.[84] The term pluralism was originally used to analyze social divisions based on ethnic, religious or linguistic membership, and not social class or ideological groupings. On the other hand, the term cleavage refers, as does pluralism, not only to primordial lines of division, but also to ideological and class or status divisions. Social classes are of course more amorphous than primordial or cultural groups, and in modern society they are also more open from the perspective of social mobility, but they cannot be ignored where such social divisions exist. This also applies to voluntary membership groups such as political movements and parties that reflect ideological cleavages which are a major source of tension and conflict. The analysis of social cleavages therefore must refer to the entire range of factors dividing society into groups and sectors.

The concept of social cleavage refers to the broader parameters of social divisions, and not necessarily to the lines of division between specific groups. This distinction is important when there are a number of groups along a certain continuum, as in the case of political parties aligned on a left-right continuum or of social classes aligned on a stratum hierarchy. In these cases too, we will refer to "class cleavages" or "ideological cleavages," even though sometimes it is clear that we are referring to a number of cleavages based on single broad parameter.

Two sets of distinction have to be made in the mapping of social cleavages; between overlapping and crosscutting cleavages,[85] and between dichotomous and non-dichotomous cleavages.[86] The distinction between overlapping and crosscutting cleavages refers to the relationship between different parameters of social divisions. Modern societies are usually characterized by partially overlapping cleavages expressed statistically by correlations showing a partial association between membership in two or more cleavage groupings. On the other hand, the distinction between dichotomous and non-dichotomous cleavages refers to divisions within one basic parameter. The question here is whether the divisions along this continuum refer to just two groups or to more than two groups. The set of concepts related to social cleavages facilitates the mapping of social structure in terms of the relations between the various cleavages and the divisions along specific lines of cleavage.

In order to analyze the impact of social divisions on the extent of separateness or interconnectedness between groups we shall employ the set of concepts associated with the term social pluralism. The scholars who developed these concepts distinguished between institutional pluralism, cultural pluralism, and social pluralism.[87] It should be noted that these concepts refer to the interrelationships between various groups along one line of cleavage, such as members of various religious or ethnic groups. The distinction between institutional pluralism and the other two types is most important: Institutional pluralism is characterized by the co-existence of separate groups within the same system that are either antagonistic or estranged from one another. Moreover, institutional pluralism usually means that the contacts between the groups are regulated by norms and sanctions enforced by formal legal means. To describe those instances where the clear-cut separation of groups is regulated by norms lacking formal legal status, we employ the term "quasi-institutional pluralism."

Cultural pluralism is reflected in differences in lifestyles or ways of life, including differences of language or accent. This concept can also reflect differences between ethnic groups or differences in patterns of socialization that are found, for example, between religious and secular groups. Social pluralism refers to more subtle differences between status groups usually related to the stratification cleavage. The distinction between social and cultural pluralism can be vague at times because social pluralism is also characterized by differences in lifestyles and behavioral codes. Social pluralism, however, is usually characterized by the restriction of group interrelations to secondary-instrumental contacts, as opposed to intimate personal relations. Still, such differences also appear in cultural pluralism. It seems, however, that the differences between social and cultural pluralism result from the differentiation that has occurred in modern societies between strata divisions and subcultural divisions. In pre-modern societies and those characterized by little or no social mobility, the two types of pluralism overlap to a large extent.

The nature of pluralism in a given society and the extent to which the cleavages provide a base for political mobilization are determined by the degree to which intergroup relations are ideologically articulated. The concept of ideology employed here is broad, and refers to a belief system linked to organized social action. Ideology is composed of three components: cognitive, normative, and prescriptive. In other words, an ideology contains a cognitive perception of the social or natural order, a normative evaluation of social phenomena, and prescribes what should be done to change or maintain that social order. This broad concept of ideology also entails a distinction between the fundamental and operative levels of discourse. The fundamental level contains basic positions and beliefs concerning the social and political order, while the operative level contains policies to be applied in a given time and place.[88] We may also distinguish between the substantive dimension of ideology, which refers to ideological issues arising in concrete historical settings, and the dimension of basic orientations of a more universal nature.[89] The first dimension refers mainly to positions concerning the allocation of social resources, type of regime, civil rights, religion and state, the boundaries of the national collectivity, and its relations to other national collectivities. The second dimension includes basic orientations to time, the relation between man and nature, and between the individual and society. These basic orientations usually emerge on the fundamental level of ideology, but the fundamental level also determines the normative assumption to which the substantive positions are anchored. The substantive positions can also include evaluations and prescriptions of an operative nature.

The Political Regulation of Social Conflict

The impact of the tensions originating in social and ideological cleavages on social cohesion is determined to a large extent by the regulative capacity of the political system. The political system mobilizes and allocates resources and commitments and regulates social conflicts.[90] The political regulating frameworks are parties, pressure or interest groups, and ideological movements that are not full-fledged parties. Politics conducted by institutionalized parties in a democratic system are called "party politics" or "parliamentary politics." Politics conducted by organizations representing organized interest groups which are not parties, particularly in the economic sphere, are referred to as "corporatist politics."[91] Politics conducted by ideological movements that are not parties are defined as "movement politics" and are usually extraparliamentary. The latter term is used here in a neutral sense without the connotation often attached that implies conduct violating the democratic rules of the game.

Another set of concepts relates to the forms of political regulation in democratic regimes. A distinction can be made between two basically different patters of political regulation: one based on majority rule in which there is a clear distinction between the government, which is politically homogeneous, and the opposition, which provides an alternative ruling group; and the other based on bargaining and compromise in the framework of coalitionary arrangements as exemplified by the consociational model which allows considerable autonomy to subcultures. In this model, social enclaves tend to form around movements which acts a secondary centers that mobilize and allocate resources and commitments, receiving continuity through socialization and indoctrination.

The effectiveness of the political mechanisms of conflict regulation and resource allocation are determined mainly by the load placed on the political system. The load or burden borne by the system is an outcome of the balance between collective goals and group demands on the one hand, and available resources, on the other. A polity overburdened with goals and demands tends to become ungovernable.

However, the proper functioning of the system can be maintained by mobilizing the resources and commitments required to meet the needs determined by the collective goals and group demands. Group demands can be instrumental, and can therefore be satisfied by the allocation of material resources. However, these demands can also be normative, demanding fundamental decisions concerning the nature of society and its central symbols. Contradictory demands of a normative nature imposed on the political system can undermine the basis of political legitimacy.

A factor making for an over-burdened polity—as a result of an imbalance between group demands, collective goals and available resources—is involvement in a protracted external conflict. In this context the question arises as to the ability of the democratic regime to handle the tensions arising between a highly-developed military and the institutions of civilian government. Two of the factors that determine the relations between these two systems are the extent to which the boundaries between the military and civilian sectors are permeable and the scope of their interrelations. The conceptual refinement required to examine this issue is based on distinctions between permeable and integral boundaries, with fragmented boundaries serving as an intermediate category.[92] Fragmented boundaries allow for permeable boundaries in certain areas of a system and integral boundaries in others. A typical case of fragmented boundaries between the military and civilian sectors is provided by a convergence between the civilian and military sectors which characterizes what has come to be known as the "nation in arms" model.[93] This is in contrast to the "garrison state"[94] in which there is a tendency to separate, in the normative and institutional sense, the military and civilian sectors and the elites that control them, thus creating more integral boundaries. However, in the "garrison state" model we find another important aspect of the relation between the military and civilian sectors, entailed in the concept of role expansion.[95] This describes the tendency of the military to broaden the areas of its activity beyond strictly military roles. Such tendencies are less pronounced in the case of the "nation in arms" where role expansion is often countervailed by political civilianization of the military.

Culture, Class, and Polity

In this chapter we have described the main characteristics of Israeli society. Central questions about Israeli society have been raised and an outline of a conceptual framework has been presented in which the case of Israel may be understood in a comparative perspective, even though this particular task is not undertaken in this book. The sets of generalizing concepts that form the conceptual framework contain several theoretical assumptions that are not always detailed or explicit. A central assumption relating to problems of collective identity and the boundaries of the collectivity, and to the ideological dimension of social divisions, posits the autonomy of the cultural factor. Theoretical approaches that offer reductionist explanations of cultural factors, viewing them as reflections of economic or even political factors, can explain neither the primordial components of collective identity nor the power of ideology as a motivational force in social movements.[96] However, our conceptual framework is not based on the opposite assumption that views economic and political phenomena as derivations of cultural factors. Our conceptual framework assumes only that in a situation where a new collectivity is in the process of formation,the emergence or existence of common cultural ties must precede the creation of political institutions, which, in turn, is subject to constraints imposed largely by economic factors. These assumptions also permit the autonomous development of the political sphere and of power which serves as the medium of exchange in this area.[97] For example, the relation of the Arab population in the occupied territories to Israel is based on the exercise of military and political power and not on a consensus based on a sense of common primordial identity. Another area where the partial autonomy of political power holds concerns the activity of elites. Among the various institutional elites, and especially the political elite, considerations based on bureaucratic cliques and personal power play a considerable role. Nevertheless, this area of activity often evades conceptual analysis, and the only reasonably valid generalizations about it concern rules of the game and styles of leadership and management.[98] Class interests rooted in economic factors can of course play an autonomous role in social mobilization, but in contrast to Marxist assumptions, there can be societies, periods or situations where this factor plays a secondary role. However, even under such conditions, economic motivations can reinforce the cultural or political factors that stimulate people to engage in organized social activity. Access to economic resources can therefore influence the outcome of social and political conflicts.

Another assumption entailed in our conceptual framework concerns the importance of consensus for determining the boundaries of the collectivity and for explaining the extent to which particularistic identities based on social cleavages are ideologically articulated. This assumption is related to another which maintains that the level of social cohesion is an appropriate point of departure for macro-social or macropolitical analysis. Social cohesion does not necessarily imply social homogeneity or harmony or absence of social tensions. Cohesion can at times be achieved through the effective regulation of conflicts. Moreover, the decision to focus on social cohesion and on processes of social integration and disintegration as a point of departure for this analysis does not imply a value preference for cohesion over lack of cohesion, or for stability over change. The preference in this case is methodological and not ideological.[99]

The definition of the characteristics of Israeli society, the identification of its central problems and the elaboration of a conceptual framework based on certain theoretical assumptions has thus prepared us for an analysis of the varied social phenomena and historical changes that have made Israel into a veritable "social laboratory" and a fascinating field for research.

2

Israel as a Multi-Cleavage Society

Social Cleavages and Social Cohesion

The establishment of the State of Israel did not reduce the extent of the social cleavages that had divided the Yishuv. On the contrary, in the transition from the Yishuv to the state, another line of division was added that had previously been external to the Yishuv—the Jewish-Arab cleavage. Other prevailing cleavages deepened or at least became more salient. For example, the religious-secular cleavage became more salient because of the need to formalize the status of religion in the state. Likewise, the importance of the ethnic cleavage heightened due to the increase in percentage of Jews of Middle Eastern and North African origin in the population brought about by the mass immigration of the 1950s. The salience of the ethnic cleavage also increased because of the high correlation that emerged between it and the fourth line of cleavage within Israeli society—status and class divisions. The fifth source of cleavage, ideological divisions, was carried over from the Yishuv and continued to generate political party divisions in the state, although some of the sharper expressions of party conflict were dulled due to the institutionalization and routinization of political life.

Each of the cleavages dividing Israeli society has a distinct structure and a substantive basis. The Arab-Jewish cleavage differs from all the other cleavages in that it is strictly dichotomous, in the sense that an individual belongs to either one group or the other.[1] The ethnic cleavage is also dichotomous if one distinguishes between the two broad groupings of Ashkenazim (Western Jews) and Sephardim (Middle Eastern Jews). However, an analysis of the social implications entailed in this cleavage will show that, in some respects, distinctions between the particular countries of origin making up the two large categories are no less important than the overall distinction between "Westerners" and "Easterners." In addition, there is a considerable group of offspring of inter-group marriages which cannot be categorized according to this dichotomous classifications.[2]

The three other cleavages are not at all dichotomous. They represent degrees of polarization along multi-dimensional continua: Between the ultra-Orthodox and those who are completely secular, there are various gradations of religious observance. The cleavage according to class and strata is not dichotomous either. It includes at least two dimensions neither of which are dichotomous: income and occupational status. (The educational component can be included in the occupational dimension or can be treated as a separate dimension.) This is also true of ideological cleavages, which represent a variety of ideological groupings that cannot always be neatly arranged on a uni-dimensional continuum.

A multiplicity of social cleavages does not in itself indicate whether the divisions will generate a degree of social conflict that can undermine societal cohesion. Indeed it is possible to argue, as many social scientists do, that the existence of multiple, crosscutting cleavages tend to mitigate the divisive impact of social polarities. According to this approach, the existence of a multiplicity of cleavages may serve to reduce the probability of the emergence of one central focus of intense conflict. By the same token, overlap among cleavages is likely to intensify conflict, since instead of distinct cleavages each with a single dimension, there is one dominant cleavage with numerous dimensions, each of which exacerbates the others.[3] For example, a national or religious cleavage that overlaps, even partially, with a social class cleavage can generate a conflict of great emotional and political intensity which would not be the case if the cleavages were crosscutting instead of overlapping. The premise that the dispersion of foci of tension mitigates social conflicts also holds for internal divisions within the same cleavage. In other words, dichotomous divisions are more likely to generate intense conflict than non-dichotomous divisions.

It should be noted that not in every case does an overlap between cleavages intensify conflicts, nor does the lack of overlap mitigate conflicts. This line of argument holds when the unit of analysis is a social group. However, when the unit of analysis is an individual with a multi-component status profile, the way these cleavages are reflected in his other identity can constitute a source of tension, precisely because the status components do not overlap.[4] For example, an individual whose social class position does not match his or her status based on ethnic membership might be subject to cross-pressures that influence any tendencies to conformity or non-conformity. Such subjective feelings of deprivation that feed non-conformity may, if they are prevalent among certain groups, have a bearing on the intensity of social conflicts even though they are not the source of these conflicts. Thus, an empirical examination of the relation between overlapping or crosscutting cleavages and the intensity of social conflicts cannot be detached from the historical circumstances and the unique social conditions of the society under study. Particular historical and social circumstances can induce deprived social groups to assume a passive stance vis a vis the existing social order while in other circumstances, the same groups may rebel against the social order. A typical example of such an effect is the tendency among passive deprived groups to resort to active protest following a relative improvement in their situation.

This phenomenon stems inter alia from the gap between the objective situation of deprivation and the consciousness of deprivation, and from the gap between an objective overlapping of cleavages and the degree of sensitivity to such overlapping. In order for individuals and groups to be motivated to seek change in the social order, the deprived group must perceive a contradiction between its situation and the principles of distributive justice in which it believes. The deprived group's principles may be identical to those held by the dominant groups in society but which are not actually applied, or they may be opposed to those held by the dominant groups.[5] The complexity of the relation between social cleavages, feelings of deprivation, and social conflicts is not only due to historical and cultural conditioning, but also reflective of the complex relationship between two dimensions of social differentiation—stratification and center-periphery. The dimension of stratification relates to an individual's position in the class and status hierarchies and to the system of rewards entailed by that position. The distinction between center and periphery relates to the distribution of power and charisma in society, both in an institutional sense and in relation to the position of social groups on the continuum that indicates their ability to participate in shaping and directing the social system. The nature of the relation between these two dimensions of social differentiation determines, to a large extent, the scope and intensity of the political manifestations of social cleavages.

Israel as a multi-cleavage society could not have achieved any degree of social and political integration if the cultural and political center had not developed mechanisms for regulating the conflicts originating in its social cleavages. Israel did inherit certain institutional mechanisms in the political sphere for regulating conflicts from the Yishuv. However, some of these mechanisms were predicated on the assumption that in the absence of sovereignty, the search for solutions to some of the conflicts could be deferred, while other conflicts could be ignored insofar as they did not have a major impact on the activities of the Organized Yishuv. The Organized Yishuv, as a system based on authority without sovereignty, dealt with conflicts over resource allocation by applying the principle of proportional representation, which was expressed in the "party key" for allocating resources and positions. Parties and political movements acted as agents of the center in the distribution of resources "imported" from the Diaspora. As for ideological conflicts, especially those between the religious and secular sectors, the Organized Yishuv developed a political culture based on bargaining and compromise and a pluralistic structure of ideological subcultures, each of which could foster its own set of values in its particularistic institutional enclave. An expression of this political culture was to be found in the separate school systems established by political movements. Moreover, some of the ideological conflicts did not require immediate treatment since the absence of sovereignty precluded their being translated into operative legal and political decisions. The religious question, for example, could not serve as a central focus of friction in the absence of the need to provide binding answers to constitutional issues concerning the status of religion in society.

In contrast to the possibility of circumventing conflicts on ideological issues, conflicts over authority stood out in their intensity given the absence of sovereignty. Conflicts over authority were dealt with by providing access to resources and participation in the decision-making processes concerning their allocation to those groups that accepted the authority of the Organized Yishuv, while denying access to groups that rejected this authority. Tensions originating in the ethnic cleavage were of limited public or political significance during the Yishuv. This was due to the dwindling proportion of Sephardim and Middle Eastern

Jews in the Jewish population after World War I and to the possibility for the non-Ashkenazim to develop particularistic ethnic subcultures within the framework of a partial ethnic pluralism.[6]

The Arab-Jewish Cleavage: 1948-1967

The transition from the Yishuv to the state significantly changed the cleavage structure of society and the conflict regulation mechanisms that were related to these cleavages. The most significant change of the transition period was the incorporation of an Arab population into the sphere of Israeli sovereignty. The size of this population in the territory controlled by the Jewish forces in May 1948 was smaller than it had been before the onset of the War of Independence in late 1947 because of the flight of many Arabs and the expulsion of others.[7] The Arab population under Israeli rule later increased as a result of the conquest of predominantly Arab areas in the Galilee and the inclusion of other areas as part of the cease-fire agreements of 1949. The dual identity of the Arab population, which was both religious (Moslem, Christian, or Druze) and national (Arab), led to a tendency in the early years of the state for the authorities to refer to the Arabs by the non-committal term "minorities," and there was even a Ministry for Minority Affairs in the early cabinets.

This state of affairs was rooted in the Zionist tradition of viewing the "Arab problem" of Palestine as an issue concerning the Arabs as individuals and not as a collective national entity.[8] Even the left-wing political party, Mapam, which upheld the goal of a binational state, expressed this perception in the 1940s when it defined Palestine under the Mandate as "the common homeland of the Jewish people returning to its land and of the Arabs of Palestine." In other words, the Jews are defined as a people, while the Arabs are regarded as a group composed of individuals with a common identity. Furthermore, at a later time when the Israeli public became more aware that "the minorities" possessed something of a national identity, the prevailing tendency was to refer to them as "Arabs" and not as "Palestinians." One of the most widely-quoted statements to this effect was made by Golda Meir, who stubbornly held that there was no such thing as a Palestinian people. Even in 1978, with the signing of the Camp David agreements recognizing Palestinian Arab rights, Prime Minister Begin insisted that the Hebrew translation of the document use the term "Arabs of Eretz

Israel" instead of "Palestinian Arabs."[9] These semantic concerns reflected the lack of clarity involved in articulating the nature of the attachment to the State of Israel on the apart of its Arab citizens and, following 1967, on the part of the Arabs in the occupied territories who were subject to Israeli rule without being citizens. As to the demographic ratio between Jews and Arabs, it should be recalled that apart from the mass exodus of the Arabs of Palestine during April and May 1948 from the areas secured or conquered by the Jewish forces, all later territorial gains for Israel involved an increase in the percentage of Arabs under its rule. The mass exodus of the Arabs during the War of Independence, whether on their own volition or because they were expelled, brought the State of Israel closer to the status of a Jewish nation-state. On the other hand, the conquests in the last stage of the war and the addition of territory as a result of the armistice agreement with Jordan, increased both the territory of the new state and its Arab population. The mass immigration of the 1950s reduced the share of the Arabs in Israel's overall population, but this percentage rose again due to the decline in immigration and to the higher rate of natural increase among Israeli Arabs compared to the Jews. (See Table 1).

Table 1
Size of Arab Population by Year

Year	*Sum*	*Jews*	*Arabs*	*% of Arabs*
1949	1,173	1,013	160	13.6
1955	1,789	1,590	199	11.1
1965	2,598	2,299	299	11.5
1968	2,841	2,434	407*	14.3
1975	3,493	2,959	534	15.2
1985	4,266	3,517	749	17.5

*The East Jerusalem population is included in the Arab population since 1948.
Source: Statistical Year Books from various years.

Despite the fact that from the very first, Israel's Arab citizens have enjoyed the right to vote and to be elected to political office, the pattern of Jewish-Arab co-existence during the first eighteen years of Israel's history was close to the pattern known as institutional pluralism. The main reason for this was the imposition of military government—ostensibly for security reasons—in the areas in which most of Israel's Arabs lived. These areas included the cities of Nazareth, Acre, and Shefaram, most of the Galilee, and the Waddi Ara area with the villages of Baka Al-Gharbiya and Umm Al-Fahm, the "little triangle" east of the

Sharon region with the villages of Taibeh, Tira, and Kafr Kassem, areas along the railroad line from Jerusalem to Tel Aviv and the Beduin areas of the Negev. Freedom of movement of those residing under military government was limited, with permits being required to leave the area. Although, in principle, this restriction applied to Jewish residents of these areas as well in practice, it was imposed only on the Arab residents.[10] The military government made the Arabs under its jurisdiction dependent on its favors both economically and politically. A paradoxical situation was thus created in which citizens who had the right to vote and could be elected to public office were deprived of the elementary right of freedom of movement which denied them access to the labor market and to the centers of government and commerce.

The security rationale for the military government weakened over the years as the situation along Israel's borders stabilized, but the military government was maintained until 1966. The military government created something akin to an Arab ghetto which, among other things, created a segmented labor market[11] that prevented cheap Arab labor from penetrating the Jewish sector. During the years of mass immigration in the 1950s, there was widespread unemployment in the Jewish sector and most efforts at rapid economic growth were aimed at providing jobs for the immigrants. The existence of the military government thus prevented competition from developing between the new immigrants and the Arabs over the limited supply of jobs.[12] This situation had a dual impact. On the one hand, it forced the Arabs to base their livelihoods on a village economy which meant a slower rise in their standard of living.[13] On the other hand, it prevented wages from dropping in the Jewish sector, which would have occurred had there been open competition between the immigrants and Arab workers. The military government also enabled the political establishment, and especially the ruling party, Mapai, to regulate political activity in the Arab sector.[14] The dependence of the Arabs on the apparatus of the military government facilitated the establishment of Arab political "lists" to run for seats in the Knesset, (the Israeli parliament) which were little more than extensions of Mapai. These lists were headed by Arab notables whose position was based on the traditional rural social structure of the Arab sector. A reciprocal relationship was thus created in which the heads of the traditional Arab clans were able to obtain various benefits for themselves and their followers in return for delivering votes for Mapai.[15] Nevertheless, Mapai was not able to prevent a considerable portion of the Arabs from supporting the Communist Party. The Communist Party, which due to its identification with the Soviet Union was the only organized political force among the Arabs which supported the UN partition plan for Palestine, was able in the early 1950s to amass a solid base of Arab support, mainly in urban areas. Communist influence was particularly strong among the Arab Greek Orthodox population in the Nazareth area.[16] The Communist Party itself, (known from its Hebrew initials as Maki), became a vehicle for the expression of Palestinian national identity and voiced its protest against the deprived status of Israeli Arabs.

Freedom of movement was not the only right denied to Israeli Arabs. Part of the Arab population who were cut off from their lands during the fighting in 1948-49 and were declared absentees, had their land expropriated and transferred to the Custodian of Absentee Property.[17] The inferior status of Israeli Arabs in the period following the establishment of the state stands out even more sharply in comparison to the Druze. The Druze, an Arabic speaking religious community whose national status is somewhat ambiguous, cast their lot with the Jewish forces during the War of Independence and were thus spared the restrictions imposed on the Moslem and Christian Arabs. The considerable Druze population in the Mount Carmel area was not put under the jurisdiction of the military government and those that did live in such areas in the Galilee, enjoyed preferential treatment. However, the most important difference in their status was that, in contrast to the Arabs, the young men of the Druze community served in the army, first as volunteers and later as draftees subject to compulsory service like the Jews. The compulsory military service of the Druze symbolized the state's formal recognition of their community as having the same rights and duties as the Jews.[18] The fact that the Arabs were not subject to the draft became the most significant expression of their partial exclusion from Israeli society. The institutional sphere of security has therefore been organized according to ethnic-national criteria rather than a purely civil criterion. In actual fact the state did not give formal legal sanction to the Arab exemption from compulsory military service. The Minister of Defense is vested with the discretionary power to call up men of military age for military service, but is not obligated to do so. The Defense Ministers have simply refrained, as a matter of policy, from calling up Arab young men for service, even though, by law, they are liable for military service. A paradoxical situation has thus been created wherein a Jew with the status of permanent resident who is not a citizen is liable for military service, but is not eligible to vote or be elected to the Knesset, while an

Arab who is a citizen may vote and be elected to the Knesset, but is not called for military service. This paradox is possible because of the gap between the legal status of Israeli Arabs and the practical considerations which determine their position in Israeli society.

Up to the time of the dismantling of the military government in 1966, no significant changes occurred in the status of the Israeli Arabs. This population remained predominantly rural, had low education levels, and concentrated in manual occupations. However, during this period, the nucleus of an intelligenstia was formed by those, albeit few, Arabs who had studied at Israeli universities. Opposition to the military government gained ground gradually and by the early 1960s the Knesset was about evenly split between the supporters and opponents of the military government.[19] Internal changes in the political party structure eventually paved the way for the abolition of the military government. The accession of Levi Eshkol to the prime ministership and the departure of David Ben-Gurion and his supporters from Mapai (to form their own Rafi party), changed the balance of forces within Mapai, and led to the dismantling of the military government in 1966. The immediate result of this step was the entry of thousands of Arab blue-collar workers into the labor market, who found jobs mainly in seasonal work in construction and agriculture and in services such as restaurants and hotels. Contacts between Jews and Arabs multiplied, the number of Arab university students grew,[20] and more and more younger Arabs became fluent in Hebrew. Knowledge of Hebrew enabled Arabs to become consumers of the predominant Israeli urban culture. Somewhat later, intensive contacts, even though limited in scope, developed within several social settings, especially in artistic and intellectual circles and the criminal underworld.

One year after the abolition of the military government another event occurred—the Six Day War—which returned the question of Arab-Jewish relations to center stage on the national agenda. Until 1967, the issue of Israel's Arabs comprised mainly a problem of the integration of a relatively small national minority into the economy, society, and political structure of Israel. Even though Israel after the cease-fire agreements of 1949 was not a full-fledged nation-state in terms of the composition of its population, it was very close to being an integral nation-state in its way of life. The influence of the Arab minority on social and political developments was quite small because of the segregation of Israel's Arabs. They had been abandoned by their elite and cut off from their brethren across the border, and were actually living in a de facto ghetto under the military government.

The Jewish-Arab Cleavage: The Consequences of the Six Day War

The outcome of the 1967 war bestowed new meaning on the national identity of Israeli Arabs. The incorporation of a large Palestinian population on the West Bank and Gaza Strip into the area under Israeli control produced a dual transformation: First, direct contact was restored between Israel's Arabs and their brethren across the cease-fire line, or the Green Line as it is popularly known in Israel; and second, Arab-Israeli relations reverted once again into a conflict between national affiliation occupying the same political-territorial entity. These changes put Israel's Arabs in a unique situation. They had a common citizenship with Israeli Jews, but shared a common ethnic-national membership with the Arabs in the occupied territories. However, neither of the components of their dual identity were complete. On the one hand, their identity as Palestinian Arabs, now that the Palestinian problem had become the focus of the Arab-Israeli conflict, made it impossible for them to identify fully as Israelis. On the other hand, their Israeli citizenship made it impossible for them to share fully in the Palestinian Arab movement since the return of the territories to Jordanian or Arab-Palestinian rule would not affect their status as Arab citizens of Israel. The inherent problems in their dual identity cannot be fully resolved as long as they are bound to live in a predominantly Jewish state. However, if they were to adopt a position denying the right of the State of Israel to exist as a predominantly Jewish state, this would undermine the basis of their claim to equal political rights in Israel. This is implied in the decision of the Supreme court that denied the right of the El-Ard group to run for election to the Knesset on a platform calling in effect for the dismantling of Israel as a sovereign entity.[21] On the other hand, adopting a position calling for the annexation of the territories and the granting of Israeli citizenship to their inhabitants would mean betraying the Palestinian Arab aspiration for self-determination. As for the third option, Palestinian self-determination alongside Israel, which is in fact supported by most Israeli Arabs, would imply a readiness to continue to live with a dual identity as Israeli Arabs.[22]

The encounter between the Arabs of Israel and the Arabs in the occupied territories thus did not resolve the problems of their dual identity, but it did intensify and radicalize their national consciousness. This process has been particularly evident among the educated elites, especially among those educated in Israeli universities. Within these circles, there is hardly any support for the Zionist political parties. Opinion in this group is divided among those favoring the establishment of a Palestinian state alongside Israel, a position advocated mainly by the Communists; and groups such as "The Sons of the Village" who adopted the extreme position of denying the right of Israel to exist and calling for the establishment of a "democratic secular state in Palestine" which is the official position of the PLO. Since those who hold the latter position cannot promote it as a basis of organized political activity in Israel, radicalization among Israeli Arabs is translated primarily into increased electoral support for the Democratic Front for Peace and Equality (Hadash), a joint list formed by the Communists and other Arab and Jewish groups. At the same time, the lists of Arab dignitaries linked to Mapai have disappeared from the political map. Nevertheless, about half of the Arab voters continued to support predominantly Jewish parties with Zionist platforms during the 1980s, most of them voting for the Alignment, the successor to Mapai, which included Arab candidates in its list.[23]

The radicalization in the nationalist outlook of Israel's Arabs occurred paradoxically as the pace of their integration into the economic, social, and cultural life of Israel accelerated. First, the rise in the standard of living among Israel's Arabs increased the interaction between the Arab and Jewish economic sectors. The low-status, low-paying jobs in Israel were filled mostly by Arabs from the territories and to a lesser extent by Israeli Arabs.[24] At the same time, more signs of Arab entrepreneurship became evident, including business under joint Jewish-Arab ownership serving mainly Jewish clienteles—restaurants, retail stores, gas stations, garages, and the like. Another major trend was the emergence of the Israeli-Arab farming sector as a significant component in some branches of Israeli agriculture. The Arab involvement in the Jewish agricultural sector increased, with Arabs serving mainly as hired labor but also in entrepreneurial roles, taking part in both the financing and marketing of crops. In the northern part of the country, Jewish farms employ Israeli Arabs, while in the south, the Arab hired workers come from the occupied territories.

The growth of the Arab population and especially the rise in its standard of living created a demand for products and services, especially those provided by professionals. This demand, in turn, has led to greater occupational diversification in the Arab sector and the creation of employment opportunities for those in the free professions such as lawyers, doctors and engineers, and for skilled manual and technical workers. However, the number of Arabs with higher education has grown faster than the number of jobs available for them.[25] One of the by-products of this situation is that many university graduates work as teachers. As a result, the tendency for the teaching profession to become the preserve of women has been less evident in the Arab sector than in the Jewish sector, and there are more teachers with academic degrees in the Arab sector than in the Jewish sector. The creation of a critical mass of demand in the Arab sector for the services of educated personnel has only partially compensated the stratum of educated Arabs for their limited access to occupations suiting their qualifications in the Jewish sector. This limited access stems, in part, from the practice of not employing Arabs in the broad range of industries and services related to defense and, in part, from problems related to cultural differences, residence, and prejudice.

In contrast to the economic sphere where there is considerable interpenetration between the Jewish and Arab sectors, in the cultural sphere this is minimal. The reason for this lies mainly in the nature of the cleavage along national lines relating to cultural phenomena such as religion, language, and common historical experiences. The gap between the cultures of different national groups is greater in traditional societies than in the modern age with all societies exposed to the pervasive influence of Western mass culture disseminated by television, radio, and movies. In Israel the gap between Jews and Arabs is also related to sharp differences in the level of modernization in the two sectors, at least where the dominant cultural orientations of each sector are concerned. The dominant orientation in the Arab sector is traditional, while the orientations of the dominant elites in the Jewish sector are modern. The gap in the levels of modernization has narrowed in respect of the younger generation of Israeli Arabs. This generation is a consumer of several cultures: Arab culture in Israel and from the region, as conveyed by television and radio from Arab countries; the Hebrew culture of Jewish Israel; and Western culture that is accessible through either Hebrew or English. Despite their exposure to Hebrew culture, only a small number of Arabs have made a name for themselves in the broad Israeli public as scholars, writers, poets, journalists, and actors. However, the exposure of young Arabs to the general Israeli culture is much greater than the exposure of young Jews to Arab culture.

Israeli Arabs and West Bank Arabs

Alienation between Arabs and Jews and manifestations of mutual hostility can be attributed to the impasse in attempts to resolve the Arab-Israeli conflict, to the impact on Jews of Arab terrorist acts, and to the tendency among Jews to ignore, at least from a social point of view, the difference between Israeli Arabs and the Arabs in the occupied territories. The "civil" identity of the Arab citizens of Israel, as distinct from their ethno-national identity, has influenced their attitudes to Israel as a socio-political entity, attitudes which contrast with those held by the Arabs in the territories. Nationalist radicalization among Israeli Arabs are usually expressed in moderate forms of political protest focused on certain key occasions such as Land Day, and have remained within the bounds of the law. Furthermore, Israeli Arabs have taken a much smaller part in acts of terror than have Arabs from the territories. Also, despite the language, religion, and culture shared by Israeli Arabs and Arabs in the West Bank and the Gaza Strip, the social boundaries between these two groups have not been blurred during the years following the Six Day War.

Another factor preserving differences between Israeli Arabs and the Arabs in the territories is their separate school systems. Israeli Arab schools use a curriculum prepared by Israel's Ministry of Education and Culture while the West Bank schools use a Jordanian curriculum and the Gaza schools use one held over from the Egyptian occupation. However, the differences between these school systems go beyond those found in their respective curricula. Israeli Arab schools, like all Israeli schools, have a predominantly modern orientation, unlike the schools in the territories. Moreover, Israeli Arab high school graduates seeking to continue their studies usually do so in Israeli universities. High school graduates in the territories, with few exception, either study in universities in Arab countries or in the colleges in the territories set up since the Six Day War. Thus there are major differences in the educational backgrounds of the Israeli Arab elites and the elites in the territories.[26]

In contrast to the cultural differences between Israeli Arabs and the Arabs in the territories shaped by their respective educational systems, the influence of the mass communication media runs in the opposite direction. Both groups watch the same programs on television and listen to the same programs on the radio which are broadcast in Arabic both from Israel and from Arab countries. Arabs on both sides of the Green Line tend to read the Arabic newspapers that are published in East Jerusalem, which because it was annexed to Israel is not subject to the same press restrictions imposed by the military government in the occupied territories.[27]

The expansion of the territories under Israeli control resulting from the 1967 war entailed creating political and economic links with an

Arab population far greater than that which had been part of Israel proper—750,000 Arabs in the West Bank and 400,000 in Gaza. Furthermore, due to the much higher birth rates among the Arabs of the occupied territories, compared to Israel in general and to Israeli Jews in particular, there is a tendency for the share of the Arabs of the West Bank and Gaza Strip in the overall population under Israeli rule to increase. During the mid-1980s, the number of children born each year to the Arabs under Israeli rule, including Israeli Arabs, surpassed the number of children born to Jews.[28] Before the Six Day War, Israel's leaders repeatedly declared that the state had no interest in territorial expansion. However, this policy did not prevent the awakening of aspirations following the war to establish some kind of permanent connection with all or part of the territory conquered. Most Israelis support the extension of the territorial aspirations of the of Zionism beyond the cease-fire lines, to incorporate at least some of the areas beyond the Green Line into Israel on a permanent basis.[29] The desire for territorial modifications, on one scale or another, was aroused during the fighting itself in the emotional reaction that accompanied the Israeli army's entry into the Old city of Jerusalem and the taking of the Temple Mount and the Western Wall—and indeed East Jerusalem was the first area to be annexed by Israel. This was carried out in two stages: In 1967 East Jerusalem was annexed to the municipality of Jewish Jerusalem, and in 1980 the Jerusalem Law declared that Jerusalem as a whole is the capital of Israel.[30] The other portions of Mandatory Palestine taken in the war—the West Bank and Gaza—remained under military government without Israel formulating an official position on their ultimate political disposition or on what Israel sought there in the way of permanent borders.

The State of Israel and the Occupied Administered Territories

The above situation has been a major factor in shaping the relations between the State of Israel and the Arabs of the territories. The occupation was temporary by nature but this was qualified from the outset by the "creation of facts" such as Jewish settlements and the employment of workers from the territories in Israel. These developments reflected a desire among a considerable portion of the Israeli public to put Israel's control over all or part of the territories on a permanent basis, whether by formal annexation or by devising arrangements that would achieve the same goal without the necessity of extending Israeli law to the territories. What has aided the consolidation and strengthening of these trends has been the duration of the occupation which has evolved into a state of "protracted temporariness." What is more, the assumption that the occupation is indeed temporary has become less and less tenable. This nebulous situation and the ideological and political divisions among Israeli Jews over the future of the territories have been reinforced by increased Jewish settlement and land purchases,[31] the integration of the economies of Israel and the territories, and by the maturing of a generation of Israeli youth who never knew an Israel limited by pre-1967 borders.

The situation of "protracted temporariness" has influenced not only the economy, society, and politics of the occupied territories, but also those of Israel. The restoration of the intercommunal dimension of the Arab-Israeli conflict have brought in its wake phenomena associated with conflicts between communities in societies with deep national cleavages. For example, a large gap exists between the degree of intercommunal economic integration and the extent of cultural and political integration.

The economic integration between Israel and the territories was accelerated by a decision made a short time after the Six Day War to allow workers from the territories to seek jobs in Israel.[32] Other political decisions that influenced this process of economic integration were the decision to make Israel currency legal tender in the territories alongside the Jordanian dinar and the replacement of the Jordanian banking system with Israeli banks. Over the years, a small number of business partnerships have been created between Israelis and Arabs from the territories. With the addition of the territories, the market for Israel's industrial goods expanded to include hundreds of thousands of Arab consumers. On the other hand, the Israeli market was not the only outlet for the surplus production of farmers from the territories or the small number of industrial plants. The opening of the Jordan bridges enabled the Arabs to export their goods from the West Bank to neighboring Arab countries, and even Israeli-made items were occasionally disguised as products of the territories so that they could be exported through this route.[33]

The decision of the Defense Minister Moshe Dayan to open the Israeli labor market to workers from the territories after the Six Day War encountered opposition in the government and especially from the Finance Minister Pinhas Sapir.[34] This opposition stemmed from the Labor Zionist tradition that sought to create an autonomous Jewish economic and class structure that would lead to the "productivization" of the Jewish people. However, these ideological objections did not stand up to the pressures of supply and demand. The emergence of economic prosperity after the war created increased demand for workers in agriculture, construction, and services such as hotels, garages, and gas stations—and this demand, in the end, determined the extent of Abab labor from the territories in the Israeli economy. As a result, a stratum of workers from the territories was created that occupied the positions carrying the lowest income and status in the Israeli economy.

These trends brought about a transformation of the stratification system within Israel. The entry of Arab workers into low-income and low-status occupations stimulated the upward occupation and social mobility of some of the Jewish workers who had occupied these positions in the past. This upwardly mobile group was composed mainly of Jews of Middle Eastern and North African origin. This group now stands alongside others such as Israeli employers of Arab workers from the territories and Israeli investors in the territories who have an economic interest in maintaining an open connection with the territories.[35]

The inclusion of the Arab population of the territories under Israeli rule also posed a challenge to the principle of the rule of law. The occupation created a situation where three sets of legal norms and procedures held sway simultaneously over a single territory: the legal system of Israel, the regulations promulgated by the military government and the legal system that had been in force under Jordanian or Egyptian rule. The mounting difficulties posed by the partial integration of the two political and territorial units, and the situation of a political uncertainty regarding the future of the links between the populations and territories of the occupiers and the occupied, created dual sets of legal norms that applied to different groups—Israelis and the local Arabs—living in the same territory. This condition of dual legal norms first emerged to cope with the problematic legal situation posed by the first groups of Jewish settlers to move in across the Green Line. For example, it was decided that crimes committed by Jewish settlers would not come under the jurisdiction of the local police and courts. Other arrangements were made to provide services such as insurance to the Jewish settlers or to enable them to pay Israeli income and social security taxes.

Another departure from the normal procedure in occupied territories was actually undertaken in order to provide access to the Israeli legal system for the Arab residents of the territories. This arrangement allows residents of the territories who are not Israeli citizens to submit petitions to the High Court of Justice, which among other things can order the government or the military authorities to desist from certain actions that violate due process of law.[36]

The military government is an arbitrary system in that it left considerable discretionary powers in the hands of military officers. The existence of legitimate security considerations for which the military is responsible for has not reduced the arbitrary use of the powers of the military government. On the contrary, in many cases these powers have created an opening for the violation of personal liberties through the imposition of curfews, searches, and restrictions on freedom of movement and economic activity. The military government is also a discriminatory system in that it may deny benefits to certain individuals at its own discretion while granting these benefits to others. For example, the military government uses the right to grant or deny exit permits to visit Arab countries as a means to manipulate the residents of the territories.[37]

This sort of arbitrariness is alien to the principles of Israeli justice and government. Israel with the occupied territories has thus become a state in which the authorities in one part of the territory under its control are not allowed to infringe individual rights, while in another part they may exercise their rule in a much more arbitrary fashion. This situation sometimes affects Israeli citizens who do not live in the territories. For example, a number of Israelis fell victim to land purchases from Arabs on the West Bank that had been carried out by fraud and extortion. These lands were then sold to Israelis, who later found out that their rights to this property were doubtful and contested.[38] The land transactions on the West Bank, particularly those carried out by private dealers, exposed another facet of Israeli rule there that has had an impact on the rule of law in Israel. A considerable segment of the public and to a lesser extent officials of the government and World Zionist Organization have developed a rather permissive attitude toward violations of the law in land transfers, and in dealing with current security matters, especially those concerning Jewish settlers, out of a sense of "patriotic" sentiment. This approach has its roots in the pre-state period when it was generally held that one should not stand on the niceties of legal procedure when Zionist interests are at stake in the conflict between Arabs and Jews. This approach, which was shaped in part by the Jewish perception of the British Mandate as an alien legal system, reappeared following the Six Day War as the

Arab-Israeli conflict returned to the intercommunal patterns of the pre-state period. This trend was most apparent in the behavior of the Jewish settlers on the West Bank. The first settlement efforts Gush Emunim involved violations of the law and confrontations with the authorities since the latter had not approved Jewish settlements in the West Bank except for the Jordan Valley, Gush Etzion, and Kiryat Arba outside of Hebron. Even after its settlement efforts gained official recognition and backing by the post-1977 government, these settlers continued their cavalier attitude to the legal process in their relations with the local Arabs.[39] This type of behavior was expressed in vigilante reprisal actions taken by the settlers against the Arabs in response to nationalistically motivated attacks and in repeated efforts to impose a significant Jewish presence in the heart of Hebron, which became something of a combat zone between Jews and Arabs. The settlers' disdain for the rule of law reached its most extreme expression in the establishment of a Jewish terror underground whose members carried out violent attacks on West Bank mayors, murdered students at the Islamic College in Hebron, and planned to blow up Arab buses and passengers in Jerusalem. The tendency to resort to violence to achieve religious-nationalistic goals emerged in its most grotesque form in the plan, which was not carried out, to blow up the Dome of the Rock on the Temple Mount, to obliterate the most important symbol of Moslem rights in Jerusalem.[40] The permissive attitude taken by the authorities to the violations of the law by the settlers in the first stage of their settlement drive was one factor that led some of the settlers to escalate their extremist actions to the point where the government had no choice but to arrest the members of the underground and bring them to trial. Still, even after their arrest, a widespread campaign was launched by their sympathizers to prevent them from being brought to trial, or at least to grant them immediate pardons.[41] Prominent political figures from the right-wing parties, the Likud, Tehiya and the religious parties took part in this activity. Likud leader Yitzhak Shamir, who was prime minister when the underground was arrested, made an unprecedented show of moral support for the Jewish terror group while their pardons were being discussed, when he invoked biblical imagery in urging the public "not to harm My anointed ones." The ambivalent attitude to the rule of law, a common feature in intercommunal conflicts, thus reached the point where the monopoly of the state over the use of legitimate means of force was challenged and violated.

The communal cleavage is the only one of the five main cleavages in Israeli society based on a dichotomous distinction between two population groups, Jews on the one hand and Arabs on the other. Nevertheless, when examining this cleavage in the context of the distinctions between center and periphery, it is apparent that the Arabs occupy various positions on this axis. The Druze occupy a less peripheral position than other Israeli Arabs; Arabs who are citizens of Israel are in a more central position than those Arabs who live in areas annexed to Israel but who have not taken Israeli citizenship; and the Arabs who live under the military government are the most peripheral, insofar as it is possible to regard them as part of this internal Israeli structure. Even so, it should be noted that certain figures among the Palestinian Arab elites in the territories have developed channels of access to the Israeli establishment, and Israeli elites have found ways to compensate these figures for their peripheral status in other ways. Thus, a connection has developed between these Arab leaders and the political center even though they do not participate in shaping the center. Despite these continuous contacts between the Israeli elites and leading figures in the West Bank and Gaza, no center or anything similar has emerged in the territories; the contacts have been carried out on an individual basis. Preventing the formation of a center or some similar body among the Arabs of the territories has formed part of Israel's systematic effort to block the crystallization of a Palestinian national leadership group in the territories. In this sense, Israel's policy has followed in the footsteps of the approach taken by the Jordanian authorities when they ruled the West Bank from 1948 to 1967.[42] And to the extent that centers representing the national aspirations of Palestinians in the territories do exist, they have been formed outside the boundaries of Israeli rule—the Palestine Liberation Organization on the one hand, and the Hashemite regime in Jordan on the other. The PLO appears to have attracted the primary nationalistic loyalty of most Arabs in the territories, while Jordan represents their affiliation framework as citizens. As a result, the Arabs in the territories maintain attachments to three separate centers, all of them outside the areas controlled by the military government. First, the Arabs in the territories have an instrumental connection to the Israeli center, whose domination rests on its coercive power. Second, the Arabs maintain a connection that is both instrumental and normative-expressive toward Jordan. And third, their connection to the national institutions of the PLO is mainly normative-expressive.[43] This phenomenon of partial connections based on different orientations to competing centers is characteristic of national communities ruled by a foreign power and to multi-communal societies.

In contrast to the straightforward relation between the Jewish-Arab cleavage and the position of Jews and Arabs on the center-periphery axis in Israeli society, the relation between the Jewish-Arab cleavage and the stratification structure is less clear. In this respect, one must distinguish between the degree of similarity between the status hierarchies of Israeli Jews, Israeli Arabs, and Arabs in the territories, and the extent, of their interdependence. The latter refers to the possibility of converting a status position in one's primary community to a status position that is recognized by all groups and which transcends the national cleavage lines. While the status hierarchies of the three groups are largely similar, there is a great difference between the Israeli Arabs and the Arabs of the territories in terms of their ability to translate status within their community to a status transcending community boundaries. The extensive similarity in criteria for determining status positions is a reflection of universal processes of modernization. To the extent that there are differences in these criteria between Jews and Arabs, particularly those in the territories, these stem mainly from differences in levels of modernization rather than from cleavage along national lines. The possibility of converting one's status within the community to a status recognized beyond the community is available more to Israeli Arabs than to the Arabs of the territories. This difference stems from the fact that since the abolition of the military government in Israel in 1966, the national cleavage in Israel proper is characterized by social and cultural pluralism, rather than institutional pluralism. On the other hand, the interrelations between Israeli society and the Arabs of the territories reflect a clear-cut pattern of institutional pluralism, at least for as long as the territories are ruled by military government.

The Religious-Secular Cleavage: Social and Legal Aspects

Religion, like national affiliation, serves as a divisive force in Israeli society. In addition to the divisions between the various religious groups in Israel—Jews, Moslems, Christians, and Druze—each group is also divided between those who adhere to religious traditions and those who do not. The religious-secular cleavage in the Jewish community differs from that in the smaller religious groups not only because it divides the dominant group in Israeli society, but also because it serves as a basis of political mobilization and social and cultural separatism. Moreover, the problem of the status of religion in Israel, even though it is relevant to all religions, usually refers to the status of Judaism in Israeli society. Thus, even though from a constitutional point of view Judaism is not the state religion in Israel, its status nevertheless determines relations between religion and state and the extent to which religion influences the political center.

The religious-secular cleavage can be examined in three different contexts: the social and political context which refers to the extent of distinctiveness and separation between the religious and the secular; the legal context which determines the formal status of religious institutions and the degree to which they may impose various aspects of traditional religious law (Halacha) on the individual and the public at large; and the ideological context which focuses on the meaning of the State of Israel as a "Jewish state." The first two contexts relate directly to social and cultural divisions between religious and secular Jews, while the third constitutes one of the several ideological cleavages in Israeli society and will be discussed separately.

The religious-secular cleavage is not dichotomous: There are no absolute lines of division but rather various shades of religiosity or non-religiosity spread out along a continuum that may be divided at different points according to various criteria. There are at least three such criteria: voting for religious parties, sending children to religious schools, and observance of religious traditions.[44] It should be noted that these criteria relate to a religious continuum based on relationships to Orthodoxy so that Jews who identify themselves as Reform or Conservative are not easily placed in the schema. This has only marginal impact on this analysis, however, since the Orthodox have a monopoly on the religious establishment in Israel and because of the small number of people who identify as Reform or Conservative. The status of Reformed Conservative Judaism in Israel is mainly an ideological issue, while in the Diaspora it has broader social and political meaning. Nevertheless, the practices of Reform and Conservative Judaism in the Diaspora are reflected in a major political-legal issue in Israel, the definition of "Who is a Jew" in the Law of Return and what this implies for the recognition of non-Orthodox conversions in Israel.

Of the three criteria of religiosity, voting is the least indicative. The vote for the religious parties in considerably smaller than the reservoir indicated by the other criteria of sending children to religious schools or of traditional observance. The religious parties generally receive about 10 to 15 percent of the vote in elections to the Knesset.[45] On the other hand, between a quarter to a third of all parents send their children to religious schools.[46] Moreover, the vote for the religious parties has fluctuated in ways that are not connected with changes in relations between the religious and the secular. Thus the percentage of voters for the religious parties dropped in 1981 because of the preference of many religious voters for other parties. Another reason why the full electoral potential of the religious parties is not expressed is because significant parts of the ultra-Orthodox community organized in the Eda Haredit and Neturei Karta boycott all elections and view the participation of Agudat Israel in the elections as a deviation from the proper religious path.

The second criterion, the percentage of parents who send their children to religious schools, is a more reliable indicator, first since it can be precisely measured and also because there are few religious parents who would send their children to secular primary schools and, conversely, even fewer secular parents who would send their children to religious schools. Nevertheless, this criterion is not as reliable as it may seem as is apparent from the fact that fluctuations in the number of pupils registered in religious schools does not necessarily reflect shifts in the religiosity of the population. The most prominent shift here has been the drop in the number of pupils in the state religious system. This system has lost pupils both to the state secular system and to the ultra-Orthodox "independent" school network associated with Agudat Israel or with other ultra-Orthodox groups. (See Table 2). This decline in the number of pupils in religious schools, however, does not necessarily reflect a decrease in the influence of religion on the population which can only be determined by the third criterion, religious observance. However, data on religious observance tends to be sketchy due to few studies having been conducted on this issue and due to unclear definitions of "religious," "traditional," and "secular," the three categories by which people are usually asked to identify their religious preference.[47]

Table 2
The Distribution of Primary School Students by Educational Stream and Year (in percent)

Year	*State School*	*Religious State School*	*Independent Religious School*	*Sum*
1953	68.5	24.5	7.0	100%
1963	64.6	28.8	6.6	100%
1978	72.9	21.3	5.8	100%
1985	74.2	19.9	5.9	100%

Source: Statistical Year Books from various years.

The differences in placement along the continuum of religiosity are also reflected in the degree of openness of the social networks of those in the religious, traditional, and secular categories. In this respect, there is a high correlation between extreme religious behavior, as reflected in very strict Halachic observance, the tendency to social and even ecological segregation, and a low degree of commitment to the national center. This is only a partial correlation, however, since there are groups within the religious Zionist sector who are not ultra-Orthodox but who segregate themselves socially, culturally, and even residentially without this being associated with a weakening in their commitment to the national center and its values. Ecological segregation, the tendency to live in separate neighborhoods, is one of the main indicators of social segregation.[48] Ecological segregation characterized the ultra-orthodox population prior to the establishment of the state. This was less pronounced among the modern Orthodox, although they did found and maintain separate agricultural settlements. However, over the years, separate housing projects or even separate neighborhoods have appeared in urban areas populated mainly by the modern Orthodox. Within the IDF, separate units for religious soldiers were formed for those studying at the Hesder yeshivas that combine Torah study with military training.

The Religious-Secular Cleavage: Orthodox Segregationism

In addition to the divisions between ultra-Orthodox, modern Orthodox, and traditional, there are others, mainly in the ultra-Orthodox sector itself which are not directly related to the continuum of religiosity. The traditional distinctions between Ashkenazim and Sephardim are expressed in certain differences in their prayers, and their having separate synagogues, and separate chief rabbis and local rabbis. Within the Ashkenazi ultra-Orthodox community, there are divisions between Hassidim and Mitnagdim, which reflect historical conflict within East European Jewry over the past 300 years. Among the various Hassidic sects, there are differences in lifestyles and dress and even in the degree of separation from non-ultra-Orthodox groups. The greatest extent of separatism is found among those ultra-Orthodox circles that seek to cut themselves off totally from any contact with values connected with the state, with the government, and even with the benefits of Israel's welfare services. This desire is expressed in minimizing interaction and points of contact with the non-ultra-Orthodox population. The separation from state institutions is reflected in boycotting elections, refusing to serve in the army, and in avoiding the use of services provided by the state. All this reflects a profound rejection of the Zionist basis of legitimacy of the state. Their rejection of Israel is not limited to contacts with the political establishment. The tendency to ghettoization among this group is marked by a high degree of autarchy in the social and cultural spheres and a fairly high level in the economic sphere. The extreme ultra-Orthodox do not only avoid marriage with secular Jews but also with Orthodox Jews who are less strictly observant in their eyes, which also includes the newly religious who have entered the fold voluntarily from secular backgrounds. They also shun all secular culture conveyed by radio, television, newspapers and books and have developed a relatively "closed" economic sector that provides most of their employment opportunities and retail consumer needs except for banking, transportation, and medical services.[49]

The extreme religious circles identified with Neturei Karta and the Eda Haredit are a minority in the ultra-Orthodox community. They represent the most extreme form of separatism from Israeli society and a virtually complete estrangement from the social and political center. In most respects, they are even more peripheral than the Israeli Arabs. Their ghettoized existence represents a form of quasi-institutional pluralism based on free choice as opposed to legally imposed restrictions.

Most of the ultra-Orthodox population however, is less cut off from the rest of Israeli society, even though it also maintains voluntary residential segregation. The moderate ultra-Orthodox associated with the political parties of Agudat Israel and Shas resemble the extremists in their strict observance of Jewish law and their stress on forms of dress that deliberately set them apart from the rest of society. This group has recourse to state funds and services and maintains its own school system, the "Independent" network, with funds provided by the Ministry of Education, even though it is not subject to ministry supervision. This school system is connected to Agudat Israel, which together with the Shas party, represents most of the moderate ultra-Orthodox. Another source of state funds for the ultra-Orthodox community are the grants for yeshivot and kollelim (yeshivot for married students) that cover not only operating expenses but also student scholarships.

The second major distinction between this population, which recognizes the institutions of the state, and the extremist element that does not, is that most of the moderates vote in elections to the Knesset. The Agudat Israel movement that has historically represented most of this group, has appeared in elections at times as a single list and at other times as two lists, one of them a workers' faction called Poalei

Agudat Israel. In 1984, however, a new ultra-Orthodox party appeared called Shas, an acronym for Sephardi Torah Guardians. Shas won the support of the Jews of Middle Eastern and North African origin in the ultra-Orthodox fold and also took votes from ultra-Orthodox Ashkenazim from the Lithuanian or Mitnagidim circles in protest against the heavy Hassidic influence, mainly by followers of the Gerer Rebbe, of Agudat Israel.[50]

As a non-Zionist party that recognizes the state of Israel, Agudat Israel is subject to ideological cross-pressures. From the direction of the Eda Haredit and Neturei Karta come sharp questions about Agudat Israel's close relationships with the "Zionist" establishment and about its readiness to enjoy the material and other benefits that it derives from this association. On the other hand, Agudat Israel has been engaged in a constant ideological debate with Religious Zionism over the former's opposition to Zionist ideology and to the tendency to attribute religious meaning to the existence of the state of Israel which is seen by Religious Zionism as the first sign of the coming redemption of the Jewish people. Agudat Israel and Shas have faced the dilemma of how to use the political bargaining power at their disposal—by securing maximal resources and other benefits for their constituency, or by pushing through legislation increasing the scope of compulsory public religious observance. The greater social segregation of the population served by Agudat Israel, as compared to the Religious Zionist constituency, has led the Aguda to concentrate more on assuring wider services and material benefits for its voters. For example, Agudat Israel has used its political leverage to secure deferments from military service for yeshiva students which, in practice, tend to become full-fledged exemptions, and to secure greater opportunities for women to qualify for an exemption from military service on religious grounds. Agudat Israel has also used its power to increase state support for its cultural and educational institutions, especially its school system. The Anatomy and Pathology Law that permits family members to prevent an autopsy from being performed on their relatives provides legal grounding for a right or privilege, depending on how one looks at it, long sought by the ultra-Orthodox.[51]

The relationship of most of the ultra-Orthodox population to the state of Israel and Israeli society thus reflects a tension between the tendency to social, cultural, and ecological separation and the exigencies of political participation that have created an attachment of sorts to the center. Another facet of this relationship is expressed in the gap between the extensive recourse of the ultra-Orthodox to services and resources provided by the state on the one hand, and their low level of commitment to the state on the other. Agudat Israel represents an extreme instance of relative centrality in terms of political influence and reliance on resources provided by the state, combined with a rather peripheral position in relation to any concrete forms of commitment to state and society, especially as reflected in the widespread ultra-Orthodox tendency to avoid military service.[52]

The Religious Zionist Sector

In contrast to the ultra-Orthodox, the broader religious population cannot be easily delineated, since it contains many of those who define themselves as traditional, in a more general sense. This group maintains a close attachment to the cultural and political center and most of it shares the Religious Zionist ideology that attributes religious meaning to the state of Israel. This group has in the past been defined as the national religious camp but this label can be misleading since it could imply a connection to the National Religious Party, the successor to the Mizrahi Party that founded the Religious Zionist movement. A more appropriate term for this group, at least in terms of its place on the continuum of religious observance, would be modern Orthodox. This group is characterized by varied voting patterns. A good portion of this group votes for the NRP (National Religious Party) or for some of the parties that have split off from it, while others vote for non-religious parties such as the Likud, Tehiya, and even the Alignment. The percentage of religious Jews voting for non-religious parties rose after the political upheaval of 1977 when the ultimate fate of the territories captured in the 1967 war became a central political issue.[53] The NRP represents the political tradition of this group concerning the place of religion in the state and the relations between the religious and the secular sectors. The tendency in this group to social separatism is much less marked than among the ultra-Orthodox, yet cultural separatism is much in evidence. However, this is not reflected in a high level of ecological segregation. The vast majority of the modern Orthodox group resides in mixed secular-religious areas, and tends not to live in ultra-Orthodox neighborhoods. The most prominent area of separation of the modern Orthodox is education. The state religious system is under the administrative and pedagogical supervision of the Ministry of Education, but enjoys a considerable autonomy in shaping its own curriculum.[54]

The multiple and varied points of contact between the modern Orthodox and the secular public are compatible with the involvement in the national center characteristic of parties sharing the Religious Zionist outlook, whether the Mizrahi and Hapoel Hamizrahi, the NRP, or the parties that split off from it such as Morasha and Tami. this involvement differs from that of Agudat Israel in relation to the dilemma between concentrating on assuring services and resources to its religious constituency or seeking to impose aspects of the Halacha on the entire Jewish population. The parties upholding the Religious Zionist outlook tend to stress the latter option. This tendency is expressed in legislative activity. The most important of these laws grant sole jurisdiction over Jews to the rabbinical courts in matters of marriage, divorce, and personal status.[55] Other religious legislation involved Sabbath observance and prohibition against pig breeding and sale of pork products. This difference between Agudat Israel and the Religious Zionist parties is actually one of degree, as both usually support particularistic arrangements assuring services for the Orthodox public and legislative initiatives expanding the scope of what is often referred to as "religious coercion." (This term is used by secular critics to describe religious legislation imposing compulsory observance, such as the monopoly granted by the state to religious courts in matters of marriage and divorce.) Moreover, the gap between the two parties in terms of the issues emphasized has narrowed over the years as a result of changes within both political camps. In the Religious Zionist camp, the stress has shifted from a desire to use the party's political leverage to strengthen the status of religion in Israel, to an approach that sees the Halacha as a source of policy guidelines for central national issues not directly concerned with matters of religion and state. Thus certain Religious Zionist groups led by Gush Emunim justify their struggle for preserving the state's hold on Greater Israel and for settlement across the Green Line, by resorting to ideological arguments based on their interpretation of the Halacha. This can be termed a transition from the "politicization of religion" to a "religiosization of politics," also involving a "theologization" of Ideology.[56]

Agudat Israel and its Knesset faction always defer to the right of its rabbinical leaders, sitting as the Council of Torah Sages, to determine the party's position on major issues. However, for Agudat Israel, which does not attribute religious significance to the state as such, these issues usually concern domestic matters. The NRP, on the other hand, does not invest its rabbinical authorities with the right to decide on political issues. They were guided by religious commitments in matters directly related to the status of religion in society, but not in matters of foreign affairs, defense, or economic policy. This situation changed after the Six Day War, and particularly after the Yom Kippur War as Halachic reasons were advanced in the debate over Greater Israel and the future of the occupied territories. The Halachic rationale for retaining the territories became a powerful tool of political persuasion in the hands of the ultra-nationalists in the party who succeeded in attaining a dominant position in the Religious Zionist camp.[57] This development granted legitimacy to the involvement of rabbis, and particularly the chief rabbis, in political processes such as the formation of government coalitions and attempts to unify the fragmented national religious political camp.

In addition to these changes in the Religious Zionist camp, changes in the ultra-Orthodox sector also helped to narrow the political gap between the two groups. Factions of Agudat Israel and Shas became supporters of the ideology of Greater Israel even though they did not accept the Zionist assumptions of the NRP or the view that regarded the state of Israel as a sign of Israel's approaching redemption. Thus another paradox emerged, that of non-Zionist Hassidim such as the Habad circles adopting hawkish views on the future of the territories. At the same time, Agudat Israel expanded the range of its political activity beyond the narrow concern for assuring the religious interests of their constituents. Agudat Israel joined the ruling coalition, even though it declined to sit in the cabinet; its leaders became involved in shaping economic policy and took on the role of mediators in coalition crises; and stepped up initiatives towards religious legislation. Shas went even further and joined the "national unity" government established after the 1984 election.

The Religious-Secular Cleavage: Constitutional and Legal Issues

The public controversies generated by the religious-secular cleavage tend to focus on legislative and legal issues. This tendency stems from the nature of the Halacha as an autonomous system of law and legal procedure. This system of Jewish law, as it is sometimes known, comprises an alternative to the civil legal system of the state. Moreover, from the perspective of the Orthodox Jew, the Halacha takes precedence over the law of the state whenever there is a contradiction between the two systems, and especially when civil law demands behavior that is contrary to Halachic rules. The nature of the Halacha as a comprehensive legal system means that the problem of defining the relationship between religion and state is not only a constitutional issue that can be resolved by the application of some sort of legal or political formula, as it is in many states, but also an issue that arises constantly in varied legal and legislative contexts. In other words, what we have here is not a problem of deciding whether or not a certain religion shall have official status, as the state religion for example, but rather of dealing with the relationship between the laws of the state and the laws of the Halacha. In this respect, Israel is an exceptional case, since although there is no state religion in Israel, neither is there separation between religion and state.

The most extreme manifestation of lack of separation between religion and state is the exclusive jurisdiction given to the Halacha and the rabbinical courts over Jews in matters of marriage and divorce. This does not confer on Judaism the status of state religion since members of other religions are also subject to the laws of their respective religious authorities in such matters of personal status. However, since this arrangement does not allow for civil marriage and divorce, it forces non-religious people in all communities to resort to religious authorities.

The arrangement that gives religious law jurisdiction over the lives of the members of the respective communities did not originate with the Israeli legislature. The Israeli laws which have conferred this authority on the religious courts of the various religious communities are continuations, in one way or another, of Mandatory law anchored in the Order in Council of 1922.[58] This law is simply another version of the Millet system governing religious minorities which was imposed when Palestine was ruled by the Ottoman Empire. The laws of personal status do not distinguish between the citizens of Israel on a national or ethnic basis, but rather a religious basis. This distinction is not of great significance for Israel's Jews because the rabbinical courts are totally under the control of the Orthodox stream in Judaism, and marriage and divorce cannot be performed under Conservative or Reform auspices, nor under civil auspices. On the other hand, the religious criterion divides the Arab population into Moslems and Christians, each with their internal divisions, and Druze. The meaning of the legal arrangements governing marriage and divorce is that this area has been removed from the jurisdiction of the secular legislature and civil courts, and Israel's Jews can have recourse only to the religious courts and traditional Jewish law. This is also reflected in the oath of allegiance

taken by judges. While civil court judges swear allegi
Israel and its laws, the religious court judges affirm a
the state of Israel. Moreover, the ordinance governin
judges states that the dayan (religious judge) is not
judicial authority except for the religious law.

Making the Halacha into the legally binding framework for marriage and divorce has created inconsistencies in defining Who is a Jew. While the Halachic definition of Jewishness is binding in reference to marriage and divorce, this is not the case with the Law of Return and the population registry. As a result, various Ministers of the Interior have issued different regulations to cover this gap. Religious ministers such as Yosef Burg and Moshe Chaim Shapiro have issued regulations in a religious spirit, while a secular minister, Israel Bar-Yehuda, ruled in 1958 that whoever declares himself a Jew can be registered as a Jew. This act, however, caused a coalition crisis and led to the resignation of the government. In the wake of this crisis, Prime Minister BenGurion sought the opinions of rabbis and Jewish thinkers around the world on the issue of "Who is a Jew," and most of them replied that with the Jewish people, one cannot distinguish between religion and national origin. In 1970, the law was changed to read that for purposes of the Law of Return and the population registry, a Jew is a person born of a Jewish mother or who has been converted to Judaism, and is not a follower of another religion. However, even after this amendment, the legal definition of Who is a Jew is not identical with the Halacha since the exclusion of the possibility of being a follower of another religion is not necessarily implied in the Halacha. The 1970 amendment was not accepted by the Orthodox since it left open the question of Reform and Conservative conversions performed abroad. Repeated attempts by the religious parties to muster a majority in the Knesset to change the law so that only Orthodox conversions be recognized have failed. It should be noted that previous changes in the definitions of "Who is a Jew" in the Law of Return also required another change in that law specifying that the non-Jewish relatives of Jewish immigrants are also eligible for new immigrants' rights. This change was made to facilitate immigration from countries with a high rate of intermarriage.

These changes were introduced in the law in response to decisions of the Supreme Court which reflected the range of ideological positions on the national and religious aspects of defining Who is a Jew. The decision to exclude as a Jew those who had been born to a Jewish mother but had converted to another religion was taken in the wake of the decision regarding "Brother Daniel" (Oswald Rufeisen), who had petitioned the Supreme Court sitting as the High Court of Justice. He argued that he should be granted citizenship under the Law of Return because he was born a Jew and still regarded himself as Jewish despite the fact that he had converted to Catholicism and had become a Carmelite monk. The majority of the court ruled that those who convert to another religion exclude themselves from the Jewish people and religion.[59] The 1970 amendments were also affected by the Supreme Court ruling ordering the Ministry of Interior to register the children of Major Binyamin Shalit as Jews despite the fact that their mother was not Jewish. The court ruled that with regard to the population registry, the law did not specify that the Halachic definition of Jewishness must apply, and that Shalit could legitimately claim that his children were Jewish by nationality.[60] The parties that joined the government following the 1969 elections stipulated in their coalition agreement that the Law of Return should be amended to rule out such options.

In order to reduce the areas of friction between the religious and the secular over legislative issues, government coalitions going back to the early years of the state adopted the principle of maintaining the status quo in religious affairs. This principle was laid down in a letter written in 1947 by David Ben-Gurion to Rabbi I.M. Levin of Agudat Israel—assuring them that the religious situation then in force in the areas of personal status, Sabbath observance, and kashrut would hold after the establishment of the state. Thus debates and controversies over religious issues were limited mainly to the interpretation of provisions of the original status quo or to new problems that arose in later years.[61]

The religious-secular cleavage is a phenomenon of cultural pluralism that has social, political, and legal implications. Certain expressions of this cleavage, especially those concerning the ultra-Orthodox, reflect the dimension of social pluralism as evident in separate areas of residence and social networks. In relation to the small group of extreme ultra-Orthodox who do not recognize the state of Israel there are also aspects of quasi-institutional pluralism present. However, despite the broad ramifications of the religious cleavage, there is very little overlap with the cleavages along class or ethnic lines; and since this involves only Jews, there cannot be any overlap with the Arab-Jewish cleavage. Further, there is no overlap between the religious-secular cleavage and ideological cleavages on socio-economic issues. There is, however, a partial overlap between ideological positions on the future of the occupied territories and the religious-secular cleavage.[62] This overlap is only partial because the ideological approach attributing religious meaning to the state of Israel—and from this deriving certain positions concerning the ideal borders of the Land of Israel—is accepted by only a part of the Orthodox public, albeit the dominant part.[63]

There are indications that during the 1970s and 1980s the religious-secular cleavage became more pronounced and increasingly dichotomous, or at least this is how the situation is perceived by both the religious and the secular sectors of the population. The spread of fundamentalism in the Religious Zionist camp has led to an increasing tendency to social and cultural separatism in this group, especially among the younger generation. Separation can sometimes mitigate conflicts in that it reduces the potential for friction. However, in this context this social and cultural separatism occurred paradoxically when the political centrality of both the Zionist and non-Zionist religious camps increased. The efforts of these groups to put their stamp on the political center resulted in a backlash which encompassed only part of the non-religious public. In this respect, there was a difference between the responses of "secular" and "traditional" groups. The considerable portion of the public that can be classed as "traditional" in one sense or another had become more receptive, especially after the Six Day War, to the religious approach that defines Jewish nationalism in religious terms. This tendency among part of the non-religious public is expressed in several ways: in a growing ethnocentrism based on the traditional concepts of the "closeness" of the Jewish people and the notion that Israel is "a people that dwells alone" and its corollary that"the whole world is against us"; an increasingly positive attitude to observant Jews as the main carriers of Jewish tradition, which led the army and some schools to open themselves up to the influence of those preaching a "return" to religion; and the reliance on religious symbols and rhetoric such as "the Divine promise" and "land of our forefathers" to ground the territorial claims of Zionism.

Thus as long as these efforts by the religious camp were perceived as attempts to provide some religious embellishments to the secular-national ethos, they did not prompt an immediate intensification of the religious-secular conflict. However, when the various religious groups carried their offensive into the more sensitive territory of imposing observance on the private sphere, a backlash occurred among the non-religious public that was expressed in criticism of the extensive allocations of resources to the religious sector, in general, and to ultra-

Orthodox groups, in particular. This brought in its wake a renewal of the ideological disputes over the place of religion in public life which had been largely dormant during the sixties and seventies.

The Ethno-Cultural Cleavage: Some Social Implications

The ethnic cleavage in Israeli society is in many ways unique, since it is rooted in the unusual social and cultural development of the Jewish people in the Diaspora. Even though this division is usually defined as an "ethnic" cleavage, it lacks the elements of national distinctiveness that usually mark ethnic cleavages. Moreover, the boundaries between the ethnic groups are not clearly defined. There are at least two ways of defining the ethnic cleavage in dichotomous terms: as Ashkenazim versus Sephardim, and as Jews of "European-American" origin versus those of "Asian-African" origin. The first of these distinctions, between Ashkenazim and Sephardim, ignores geographical factors and is based on differences in prayer and ritual. The second is based on geographical and cultural origin, and thus some Sephardim, mainly those from the Balkans, are included in the category of Jews of European-American origin.

In addition to these dichotomous distinctions, there are non-dichotomous formulations such as the triad of Ashkenazim, Sephardim, and Afro-Asian Jews—which was current during the pre-state period—and a four-way classification putting the Yemenite Jews in a category of their own. There are also groups which cannot be placed clearly in any of these categories, such as the Jews from Georgia and other Asian republics of the Soviet Union, the Ethiopian Jews, and the Bene Israel from India. The latter two groups, cut off for long periods from mainstream Judaism have distinct racial features. Other common ethnic distinctions are based on differences between specific countries of origin, areas, or cities within a single country. Another factor blurring the lines distinguishing ethnic groups are the marriages between them. About a fifth of all marriages among Jews in Israel are between those Afro-Asian origin and those of European-American origin. There is thus a growing population of second and even third generation offspring of these marriages for whom the dichotomous distinctions do not apply.[64]

The essence of ethnic pluralism in Israel is basically cultural. It is nevertheless accompanied at times by social pluralism which is expressed through social networks within ethnic groups. Ethnic ecological segregation appears in neighborhoods and towns which have a high concentration of Afro-Asian Jews or even of Jews from one specific country. These ethnic residential concentrations were formed in two ways: by those of the same background choosing to live together, or by those who arrived in Israel together from a certain country being directed to a specific area by the authorities.

Ethnic neighborhoods formed as a result of administrative decisions include the development towns set up in the 1950s and the urban neighborhoods which replaced the immigrant transit camps (maabarot) in the late 1950s. The creation of ethnically homogeneous residential areas was largely a matter of chance and did not reflect a specific policy on the part of the housing or settlement authorities, except in the case of certain moshavim (co-operative farming villages).

The issue of ethnic separatism or the formation of social ties across ethnic boundaries is not just a matter of residence. No less important in this context are the social connections within and outside the ethnic group that are maintained by individuals and families. Such connections that are not simply a one-time affair are viewed as social networks which can be compared according to their duration, density, and intensity of contact. In the context of ethnic separatism, two kinds of social networks represent two opposing tendencies: internal networks that strengthen the cohesion of ethnic groups and networks across ethnic lines that indicate a low degree of separatism. Three factors determine the nature of these two kinds of social networks: differences between various countries of origin, status differences, and generational differences, with the latter mainly affecting differences between immigrants and those born or raised in Israel.

Among those born in Europe, social networks based on country of origin play only a small role. An exception here are the "landsmanschaften" comprised of immigrants from Hungary, Germany, and Romania which stress social ties based on a common language. Homogeneous social networks based on those from a specific country of origin are much more widespread among Afro-Asians. The persistence of the extended family among Middle Eastern and North African communities is a major factor in the creation of these homogeneous networks, as is residence in the same town or neighborhood. These internal social networks are also strengthened by the Afro-Asian practice of attending synagogues based on specific countries of origin.[65]

The second factor related to the tendency to form social networks is social status which has a complex and varied influence. On the whole, however, one may say that the higher the status of individuals and families, the less their tendency to form ethnically homogeneous social networks. This tendency is most pronounced among those with higher education, as indicated by the high inter-ethnic marriage rates for this group. Inter-ethnic marriages are the clearest indicator of social networks that cross ethnic lines. It should be noted that in addition to the marriages between Ashkenazim and Afro-Asians, the marriages between Afro-Asians of specific countries are an important indicator of a tendency to broaden social networks.

Generational status is an important factor determining whether social networks will cross ethnic lines. This factor is common in all immigrant societies and affects all country of origin groups to one extent or another. Among Ashkenazim, at least in non-Orthodox groups, the country of origin of the parents has no influence in shaping the social networks of their children. Among second-generation Afro-Asians there is a decreasing tendency to maintain social networks based on a specific country of origin. The many points of social contact, mainly in the schools and the army, between those of different countries of origin also contribute to blurring the differences between them. Nevertheless, among second-generation Afro-Asians who are not socially mobile and who lead a religiously traditional way of life, social networks based on specific countries of origin are still strong. Even though differences based on specific countries of origin are almost completely blurred in the second generation, generalized differences between "Ashkenazim" and "Sephardim" (as these are colloquially expressed) are still apparent in the second generation, although to a much lesser extent than in the first generation. This phenomenon is generated usually by status differences such as education and income rather than by ethnic stereotypes. However, these differences in income and education tend to stigmatize those of lower status when they are linked with external indicators of ethnic background such as physical appearance and type of Hebrew accent. At any rate, the increase in inter-ethnic marriages and the increased social mobility among Afro-Asians indicates that the generalized distinctions between Ashkenazim and Sephardim do lose much of their impact in the second generation.

Ethno-Cultural Consciousness as a Political Resource

Ethnic separatism generates ethnic consciousness even if, on the whole, there is no direct connection between the extent of separation and the intensity of ethnic consciousness. However, ethnic consciousness, more than the fact of ethnic separation itself, means that people find a common bond in culturally distinctive symbols which, in turn, can prepare the ground for the conversion of ethnicity into a political resource. In other words, the extent to which social, political, and cultural mobilization can be grounded in an ethnic basis reflects the strength of ethnic consciousness. Research conducted in Israel reveals varied expressions of ethnic consciousness especially among Afro-Asians, as in this group it tends to be related to feelings of socio-economic deprivation.[66] This connection provides a basis for social, cultural, and political mobilization among Afro-Asians. Nowadays, social organization on an ethnic basis beyond social networks is much more limited than it was during the period of the Mandate.[67] Exceptions to this are religious expressions of ethnic mobilization such as synagogues organized according to country of origin. Ethnic organizations that do not focus on religious activities, such as the various national committees purporting to represent the Sephardi, Moroccan, or Kurdish Jews, have little impact on the daily lives of most members of these groups with the exception of the handful of public figures who are active in these bodies. Nevertheless, these organizations represent an attempt to preserve and cultivate ethnic consciousness by publishing journals and books, encouraging research on a group's ethnic heritage and promoting ethnic folklore through social events and special festivities. The annual ethnic celebrations of the Mimouna for the Moroccans and the Saharana for Kurdish Jews serve as focal points of cultural mobilization for Afro-Asian Jews.[68] Other expressions of cultural mobilization are performances by song and dance groups which seek to cultivate the Afro-Asian artistic heritage. This stress on an ethnic cultural heritage, its revival, and preservation, reflects an attempt to compensate for feelings of deprivation or inferiority held by many Afro-Asians toward the dominant culture. These activities also represent attempts to convey the cultural heritage of an ethnic group to the public at large in order to attain recognition for the group as a legitimate component of Israeli culture.

This attempt to transform the folkloristic elements in an ethnic cultural heritage into general cultural values, like the attempt to teach about the Afro-Asian cultural heritage in the schools, sometimes takes on the artificial quality that marks other efforts at cultural creation that are initiated and sanctioned by the establishment and are politically motivated.[69] The use of ethnic sentiment and loyalties for political mobilization reflects, on the one hand, the awareness among politicians of the power of such feelings in Israeli society and, on the other, the increasing electoral significance of Afro-Asian voters. The increase in the size of the Afro-Asian population, due to their birth rates being higher than that of the Ashkenazim, has gradually increased their weight among the voting population.[70]

There have been two main aspects to the exploitation of ethnicity for political purposes. The first refers to political organization that is explicitly or implicitly ethnically based. Examples of this are the electoral lists of the Sephardim and Yemenites that were active until the early 1950s (which, paradoxically, disappeared at the height of the mass immigration from Middle Eastern countries) and parties such as Tami and Shas which appeared in the 1980s.[71] The second and more prevalent aspect of the use of ethnic consciousness to rally political support is reflected in attempts to cultivate ethnic identification with certain parties that are themselves not ethnically based.[72] Attempts to forge these kinds of ties are facilitated by feelings of ethnic social deprivation. Parties such as the Likud have presented themselves as the spokesmen of the aspirations of the deprived Afro-Asian groups, known as the "Second Israel," for an improvement in their socio-economic, cultural, and political status. The common point of departure for both strategies of utilizing ethnic consciousness for political mobilization is the extensive overlap between the ethnic cleavage and the cleavage along class lines. However, these strategies point in entirely different directions, with one being separatist and the other integrationist.

The greater success of the integrationist strategy indicates that most Afro-Asian Jews do not seek political-ethnic separatism. The integrationist strategy is fed by the embittered feelings of many Afro-Asians against the political establishment that was dominant in the 1950s and 1960s, which in their eyes shunted them into a peripheral social and political position.

It should be noted that support for parties which base their appeals on feelings of ethnic deprivation does not necessarily represent an act of instrumental voting based on a concrete expectation of social or economic advancement. It is usually an expressive act that conveys social protest or that seeks compensation for wounded ethnic pride by identifying with symbols of national unity, thus gaining symbolic access to the cultural and national center that was denied them by the establishment. The extensive use of ethnic symbols and sentiments for political mobilization has created a high correlation between ethnic origin and party voting preferences. This correlation was at first more evident among Afro-Asians but also appeared later among those of European-American origin, so that ethnic polarization has generated political party polarization as well. It is noteworthy, however, that the correlation between ethnicity and party applies in voting patterns but is not reflected in the composition of the parties' lists of candidates to the Knesset.

The Ethno-Cultural Cleavage: The Impact of Mass Immigration

The ethnic cleavage originated during the Ottoman period in the separate ethnic organizations for Ashkenazim and Sephardim maintained within the Old Yishuv. The Jews from Eastern Europe who came with the early waves of Zionist immigration did not become part of the institutional frameworks of the Old Yishuv, but established new frameworks such as agricultural settlements, political parties, workers organizations, modern schools, and so forth. As for the Afro-Asian Jews who came to Palestine at that time, some found their niche in the institutions of the Old Yishuv, while others became part of the life of the "New Yishuv." These processes—the growth of the Ashkenazi population, the expansion of the new institutional network and the partial integration of Afro-Asians with it—continued during the period of the Mandate. The portion of Sephardim and Afro-Asians in the Jewish population declined from 40 percent to 20 percent during the 30 years of the Mandate.[73]

The institutions of the New Yishuv were based on the ideology of the "ingathering of the exiles" which totally rejected separatist ethnic organization. Nevertheless, during this period the communal institutions of the non-Ashkenazim flourished and became the focus of political organization. Despite the fact that ethnic parties elected delegates to Knesset Israel and the local authorities, the ethnic cleavage was far from the main item on the agenda of the Yishuv during the Mandate. The involvement of the organized Sephardic community in building the institutions of the New Yishuv and in the political decisions taken by the Organized Yishuv was rather small, and the power struggles at that time were between political-ideological forces, workers and employers, and ultra-Orthodox and secular Jews. Another reason for the low salience of the ethnic cleavage under the Mandate was the low extent of overlap between ethnicity and social class, particularly in the 1920s. Many of the East European immigrants were without means and supported themselves by a variety of occupations, including unskilled manual labor; while the veteran Sephardic population included businessmen and property owners, in addition to manual laborers, craftsmen, and small merchants.[74]

This situation changed radically after the establishment of the state. The ethnic problems to emerge after 1948 were only slightly connected with the ethnic organization of the Sephardim from the period of the Yishuv. The mass immigration of the 1950s made a deep impact on both the ethnic cleavage and the social class cleavage and above all, on the emerging correlation between them. The mass immigration of the early 1950s marks a turning point in the development of Israeli society because of its broad scope, its rapid pace and the diversity of the groups that arrived during that brief period. During the first eleven years of Israel's existence, close to a million immigrants arrived, thus swelling the population of 650,000 Jews who lived in Israel when the state was established. Most of the immigration came during 1949-51, so that by 1952 Israel's Jewish population had doubled compared to 1948. The growth rate of the Jewish population during 1932-36 was actually higher than in the first years of the state but it should be recalled that since the Jews were a minority then, the growth rate of the entire population—Jews and Arabs alike—was smaller than the growth rate of Israel's population in the early 1950s. (See Table 3).

Table 3
Annual Rates of Jewish Immigration per 1000 Jews in Palestine (until 1948) and Israel (1948-1958)*

Year	*Rate*	*Year*	*Rate*
1919	32	1937	27
1920	135	1938	32
1921	115	1939	64
1922	104	1940	18
1923	91	1941	13
1924	146	1942	8
1925	285	1943	17
1926	93	1944	27
1927	20	1945	23
1928	14	1946	30
1929	34	1947	35
1930	30	1948	117
1931	24	1949	266
1932	53	1950	154
1933	144	1951	132
1934	166	1952	17
1935	192	1953	8
1936	80	1954	12

*Average population for each year.
Source: "The Demographic Development of Israel," *The Economic Quarterly*, Vol. 2, No. 8, June 1955, p. 380 (Hebrew).

The immigration of the 1950s also differed from the immigration of the previous two decades in terms of the countries of origin of the immigrants. While the immigrants of the 1930s and 1940s were mainly from Central and Eastern Europe, the immigration of the 1950s was more heterogeneous—about half came from Europe and half from Islamic countries. (See Table 4). The first wave came during 1948-51 and numbered about 700,000 people. This wave crested in 1949 when 240,000 immigrants came, about half of whom were from Eastern Europe, including the internees of the "illegal immigrant" detention camps on Cyprus, residents of the Displaced Persons camps in Europe, and the Jewish communities of Bulgaria and Yugoslavia. The other half came from several Asian and African countries, mostly from Iraq and Yemen. The first wave of immigration dwindled to a trickle during 1952-54, with the low point reached during the first half of 1953. During that time, the number of those leaving the country exceeded those entering. Those leaving were composed mainly of recent immigrants from Morocco and Eastern and Central Europe. The next wave began in 1955 and continued until the end of 1957, bringing a total of 165,000 immigrants. Most of this wave came from Morocco, with others from Romania and Hungary. This wave also included Polish Jews who had taken refuge in the Soviet Union during World War II. In the next phase, about 25,000 immigrants came in each of the following two years until the end of the decade. In 1961 immigration rose again, and during the next two years 40,000 immigrants came from Europe and close to 70,000 from Asia and Africa.

Table 4
Immigrants by Country of Birth and Year of Immigration, 1948-1985 (percent)

Country of Birth	*1948*	*1949*	*1950*	*1951*	*1952*	*1953*	*1948-1953*
All Countries	100.0	100.0	100.0	100.0	100.0	100.0	100.0
Asia	5.3	30.5	34.4	59.5	28.7	27.8	35.3
Turkey	4.8	11.2	1.4	0.7	1.5	2.6	5.0
Iraq	0.0	0.7	19.3	51.3	4.1	4.1	17.8
Iran	0.1	0.8	6.3	5.4	17.9	10.6	3.9
Yemen & Aden	0.3	16.3	5.4	0.6	0.6	0.8	6.9
Other Countries	0.1	1.6	2.0	1.5	4.6	9.7	1.7
Africa	9.1	16.7	15.2	11.5	42.9	67.3	15.4
Tunisia, Algeria & Morocco	7.6	7.4	5.6	6.5	32.3	35.1	8.0
Libya	1.2	6.1	5.2	3.8	5.1	2.3	4.6
Other Countries	0.3	3.2	4.3	1.2	5.5	9.9	2.8

Table 4 (continued)
Immigrants by Country of Birth and Year of Immigration, 1948-1985 (percent)

Country of Birth	*1948*	*1949*	*1950*	*1951*	*1952*	*1953*	*1948-1953*
Europe	85.1	52.1	49.8	28.6	26.2	19.6	48.6
USSR	1.3	1.4	1.6	0.4	0.8	2.1	1.2
Poland	32.0	20.2	15.8	2.0	2.7	3.8	15.3
Romania	19.6	5.8	27.6	23.1	15.5	0.8	17.4
Bulgaria	16.8	8.6	0.6	0.7	1.9	3.3	5.4
Yugoslavia	4.6	1.1	0.2	0.4	0.4	0.1	1.1
Germany & Austria	2.0	3.0	0.8	0.4	1.1	1.8	1.6
Czechoslovakia	2.3	7.6	0.4	0.2	0.4	0.3	2.7
Hungary	3.9	2.0	1.6	0.7	0.9	2.2	2.1
Other Countries	2.6	2.4	1.2	0.7	2.5	5.2	1.8
American & Oceania	0.5	0.6	0.6	0.4	2.2	5.3	0.7
USA	0.3	0.2	0.2	0.1	0.4	0.7	0.2
Other Countries	0.2	0.4	0.4	0.3	1.8	4.6	0.5

Source: M. Sicron, *Immigration to Israel.* Jerusalem, Falk Institute and Central Bureau of Statistics, Table A33

Ethnically speaking, 1951 was the turning point marking the first time since the Zionist waves of immigration at the end of the nineteenth century that Europeans formed a minority of the newcomers. Following a transition phase of one year when immigrants from Asia comprise the largest group, in the remaining years of the decade immigrants from North Africa comprised the largest group of newcomers. These changes in the composition of the countries of origin of the immigrants reflect the radical demographic changes that took place then in Israeli society. These changes had many aspects. Among the most important was drastic increase in average family size as many large families arrived in Israel, and a change in age composition that increased the number of young children and the aged. These changes had significant ramifications for participation rates in the labor force, and led to a drop in the number of breadwinners and an increase in the number of dependents.[75]

The problems that stemmed from the age structure of the immigrants were compounded by their poor state of health. The number of chronically ill and invalids of all ages, but particularly among the elderly, reached such proportions that the country's health services could not cope. The country had never been faced with medical problems of such scope and severity. During the first seven years of the mass immigration, about 15 percent of the immigrants—110,000 out of 745,000—were officially listed as disabled, and most of these were chronically ill, unable to contribute anything at all to the work force.[76] This population evolved over the years into the hard core of Israel's social welfare cases. The combination of material hardship and unemployment, due to a serious lag in preparing an economic infrastructure for the immigrants, together with the enormous problems faced by health and welfare agencies, led the absorption authorities to consider a policy of selective immigration. Such a policy was adopted following considerable debate and political controversy, with eligibility for immigration based on state of health, ability to work and the age of the family's chief breadwinner. These selective criteria could not be applied in the mass evacuations of the Jews of Iraq and Yemen, which appeared to be Israel's only chance to save these communities, so it was applied mainly to immigrants from Morocco and Iran. However, this policy lasted only a short time because of the decline in immigration and the pressure from families of those who had not been allowed to come.[77]

The scope and rapid pace of immigration created a lag of several years before immigrants could be properly employed, housed, and provided with the necessary social services. This lag meant that the absorption authorities had to provide the basic needs of hundreds of thousands of people under conditions of temporary housing and employment with the newcomers cut off socially and culturally from the mainstream of society. The immigrants were indeed provided with housing, employment, and education for their children, but these were of minimum quality that placed them on the bottom of the social status hierarchy.[78]

The Ethno-Cultural Cleavage: Cultural Traditions and the Israeli Culture

The constraints faced by the absorption authorities and the resulting policies were not the only factors that influenced the immigrants' position in the stratification structure or on the center-periphery axis. Factors of no less importance were the specific characteristics that the immigrants brought from their countries of origin and their ability to use these as resources to facilitate their social, cultural, occupational, and political integration. The first aspect included demographic characteristics such as age, family size, vocational training, and formal education. The second aspect included cultural orientations usually connected to the concept of "modernity": a sense of enterprise and the ability to delay gratification of material needs while working toward personal goals for the future. The third aspect refers to personal qualities or resources facilitating easy access to the Israeli establishment—what is known colloquially in Israel as "protecksia"—which might be a common spoken language, shared forms of behavior, or personal connections through social networks based on country of origin.

The cultural differences between the immigrants from Europe and those from the Islamic countries, and the differences between the traditional orientations of most Afro-Asian immigrants and the dominant values of Israeli society, forced both the immigrants and the veterans to confront the dilemma between a "melting pot" approach to absorption and an approach of cultural preservation and pluralism.[79] A similar dilemma existed during the Yishuv, but then, since aliyah had been a matter of personal ideological choice for most immigrants, the expectation that the newcomers would seek to adapt to the emerging culture of the Yishuv was taken for granted. Furthermore, the immigrants themselves sought to take an active part in shaping the society and ways of life in the Yishuv. An exception to this trend was the aliyah from Germany in the mid-1930s, following Hitler's rise to power. The German immigrants thus had to adapt to the dominant culture and political system shaped by other immigrants mainly from Eastern Europe whom they regarded as their inferiors in terms of education, skills, and cultural traditions. However, since the German immigrants possessed high levels of education and professional training, they developed channels of economic and cultural activity that had not yet been fully developed prior to their arrival—banking, industry, art, and science.[80]

The possibility of overcoming cultural estrangement by opening up alternative channels of activity and mobility was not available to the Afro-Asian immigrants after the establishment of the state. These immigrants lacked what the Germans had possessed in terms of formal education and training and cultural norms instilled in early socialization termed by social scientists of the 1960s as "achievement syndrome."[81] Furthermore, the paternalistic approach of the absorption authorities did not facilitate their adaptation to the dominant society since the Israeli cultural norms imposed on them were perceived by the newcomers not as universal values but as expressions of Ashkenazi dominance.[82]

A paradox was thus created: While those elements that shaped the new Jewish way of life to emerge in the Yishuv, and particularly those who adhered to the lifestyle and value orientations of the Labor

Movement regarded their culture as a successful expression of the radical Zionist aim of "negating the Diaspora," the immigrants from the Islamic countries saw all this as having nothing to do with them—it was a matter of importance only for those who came from Europe. Since most of the Afro-Asian immigrants adhered to a traditional religious life, the dimension of modern Israeli culture that reflected the "negation of the Diaspora," with all its anti-traditional overtones, was alien to them. Indeed, they were not even aware of it.

The outlook seeking to achieve a cultural revolution as part of the Zionist movement of national renewal, which also spoke of the need to create a "new type of Jew" to replace the type corrupted by centuries of exile, provided much of the impetus for the paternalistic policies of immigrant absorption reflected in the "melting pot" concept. When the "melting pot" policies were dropped, however, it was not because the ideological principle of the "negation of the Diaspora" had been abandoned. It was due rather to the pragmatic recognition that the frontal assault on the cultural heritage of the Afro-Asian immigrants was hampering rather than facilitating their integration into Israeli society. This realization spread fastest among the political establishment which faced the practical problems of mobilizing the immigrants into political party frameworks.[83] The political parties and social frameworks such as the moshav movement which worked to absorb the Afro-Asian immigrants found that the strategy of cultural confrontation aroused opposition and even rejection. Moreover, within Israeli society as a whole, and particularly its political establishment, there was no agreement on the precise contours of the new cultural model that the immigrants were supposed to embrace. Religious circles, which naturally objected to the secularizing thrust of the Zionist cultural revolution, viewed the Afro-Asian immigrants' traditional background in a positive light. Even here, however, there was a strong paternalistic element in the approach of the Ashkenazi religious establishment. These groups regarded the Ashkenazi religious tradition in all its aspects—Halachic, ceremonial, and intellectual—as the mainstream of Jewish tradition, while the Afro-Asian religious traditions were seen as secondary or lacking in depth. The Afro-Asian Jews, however, saw their traditions as the authentic complete expression of Judaism. From these trends there emerged a form of cultural pluralism that was not based on a sense of cultural equality, but rather on mutual estrangement based on unflattering mutual stereotypes.

Over the years there were three major changes in the cultural aspect of the ethnic problem:

1) In the second generation, the differences between specific countries of origin became blurred and the tendency increased to stress the dichotomous distinction between Ashkenazim and Afro-Asians. This distinction, which had lost much of its political relevance in the 1950s, achieved renewed significance in the 1970s and 1980s as symbols of ethnic identity became important tools of political mobilization, although not necessarily by ethnic parties. The increased public references to the dichotomous distinction between Ashkenazim and Afro-Asians were also connected to a sharpening of mutual stereotypes, expressed mainly in the images of the violent, crude Levantine on the one hand and the snobbish, do-gooder liberal on the other.

2) The political establishment initiated a program, which did not get very far, of cultivating the "heritage of Afro-Asian Jewry" mainly through a special curriculum prepared for the schools. The difficulties encountered by this program stemmed from the process of cultural decline that had afflicted Sephardic culture following its peak period of the Golden Age in Spain and the expulsion from Spain in 1492. Thus, the material representing the Afro-Asian cultural heritage of the nineteenth and twentieth centuries included in this program could not match the same standards of quality which exemplary works of European Jewish culture at that time reflected. As a result, the folkloristic elements of the Afro-Asian heritage had a greater weight in the curriculum than works representing "high culture."

3) Under the universal impact of western popular culture, the second generation of both Ashkenazi and Afro-Asian backgrounds increasingly resemble each other. Patterns of cultural consumption and leisure activities such as the movies, television, pop music, and spectator sports created common cultural channels that made differences in cultural background less relevant in everyday interaction between members of the two groups. Thus the renewed stress on the uniqueness of Afro-Asian culture occurred at a time when the significance of cultural pluralism as an expression of distinct life-styles and patterns of behavior was rapidly fading.[84]

The third category of personal and group characteristics that shaped the positions attained by the immigrants in the stratification structure and on the center-periphery axis refers to the differences in social networks between those of European and Afro-Asian origin. These differences determined the ability of the two groups to attain direct access to the Israeli establishment. In Israel of the 1950s an administrative culture held sway that was based on patterns inherited from the Yishuv which gave much more weight to particularistic connections between public bureaucracies and their clientele than to universalistic standards of access and treatment. These particularistic connections were based on common movement membership, length of residence, common language, personal and family acquaintances, common place of birth, and so forth. The European immigrants of the 1950s had an advantage over the Afro-Asian immigrants in all these connections, since the social networks of the former were connected at least in some ways to those of the veteran population. Because they lacked these social networks, the Afro-Asian immigrants became more dependent on the public bureaucracies that expanded considerably then and which also dealt directly with immigrant absorption.[85] Since the public bureaucracies then were run and staffed according a "political party key," political channels of access could substitute to some extent, for the missing personal channels of access. Thus, the politicization of the public services facilitated the entry of the Afro-Asian immigrants into the particularistic ethos that dominated public life then, while the depoliticization of the public bureaucracies that occurred in later years deprived them of one of their channels of access to the establishment. On the other hand, the emergence of universal mechanisms of resource allocation compensated somewhat for the weakness of their social networks.

The Ethno-Cultural Cleavage: The Dilemma of the Israeli Establishment

The problems of integration faced by the immigrants of the 1950s, and especially those from the Asia and North Africa, were not theirs along. The establishment also faced some serious dilemmas in those days, the most important of which was the choice between pursuing policies of rapid integration, or reconciling itself to the existence of cultural pluralism and accepting it as fact. This dilemma was particularly pronounced in two spheres, the political and the educational. The political sphere was the first to abandon the more radical expressions of the melting pot. The opposition to ethnic parties was shared by the entire political elite, both the ruling parties and the opposition, but this did not prevent them from manipulating the traditional ethnic frameworks for mobilizing political support. On the local level, the local party leaders utilized the traditional kinship networks of the immigrants and ethnically-based neighborhood solidarity to recruit party members or at least to get their supporters to the polls on election

.[86] The parties that comprised the ruling coalition usually obtained ,e support of the older generation of leaders among the Afro-Asian immigrants, so that younger people with political ambitions found these channels blocked. Some of these younger people turned to opposition parties as an outlet for their ambitions, primarily to the main opposition party Herut, whose attractiveness for the immigrants was enhanced by the feelings of deprivation generated by the absorption processes of the 1950s and by the resentment felt by many immigrants against the traditional leaders who had allowed themselves to be co-opted by the establishment. The "social underdogs" thus sought to improve their condition through an alliance with the "political underdogs."

In addition to the growing support for opposition parties, the currents of ethnic social protest found expression, at times violent, in extra-parliamentary politics. The most important expressions of this trend were the disturbances in the Waddi Salib slum in Haifa in 1959 and the emergence of the Black Panthers in Jerusalem in the early 1970s. The confrontations between demonstrators and the police in Waddi Salib, following an incident in which a local resident was injured by policemen, were largely spontaneous and left no organized protest efforts in their wake.[87] It should be noted nevertheless, that a local leader who took a prominent role in these events almost succeeded in getting elected to the Knesset on an ethnic list in 1959. Waddi Salib, however, had another impact on the elections by increasing the support for Herut in concentrations of North African immigrants. A second wave of ethnic protest broke out in the early 1970s. The Black Panthers, who sparked this second wave, represent a different case since their appearance was not the result of one incident but rather the outcome of deep feelings of deprivation experienced by the second generation of North African slum-dwellers. This movement managed to maintain an organized political effort for three years. Its successful showing in the 1974 elections for the Histadrut prompted the government to make considerable increases in budgets for housing, education, and welfare, out of concern for the social and political repercussions that might result from the spread of militant ethnic protest.[88]

The crisis brought on by the Yom Kippur War overshadowed the rising ethnic tensions and in the Knesset elections held two months after the fighting, the Panthers did not succeed in repeating their achievements in the elections to the Histadrut. Following this defeat, the movement began to break up into various factions and several of its leaders joined leftist anti-establishment parties. The appearance and limited success of the Black Panthers was exceptional in that most of its leaders and activists leaned toward the left. The main body of ethnic-political protest had for years been expressed electorally in support for Herut, which is identified as a right wing party—despite the fact that most of its voters are low income white-collar and blue-collar workers. Election results over the years have shown that the vast majority of the public tends to vote for parties with an ethnically heterogeneous composition. Nevertheless, the high correlations between Afro-Asian background and voting for Herut (and its successor, the Likud) and Ashkenazi background and voting for Mapai (and its successor, the Alignment) came to be firmly established over the years.[89] This represents another paradox: Particularistic identities found political expression through support for parties that share an integrative orientation and that articulate their values and goals in universal terms.

It was in the educational sphere that the dilemma was sharpest between the desire for rapid integration that would put an end to ethnic distinctions and the willingness to accept cultural pluralism. Moreover, in the educational sphere it was easier than in other spheres to translate ideological positions into concrete policies or to conduct controlled experiments to evaluate the success of educational reforms. The first stage in the educational absorption of the immigrants was expressly governed by a drive for uniformity that ignored the differences in cultural and social backgrounds. This influenced the ability of pupils to adapt to the demands of formal education and to absorb the contents conveyed by the curriculum. Education policy also sought to provide equal inputs throughout the system, but found this difficult to achieve because of the shortage of qualified teachers willing to work in the outlying areas. Educational policy-makers at that time did not take into account that providing formal equality in educational inputs would not lead to equal educational achievements by pupils from different cultural backgrounds and, in fact, would achieve the opposite result by increasing the gaps between groups of pupils. It was soon noticed that this policy had created a situation where immigrant children finishing their eight years of compulsory education could come out as "functional illiterates."

When the failure of this approach was acknowledged, it was replaced by an approach that provided extra educational resources to schools with a high concentration of those defined as culturally deprived, on the assumption that unequal inputs would lead to more equal outputs. However, from the perspective of the dilemma between integration and cultural pluralism, this policy too sought a homogeneous type of educational product uninfluenced by cultural background. This integrative approach was reflected in the key terms used to define this policy of helping the "culturally deprived" advance through "enrichment." In other words, cultural differences were perceived as a sign of cultural backwardness.[90]

Another problem to arise with the policy of formal equality in education was the attempt to get around some of its consequences by establishing differential criteria for acceptance into academic high schools. A lower set of entrance requirements was defined for pupils of Afro-Asian background. This measure created problems because it led to the growth of unrealistic expectations among the Afro-Asian youths accepted on the basis of lower entrance criteria to academic high schools who often came unequipped to handle the challenges of these elitist institutions.[91] Later the educational authorities acknowledged the difficulties of attaining equal achievement levels in the schools, but sought to use the schools as a tool for social integration that would reduce the social barriers among children of different cultural backgrounds. An integration policy was thus adopted that called for the enrollment of children of different backgrounds at the same school, while making provision for differential teaching methods to be employed in certain subjects. These methods included distinctions between homeroom classes and classes grouped according to ability level for the teaching of certain subjects, and classes grouped according to average achievement levels. This often created a de facto separation of classes within each grade level according to ethnic background.[92] The common thread running through all these stages of educational policy was the desire to provide the same educational opportunities to children of all backgrounds. Thus, even when recognition of cultural pluralism led to the inclusion of lessons on the Afro-Asian Jewish heritage in the curriculum, these were provided for all children irrespective of their background.

There was only one exception to the policy of a common, unifying curriculum, and this was not related to ethnicity. Separate educational frameworks teaching different curricula were adopted to handle the problems created by the religious-secular cleavage. The creation of a religious framework within the state school system was not perceived as opposing the principle of the ingathering of the exiles, because the difference between the two school systems was ideological rather than ethnic. The only sector that openly maintained separate ethnic frameworks in the sphere of education was the ultra-Orthodox education system. In this sector there are many Ashkenazi yeshivot with very small numbers of Afro-Asian students, and Sephardic yeshivot and kollelim which have no Askenazi students. In the state schools, the prevailing orientation remained integrationist rather than pluralist, irrespective of the changes in the educational strategies adopted in the context of this orientation.

The blurring of most differences between Jews of Western origin and Jews of Middle Eastern and North African origin is not possible as long as there is a pronounced correlation between the achievement components of status—such as income, education, and occupation—and the ascriptive components such as ethno-cultural background. This correlation is usually expressed through the concept of the "ethnic gap," which surfaces in public discussions of social and political issues. The existence of such a gap during the period of mass immigration was an inevitable result of differences in personal resources such as education, occupational skills, and family size, on the one hand, and the authorities' preference for a process of absorption that stressed speed and quantity rather than quality, on the other. These status differences persisted over the years and continued into the generation of those born and educated in Israel despite the blurring of distinct group identities during that time. Studies of the relationship between status and country of origin have shown that all groups have progressed in terms of their level of education, occupational status, and income but this progress has not been accompanied by a narrowing of the gap in all areas. On the contrary, since those of European origin have advanced further and faster than the others in some areas, the gap remained stable or has even increased in the second generation. The gap in occupational status is especially pronounced in the second generation as this is reflected in the prestige attached to the occupations held by members of the two groups.[93] The data on income differences are less clear-cut due to problems in obtaining accurate data as well as to the significant number of high-paying occupations that carry low prestige. Since most of those who have such occupations are of Afro-Asian origin, it may be presumed that the gap in income has narrowed to a greater extent than with education and occupational prestige.

In Israeli society, a wide variety of differential mobility rates have emerged: in mobility rates of different ethnic-national groups; in mobility rates as measured by various status components; and in changing rates for different periods. Differential group mobility rates have emerged between cultural origin groups in the Jewish population and between Jews and Arabs. These differential rates apply to all three main status components, income, education, and occupation, but not to the same extent in each one. In the area of education, those of Afro-African origin have increased their representation at all levels of education achievement—as measured by years and levels of learning—but the relative gap between them and those of Western origin has persisted in the second generation.[94] The greatest mobility for the Afro-Asians occurred in secondary education where they significantly increased their achievements relative to the immigrant generation. The percentage of Afro-Asians with a secondary education now approaches their share of the entire population. On the other hand, the Afro-Asians are still significantly underrepresented among university students, despite the increase in the percentage of Afro-Asians in the student population over the years.[95]

Another major trend has been the narrowing of education gaps in the second generation among various groups of Afro-Asian origin and among groups of European origin. In the immigrant generation, for example, there were significant gaps in education levels between those from Iraq and Egypt and those from Yemen, Morocco, and Iran, which have almost disappeared in the second generation. This is also true of the differences in education levels that once distinguished immigrants from Poland and Romania from those from central Europe and Russia. The educational advantage of the latter did not continue into the second generation. Major advances occurred in the education levels of women of Afro-Asian origin compared to men of this background. As in the area of education, the gap between Afro-Asians and Westerners in occupational attainments was not reduced over the years. What is more, the gap between the two groups in the second generation was even larger than it was for their fathers in respect of both salaried workers and the self-employed.

To complete this discussion of differential group mobility, one must consider the ability of a group to convert the resources of education attainments into occupational status and a higher standard of living. The ability of second generation Afro-Asians to convert their educational resources, which were attained mainly at the secondary level, into other status components was impaired by the decline in the market value of the high school diploma. This occurred because of the growth in the number of academic degree holders, which in turn led employers who previously would settle for high school graduates, to make the educational requirements of various jobs more demanding. Thus, the number of occupations requiring university education increased over the years.[96] And since education is related to occupation, which, in turn, is related to income, the ability of Afro-Asians to convert their educational resources into higher income tended to decline. However, because of the availability of channels of economic mobility that were not dependent on education, it was possible for some of them to improve their income even with limited educational resources.[97] The limited ability to convert educational achievements to occupational and income attainments points to the fact that the pace and extent of mobility in themselves may not be sufficient for closing economic and social gaps. The timing of mobility also has a major influence, since it determines the extent to which the availability of certain resources on the job market is synchronized with a demand for these resources. Educational achievements that at one time could ensure economic and social mobility were no longer sufficient once the supply of educational abilities of all types exceeded the demand. This trend hurt mainly those who had succeeded in reaching medium educational levels, to discover that the positions to which they had aspired had been taken in the meanwhile by those with higher educational qualifications. It should be noted that the conversionary potential of resources does not operate in one direction only. Income can be at least partially converted into education, and a tendency exists among the economically successful who lack a university education to make sure that their children attain an academic degree. Since this possibility relates mainly to the third generation of Afro-Asian immigrants, starting with those who came to Israel in the 1950s, it is not possible at this stage to point to definite trends. Nevertheless, studies of attitudes and expectations point to the existence of such a tendency.

The Class Cleavage: The Decline of Class Consciousness

An examination of the social class cleavage in Israel reveals a paradox: Since the establishment of the state, inequality in the distribution of income and property has increased considerably, while the consciousness of class differences has decreased. (See Tables 5 and 6). In the prestate period, ideologies of social class served as the basis of political organization. There was a considerable degree of correspondence between social class and political affiliation, whether among the workers with their ties to the Labor Movement or among property owners and employers with their ties to the Ezrahim camp. In the early years of the state, comparative figures show that Israel was among the most egalitarian countries in the world in terms of income distribution. this situation changed within Israel's first decade. The deliberate encouragement of the private sector by a government dominated paradoxically by a socialist party created a stratum of nouveau riche and a broad middle class of small employers.[98] At the same time, the income gap grew among various categories of employees. As a result of these changes, income distribution in Israel came to resemble the patterns common to other developed societies.

Table 5
Income by Deciles Before and After Transfer Payments and Gini Coefficient

Decile	*1977*		*1979*		*1980*		*1981*	
	*Before T.P.**	*After T.P.**	*Before T.P.**	*After T.P.**	*Before T.P.**	*After T.P.**	*Before T.P.**	*After T.P.**
1	1.9	3.1	1.7	2.6	1.7	2.5	1.7	2.4
2	3.5	4.3	3.3	3.9	3.4	4.0	3.4	3.9
3	4.7	5.2	4.6	5.0	4.7	5.1	4.6	5.1
4	6.0	6.3	6.0	6.2	6.0	6.2	5.9	6.1
5	7.3	7.5	7.4	7.5	7.4	7.5	7.2	7.4
6	8.9	8.9	9.0	9.0	9.1	9.1	8.9	8.9
7	10.9	10.7	11.0	10.9	10.9	10.7	10.9	10.8
8	13.4	13.0	13.6	13.2	13.4	13.1	13.4	12.9
9	16.9	16.1	16.8	16.1	16.9	16.2	16.8	16.2
10	26.3	24.8	26.6	25.6	26.5	25.6	27.2	26.3
Gini Co-efficient	0.2838	2.2418	0.3075	0.2709	0.3131	0.2759	0.3202	0.2812

*T.P. = Transfer Payments
Source: The National Insurance Institute. *Annual Survey, 1981,* Table 9.

Table 6
Income Distribution of Wage and Salary Earners and all Jewish Urban Population: 1954 and 1957-58 (percent)

Decile	*Urban Employees Personal Income*		*Net Income*		*All the Urban Population Personal Income*	
	1954	*1957-8*	*1954*	*1957-8*	*1954 Families*	*1957-8 Observation Units*
1 Lowest	3.3	2.6	3.5	2.7	2.5	1.6
2	5.2	4.2	5.5	4.9	4.5	3.3
3	7.0	6.0	7.5	6.7	6.3	5.0
4	8.3	7.4	8.6	7.7	7.6	7.0
5	8.9	8.3	9.3	9.4	8.7	8.9
6	9.4	9.6	9.3	9.6	9.5	9.3
7	10.7	10.3	11.2	11.1	10.4	10.7

Table 6 (continued)
Income Distribution of Wage and Salary Earners and all Jewish Urban Population: 1954 and 1957-58 (percent)

Decile	*Urban Employees Personal Income*		*Net Income*		*All the Urban Population Personal Income*	
	1954	*1957-8*	*1954*	*1957-8*	*1954 Families*	*1957-8 Observation Units*
8	11.9	12.2	11.4	12.4	12.5	12.5
9	14.2	17.0	14.3	15.2	15.3	17.5
10	21.1	22.4	19.4	20.3	22.7	24.2
Sum	100.0	100.0	100.0	100.0	100.0	100.0
Average Annual Income (IL)	2,531	3,330	2,336	2,928	2,618	3,196

Source: M. Zandberg, "Income distribution of the Jewish population." *The Economic Quarterly,* No. 25-26, January 1960, p. 65.

These developments could conceivably have led to a deepening of class consciousness and to increased political mobilization on a class basis but this did not occur. On the contrary, utilization of the rhetoric of social class as a means of mobilizing political support declined. Symbols of working class identity cultivated by the Labor Movement during the period of the Yishuv, such as May Day celebrations, the red flag, and the Internationale either disappeared altogether or remained as rituals emptied of their expressive and mobilizing power. To the extent that terms with social class overtones such as "the working class" were used in public discourse, they were usually used in the context of labor relations between the Histadrut as a trade union with the government or the private sector, in negotiations over wages and working conditions. Such terms had lost much of the force of their political connotations.

Even more important was the severance of the connection between social class and voting patterns, a process that occurred in two stages. In the first stage, Mapai shifted from being a fairly homogeneous party in terms of its class composition to being a heterogeneous party. Along with its traditional working class electorate, Mapai voters now included voters from the middle class and the professions. At the same time, the social base of the parties on the right wing of the spectrum also became more heterogeneous. While the General Zionists and its successor the Liberal Party remained parties of the bourgeoisie in terms of their electorate as well as their economic orientation, an increasing number of workers joined the ranks of Herut's electorate. In 1965, Herut formed a political bloc with the

Liberal Party and eventually became the dominant partner with the Liberals in Gahal and later the Likud. In the 1960s, workers began to desert Mapai and flock to Herut. As a result of these changes, the situation that held in the early 1950s was gradually turned on its head. Most of the workers, and particularly those with low incomes, became supporters of Gahal and later the Likud, while Mapai and later the Alignment came to have an "excessive" amount of middle class supporters which included businessmen and professionals as well as employees in the high income brackets.

The weakness of class consciousness in Israel and the distinction between class membership and political party affiliation pose a quandary, since these phenomena depart from the common European pattern of a close connection between working class affiliation and socialist or communist political leanings—a pattern which shaped the political outlook of the veteran elites in Israel. The peculiarities of the association between class and political affiliation in Israel can be explained by a variety of economic, social, cultural, political, and ideological factors, each of which supplements the others:

1) The economic explanation points to the close structural connection between economic development and national capital in the Yishuv and in the State of Israel. Already in the 1920s labor leader Chaim Arlozoroff was able to foresee that class struggle in the Marxist sense would not play a major role in the emerging Jewish society in Palestine since most of the capital was imported from abroad rather than accumulated from internal sources.[99] According to this approach, the source of capital has a dual influence on class consciousness. First, the distribution of wealth is determined by central political mechanisms no less than by relationships between labor and capital. And second, a considerable portion of the imported capital is invested in frameworks under public ownership, where the traditional concept of class struggle does not hold.

One of the results of this situation can be seen in the structure of ownership. The Israeli economy has developed from the outset as a multi-sector economy and most of the workers are employed by firms under some form of public ownership. As a result, the hostility of the working class stemming from a sense of economic deprivation is not aimed, for the most part, at private employers or at the "bourgeoisie" as a whole, but rather at the political establishment that is responsible for allocating resources and for managing the publicly-owned industries and services which employ most of Israel's workers. It should be noted in this context that most of the capital now in private hands originated as capital imported by public institutions and was allocated to private entrepreneurs to encourage investment.[100] These developments negated the validity in Israel of the Marxist notion that politics is but a superstructure that rests on the base of economic relations. To the extent that there is a uni-directional connection between economics and politics, in Israel, it is upside-down, i.e., economics is rather a superstructure that rests on a base of political relations.

Another result of imported capital that also weakened class consciousness was the prolonged process of economic growth in which considerable and steady increases in the national product were attained from the early 1950s until the early 1970s. This process of growth led to an increase in real income and in living standards for the entire population. (See Table 7). However, no less important, from the standpoint of class consciousness, were the possibilities for upward economic mobility opened up by these processes. The increase in inequality appeared as wage levels rose at different rates, but with no group becoming impoverished in the process. Opportunities for upward mobility were found not only in larger wage differentials but also in the availability of new job opportunities. However, the increase in the number of jobs was not the same at all levels. An occupational structure emerged where senior posts increased at a greater rate than more junior positions, compared with the situation in the early 1950s.[101] This "open frontier" in the economic sphere was made possible by an import of capital that swelled the size of the public sector. A considerable portion of those at the top of this status hierarchy had only recently succeeded in "making it," and thus had not managed to cultivate a set of status symbols that would set them apart as an exclusive group. In such a fluid hierarchy, the individual's hopes for improvement in his status could be pinned on individual mobility rather than on a transformation of the class structure that would necessitate collective consciousness and action.

Table 7
Private Consumption and Gross National Product
Per Capita: 1950-1985

Year	*Per Capita (NIS)**	
	Private Consumption Expenditure	*Gross National Product*
	At 1980 Prices	
1950	5.39	7.70
1951	5.60	8.47
1952	5.60	8.25
1953	5.64	7.88

Table 7 (continued)
Private Consumption and Gross National Product
Per Capita: 1950-1985

Year	*Per Capita (NIS)**	
	Private Consumption Expenditure	*Gross National Product*
	At 1980 Prices	
1954	6.34	9.22
1955	6.61	10.14
1956	6.91	10.60
1957	7.00	10.90
1958	7.44	11.27
1959	7.93	12.32
1960	8.26	12.79
1961	8.86	13.63
1962	9.36	14.36
1963	9.90	15.37
1964	10.53	16.21
1964	10.27	15.88
1965	10.83	16.74
1966	10.75	16.44
1967	10.65	16.28
1968	11.68	18.18
1969	12.52	19.93
1970	12.50	20.85
1971	12.82	22.45
1972	13.66	24.46
1973	14.33	24.64
1974	14.95	25.15
1975	14.65	25.48
1976	15.02	25.41
1977	15.40	25.46
1978	16.31	25.86
1979	17.18	26.28
1980	16.29	26.51
1981	17.85	27.17
1982	18.65	26.47
1983	19.71	26.50
1984	18.01	26.05
1985	17.58	26.47
	At current prices	
1985	3,873.91	5,779.74

*NIS thousand, unless otherwise stated.
Source: Statistical Abstract of Israel, 1986, No. 27, p. 171.

Another economic factor that helped mitigate class conflicts was the role played by Israel's welfare state in the redistribution of resources. This mechanism was not able to prevent the upper strata from increasing their share of income, but it did reduce extreme manifestations of poverty in Israel.[102] Moreover, the welfare apparatus assured minimum levels of health and educational services to all, and through National Insurance provided a minimum assured income, old age pensions, child allowances, and grants to widows. In addition, local welfare services provided help with personal and family problems which could include material aid if necessary. Besides resource allocation, Israel's welfare system also attempted, through various forms of community work, to provide a focus for social and cultural life in disadvantaged areas. These activities, which had varying degrees of success, included community centers, youth workers for street corner groups, and neighborhood organization through Project Renewal, which provided social and cultural services in addition to improving housing conditions.[103]

The Israeli political establishment was aware of the role of the welfare state in mitigating class tensions and conflicts. Thus government allocations for welfare tended to increase following outbursts of social tensions which were usually accompanied by expressions of ethnic protest. This occurred following the disturbances in Waddi Salib in 1959 and the protests of the Black Panthers in the early 1970s.[104] The initiative taken by the Likud government in establishing Project Renewal in the late 1970s was, in part, due to its desire to fulfill its political obligations to the low-income and low-status groups that had played an important electoral role in the downfall of Labor and the rise of the Likud in 1977.

2) The political explanation for the weakness of class consciousness in Israel is based on the perception that holds the political establishment responsible for the deprivation suffered by the weaker groups. The members of these groups, who saw themselves as rejected by the parties comprising the establishment, found a way to express their collective protest by supporting parties seeking to depose the dominant establishment and become an alternative ruling group. In other words, the Labor movement paid the price for being the ruling party when the economic and class structure of Israel was shaped, while Herut, which had been cast out by the establishment, became a convenient rallying point for those who felt that they were being treated as social and economic outcasts. Moreover, because of the partial correspondence between class cleavages and the ethnic cleavages, this mode of protest was chosen mainly by Afro-Asian immigrants from the 1950s and their children.

3) The social explanation of the weakness of class consciousness is rooted in the different conceptions of the social order found in Israel. The conception that views society as based primarily on class divisions

stems from the social and cultural traditions of Europe. The transformation of feudal society into capitalism and the industrial revolution in Europe were connected to the struggle waged by social classes for political rights, first by the bourgeoisie and later by the workers—a process which converted economically distinct strata into groups that were also distinguishable from a social, political, and cultural point of view. Under the impact of industrialization, democratization, and secularization, an ascendant culture based on universalistic values shook off the declining remnants of particularistic attachments. Moreover, because of the historical tradition that linked class struggle to the struggle for political rights such as suffrage, a division between classes took root in Europe which separated them into distinct subcultures.

This approach was adopted as part of the ideology of the Labor Zionist Movement, but it did not correspond to the social and economic developments in Israel which gradually created a multi-strata structure that lacked clear-cut boundaries between classes. As a result, a non-dichotomous stratification structure developed in Israel that was closer to the American model which was based on status groups, rather than to the dichotomous Marxist concept, which was rooted in Europe. This reality was not fully reflected at the ideological level, but it did weaken the political appeal of class symbolism stressing the sharp division and conflict between workers and capital.

Another social factor that weakened class consciousness in Israel was the conception of the social order held by the Afro-Asian immigrants who formed the bulk of the workers and low-income groups in Israel. These immigrants did not view society as divided primarily into social or economic strata, whether on a dichotomous or non-dichotomous basis. In their countries of origin, the social order was conceived in terms of attachments to particularistic groups—family, religious community, and/or ethnic group. Thus, in Israel, when a considerable overlap emerged between country of origin and socio-economic status, the social and political response of the Afro-Asian immigrants and their children was expressed mainly in ethnic rather than in class terms. Thus a concept of social-ethnic stratification emerged as an alternative to a class-based concept, but the "ethnic" concept happened to be based on a dichotomous division between Ashkenazim and Afro-Asians.

4) The ideological explanation for the weakness of class consciousness relates to changes that occurred in the ideology of the Israeli left, which of course was the main carrier of a class-based concept of social

structure. Already in the early days of the Yishuv, the Labor movement did not regard the class struggle in its European sense as the main political path to the realization of socialism. The Labor movement preferred the path of building a socialist economic sector from the ground up. The drive to build up a workers' economic sector gradually, by means of national capital, was defined as "socialist constructivism," which was to be implemented through the political dominance of the Labor movement. In addition, once Mapai attained this goal of political dominance in the Yishuv in the mid-1930s, it began to cultivate national values instead of class-based values, thus weakening the legitimacy of the Labor movement's particularistic culture and institutions. Later, this trend was expressed in reducing the functions of the Histadrut and transferring some of them to the new state frameworks, such as the decision to abolish the separate workers, schools and to integrate them into the state school system. The most prominent Labor movement advocate of this approach was David Ben-Gurion who made the concept of "statism" (mamlachtiut) into a pillar of his political philosophy. Under the impact of this concept, the ideological distance decreased between the Labor movement and its right-wing and centrist rivals.

The weakness of class consciousness does not mean that economic status has no influence in shaping social relations in Israel. There are indications that social class has a considerable influence on shaping social networks and other forms of interaction. There is also evidence linking social class to consumption patterns and use of leisure time. There seems to be considerable social sensitivity in Israel to status differences based on occupational and income variables, but this sensitivity does not necessarily influence conceptions of the ideal social order.

Given the absence of a tendency to translate class situation on the micro level into a generalized dichtomous conception of social order at the macro level, the tendency prevails to perceive class differences as part of a multi-strata, multi-dimensional structure. This non-dichotomous concept more faithfully conveys the Israeli reality than the ideological model rooted in the fundamental distinction between labor and capital. Social class differences are reflected in partial ecological separation (due to housing market factors),[105] cultural differences reflected in consumption patterns, and differences in the composition of social networks. Nevertheless, the tensions arising from social class differences are less than those stemming from other cleavages. Social class differences in Israel are expressed more by means of the outward signs of status—objects appropriated by would-be status groups to set themselves apart from others—rather than by established status symbols, which are long-term expressions of the cultural differences dividing classes. Thus, the absence of a historical tradition of status groups reinforces the multi-strata structure and blurs the lines between strata. In addition, the import of capital has facilitated a rise in the standard of living for the entire population and considerable upward mobility for some parts of the population. Under these conditions, class consciousness has not become a major source of tension in Israeli society.

Elites and the Articulation of Group Identities

The very existence of social cleavages entails a potential threat to the cohesion of society. The extent to which the cleavages actually serve as a source of social and political tension and conflict is closely related to the extent to which the collective identities of the nation, on the one hand, and the social groups within it, on the other, are articulated. A central role in the articulation of these collective identities is played by elites in society whether these are elites that occupy the political and social center or whether they are elites outside the establishment that emerge on the periphery and represent subcultures.

In this context, it is important to note the difference between the cultural and political center that emerged in the Yishuv and the cultural and political center of the State of Israel. The center, in the period of the Yishuv, was not a simple reflection of the cleavage structure, but neither was it homogeneous. The dominant divisions among the cultural elites reflected their opposing visions of the ideal society more than they did the social cleavages among the population.[106] After the establishment of the state, however, the correspondence between the structure of elites and the structure of social cleavages increased, or at least the demand to attain such a correspondence increased. This trend was connected to a decline in the influence of the veteran ideological group oriented to the political center. As its ability to mobilize support decreased, its responsiveness to pressures from the periphery increased. Its composition gradually became less homogeneous as new groups joined the elite, mainly from among the immigrants of the 1950s. When the Likud, which had been partially excluded from the establishment, rose to power and took over the center, the composition of the center changed even more.

During the Yishuv, politics penetrated into all spheres of life, which made the political elite the dominant elite in society. Its dominance was expressed in its power and in the multi-dimensionality of its activity. It was reinforced by the existence of a reservoir of professional politicians who could be called upon to fill key positions in the elite structure.[107]

The cultural, economic, and administrative elites did not actually enjoy an autonomous status because of their extensive politicization and because these areas had not yet been sufficiently developed in their own right. In the cultural sphere there were small groups, mainly among scholars and professionals such as lawyers, which preserved their political independence. Elementary education, on the other hand, was split among ideologically-oriented school systems. Political influence was also apparent in secondary education. In the area of literature, the political commitments of writers were frequently expressed, and some of the literary creations of the Yishuv were written in the service of a political cause.[108] Traditional elites that did not have a political or ideological base had a marginal impact on the public at large, although their influence was felt within socially distinct circles, as in the case of rabbinical scholars and Hassidic rabbis among the ultra-Orthodox and the veteran Sephardic elite among Afro-Asian Jews.

Because of the extensive penetration of politics into culture, economics, and administration, the dividing lines between ideological movements also influenced the composition of social networks among these elite groups. Ideological and political attachments often had more influence on the social networks and life-styles of the elites than their educational or professional backgrounds.

The establishment of the state provided a much broader supply of positions that could be defined as elite. New elite positions were created in areas not encompassed by the institutional framework of the Yishuv, such as the courts and the police, and the number of positions in other areas rose because of the increase in population and the rapid pace of economic growth. The import of capital permitted the growth of public services faster than the rate of population increase; thousands of officers and other key defense personnel were needed to man the new security establishment; and the development of a welfare state created the demand for elite positions in education, health, and social services.

The composition of the new elites that emerged in the early years of the state was not essentially different from the composition of the elites of the Yishuv in terms of their ethnic and social backgrounds. The veterans and their children from the Yishuv had advantages in the competition for these elite positions that gave them a virtual monopoly on them—their mastery of Hebrew and their familiarity with the institutional maze that the Yishuv had bequeathed to the state. This enabled many of the veterans to move from blue-collar to white-collar occupations, and from junior to senior white-collar positions. The connection between length of residence and preferential access to elite positions was not new—it has existed in all immigrant societies and was also present in the New Yishuv from the outset. For example, the veterans of the Second and Third Aliyah were over-represented in senior political positions in the Yishuv and in the institutions of the state.[109]

The concentration of veterans in the political elite and the differential dispersion of different waves of immigration in various institutional spheres—those from the Fifth Aliyah in economics and academic life; and those who were born or grew up in the country in defense, administration, and later, academic life—reflects patterns of institutional development in the Yishuv and the state. Each wave of immigration or generational group was able to put its stamp on an institutional sphere still open to enterprise and innovation.

Over the years, an association has emerged between the expansion of institutional spheres in a certain period and the ability of certain groups, such as the native-born or the immigrants of the 1950s, to secure legitimacy for their demands to gain access to elite positions. This legitimacy was usually influenced by internal changes within the rising groups, such as the increased educational levels of the immigrants, and by conflicts within the veteran political elites, which made them more responsive to pressures from below.

Old and New Elites

The end of the period of mass immigration and rapid economic growth also concluded the era of rapid institutional expansion that characterized Israel until the mid-1960s. As a result, channels for the rapid advancement of new groups became clogged and the opportunities for the rising generational groups to put their own stamp on central areas of social activity were severely reduced. The turnover in elite positions was slower, and the process of advancement became institutionalized and was based to a large extent on seniority. By its very nature, such a process of advancement reduces the potential for innovation in organizational forms and institutional activity. The new elites of the 1950s introduced comprehensive organizational changes in the areas of defense, public administration, and higher education.[110] However, change of such broad dimensions did not recur, and the Israeli institutional system continued to operate according to patterns shaped, at the very latest, in the 1950s. The progress that the Afro-Asian immigrants made in moving up the political hierarchy was directly connected to their ability to utilize their electoral bases of support, which gave them leverage at least on the local level. Moreover, the tendency for political channels of mobility to assume a more prominent role for Afro-Asians than other channels, apart from sports and entertainment, led to a renewed articulation of ethnic identities. This articulation, in turn, made the political sphere more sensitive to the tensions generated by the ethno-cultural cleavage than it had been in the past. As a result, in the 1970s and 1980s, a high correlation emerged between voting patterns and ethnocultural background; and small ethnic parties succeeded in gaining representation on the national level, a phenomenon that was present in the early years of the state but had died out by the mid-1950s.

A second group that was denied the opportunity of making a distinct contribution as a generational group on the central institutions of society was the generation that grew up after the establishment of the state. Strong feelings of deprivation emerged among the better-off segments of the young of European background, who were in many ways similar to the generation which had had the opportunity to shape the areas of defense, public administration, and higher education in the 1950s. Members of the younger group were able to advance on a personal basis, but at a much slower pace than their predecessors and only through the routine channels of an established institutional structure.[111] From their perspective, the innovators of the 1930s and 1940s had become the conservatives of the 1960s and 1970s.

There is an important exception to the patterns in which the generation that matured in the 1960s and 1970s adjusted to existing institutional frameworks. In the Religious Zionist sector, a social and cultural transformation occurred in the 1970s in which the younger generation not only deposed most of the older generation of political leaders, but also refashioned the ideological emphases and cultural and political style of this sector.[112] No comparable group of young innovators has managed to attain leadership positions in the non-religious sector.

There are, however, secondary areas of cultural activity where those who grew up with the state have managed to make an impact, the main one being mass communications. This area is regarded as secondary because the elites which control it act as intermediaries, transmitting messages in both directions between the centers of social and political power and the public in the periphery. The secondary status of communications as an intermediary sphere means that innovation refers to style rather than substance. The innovative style of the communications elite in radio and television, and to a lesser extent in the press, is expressed primarily in being more responsive to the desires and tastes of the public than to the concerns of the establishment. This change in orientation has meant an end to the paternalistic, ideological, and educational controls over the dissemination of information and culture that had previously been in force. The change has also been expressed in a greater stress on cultivating popular as opposed to high culture and the use of popular styles of speech in the mass media. Despite the fact that changes of style rather than substance are involved here, this shift has led to tensions between a considerable portion of the political establishment and most of the new mass communications elite. The tensions themselves have led, in turn, to the introduction of substantive issues into the confrontation, with the media elites being accused of conveying radical messages and of being a "leftist mafia," and the establishment being accused of having authoritarian leanings and seeking to hamper freedom of information.[113]

Among the elites of Israel, one in particular is exceptional in a number of ways: the economic elite of the private sector. First, it is difficult to point to a distinct group of founding fathers among this elite, since each entrepreneur is something of a founding father in respect to his own business. Second, the elite lacks a pyramidal structure since criteria of membership and prominence within it tend to vary. These criteria can include the size of one's economic assets, the volume of a firm's business activity, holding top executive positions in leading firms or influential positions as stockholders, or a combination of ownership and executive control. Third, because Israel's economic development has been continuous, mobility within this sector has also been more continuous and less sporadic than in other areas. As a result, generational groupings are virtually non-existent among the economic elites. Fourth, the economic elite has a more varied background than other elites. While those who manage, but do not own large firms are similar in social background to the top managers in the public sector, and are often recruited from the ranks of the latter, the owners themselves have a less distinct social profile, even if they are not necessarily representative of the population as a whole.

The changes that have occurred over the years in the social status of the economic elite of the private sector are directly related to the drastic decline of social class as a basis of political mobilization. The paradox of declining class consciousness occurring simultaneously with growth in economic inequality has enabled the economic elite to enjoy a position of high prestige. The decline in public entrepreneurship and the encouragement of private initiative by the state—which was until 1977 dominated by the Labor movement—meant removing the ideological stigma which had been attached earlier to "bourgeois" occupations. A related development has been the rise in the importance of personal economic success as a source of prestige. As a result, the ideological stigma attached to the status symbols of economic success, such as conspicuous consumption, have also disappeared.

The economic elite of the private sector has thus become a highly esteemed status group. Nevertheless, it has not developed a strong tendency to articulate its identity in class and political terms. This elite's close relations with the government and the circumstances under which it emerged, have prevented it from becoming a closed social class group. Its social networks continue to interconnect with a variety of political and sectoral groups. In other words, on the propertied side of the social class cleavage line, there has emerged an elitist pressure group that has not cultivated its own class identity. In addition, the private economic elite has continued to expand after other elites had reached their saturation point. The accumulation of wealth, assisted by government incentives and inflation, and made possible by the wasteful use of foreign aid, reached new heights in the period of hyper-inflation in the early 1980s under the Likud when the stock exchange became a popular avenue for making easy money. However, this channel of rapid economic mobility was blocked for the most part by the economic austerity program imposed by the national unity government in 1985.

The short-lived opportunities for rapid economic mobility notwithstanding, the basic trend in Israel of the 1970s and 1980s has been marked by a decreasing supply of elite positions and opportunities for social mobility. The end of the era of rapid population growth, institutional expansion and economic growth severely constricted the wide-ranging and rapid possibilities for rising to elite positions. It is reasonable to posit that this slowdown, which reduced the turnover in elite positions, was also one of the factors in the decline in enterprise and innovation in Israeli society.

3

Ideology and Political Culture

Basic Ideological Orientations: The Time Dimension

The State of Israel has been shaped both by ideological consensus and dissensus. Zionist ideology was the common ground shared by the political parties and movements that laid the foundations of the Yishuv as a community seeking cultural and political autonomy.[1] As a revolutionary movement, Zionism sought to uproot people from their traditional surroundings and to sever their traditional social and cultural ties. Zionism sought to infuse an ancient people with the spirit of cultural, social, and political renewal. This spirit was based on the following shared ideological essentials that formed the minimal ground of Zionist consensus: The desire to establish a Jewish national center in Palestine through immigration and settlement and to weld the settlers into an organized community with its own distinct cultural and political life, while maintaining close ties with the Jewish people throughout the world.

Beyond this minimal consensus, opinions within the Zionist movement were divided over the nature of the Jewish society to be eventually established in Palestine, and the nature of the intermediate stages leading up to this goal, and the means to achieve both the ultimate goal and the intermediate stages. A well-known Israeli author described Zionism as a family name and not a proper name, with the members of this family being Religious Zionism, Labor Zionism,

Revisionist Zionism, and so forth.[2] However, even though Israel is occasionally referred to as a "Zionist state," a test of commitment to Zionist ideology as a prerequisite for citizenship or for any other purpose does not appear anywhere in Israeli law. Parties with non-Zionist platforms may take part in Israel's political life unless they actually deny the state's right to exist or its connection to the Jewish people.[3]

Ideology as a central factor in the development of the Yishuv and Israeli society has thus played both a unifying and a divisive role as is reflected in the historiography of the Yishuv and the state. The many examples of tensions generated by ideology are of two kinds: those between ideological imperatives and constraints on implementations, and those between ideological agreement and disagreement among the various parties and movements. The centrality of ideology and the recognition of legitimate variants within the framework of the Zionist consensus led to the emergence of ideological subcultures with their own institutional manifestations.[4] The most prominent of these institutional arrangements were the separate school systems or "trends" during the period of the Mandate, with political ideology being recognized as a legitimate basis of social and cultural distinctiveness. The existence of institutionalized social "enclaves" based on ideological subcultures became a major problem during the transition stage from Yishuv to state generating tensions between the particularist orientation of the enclaves and the universalist demands of the emerging statist ideology.

There is no agreed formula among social scientists for defining the concept of ideology. However, most formulations used today usually contain three components pertaining to the relation between a set of ideas applied to organized social activity: cognitive, evaluative, and prescriptive.[5] The relative emphasis placed on each of these components varies among ideologies. Another way to grasp the analytical dimensions of ideologies is to identify their orientations to time, the relations between man and the environment and the relations between the individual and society. In addition, ideologies may be distinguished by their substantive approaches to the social, cultural, and political order in concrete historical settings.[6]

The relation to time expressed in an ideology has three aspects: the first is the relation to past, present, and future; the second relates to tempo or pace of time; and the third deals with the concept of timing.

The relation to past, present, and future is a central problem in the Zionist ideology which has had to wrestle with the central issue of the historical continuity of the Jewish people. The concept of renewal in Zionism treated the present as a passageway to the future. The relationship to the past was more complex. Acknowledgment of the past as a source of legitimacy for the Jewish national movement was a notion common to all streams within Zionism since it was implied in the Zionist pursuit of new ways to assure the continued existence of the Jewish people as a cultural entity. Nevertheless, the immediate past of the Jewish people in the Diaspora was perceived as an undesirable state in which the dispersion of the Jews and their lack of political independence had converted them from an active subject to a passive object in historical processes shaped by others.

Some currents within Zionism viewed the condition of Exile as flawed only in a political sense, but others viewed it as socially and culturally deficient as well. These differences were reflected in the specific periods of the past selected by various ideological currents as a source of inspiration and legitimacy for the social and cultural revitalization they sought for the Jewish people. For example, those who totally negated the Diaspora adopted a selective vision of Jewish history that pointed toward their ideal future. Thus, they viewed the emergence of the ancient kingdom of Israel and its restoration in the period of the Second Temple as their sources of inspiration. These currents tended to link these periods with the modern return and restoration, while frequently ignoring the cultural heritage developed in the diaspora during the intervening 2,000 years.[7]

The "Canaanite" ideology took this approach to an extreme by taking as its model the Hebrew culture of the early period which was shaped not only by the ancient Israelites but also by other nations in the region. This ideological approach was propounded by only a handful of intellectuals, but its indirect impact was felt in literature, art, and social commentary.[8]

Parts of the Zionist movement saw Jewish history as a continuum stretching from the distant past to the immediate past leading directly, on this same continuum, into the future. The future realization of Zionism was intended to create the conditions that would ensure the preservation and continuity of the Jewish heritage, especially those parts shaped in the Diaspora. This approach was developed primarily by Religious Zionism which wrestled with the question of how to reconcile an active, future orientation with a traditionalist stance that sanctified values and institutions mainly by virtue of their roots in the past.[9] Thus, the Religious Zionist parties were torn by conflicting pressures created, on the one hand, by those who rejected the Diaspora, and on the other, by the anti-Zionist ultra-Orthodox, who regarded future-oriented Zionist activity as a heretical denial of the doctrine that the Jewish people would be redeemed only at the divinely appointed coming of the Messiah.[10] Religious Zionism found a way to resolve the tension between traditionalism and futurism by adopting a gradualistic notion of redemption (athalta d'Geula),[11] in which future-oriented acts in the present formed part of a sacred historical progression toward the end of historical time.

The two extremes of the Zionist spectrum in relation to past, present, and future thus edged toward positions that countered the Zionist consensus: the ideal of the pre-exilic Israelite past upheld by the Canaanites which totally rejected the Diaspora as a model for the future of the Hebrew nation; and the ultra-Orthodox veneration of tradition to the extent that it totally rejected all Jewish initiatives to speed up historical processes toward the future. In between these extremes could be found the many variants of the Zionist ideal which, in one way or another, sought to blend a future orientation with historical continuity. The stress on the future and the related thrust toward social innovation was most pronounced in the ideology of the Labor Zionist movement which sought to harness the task of building a new social order to the goal of shaping a new Jewish nation. On the other hand, the parties of the right and center, known then as the Ezrahim, sought to limit their future orientation and its related emphasis on change to the national dimension alone. However, their image of an ideal society did not exactly match the emerging social structure of the Yishuv in which the capital mobilized by the national institutions and the Histadrut constricted freedom of action in the private sector.[12]

The ideological gap between the social democratic Mapai, the dominant party in the Labor Zionist movement and the bourgeois parties, such as the General Zionists, narrowed after the establishment of the state. The future orientation in the social sphere, which was quite pronounced throughout the Labor Zionist movement before 1948, did not suit Mapai's interests as a ruling party seeking to promote political conformism. Too much talk about the flaws of the present social order were considered likely to arouse doubt as to the course of the ruling party and the wisdom of its leaders. As a result, the party's goals of social change were played down and slogans such as "socialism in our time," propagated by Golda Meir in the early 1950s, gradually disappeared from Mapai's political lexicon.[13]

The second ideological aspect of the relation to time refers to the optimal tempo or pace of change. Do the substantive imperatives of a given ideology demand a rapid pace or a slow one? Is the historical process traversed gradually or in leaps and bounds? The aspects of tempo can be broken down into two elements, the overall pace of change demanded by an ideology, either slow or rapid and the pattern of change, either a gradual movement at a uniform rate or an alternating movement of radical change and periods of slower development. In the pre-state period, opinions were divided between advocates of an incremental approach to the goals of Zionism aimed at building up a Jewish presence in Palestine step by step, and the advocates of a radical approach aimed at rapid realization of these goals, in one fell swoop if possible. Adherents of the first approach included the Labor movement and its partners in the World Zionist Organization—the General Zionists and both the labor and bourgeois segments of the Mizrahi or Religious Zionist movement, while the latter approach was upheld by the Revisionists and the underground organizations of the IZL (Irgun Zvai Leumi) and LHI (Lohamei Herut Israel) which were ideological offshoots of Revisionism.

The debate concerning the tempo of movement toward the goals of Zionism between the radicals and the pragmatists focused on several issues: whether the Zionist movement should publicly proclaim its ultimate goal of establishing a Jewish state in Palestine;[14] The need for a rapid mass "evacuation" of European Jewry as opposed to selective immigration in accordance with the economic absorptive capacity of Palestine;[15] achieving statehood through a process of settlement and building autonomous political institutions as opposed to seeking it through the bestowal of an international charter or, failing that, by military force.[16]

The incremental approach to the realization of ideologically-inspired goals was followed by the Labor movement not only in the international sphere, but also in the sphere of internal social change. This was expressed in the notion of "socialist constructivism" that called for the establishment of a society based on labor through the gradual emergence, from the ground up, of an autonomous workers' economy funded by capital raised through the Zionist movement—as opposed to a class struggle leading to a revolutionary seizure of power by the workers.[17] Thus, the constructivism of the Labor movement in its socio-economic platform paralleled its constructivist approach in national affairs known as "practical Zionism."

The attainment of the political goal of Zionism—the establishment of Jewish sovereignty in Palestine—put an end to the dispute over the appropriate path and rate of advancement toward this goal. Issues concerning the tempo of movement toward Zionist goals henceforth focused on the pace at which the ingathering of the exiles should take place, with the alternatives being mass immigration carried out within a short time, or a continuation of gradual, selective immigration in accordance with the absorptive capacity of the country. A dramatic change occurred here following the establishment of the state: the gradual, selective approach quickly gave way to urgent operations in which entire Diaspora communities were brought to Israel within a space of several months. This shift was based on the assumption that persisting in the gradualist approach might mean the loss of precious, one-time opportunities to bring large numbers of Jews to Israel. Therefore, the need to bring them to Israel as fast as possible took precedence over the preparation of optimal material conditions for their absorption. The quality of their treatment, once the immigrants arrived, was thus unavoidably sacrificed to the need to absorb them as quickly as possible.[18]

The enormous demands imposed by the mass immigration and absorption efforts did not permit the Labor movement to launch a simultaneous attempt to reshape the social order in accordance with its socialist ideals. Therefore Mapai, the dominant party in the government coalitions of the 1950s, abandoned in practice, if not in theory, its commitment to the gradual establishment of an egalitarian "workers' society" based on the principles of socialist constructivism. The constructivist approach nevertheless left its imprint on Mapai's efforts in the social sphere to establish a welfare state.

It should be noted, however, that in the national sphere, the incremental strategy of building up settlements for the gradual attainment of Zionist goals was revived in a new format after the Six Day War. The context this time, however, was not the attempt to attain political independence, but rather an attempt to extend the boundaries of Israeli sovereignty over the territories conquered in the Six Day War. Paradoxically, the ideological imperative calling for a gradual effort to "create facts" in the territories as a means to attain long-term political goals was not at this time characteristic of the moderate wing of the Zionist movement, which includes the Labor movement, but rather of the radical nationalist adherents to the goal of Greater Israel. The militant Religious Zionists and Gush Emunim adopted the strategy of using settlements as a means to redraw the map of Jewish sovereignty, while the moderate camp called for territorial compromise that would be achieved as a one-time political act in the framework of a peace treaty.

The changes that occurred in relation to the pace of movement toward Zionist goals also reflected the connection between the desired pace of change and the question of timing. The question of timing usually appears as a problem of synchronizing rates of change in different spheres, such as the economic and political. During the period of the Yishuv, for example, the adherents of practical Zionism argued that as long as a solid social and economic base for Jewish sovereignty had not been formed in Palestine, the ultimate aim of setting up a Jewish state should not be publicly stressed. Leader such as Ben-Gurion saw no contradiction between this position adopted on pragmatic grounds in the 1930s, and the drive for a Jewish state launched in the 1940s which culminated in the decision to declare the establishment of the state in 1948 despite heavy international pressure to postpone the move. The change in the tempo of immigration after 1948 was also justified by considerations of timing which meant that the possibility of synchronizing immigration with the process of absorption was sacrificed to what was believed to be a one-time opportunity.[19]

After the Six Day War, the relation between the tempo of realization of ideological goals and the problems of timing was expressed in several contexts. One was the above mentioned decision by the radicals to adopt a strategy of creeping annexation to achieve a goal that could not be attained immediately in a single blow. The future of the occupied territories was also connected to a problem of synchronizing socio-economic and political developments. The question was posed as an issue of national priorities: Should Israel give preference to solving its pressing social and economic problems, or to the political goal of settling the territories? The proponents of Greater Israel, out of considerations of timing related to the prospects of their political struggle over the territories, sought to hasten the pace of settlement there even though this meant slowing the pace of dealing with long-standing social problems, especially the need to provide a sound social and economic base to the development towns established during the period of mass immigration.

The Six Day War aroused ideological issues of tempo and timing not only on the operative level of ideology, but also on the fundamental level. The outcome of the war was viewed by part of the Religious Zionist sector, especially those groups attracted to Gush Emunim, not only as a confirmation of the doctrine that the State of Israel is part of the process of redemption, but also a sign that the day of the Messiah may be at hand. Messianic currents began to sweep through these groups to such an extent that some even began to speak of the possibility of the complete redemption of the Jewish people occurring in this generation. Such sentiments, which are considered highly controversial even among believers, induced heightened Messianic expectations among some Gush Emunim firebrands, who became ready to carry out collective acts of defiance that would, they believed, help bring on the end of days. The most extreme manifestation of such beliefs appeared among the members of the Jewish terror underground who plotted to blow up the Dome of the Rock, a sacred Moslem shrine located on the site of the ancient temple in Jerusalem. This act, they believed, would lead to a holy war between Israel and the Moslem world that would force divine intervention and thus hasten the coming of the Messiah. This change in their historical time perspective, which was believed to reflect the will of God, thus led ultimately to a change of theological time perspective.

An ideological position assuming that essentially long-range objectives appear to be quickly attainable through collective action, was not the monopoly of the messianic wing of the maximalist camp. Similar strivings burst forth at the opposite end of the political spectrum, but without the theological trappings of Gush Emunim and, at times, without any sort of dogmatic ideological doctrine. Certain elements within the dovish camp, so-called because of the moderate views held by it on the Arab-Israeli conflict, were no longer willing to relegate their deep desire for peace to the level of aspirations alone. The fear that historical opportunities for peace might be lost created a sense of urgency among these circles that reflected in their adoption of the slogan "Peace Now."[20] Thus, the willingness to settle for a gradual attainment of ideologically-rooted goals weakened after the Six Day War at both ends of the political spectrum.

Basic Ideological Orientations: Man-Environment Relations

A future orientation is compatible with an active orientation vis a vis the natural and social environment. The distinction between an active and a passive orientation toward the natural and social environment provides an additional tool for classifying ideologies. Zionism in its very essence, which stressed the self-emancipation of the Jews, was active in orientation. However, there were differences among the ideological currents in Zionism as to the extent to which man has the capacity to shape or reshape his world through voluntary action.

A characteristic dispute between these two orientations revolved around the predictions of experts who cast doubt on the ability of the Zionist movement to overcome obstacles in the areas of economics and settlement and who stressed the narrow limits of the economic capacity of Palestine to absorb large numbers of immigrants. The activists countered with the argument that the experience of the Yishuv shows that it is possible to break through environmental barriers by mobilizing intense dedication and the volunteer spirit—or in other words, by selecting and shaping the best people to do the job. These ideas crystallized into the concept of pioneering (halutziut) according to which it is deemed possible to summon up extraordinary powers in people that will enable them to conquer obstacles that otherwise appear to be immovable. Ben-Gurion put a rather extreme interpretation on this notion in the 1950s when he argued that there was no such thing as economic "laws." He based this claim on the experience of the Yishuv and the state which had refuted the predictions of economic experts, giving as an example the success of the Zionist movement in reversing the "natural" tendency of people to migrate from village to town.[21] The critics of this idealistic approach responded that the social and economic achievements of Zionism that were purportedly attained by challenging the laws of economics were actually brought about by the import of capital from the Diaspora. One of the major spokesmen for the realists in the 1920s and 1930s was Chaim Arlozoroff who wrote that the Yishuv had to choose between "heroic economics" and "rational economics."[22] A leading American sociologist reacted in similar fashion to Ben-Gurion's denial of the validity of the laws of economics, by saying that "a piece of paper carried by the wind does not invalidate the laws of gravitation."[23]

The stress of human will as the decisive factor in overcoming environmental challenges and a scarcity of material resources appeared not only in relation to economics, but also, and perhaps even more so, in the military sphere where the ethos of the struggle of the few against the many has been cultivated. The supreme expression of this ethos came in the War of Independence when it influenced strategic thinking, such as the decision not to evacuate isolated settlements in order to shorten lines of communication.

The arguments of the activists in the sphere of economics or defense were not always grounded in fact: Despite the campaign to ensure that only Jewish labor would be employed in the enterprises of the Yishuv, there were always employers ready to break ranks if it meant increasing their profits;[24] non-viable enterprises did go bankrupt despite the presence of the pioneering spirit; and research into the War of Independence has shown that the balance of forces in the later stages of the war did not always support the myth of the "few against the many." Nevertheless, the persistent faith of the activists in the ultimate triumph of the human factor had a cumulative social impact. The constant repetition of Herzl's famous phrase, "If you will it, it is no legend", was a part of the process of indoctrination that increased the ability of the Yishuv, or at least of certain groups, to mobilize their energies for collective tasks.

The epitome of the activist orientation on the Zionist left wing was the concept of pioneering which entailed elements of elitism, service to the collectivity, asceticism, and an almost total commitment to movement goals. On the nationalistic right wing, in the Revisionist movement, and its offshoots in the IZL and LHI, the activist orientations were expressed as faith in the military struggle to bring about the establishment of the state within the boundaries of Greater Israel. This ethos was fed by romanticization of life in the underground, prison—and the gallows.

The romantic elements in the activist orientations of left and right were not the same. While the militant nationalistic ethos stressed the role of force in changing the pattern of politics and history, the pioneering ethos stressed the creative, constructive element in efforts to reshape man and his world.

These differences were also expressed in literature. The longing for expressions of Jewish power to compensate for the helpless condition of Diaspora Jewry appeared frequently in writers associated with the nationalistic right. The most prominent of these writers was Uri Zvi Greenberg whose poetry is laden with expressions of power as the sacred embodiment of Jewish national renewal, and seethes with contempt for the mundane concerns that occupy the proponents of constructivism.[25] In the literary work of the Labor movement, on the other hand, there is a tendency to idealize the creative acts embodied in settlement as the key to changing man and the environment.

The establishment of the state brought about certain changes in the ideological orientations to man's struggle with his environment. In the early years of the state, the utopian strands in Zionism were still very influential. The act of bringing in hundreds of thousands of immigrants within a few years without prior assurance that proper facilities would be available for their absorption flew in the face of the approach stressing the need to adjust goals to limitations of reality. The ideology of dispersing the immigrants in new towns and border settlements, and the call to the younger generation to settle the Negev wilderness, also drew heavily on the ethos that saw pioneering as the key to unlocking new worlds. However, gradually, a more realistic outlook emerged in all areas of activity as expressed in a growing tendency to adjust intermediate social, economic, and political-military goals to constraints rooted in the environment or to the difficulties of mobilizing the immigrants for such ambitious tasks. In the political sphere, the trend toward greater realism began even before the establishment of the state. The Zionist movement gradually abandoned the maximalist goal of setting up a Jewish state in all of Mandatory Palestine—or in the words of the Biltmore plan, converting Palestine into a "Jewish Commonwealth"[26]—and moved toward acceptance of the idea of partition. The readiness to accept a "Jewish state in Palestine," as opposed to "Palestine as a Jewish state" became official policy at the Zionist Congress of 1946.[27] This principle guided the Zionist movement in formulating its policy to the United Nations Commission and later to the UN General Assembly in 1947.[28] The decision of the General Assembly of November 29, 1947 that recommended the partition of Palestine into an Arab and a Jewish state was enthusiastically welcomed by most of the Yishuv as well as by the Zionist movement in the Diaspora. Even those groups which continued to uphold the ideal of Greater Israel, such as the IZL and later Herut, eventually decided to take part in the political life of the "partition state," as they called it.

A greater willingness to adapt to the constraints posed by the physical and social environment was also apparent in the economic sphere. Following a brief effort of several years to direct economic behavior through massive governmental controls as part of an austerity program, a new economic policy was adopted that took into account not only the scarcity of resources but also the constraints stemming from the public's limited ability to bear the harsh burdens entailed in a "mobilized economy."[29] The turning point in the political process leading to this economic shift occurred in the elections to the Second Knesset in the fall of 1951. The election results, especially the dramatic gains for the General Zionists, were perceived as an expression of the public's longing for a respite from the harsh economic demands of the government. The faith in the ability of the government to impose severe belt-tightening on the public in order to mobilize the resources needed for collective tasks turned out to be unrealistic, both economically and politically. The hope voiced during the austerity period that the public would voluntarily respond to the government's appeal to restrain consumption, and thus reduce inflationary pressures, gave way to a painful disillusionment.[30] The government formed after the elections of 1951 quickly began to ease controls and to give greater play to market forces.

This failure to direct the economy through administrative channels reflected the demise of the ideological orientation which sought the blend mass participation in efforts to attain collective goals with the coercive mechanisms of the state. This faith in what may be called regimented voluntarism was not limited to the sphere of macro-economic policy. For example, Ben-Gurion sought to solve the problems of tens of thousands of jobless immigrants by organizing them in "labor battalions."[31] These frameworks would carry out public works projects to develop the Negev, while teaching the immigrants Hebrew and a trade, getting them used to the regime of work and instilling them with national discipline. Despite the fact that this proposal was soon abandoned, it reflected the ideological tradition that sought to overcome social and natural barriers by means of organized social action. The proposal did depart, however, from a traditional stress on the virtues of voluntary action, replacing it with state organization imposed from above. The original Labor Brigade in the 1920s, which was evidently Ben-Gurion's model for this idea, was forged from the voluntary discipline of idealistic young pioneers, while the plan envisioned for the immigrants was based on a military regime to be organized by the army.[32]

The appeals by the country's leaders to the veteran population to volunteer in the national effort to absorb the immigrants did not achieve an overwhelming response. The most successful effort here was a project in which young people who had grown up on the older moshavim co-operative farming villages volunteered to work for limited periods on the immigrant moshavim as agricultural instructors and community organizers.[33] The project to mobilize veterans to teach the newcomers Hebrew and wipe out illiteracy among them met with less success.[34] By the end of the 1950s, hopes were gradually abandoned of overcoming physical and social constraints by resorting to the coercive powers of the state or by relying on the success of appeals for voluntary action.

As in other areas, the Six Day War proved to be a turning point in terms of ideological approaches to the relation of man and his environment. The dramatic contrast between the pervasive anxiety bred by the tense "waiting period" leading up to the outbreak of the war, and the impressive victories achieved in only six days of fighting, reawakened belief in the collective ability to change history and overcome awesome obstacles. Activist orientations in politics, defense, and settlement were once again in fashion.

The optimistic mood created by the Six Day War was shattered by the Yom Kippur War of 1973 which again exposed the web of military, political, and demographic constraints that limit Israel's room for maneuver. The reaction to this event was sharply divided at the nationalistic end of the political spectrum. Pressures rose to increase the pace of "creating facts" to bolster Israel's hold on the territories, whether by building new settlements or by legislative measures formalizing Israel's hold on Jerusalem[35] and the Golan Heights.[36] At the other end of the spectrum, warnings were increasingly voiced of the dangers of ignoring basic political constraints; for example, the impossibility of striving for peace and seeking to preserve Israel as a democratic state with a Jewish majority[37] while at the same time adhering to the ideal of Greater Israel. The activist line was energetically advocated primarily by Gush Emunim, with the support of the Likud and Tehiya parties. The more cautious line was voiced primarily by the Alignment, while the demand to adopt an active peace policy was raised by Peace Now. Common to both ends of the spectrum were predictions of the dire consequences should the positions of the other side be adopted, with the right warning of the dangers of faint-heartedness and the left warning of the dangers of Messianic adventurism.[38]

Basic Ideological Orientations: Collective and Individualistic Approaches

The confrontation between active and passive ideological orientations was linked, in the pre-state period, to the dilemma between a collectivist versus an individual orientation. The lack of sovereignty and a coercive framework of state power at that time posed a major problem in the mobilization of human and other resources for the Yishuv and the Zionist movement. The attainment of collective goals was thus dependent on the emergence of a strong collectivist ideological orientation to provide the motivational element for organized voluntary activity. The commitment to ideological goals was not defined in terms of commitment to abstract, universal values, but rather as dedication to serving a concrete collectivity. On the fundamental level, this could be the "nation" or "class," or both; on the operative level this could be the "movement" or "party" embodying the collective needs as conceived by the elites who were the carriers of a particular ideology. The view of the individual as the carrier of collective ideals and as subordinate to them was a common thread characterizing the otherwise antagonistic camps of the left-wing pioneers and the right-wing nationalists. Both ideological approaches demanded from the individual, albeit in different ways, to be prepared to sacrifice personal interest and put him or herself at the service of the movement which embodied the needs of the collectivity. In the Labor movement, this approach was expressed through frameworks in which the individual was fully mobilized in the service of class and nation. The primary manifestation of this approach were the kibbutzim which were expected to submit to the collective discipline of their respective national kibbutz movements and to help other kibbutzim when requested to do so. A strong collectivist orientation was also evident in the radical nationalistic right wing. For example, the constitution of the New Zionist Organization, founded by the Revisionists, declared that the national redemption of the Jewish people took precedence over the interests of the individual, group, or social class.[39] A more poetic expression of this idea appeared in the LHI hymn "We shall work for the cause, our whole life long, and only death can release us from the ranks."[40]

The collectivist orientation of the rightist camp, however, was limited to the struggle for national liberation. On social and economic matters, the Revisionists accepted the ideology of the bourgeois Ezrahim, that the Yishuv should be built by private enterprise.[41] The Ezrahim, however, went beyond the Revisionists in their stress on individualism, since sectoral and professional economic interests were considered a legitimate basis of political organization.[42] Thus we see that on the left, the commitment to the collectivity demanded of the individual was both extensive, including several spheres of activity, and intensive reaching into the individual's private life, while the commitment sought by the right was limited to collective political goals. These different ideological conceptions of the scope of commitment demanded for the collectivity were also related to the nature of the collectivity in question. While the Revisionists and the Ezrahim saw a person's affinity to the nation as the prime focus of commitment,[43] the Labor movement fostered a dual commitment, to class and to nation. The Revisionist Movement resembled the Labor movement in the intensity of the commitment it demanded of its members, but like the Ezrahim, limited the commitment to one sphere.

Even before the establishment of the state, an ideological shift had begun in the Labor movement, in particular within Mapai, concerning the relative emphasis to be placed on the commitment to the nation, as opposed to the commitment to the working class. The particularistic framework of the working class ceased to be the exclusive focus of collective action aimed at achieving national goals. This shift was legitimated and reinforced by the slogan coined in the 1930s by Mapai leader Ben-Gurion, "from class to nation." The conception entailed in this slogan paved the way for Ben-Gurion's shift after the establishment of the state when he gave preference to the mobilizing frameworks of the state over those of the movement.

Labor's collectivist orientation also underwent a transformation after the establishment of the state. Instead of the voluntary connection to movement frameworks through which the individual expressed a commitment to the collectivity, there arose a tendency to compel the individual, by legislative means, to take part in the national effort. As in other states, compulsory military service and reserve duty, in addition to income tax and other levies, are basic tools at the disposal of the Israeli government for mobilizing the resources and energies of its citizens toward its collective goals. However, the exceptional duration of military service demanded of Israeli citizens, both as conscripts and reservists, and the unusually high taxation rates, reflect the broad range of goals the state has assumed as part of its commitment to Zionist ideology, as well as the necessity of meeting the demands of a protracted military conflict.[44] The gradual process of replacing the reliance on individual commitment to the collectivity with reliance on the formal powers of the law was also reflected in the transfer of societal functions from voluntary movement frameworks to those of the state.

One of the expressions of the changing expectations in regard to volunteering could be seen in the relation between elitist attitudes and demands to contribute to the collective good. The association between excellence and volunteering, which has been the essence of the idea of "pioneering," shifted primarily to the sphere of security. This tendency was not welcomed, however, by the original adherents of the concept of pioneering, who claimed that it slighted other national tasks, primarily those connected with settlement. Indeed, the overall shift in the focus of the collectivist service orientation did occur to a considerable extent at the expense of the kibbutz movement. The kibbutz sector continued to cultivate the ties between the individual and the collectivity as the basis for communal life. But the sector's self-image of its centrality in Israel's national life was impaired by a widely-held perception that kibbutz membership in and of itself was no longer intrinsically related to the attainment of national goals. This change led in turn to a modification of the kibbutz ideology. The image of the kibbutz member as a pioneer in the service of the collectivity gave way to emphasis being put on the quality of the cultural and material life provided by the kibbutz, especially the contribution of the values of cooperation and equality to the material security and social welfare of the individual member.[45] The rupture of the link between the members' affinity to the kibbutz movement and their wider commitment to the national collectivity ultimately created centrifugal pressures that pushed the kibbutz movement further out on the center-periphery axis. Under the Likud government, this process led to an unprecedented alienation between the kibbutz movement and the political establishment. One of the indirect effects of this alienation was the decline in the willingness of soldiers from kibbutzim to volunteer for the officer's corps which entailed signing on for an extra tour of duty. Nevertheless, hardly any change occurred in the willingness of kibbutz youth to volunteer for elite combat units.

The transfer of responsibility for the attainment of national goals to the frameworks of the state created a situation in which the political movements largely shed their responsibilities for recruiting people to serve in voluntary positions. This gap was partially filled in areas where the state is unable or unwilling to function by non-political voluntary associations which recruit people mainly by appealing to the norms of "good citizenship." However, in this type of voluntary activity, too, national security concerns played a central role, as in the case of the volunteer Civil Guard which helps the police and the security forces in the fight against terror.[46] In wartime, volunteer efforts flourish in a broad range of areas, including service offered by young people from the Diaspora. The reappearance, in times of crisis, of the feeling that Israel is a "society under siege" becomes a spark to rekindle, if only for limited time, the collectivist spirit of yore.

Consensus and Dissensus: Ambiguities and Contradictions

The futurist, activist and collectivist orientations found, to one degree or another, in all ideological currents within Zionism are related to the circumstances in which Zionism itself emerged. Zionist ideology was born in the Diaspora, but its tasks were to be carried out in Palestine. The social, political, and cultural differences between the context in which Zionism emerged and the context in which it was to be realized meant that the basic Zionist consensus referred only to agreement on several broad, abstract principles. The central and most basic principle of Zionism is the ideal of the "Return to Zion," the ingathering of Jews from around the world to join in building an autonomous Jewish society in Palestine. And even if this was not always explicitly stated, for most Zionists, Zionism also entailed the aim of establishing Jewish sovereignty in the form of a nation-state. Since this goal involved the creation of a new society, one not based directly on the remnants of older Jewish communities already in Palestine, the Zionist idea also became associated with concepts of social justice based on universal values. These were to be expressed in the form of a democratic polity based on the principles of political participation, civil rights, and the rule of law. The utopian elements contained in this vision of the desired social order was to constitute part of the realization of Zionism. This ideological foundation was actually problematic from the outset, in three respects:

1) The substantive concepts comprising Zionism's ideological foundation were ambiguous. There were various ways to define Judaism, social justice, and democracy, and these differences were expressed in the various currents of Zionist thought. In relation to the concept of Judaism, the issue touched on basic questions of Jewish identity or Jewishness. Was Jewish nationhood a secular or a traditional-religious phenomenon, or was there a basic difference between the Diaspora expression of Jewishness, which was primarily religious, and the form that Jewish culture would assume once the goal of the Return to Zion was achieved? Another source of ambiguity related to the future of the Diaspora. Was the Diaspora expected to disappear, either through the ingathering or from assimilation and persecution, or was the future Jewish society in Palestine destined to serve only as a center for Jewish communities still dispersed around the world?

No less vague was the concept of social justice which was to be one of the guiding principles of the emerging Jewish society in Palestine. Did this refer only to the basic civil rights stressed by classical liberalism, or did it also imply the values of cooperation and equality stressed by democratic socialism? As for democracy, did this concept imply simply the formal mechanisms of government, such as an elected legislature, or did it also entail a broad range of individual rights such as freedom of expression and association and the equality of all citizens before the law?

2) There were some inherent contradictions among the basic elements of Zionist ideology, the most blatant of these being between the value of Jewish particularism entailed in the aspiration of creating a Jewish nation-state and universal values related to the humanist and liberal traditions, which inspired the founding fathers of Zionism. This contradiction emerged with full force when it became apparent that the process of Zionist settlement would not be taking place in a "land without a people," as an early advocate of Zionism put it,[47] but in a

country with an indigenous Arab population whose aspirations for self-determination were incompatible with Zionist goals. The particularist tradition within Zionism was manifested in the separatist tendencies of the Jews in binational Palestine that led them to establish a separate communal structure within the state framework of the Mandate. This separatism became problematic when the attainment of Jewish sovereignty led to the establishment of a state, not all of whose citizens were Jews. Would the particularist tradition of Jewish communal separatism persist within the state as well, or did the achievement of national sovereignty ("auto-emancipation") mean that the Jews would also liberate themselves from their protective particularist shell, and apply universalist values in the public life of the state? This value contradiction touched directly on the question of the equality of all citizens before the law. Would the non-Jewish citizens of the Jewish state enjoy the same rights and liberties as the Jews, including the right to use the legislative process to change the Jewish character of the state? Would marriages between Jews and non-Jews be permitted in the Jewish state, or would a person's personal status continue to be determined by his religious-communal affiliation, as it was under the Mandate?

3) The broad Zionist consensus on basic ideological principles applied only to the fundamental level and not to the operative level. In other words, the basic aims of Zionism were held in common, but not the means by which they would be realized. The lack of guidelines for linking ends and means quickly led to a split over the question of how to implement Zionism's goals.

The ambiguities, contradictions and lack of consensus on the relation between ends and means meant that the boundaries of the operative Zionist consensus could shift depending on the issue involved. During the period of the Yishuv, for example, political conflict stemmed not only from the rift between Zionists and non-Zionists, such as the extreme Orthodox, but also from the division between those who accepted the authority of the Organized Yishuv and those who refused to accept it. After 1948, attitudes towards the State of Israel itself also became an issue in regard to the boundaries of legitimate authority. Groups that denied the right of Israel to exist have been declared illegal. Israel's Supreme Court in 1965 denied an Arab list called El-Ard the right to organize as a political grouping. The judges' reasoning concerning the limits of political legitimacy stressed the "even if political theory holds that freedom of association is one of the basic principles of democracy and one of the basic rights of the citizen, especially considering the lessons of history in our times, no form of rnment based on freedom can allow itself to support or recognize a movement seeking to undermine the regime itself,"[48] It should be noted that the question of the legitimacy of groups denying the right of Israel to exist has arisen as a practical legal problem only in the context of groups seeking to take part in national elections. Thus, for example, there is no legal ruling concerning the ultra-Orthodox sect that denies the legitimacy of the state, Neturei Karta, since it refuses, as a matter of principle, to participate in elections. In relation to such groups, an informal policy of "mutual non-recognition" holds: They do not recognize the state, and the state behaves as if they do not exist.

A special problem concerning the boundaries of the Zionist consensus is posed by those groups which define themselves as Zionist, but are so radical in their approach that they do not accept the constraints imposed by Israeli democracy and the rule of law. Members of a radical right underground organization in the 1950s calling itself "The Kingdom of Israel," and members of the terrorist groups organized by Jewish settlers in the West Bank in the 1980s, were sent to prison for their illegal activities. On the other hand, the attempt by the authorities to prevent the racist, anti-democratic list headed by Rabbi Meir Kahane, called Kach, from taking part in the 1984 elections failed. Following Kahane's election, however, a law was passed enabling the state elections committee to reject lists of candidates which espouse a racist ideology or which do not recognize Israel as the state of the Jewish people. The legislature has thus denied legitimacy both to racist Jewish groups and to radical Arab groups which explicitly reject Israel as a Jewish state.

Jewish Nationalism as an Ideological Issue

The establishment of the State of Israel was perceived by Zionists as a fulfillment of Jewish aspirations to become a self-governing nation. However, the very establishment of the state brought to light certain problematic aspects of the goals of the Jewish national movement. These problematic aspects were interwoven with a fundamental issue that appeared in various ideological and political contexts: Is Jewish nationalism intended to satisfy the desire of the Jewish people to achieve equal status among the family of nations? Or does Jewish nationalism represent the particularistic tradition of the "chosen people" destined to remain apart from other nations so that the realization of Jewish rights does not depend on avoiding infringement of the rights of others.

The operative manifestations of this issue were an outcome of the fact that Arabs constituted the majority of the population in Palestine before 1948. The Jewish encounter with this population and the confrontation between the two national movements posed ideological and political dilemmas for Zionism which were related to fundamental conceptions regarding the nature of Jewish nationalism.[49]

The ideological positions that emerged in the Zionist movement reflected the two conflicting conceptions of modern nationalism that left an indelible mark on the history of the twentieth century: On the one hand, the conception that recognizes the universal right of all nations to self-determination, and on the other, the ethnocentric conception stressing national "egoism."[50] This ideological conflict was particularly relevant in the historical context in which Zionism arose and developed: The universalist conception adopted by liberal and social-democratic groups stressed the cooperative elements in relations between people but the ethnocentric concept, adopted by the radical right, stressed the antagonistic or conflictual elements in international relations. These opposing approaches played a significant role in the formation of attitudes toward the challenges of Arab nationalism. In the pre-state period, the proponents of the ethnocentric approach advocated territorial maximalism in which the Jewish state would include all of western Palestine in addition to lands east of the Jordan River, and stressed a power orientation in their search for means to achieve Zionist ends. In contrast, the proponents of the humanist-pluralist approach sought compromise solutions that would achieve a modus vivendi between Zionism and the Palestinian Arab national movement. The latter approach stressed political solutions more than solutions relying on the exercise of superior force.[51]

The ethnocentric approach had religious and secular facets, both of which drew inspiration from the ideas, deeply rooted in Jewish tradition of the "chosen people" and "a people that dwells alone." As long as the Jews were bereft of political sovereignty and were militarily powerless, these concepts were interpreted in a defensive way that was expressed in a "ghetto mentality" seeking to preserve and protect Jewish social and cultural uniqueness in a hostile gentile environment. The interpretation of Jewish traditional religious law (Halacha), in its rules governing relations between Jews and non-Jews in the Diaspora, reflected the assumption of assymetrical relations between the vulnerable Jewish minority and the dominant gentile majority.[52] The attainment of sovereignty and the arrogance of power that grew along with Israel's military victories and conquests stimulated reformula-

dea of the "chosen people" that stressed its offensive in rabbis and thinkers on the radical right dredged the reveal and promote its non-humanistic components. Militant Jewish ethnocentrism thus received religious sanction for extreme notions that went as far as legitimating a Jewish doctrine of genocide. The contemporary enemies of Israel were to be regarded as descendants of its biblical nemesis Amalek, which the Israelites were bidden to destroy down to the women and children. A less extreme expression of the same ideological thrust was the attempt to redefine the status of non-Jews under Jewish rule, with the aim of finding support in traditional texts for denying civil rights to non-Jews.[53]

The secular facet of Jewish attitudes of hostility and superiority toward the gentile world was nourished by the collective traumas suffered by the Jews throughout their history, especially in the Holocaust. The widespread image of Israel as a nation under seige ("The whole world is against us") was reinforced by currents of mass xenophobia aimed mainly at the Arabs, and by a sense of national superiority bolstered by Israel's military achievements and by expressions of the "Jewish genius" found in the contributions made by Jews to Western culture.

The establishment of the state shifted the confrontation between opposing concepts of nationalism into different contexts. The most important context concerns the dual nature of Israeli identity, with its civil and national-ethnic components.[54] This dual identity and its attendant contradictions are accepted by the vast majority of ideological groupings in Israel. Only marginal groups such as the Canaanites and Communists on the one hand, and Kach, on the other hand, have advocated doing away with this duality, either by severing the state's connection with the Jewish people, or by abolishing equal civil rights for the Arabs within Israel. Israel's conquest in 1967 of the parts of Mandatory Palestine that had been under Jordanian and Egyptian rule since 1948 reawakened ideological disputes that had been largely dormant during those nineteen years. They erupted as a result of a feedback from the operative level to the fundamental level of ideology. The sudden availability of new options on the operative level created dilemmas that had to be resolved on the fundamental level: For the first time in the history of Zionism, the Jewish side to the conflict over Palestine possessed territorial assets that could either be retained or given up in return for a political compromise.

Under these circumstances, a reawakening of the debate over the territorial boundaries of Zionist aspirations was unavoidable. The first point in dispute revolved around the question of whether the aim of Zionism was primarily to build a Jewish nation-state or to return to the Jewish people its entire ancient homeland. Among the phrases coined in the course of this debate was the opposition set up between "liberating a people" versus "liberating territory," or "social Zionism" versus "territorial Zionism."[55] The second point in dispute concerned the notion of "historic rights" in international relations. The two extreme positions on this issue were, on the one hand, that the Jewish people has an absolute, inalienable, and indivisible right over Eretz Israel,[56] and on the other, that there is no such thing as objective rights possessed by nations over territories, only subjective attachments.[57] A third position, held by most of those favoring a territorial compromise, recognized historic rights over territory, but argued that this also includes the option of giving up some territory out of consideration for the rights of others or because of the pressures of Realpolitik.[58] This third position combined the main fundamental argument of the first position with the operative conclusions of the second position. One of the main arguments used by advocates of the hard-line position was that willingness to yield historical rights on territory undermines the entire raison d'etre of Zionism. This position reflected the inclination among radical nationalists to take the concept of a right to territory out of its historical and political context and elevate it to a level of a primordial imperative.

The opponents of this position rejected these basic assumptions on historical, pragmatic, and humanistic grounds. The historical arguments marshalled against the territorial fundamentalists stressed the lack of a fixed boundary delineating this entity called Eretz Israel, whether in the earliest period of Jewish rule in biblical days or in the later periods of foreign rule. The pragmatic arguments stressed considerations of Realpolitik which limit Israel's room for maneuver, and particularly the demographic balance between Jews and Arabs within Greater Israel. Partition thus came to be perceived as a means of assuring the Jewishness of the state in terms of population ratios. The advocates of repartition make reference to statistical data that since the mid-1980s more Arab children are born each year within Greater Israel than Jewish children. However, demographic forecasts indicated that, given existing birth rates, the gap between the Jewish and Arab populations would close within about thirty years.

The humanistic argument against annexation of the territories or other forms of maintaining Israeli control over them focused on the rights of the Palestinian Arab population. On one level, the argument revolved around the relative nature of historical rights in a case of conflicting claims by two nations for the same territory. On another level, it simply emphasized the immorality of imposing foreign rule by force over an unwilling population.

The third area of disagreement is related to the second. Is the source of legitimacy for the Jewish national movement, which of course includes its attachment to the land, religious or secular? This conflict revolved around the question whether religious significance should be attributed to the State of Israel, seeing it, for example, as the "beginning of Israel's redemption"; or is the state a secular entity that has no need of transcendent legitimacy? The issue of the religious significance of the state is closely related to the conflict over its appropriate boundaries that has raged since the Six Day War. The argument that voluntarily relinquishing any part of Eretz Israel that is under Jewish control is against the Halacha bolstered the hawkish tendencies among the Religious Zionist sector, especially among the younger generation. Gush Emunim emerged from this group and became a leading force among the proponents of Greater Israel and among the settlement movement in the occupied territories. Such a position was not typical of the entire Orthodox community. Leading rabbis in the ultra-Orthodox sector were strongly opposed to the Halachic reasoning of the militant Religious Zionists on the territorial question. Two counter-arguments were raised by the ultra-Orthodox: first, they rejected attributing religious significance to the state; and second, they believed that when the loss of human life, which might be entailed by keeping the territories by force, is weighed against the ideal of Greater Israel, the consideration in favor of saving lives take preference. The difference in fundamental positions that determined perceptions of the nature of the Arab-Israeli conflict also determined positions on the territorial question. However, the operative implications of these fundamental differences went beyond territory. They included, among other things, the problem of who is authorized to speak for the Arabs in the territories—Jordan, the PLO, or the local leadership?[59]

The perception of the Israel-Arab conflict as a conflict between states continued to shape the government's security policies until after the Yom Kippur War of 1973. After the Likud came to power in 1977, however, a shift in perceptions occurred that was due largely to the personal views of Menachem Begin as prime minister. While security policy under the Alignment had focused on the threat entailed in the combined might of the regular Arab armies, under the Likud, the focus shifted to the threat posed by Palestinian terrorism. This threat also provided the jurisdiction for the war launched by Israel in Lebanon in 1982 which was the first fought by the State of Israel whose objectives stemmed from the inter-communal perception of the Arab-Israeli conflict. The objectives of the war included not only the destruction of the military infrastructure of the PLO in southern Lebanon, but also its political infrastructure in Beirut.[60] The assumption underlying this policy was that by weakening the PLO not only militarily but politically as well, there would be less resistance among the Arabs of the occupied territories to acceptance of continued Israeli rule there. "It should be noted that the "Palestinization" of the conflict from Israel's perspective occurred after the Arab states underwent a "Palestinization" of their own perceptions, for example, in the Rabat Arab summit in 1974.[61]

Another aspect of the perception of Jewish nationality that came to the fore only after the establishment of the state was the relation between Israel and Diaspora Jewry. The question of the relationship between the emerging national center in Palestine and the Diaspora occupied the Zionist movement even before 1948. This question had several aspects: the issue of dual loyalty of Jewish supporters of Zionism who did not immigrate to Palestine; the status of the Zionist movement in the Diaspora vis a vis the Jews of Palestine which, among other things, entailed conflicting interests between the Zionist leaders abroad and the leaders of the Yishuv; and the shaping of the emerging national center as a spiritual center for the Jewish people. The controversy surrounding these issues increased after the establishment of Israel since the Zionist movement had now turned into a sovereign state with its own interests which were not always compatible with the interests of the states where the Jews of the Diaspora continued to live.[62]

Another aspect of Israel-Diaspora relations concerned the status of the Diaspora vis a vis Israel. Jewish solidarity with Israel expanded beyond the bounds of the Zionist movement after the establishment of the state. However, not only did non-Zionist pro-Israel elements among Western Jewry refrain from moving to the new state, many who had identified as Zionists also stayed away. As a result of this trend, the question arose in Israel as to whether there was any meaning at all to the term "Zionist" following the establishment of the state. Ben-Gurion took an extreme position in the 1950s that the existence of the state had removed the raison d'etre for the Zionist movement in the Diaspora.[63] There were two important implications to this argument: One, that from the perspective of Israel, only those who personally realize the Zionist ideal can legitimately seek to be involved in the building of the Jewish state; and two, that from the perspective of the Diaspora, there is no difference between a supporter of Israel who does not identify as a Zionist and a Zionist who does not make a personal commitment by going to live in the Jewish state. This approach would have reshaped Israel-Diaspora relations in accordance with the model of a mother country that maintains ties with its emigrant sons abroad, such as Ireland. There was a strong "normalizing" element in this approach according to which the establishment of a Jewish state would make the Jews more like "all other nations."[64] Ben-Gurion's viewpoint was not accepted by other Israeli and Zionist leaders, but developments since then in Israel and in the Diaspora have shaped their relations along the lines that Ben-Gurion originally proposed, even if this has not been expressed in official Zionist ideology. Expressing support for Israel among Diaspora Jews has become one of the main components of their Jewish identity without it implying any ideological commitment to Zionism or any moral obligation to even consider immigration to Israel. At the same time, however, in the two largest Diaspora communities, the United States and the Soviet Union, there has been an accelerated process of assimilation expressed in mixed marriages and reduced institutional identification, which is reflected in lower rates of organizational affiliation in the United States and in changes in nationality registration in the Soviet Union. Lower Jewish birth rates have also reduced the effective size of the Diaspora.[65] Thus, the "territorial concentration of the Jewish people in Palestine," one of the goals of classical Zionism, appears to be coming about, but not through immigration from the Jewish periphery to the national home. It is occurring because of demographic and cultural processes that have increased attrition among Jewish communities in the Diaspora.

The ideological controversies over the question of Jewish nationality have also been stimulated by the historical experience of the Jewish people with an enormous impact made by the traumatic events of World War II and the destruction of European Jewry. The impact of this historical experience is to be found among all ideological currents in Israel but the lessons drawn it have not been uniform. A slogan such as "Never Again," referring to the Holocaust, resonates in different ways among the advocates of various fundamental positions on the question of Jewish nationalism. Advocates of the ethnocentric position have stressed that the Jewish people cannot afford to rely on anything but its own power. For the humanists, the Holocaust has taught a terrifying lesson in the dangers inherent in racism, power-hungry nationalism, and the tendency to dehumanize one's enemy. These contrasting conclusions drawn from the greatest historical tragedy to befall the Jewish people only serve to reinforce the fact that the nature of Jewish nationalism, which was supposed to guide the Jewish state in its relations with the nations of the world, is still subject to deepseated controversy.[66]

The Social Structure as an Ideological Issue

Israel has become known over the years as a laboratory on a grand scale for various social experiments, many of which began in the days of the Yishuv. It appeared then to the settlers and Zionist leaders that the new Jewish society in Palestine could be built literally from the ground up by following ideologically-inspired blueprints as guides to institution-building

The movement that was best able to utilize its general ideological principles and innovative capacities, in both the social and national spheres, while adapting them to the unique conditions of the Yishuv, was the Labor Zionist movement. Its basic approach was to apply the ideological principles of constructivism and cooperation to various levels of social organization, ranging from the country-wide labor federation, the Histadrut, to the communal patterns of the kibbutz. The application of this approach on the national level turned the Labor movement into the leading political force within the practical Zionist camp which regarded steady efforts to increase immigration and settlement as the main path to the ultimate political goals of Zionism. The alliance between the Labor movement and Chaim Weizmann and his supporters, who shared a common constructivist approach, eventually paved the way for the Labor Party to become the dominant political force in the Zionist movement and the Yishuv.[67] In the social sphere, the Labor movement's general approach was translated into socialist constructivism which, for most of those in the movement, meant the goal of building a worker's society from the ground up by means of capital provided by the national institutions. Opposed to this strategy was the approach that saw private capital as the exclusive agent of economic development in the Yishuv. Within the Zionist movement in the Diaspora, the American Supreme Court Justice Louis Brandeis[68] and his followers represented this approach, while in the Yishuv it was advocated by the group known as the Ezrahim. Views supporting the capitalist path of development for the Yishuv were also voiced on occasion by the Revisionist leader Zeev Jabotinsky, who proudly referred to himself as a "scion of the bourgeois."[69]

On the other hand, socialist constructivism was also opposed to the path of class struggle advocated by those in the Labor movement under the sway of Marxist doctrines. The leftist Poalei Zion group, for example, held that a new Jewish society in Palestine could be built only through the accumulation of private capital. Therefore, one could not and should not try to skip over the capitalist stage of development and its corollary of class struggle.[70] Thus two broad ideological coalitions emerged within the Zionist movement, despite the absence of formal political ties between the members of each group. One coalition started from this assumption that, for various reasons, the economy of the Yishuv would develop along capitalist lines through private enterprise. This coalition was composed paradoxically of groups from the extremes of the political spectrum, the right-wing petty bourgeois and the Marxist left. The other coalition, which accorded a leading role to national capital in the building of the Yishuv, was composed of groups leaning more toward the center: the mainstream of the Labor movement and the part of the General Zionists which supported Weizmann.

The two approaches clashed face to face for the first time at the London Conference of the World Zionist Organization in 1920.[71] The group which favored private enterprise was represented by American Zionists led by Brandeis, and the group which favored national capital was led by Weizmann and members of the Labor movement. The latter approach emerged triumphant at the conference, but this victory was not sufficient to lead all segments of the Labor movement to agree on the necessity to take part in the Zionist Executive. Only with the establishment of Mapai in 1930 following the unification of Achdut Ha'Avodah and Hapoel Hatzair was the new party ready to concentrate its efforts on seeking a leading role in the Zionist movement. The new approach was expressed by Ben-Gurion in the slogan "from class to nation."[72]

The ideological coalition that included Mapai and those elements among the General Zionists and Religious Zionism willing to cooperate with the Labor movement took over the key positions in the Zionist Executive in the early 1930s, thus obtaining a dominant role in allocating the money raised from the national funds. However, this coalition was forced to share power with some elements in the opposing coalition, namely the General Zionist B party identified with the Ezrahim as well as the Religious Zionist Mizrahi party. The Revisionists were left out of the Zionist Executive and eventually withdrew from the Zionist Organization to set up a rival movement. The political dominance achieved by Labor thus gave it control of most the national capital raised, but in the 1930s, most of the capital imported into Palestine was from private sources.[73] Moreover, the import of private capital increased after the rise of Hitler to power when Germany allowed immigrants to move some of their capital to Palestine under the Transfer Agreement.[74] Thus, two economic sectors began to develop side by side: the public sector financed by national capital and the private sector funded by imported private capital. Despite the continuing debate between the proponents of the public and private approaches to building the Yishuv, both sides eventually became reconciled to the dual structure development. The coexistence of two economic sectors thus became part of the political consensus which persisted after the establishment of the state.

The state came into existence at the point where the public sector, led by the Histadrut, had reached the peak of its power. Economic developments during World War II weakened the private sector and strengthened the public sector. The import of capital from Europe stopped altogether, while the import of public capital grew considerably due to the increase in donations made by American Jewry during the war. The establishment of the state and the departure of most of the Arabs in the Jewish-held areas during the War of Independence created another type of public sector, controlled by the state, that took possession of public lands and the lands abandoned by the Arabs. The state sector also controlled large firms such as the electricity company, the Dead Sea potash works, the Haifa oil refineries and the ports. Over the years, the development of the defense industries—including the country's largest industrial firm, the Israel Aircraft Industries—further increased the size of the state sector.[75]

The large combined share of the state and public sectors in total capital assets and employment, plus the control exercised by the government over the economy as a whole, aroused renewed hopes among some parts of the Labor movement for the realization of "socialism in our time." However, political trends that brought large electoral gains to the General Zionists in 1951, together with the shortage of capital that led the government to court private investors, forced the leaders of the Labor movement to abandon its policy of giving clear preference to the expansion of the public sector. The Mapai leaders who served as Minister of Finance—Eliezer Kaplan, Levi Eshkol, and Pinhas Sapir—consistently followed a policy of providing government support to encourage private investors.[76] Thus, investments in both the public and the private sectors were actually financed mainly by capital imported through national channels. These changes in economic policy were accompanied by new ideological emphases that went hand in hand with the"statist" outlook of Ben-Gurion which stressed the national responsibility of the Labor movement as the country's ruling group. In this context, Ben-Gurion also sought to transfer certain economic and social service functions from the workers' sector, the Histradrut, to the state sector. The transfer of the Labor Movement's school system to the state and the establishment of state agencies parallel to existing Histadrut enterprises such as the government's Public Works Department and housing companies, reflected a new perception of the role of the Histadrut. The Histadrut was no longer the central instrument for carrying out national tasks and the nucleus of a future socialist society, but rather a particularistic framework that belonged to the Labor movement.

This transformation did not go unopposed in the Labor movement. Although some of the opponents were to be found in Mapai, mainly among its veteran settlements, the main focus of resistance—both to the statist approach of Ben-Gurion and to the government's economic policy that encouraged private investors—was in Mapam.[77] There were two facets to Mapam's critique representing two strains in its ideological background that were not always mutually consistent. The first facet stemmed from the concept of "class struggle" that represented the Marxian heritage of the left wing of the Yishuv and Israel. This approach left Mapam to encourage militant trade union struggles, the most radical of which was the seamen's strike of 1951, and to organize protest demonstrations among the unemployed calling for "Bread and Work." This militant line in labor conflicts conformed with Mapam's largely vain attempt to become part of the "forces of world revolution" headed by the Soviet Union and to declare its allegiance to the doctrines of what was known then as Marxism-Leninism.[78] The other facet of Mapam's critique of the government's economic policy stemmed from its role in the Yishuv as an advocate of the ideological school of socialist constructivism. In this context, Mapam appeared in the 1950s as a diehard defender of the idea that the Histadrut—including its unions, economic enterprises, and services—should regard itself as the nucleus of a labor commonwealth that would one day encompass the entire society. In an attempt to reconcile the two opposing components in its ideology, Mapam leader Meir Yaari formulated a concept of a multi-staged process of Zionist-Socialist development. According to this doctrine, during the stage when the economic foundations of the new Jewish society are laid, cooperation with the bourgeoisie is necessary, even though this will eventually give way to a class struggle.[79] Nevertheless, constructive efforts should not be neglected, for only through them will it be possible to prepare the ground for socialism, by creating elements of a worker's society such as Histadrut-owned enterprises and the kibbutzim to serve as the "prototypes" of the socialist society of the future.

Political developments after 1948 led Mapam to intensify its stress on both facets of its ideology, the constructivist and the Marxist. The constructivist elements assumed a central position in Mapam's dispute with Mapai over the need to preserve the integrity and autonomy of the Labor movement's institutions which Ben-Gurion's statist approach had undermined. Mapam's stress on class struggle intensified as it was drawn closer into the ideological orbit of the Soviet Union, which in turn led to an excessive outpouring of Marxist rhetoric, especially among one of the components of Mapam—Hashomer Hatzair. These trends were cut short by developments in the mid-1950s: the thaw in the Soviet Union following Stalin's death; the split in Mapam, particularly the defection of an ultra-left group headed by Dr. Moshe Sneh to the Communists; and the decision of Mapam and Achdut Ha'avodah, now separate parties, to join the ruling coalition. This tendency of Hashomer Hatzair led eventually to the split of Mapam into its two component parties. Hashomer Hatzair was led by Meir Yaari, on the one hand, and Achdut-Ha'avodah was led by Yitzhak Tabenkin, on the other hand. The two parties joined the ruling coalition after the elections of 1955. All this considerably blurred the Marxist components of the ideology of the left wing of the Labor movement, which in any case had, throughout its history, kept open numerous channels of communication with the Israeli political establishment headed by Mapai.

In retrospect, the Marxist elements in the ideology of Hashomer Hatzair served mainly as an educational tool in its youth movement and as an expression of ideological collectivism in its kibbutzim. Even when Hashomer Hatzair sought links with the Communist bloc, it tried to do so without sacrificing its own identity. Thus, when Mapam shook off the radical mood that colored its activities in the early 1950s, it did so rather rapidly, so that by 1956 it refrained from walking out of Ben-Gurion's government when it conspired with the "imperialist powers" of Britain and France against Egypt in the Sinai Campaign. After the Six Day War, Mapam drifted even further from its earlier radicalism and set up a joint electoral list of candidates with the Labor Party which had succeeded Mapai as the dominant party in the Labor movement. The Marxist strain in Achdut Ha'avodah was always weaker than in its erstwhile partner Hashomer Hatzair. Actually, the Marxist formulations in the ideological writings of Yitzhak Tabenkin, the leader of Hakibbutz Hameuchad and Achdut Ha'avodah, were mainly to express his radical socialist leanings and were not marked by the dogmatism usually associated with the communist version of Marxism. In addition, the maximalist nationalism of Hakibbutz Hameuchad frequently overshadowed themes of class solidarity and class struggle in Tabenkin's ideology, especially in relation to the internationalist stress in Marxism.[80] Thus, it was easier for the leaders of Achdut Ha'avodah and Hakibbutz Hameuchad than it was for the leaders of Hashomer Hatzair to slough off their radicalism of the early 1950s. Achdut Ha'avodah joined a coalition led by Mapai in 1961, set up an electoral alignment with Mapai in 1965 and merged with Mapai and the Rafi party to form the Labor Party in 1968.

The two left-wing parties of Mapam and Achdut Ha'avodah, which became independent parties after their partnership broke up in 1954, were both based on kibbutz movments. Mapam after the split was associated with Hakibbutz Ha'artzi-Hashomer Hatzair, while Achdut Ha'avodah's political base was Hakibbutz Hameuchad. Achdut Ha'avodah came into being following a split in Mapai in 1944, and was part of Mapam between 1948 and 1954. However, Hakkibutz Hameuchad retained its unity until 1953 in spite of the fact that it was composed of members of both Mapai and Achdut Ha'avodah. However, the pervasive influence of party politics and the deepening of the ideological rift between Mapai and Mapam triggered a bitter internal struggle for power that ended, in 1953, in a split in the Kibbutz Hameuchad federation as well as in many of its settlements.[81]

One of the consequences of the deflation of the ideological pretensions of the Histadrut as a result of BenGurion's statist orientation was a shift in the relative importance of its three main functions as trade union, social service network, and economic conglomerate. The Histadrut's trade union function grew in importance as it won legal recognition as the workers' representative. Its social service function was reduced as the Labor movement school system was "nationalized." The Kupat Holim health fund, however, remained under its control along with its pension funds, but with the formation of the National Insurance Institute, the state also became a leading force in the field of social security.[82] The Histadrut economic empire continued to benefit from considerable government support that enabled it to take on risky economic ventures that the private sector would not dare to undertake.[83] However, the Histadrut sector was not the exclusive beneficiary of government aid, and had to share it with the private sector.[84]

The Social Structure: Ideology and Practice

After the establishment of the state, those who had shaped the Labor movement's ideology had to confront three problematic issues: the Histadrut's overall status in the state, the social character of the Labor economy, and the unique cultural identity of the Labor movement.

The first issue concerned the need to redefine the Histadrut's autonomous organizational role in the context of a sovereign state. This problem arose because of unique pattern of development of Israel's labor movement that focused its efforts on building what was to be the worker's society of the future from the ground up. Thus a situation was created in which the Histadrut was often referred to as a "state within a state." In this respect, the Israeli labor movement differed from other Western labor movements which stressed the need for the government to nationalize the economy or at least to intervene forcefully in order to achieve a more equitable distribution of income. In other words, while labor movements elsewhere sought to strengthen the state at the expense of private capital and private enterprise, in Israel strengthening the state, in many cases, meant weakening the autonomous organs of the Histadrut. In such circumstances, where the Histadrut stood for "class interests" in relation to the broader range of interests represented by the state, it is not surprising that the left wing of the Labor movement was the most strident opponent of transferring functions from the "voluntary" framework of the Histadrut to the"coercive" agency of the state.[85]

The ideological argument advanced in favor of preserving the autonomy of the Histadrut stressed the danger of concentrating too much power in the government, which could lead to "statism."[86] In response, the proponents of a statist approach stressed the responsibility of the Labor movement as the leading force in society as a whole. Each of these positions contained its own internal contradictions. Depicting the Histadrut as a "voluntary" organization that would be a counter-weight to the power concentrated in the state bureaucracy, as was done by Histadrut leaders Pinhas Lavon and Yitzhak Ben-Aharon and by spokesmen of Achdut Ha'avodah and Mapam, bore a paradoxical resemblance to the arguments against nationalization raised in other countries by conservatives. The advocates of statism on the other hand, which emphasized Labor's responsibility to the nation as a whole, tended to lose sight of the working class perspective grounded in socialist ideology. Eventually, a modus vivendi was worked out between the two approaches. In the sphere of wage policy, the Histadrut joined the government and private employers as a partner in corporatist practices of shaping policy. In addition, the Histadrut took upon itself the task of regulating wage demands from specific sectors, seeking to make them compatible with overall wage policy. However, this task proved at times to be beyond the capacity of the Histadrut as groups of workers with an independent base of bargaining power flouted its authority in wage disputes.[87]

The second ideological issue to occupy the Labor movement was the unique character of the Histadrut enterprises in a tripartite economy. The enterprises run by Hevrat Ha'ovdim were supposed to be ideologically directed towards national and social goals: contributing to the attainment of national goals and furthering the welfare of the workers. This outlook implied that profit was not the only criterion of success for the Histadrut enterprises. The readiness to be mobilized for essential tasks of national development was understood to imply a greater willingness on the part of the Histadrut than in the private sector to take the economic risks entailed in such efforts. The ability of Histadrut enterprises to take these risks was dependent, in large measure, on its access to sources of national capital raised for development purposes and not necessary for profit. As access to these sources of capital declined over the years, so did the willingness of the Histadrut enterprises to take on economically risky projects.

The ideology of the Labor movement posed challenges to the Histadrut economy which it found difficult to meet. First, the Histadrut found it difficult to develop a unique pattern of labor relations between workers and employers. The worker's sense of partnership in an enterprise was usually no greater than that to be found in private or state-owned firms. Attempts to increase this sense of partnership by instituting various forms of "industrial democracy," which usually meant worker representation in management forums,[88] did little to reduce alienation between workers and managers.

The third ideological issue that the Labor movement had to confront after the establishment of the state concerned its special cultural character. The image of the ideal social order contained in the ideology of the Labor movement was not confined to the political and economic spheres, but also included cultural values and symbols. Like other movements with a radical, comprehensive ideology, the Labor movement sought to mold a new type of man: productive, loyal to both the movement and the nation, ready to sacrifice for the future, highly cultured, and able to keep his material demands within modest limits. This image of the "pioneering" type of man was somewhat elitist in its pretensions.[89] At any rate, the cultivation of the new Labor Zionist-inspired culture required the creation of socializing frameworks controlled by the Movement: youth movements, ideologically oriented schools, seminars for movement activists, cultural enterprises, newspapers and magazines, books, and the theater. These cultural media were supposed to shape a unique Labor movement life-style and outlook which included manners of speech and dress, leisure time activity and literacy and artistic tastes. A Labor subculture emerged during the Yishuv which drew its greatest strength from the ecological or institutional enclaves where the daily lives of the residents were shaped by these values and symbols: the kibbutzim, moshavim, cooperatives, and workers' housing projects in the towns.

One of the characteristic elements of the Labor movement subculture was the cultivation of a system of symbols and ceremonies that set apart those attached to the Movement from the rest of the Yishuv. A characteristic example of this use of symbols and ceremonies was the refashioning of traditional religious festivals in secular national garb.[90] Thus, the kibbutzim reshaped the meaning and observance of traditional festivals, for example, celebrating Shavuot as a harvest festival instead of as a commemoration of the revelation of the Torah at Mt. Sinai. Such attempts at cultural innovation were quite far-reaching—more so than the cultivation of special Labor holidays such as May Day—since they entailed creating a particularistic variant of a national "civil religion".

The symbolic expression of the Labor Movement subculture was not confined to public ceremonies but also included the "presentation of self in everyday life."[91] The manner of dress and appearance by which one could identify an adherent of the Labor Movement reflected the ascetic component of the pioneering ideology. The ascetic elements in this lifestyle reflected the deliberate rejection of "bourgeois" patterns of consumption which were regarded as extravagant and wasteful. In this sense, the Israeli Labor movement anticipated the rejection of the consumer society that emerged in the West as part of the counter-culture of the 1960s. While the ascetic spirit of the pioneers permeated the area of dress, the use of leisure time in the Labor movement strongly reflected its collectivist values: group singing and dancing, especially the hora, and group hikes around the country. The pioneering tough movements rejected the bourgeois "salon culture" of private parties, ballroom dancing, and other activities that stressed individual gratification or expression.[92] In the area of literary and artistic taste, the Labor subculture did not reach the level of "socialist realism" of the Soviet Union that formulated explicit asthetic standards for distinguishing between "good" literature and "bad." Nevertheless, certain literary works became popular in the Labor movement, not necessarily due to their high esthetic standards. These literary works conveyed a cultural message that answered the cultural needs of the movement or of particularistic groups within it.[93]

The ties between the Labor movement and literary circles were much closer than its ties to intellectual and academic circles. Some of the leaders of the Labor movement regarded themselves as serious thinkers and intellectuals even thought they lacked formal academic training. Characteristically, the leading intellectual singled out by the Movement as a spiritual guide was Aharon David Gordon[94] whose influence had more to do with the ideological halo spun around him by the Movement than with his writings since he came to Palestine at a relatively advanced age and spent his last years as a farmer in the collective settlement, Kinneret. By contrast, the Labor movement's ties with scholars reflected its ambivalence toward the academic world.[95] Certain leading Labor movement intellectuals such as Berl Katznelson and Zalman Shazar were personally close to prominent Hebrew University scholars such as Martin Buber, Gershom Sholem, and Hugo Bergmann, as they were to prominent writers such as S.Y. Agnon.[96] However, despite these scholars' positive attitudes toward the Labor movement, they never became accepted as part of the Labor subculture. This was due to the movement's ambivalence to the academic establishment—the rootedness of the pioneer was contrasted to the alienation of the scholar—this in addition to the rejection of the political views of the above scholars, who were either members of or close to the Brit Shalom circle that was prepared to make far-reaching compromises with Arab nationalism.[97]

The unique cultural milieu and lifestyle created by the Labor movement during the Yishuv had not become sufficiently entrenched by the time the state was established to meet the challenges of the changed historical conditions after 1948. Actually, the establishment of the state spelled the end of the period in which the Labor movement subculture was able to put its stamp on the culture of the Jewish community as a whole. Indeed, certain features of Israeli society that supported the dominance of the Labor movement weakened in the cultural sphere sometime before they declined in the political sphere. Several factors contributed to this decline:

First, the Labor subculture was elitist in character and appealed to people who had reached Palestine through a process of selective immigration after they had already received political and cultural socialization in Movement frameworks in the Diaspora. In contrast, the mass immigration that began immediately after the establishment of the state—both the Holocaust survivors from Europe and the Jews from Islamic countries—was not prepared to respond to the messages transmitted by the Labor subculture. On the contrary, the crude individualism that characterized many of the newcomers from Europe and the strong attachments to family, religious tradition, and ethnic group that characterized most of the Afro-Asian immigrants effectively immunized them against most attempts to mobilize them into the ranks of the Labor subculture.[98]

Second, the institutional transformations resulting from the advent of statism weakened the Labor movement's political institutions as well as the organizational and symbolic bases of the Labor subculture. The absorption of the Labor schools into the new state education system and the creation of state frameworks for youth socialization such as the Gadna (a paramilitary youth organization) was, according to the advocates of Ben-Gurion's statist outlook, supposed to impart the pioneering values of Labor to the society as a whole.[99]

The limited success in diffusing the elements of the Labor subculture had its cost. The blurring of the uniqueness of this subculture undercut the social and organizational base that had originally generated and nurtured it. Cut off from its organic roots, the Labor subculture lost the ability to renew itself, thus increasingly becoming an object of nostalgia that no longer had the power to inspire people to work for social change.

Third, a change occurred in the composition of the groups which supported the parties of the Labor Movement. This change stemmed mainly from the "embourgoisement" of the veteran Ashkenazi population, most of which had reached middle class status, and from the shift in electoral preferences among middle-class voters from the General Zionists to the Labor Party.[100] The groups identified with the Labor movement now included not only a good part of the middle class and professionals, but also most of those who staffed the public bureaucracies of the government, the municipalities, the Histadrut, and the

Jewish Agency.[101] On tun other hand, manual labor, skilled and unskilled, became mainly the province of Afro-Asian immigrants, most of whom felt that the cultural heritage of the Labor movement had little to offer them. A paradoxical development thus occurred in which manual workers abandoned the movement which saw them as the mainstay of society, while growing numbers of middle-class people and white-collar workers gave the movement their support. Even the support of the public bureaucracies for the parties of the Labor movement was not related to the consistent pursuit of its ideological goals since some of this support stemmed from the bureaucrats' view of Mapai and the later Labor Party as the "natural" ruling party that would assure political stability and continue to provide the benefits needed to maintain their middle-class life-style. The "hotbed of political conformity" represented by the public bureaucracy was not exactly the source of electoral support appropriate for a party with ideological pretensions of striving for social change which implied more of a nonconformist thrust.[102]

Fourth, after the establishment of the state, Israel became exposed to more intensive contacts with Western culture, which influenced all levels of Israeli culture, from the intellectual elite to popular culture. One of the intellectual elite groups to become prominent after the establishment of the state was the academic elite composed of those either born or raised in Israel or the Yishuv. This elite, whose reference group was the international scholarly and scientific community, imparted to its students the values and ways of thinking characteristic of the post-World War II intellectual world. The cultural orientations of the academic elite combined positivistic or value-free methodological approaches in their theoretical and applied work with liberal or social-democratic positions on issues of public controversy. The technically-neutral approach of the academic elite in their roles as researchers and advisors was emulated by the technocratic elites who gradually assumed key positions in the public service. The approach characteristic of these elites in the fields of social and economic policy was skeptical of the possibility of using ideological blueprints to shape the country's economy and society. They tended to stress the "professional" rather than the evaluative dimension of issues in their inputs on the social and economic questions to be handled by the political decision-makers. In other words, the ideological and voluntaristic traditions of the Yishuv were considered by the technocrats to constitute obstacles in the path of realistic policies that take into account environmental constraints. Political leaders of the young generation also adopted this approach, termed "bitzuism"[103] by their critics, which implied a stress on "getting things done" without getting bogged down in ideological disputes.

The popular elements of Western culture found a receptive audience at all levels of Israeli society. The only group to remain more or less closed to these influences was the ultra-Orthodox sector. Otherwise, all classes and communities whether from Europe or the Middle East, adopted the patterns of consumption and leisure of the all-pervasive American way of life. Most of the younger generation that grew up since 1948, whether from East or West, adopted the Western style of entertainment, consumption, and inter-personal relations—at least as this style is reflected in media of mass communications. In sum, whatever original cultural expressions that had managed to emerge in the relatively isolated enclave of the Yishuv were eventually submerged or swept away in the tidal wave of popular Western culture that swept over the "global village" of the post-war world.[104]

It is no accident that this discussion of ideological conceptions of the social order has focused on the social thought and cultural inclinations of the Labor movement. Not only was this movement the politically-dominant group in the Yishuv and Israel from the mid-1930s until 1977—over forty years—but it was virtually the only major movement to engage in intensive ideological activity. The ideology of the Labor movement was thus the only body of ideological teaching that was constantly faced with the need to redefine itself in light of changing political, economical, and social constraints. The right—which included the General Zionists and their successors the Liberals, along with part of Herut—advocated a free enterprise economy with more autonomy to be granted to market forces. However, their reiteration of these principles over the years did not add up to a systematic body of ideological teachings. Moreover, the bourgeois right in Israel—as opposed to the nationalistic right—pursued a rather moderate line on the issue of government intervention in the economy, compared with other right-wing parties in the West. This moderation was related to the fact that the government's massive influence in Israel's economy stemmed in large measure from the resources that it raised abroad from philanthropy, foreign aid, and German reparations—much of which was channeled to the private sector in an effort to encourage investment.

A major factor in the ideological slackness of the bourgeois parties was the lack of a politically cohesive constituency. The tendency of much of the middle class and even many private businessmen to vote for Mapai and later for the Labor Party, with others from these groups voting for the right-wing nationalist Herut, was a constant source of weakness for the General Zionists and their successors, the Liberals. Private businessmen generally preferred to bargain with the government and the Histadrut through ideologically-neutral bodies such as the Manufacturers' Association, rather than to fight their battles through the political party system. The weakness of the bourgeois parties led them to lose the electoral primacy on the right that they enjoyed since the early 1950s, gradually surrendering it to the nationalistic Herut. The bourgeois right was gradually swallowed up by the nationalistic right starting from 1965 when Herut and the Liberals established a joint electoral list called Gahal. This process was accelerated after the Six Day War when socio-economic issues were pushed aside by the sudden intensification of ideological conflicts over national questions such as the disposition of the occupied territories. During this time the status of the Liberals within Gahal, which was succeeded by the Likud, weakened to the point where they no longer felt capable of running as a party in their own right, their potential electoral constituency having long since dwindled.

In contrast to the General Zionists or Liberals, Herut was far from homogeneous in its social composition and ideological tendencies. Even though Herut's ideological heritage from the Revisionist movement of Zeev Jabotinsky was explicitly "liberal-bourgeois," Herut could not ignore its electoral constituency. This was composed of numerous lowincome and lower-status elements in Israeli society, including not a few wage-earners. Moreover, like radical nationalist right-wing movements in Europe or Latin America, Herut's political style contained a strong populist thrust. For this reason, Herut was never opposed to the development of state welfare services. Moreover, Herut demanded that the social services of the Histadrut, especially its health fund Kupat Holim, be nationalized. This demand echoed the traditional Revisionist opposition to the Histadrut as a labor organization combining the functions of trade union, welfare agency, and ownership of economic enterprises. This opposition was rooted, first of all, in the Revisionist rejection of the Labor movement's basic goal of building up Hevrat Ha'ovdim as the economic base of a future socialist society,[105] a position that was sharply articulated by Jabotinsky in the 1930s when he called on his followers "to break" the Histadrut. This position was moderated after the establishment of the state when it became apparent to Herut that a significant number of their voters had joined the Histadrut to benefit from its health services and to seek trade union protection. This situation led Herut to accord de facto recognition to the Histadrut and to form a list to compete in the elections for the Histadrut's ruling bodies. After Herut joined the Histadrut, it continued to voice its traditional ideological opposition to the broad social goals of the Histadrut and to demand the trade union function be separated from its ownership of enterprises, and that a national health insurance system replace the sectoral health programs.

The ideological positions of Herut remained on paper and were not activated when Herut, as the dominant component in the Likud, came to power in 1977, thus ending twenty-nine years of Labor movement rule. The reality of the tripartite economy and the division of welfare services between the state and other bodies proved to be stronger than the principles nurtured by Herut during its long years in opposition.

Herut's rise to power in 1977 as the leading component in the Likud was brought about by several electoral shifts that began in the 1960s and had changed the social composition of Herut's constituency. The proportion of semi-skilled and unskilled manual laborers in Herut's electoral constituency increased along with the proportion of small businessmen, while the percentage of its affluent middle class voters declined.[106] This change in social composition implied a shift in the ethnic background of Herut's voters as well, with most of the party's votes coming from Afro-Asian Jews who, a as a group voted, for the most part, for Herut. Herut's positions on social issues changed accordingly with its traditional liberalism declining in favor of populism. Herut's populism was epitomized by its aim "to make things better for the people," a slogan coined by Herut leader Menachem Begin. In contrast to the constructivist ideology of the Labor movement which stressed economic growth and development and the need to give preference to investments over consumption, Herut came increasingly to advocate a kind of economic permissiveness that created conditions for increasing demand and encouraging consumption.

The course taken by Herut's populistic policy, which reached its high point in the early 1980s, also reflected a long-standing tendency in the party's ideology for its social component to be disassociated from its national component. The unavoidable outcome of economic permissiveness was to increase Israel's financial dependence on the United States which, in turn, hampered Israel's political freedom of action. This lack of consistency between ideological components was inherited by Herut from the Revisionist movement which had lacked the pragmatic and incremental approach of the Labor movement.

Labor had always refrained from giving flight to ambitious ideological goals that came to have a life of their own and could not be backed up with concrete economic or political assets. This difference in the ideological approaches of the two movements can also be encapsulated in the distinction between expressive and instrumental orientations. In the Revisionist ideological heritage of Herut there were strong romantic, expressive urges dubbed as "declarative Zionism" by the movement's critics. This was contrasted to "realistic Zionism," which maintained that the goals of Zionism could not be realized just by making passionate statements about what should be done. This expressive tradition was a key to Herut's success in mobilizing popular electoral support among Afro-Asian Jews. Despite the fact that the gaps in income, education, and social status between Ashkenazim and Afro-Asians were not narrowed at all during the Likud's years in power, the party managed to entrench its support among the Afro-Asians by conveying the feeling that it had succeeded in restoring their pride. Their sense of group pride had supposedly been trampled on in earlier years by the Labor-led establishment which was accused of having manipulated them politically and treated their culture with contempt. The message conveyed by Herut to this socially peripheral constituency—that there is no need for either social change or economic restraint—was interpreted to mean that there is no need to invest a special effort to improve the situation of the individual or the collectivity. Making demands on these peripheral groups to sacrifice and work to change their situation was seen to represent "arrogance" on the part of the culturally dominant group that had been held responsible for wounding their pride.

Ideological Issues: Religion, Society, and State

The issue of religion and state and religion and society is closely connected to the cleavage between the religious and secular, which is essentially ideological. However, even though a religious world view can be treated as an ideology, it differs from other types of ideology since its adherents consider themselves as bound by a transcendent source of authority and are not free to modify their beliefs at will. However, acceptance of the Jewish religious outlook also obligates one to follow a code of conduct grounded in what are considered to be divine commandments, the Halacha.

The first ideological dispute concerning the status and role of religion in Israel focuses on the definition of Judaism: Is it possible to sever Jewish nationalism from the Jewish religion? This question has both an ideological and historical aspect. Historically, it is clear that in premodern times at least, Jewish identity was defined in religious terms. The act of abandoning the Jewish faith and converting to another religion meant leaving the Jewish people. However, the dawn of secularization in the West and the rise of modern nationalism opened up other ideological options. First, it became possible to combine adherence to the Jewish faith with national identification with another people. This option, proposed by the Enlightenment movement in Germany, was epitomized in the formula that described Jews as "Germans of Mosaic persuasion."[107] The second option appeared later, in no small part as a result of the disillusionment that set in after it was realized the civil emancipation had not solved "the Jewish problem." This option proposed a modern nationalist interpretation to Jewish identity that would make it possible to feel a part of the Jewish people without necessarily being committed to religious belief and observance. The possibility of establishing a secular Jewish nationalism was acknowledged by most adherents of the Zionist movement. From the perspective of the secular Zionist, the modern Return to Zion was intended to create the conditions for defining Jewish identity in political-territorial terms instead of in religious-communal terms.

The voluntary aspect of secular Jewish identity that legitimizes Jewish atheism was one of the reasons why most religious Jews in the Diaspora reacted negatively to the emergence of the Zionist movement, even though their opposition was justified in formal terms by their rejection of the notion of self-emancipation which violated the doctrine that only God could ordain the timing of the redemption of the Jewish people. Religious Zionism thus found itself between the hammer of secular Zionism and the anvil of traditionalist anti-Zionism. Religious Zionism had tried to resolve this problem by attributing religious meaning to the modern Return to Zion, viewing the establishment of the state as the "beginning of the redemption." It's adherents see it as a way of providing a political-territorial supplement to the traditional national-religious component of Jewish identity.[108]

In the State of Israel, this approach formed the basis of a Supreme court decision rejecting the appeal of Oswald Rufeisen (Brother Daniel), a Catholic priest of Jewish origin, who sought to acquire Israeli citizenship under the Law of Return and be registered as a Jew by the Ministry of the Interior.[109] On the other hand, the approach of secular

Zionism was ambiguous on the question of whether the state should consider family members of Jews, who are not Jewish according to Halacha, as Jews nonetheless. These were some manifestations of the question, known in Israeli public life as "Who is a Jew?" which has appeared in various forms over the years.[110]

The issue of the essence of Judaism and Jewishness has arisen in the legal arena as well as in the public expression of symbolic attachments to Jewish tradition. The approach identifying Judaism with the religious tradition is not the exclusive province of the Orthodox but is also shared by some non-observant Jews as well. This approach has influenced a number of symbols and ceremonies of a national or government nature. While during the Yishuv and the early years of the state, the tendency was to maintain the secular character of such collective ceremonies—thus leading some scholars to speak of an emerging "civil religion." The use of religious symbols increased later on, and with it, the tendency to impart a religious tone to public ceremonies. Thus, following the Six Day War, the swearing-in ceremonies for elite military units came to be held at the Western Wall in Jerusalem, while previously the ancient stronghold of Masada was thought to be a more appropriate site. This is not the only instance of the Western Wall being used as a national symbol and becoming the site of official state ceremonies. Similarly, the role of the military chaplaincy in IDF ceremonies has also increased since 1967.

An equally conspicuous trend that has taken hold in recent years is the custom of secular political figures making courtesy calls on rabbis and inspirational religious figures in a way that conveys the respect rendered by the temporal power to the spiritual power. The educational message indirectly conveyed by this homage paid to religious figures and symbols has reinforced the explicit educational policy of instituting lessons on "Jewish consciousness" in the state secular schools.[111]

The growing tendency to identify Jewish culture with Jewish religion has paved the way for increasing political demands on the part of religious groups. Thus the demand to exempt yeshiva students from conscript military service was justified on the ground that it was the tradition of intensive Torah study cultivated in the yeshivot that had preserved the Jewish people in the Diaspora. The same tendencies also boosted the popularity of the "back to religion" movement that took hold in the 1970s and 1980s, in which thousands of people, including army officers and well-known entertainers, abandoned their secular lifestyle and joined ultra-Orthodox communities.[112]

The ideological controversy over the place of religion in Zionism and the State of Israel has, fro the beginning, been conducted in an atmosphere of a looming threat to Jewish solidarity referred to as Kulturkampf. Thinkers and political leaders in the Yishuv and in the State of Israel have expressed repeated concern over the question of the extent to which secular culture and religious culture can live side by side without being embroiled in constant conflict.[113] The desire to prevent a Kulturkampf that would create a split within the Jewish people became the basis of the willingness of secular groups to make certain concessions to the religious. This same sentiment also led the Knesset to impose religious laws relating to personal status on secular Israeli Jews—laws which at times conflicted with modern norms such as the equality of women and the right of any person to marry as he or she chooses. Other less salient instances of the secular public being forced, against its will, to abide by religious laws include some compulsory public observance of the Sabbath and the dietary laws (kashrut), infringement of a women's right to have an abortion, censorship of films and plays, and restrictions on the freedom of scientific research in the areas of medicine and archeology. Despite the pragmatic compromises that have been made between the religious and secular aimed at avoiding a Kulturkampf, it has not proved possible to bridge the gap on the fundamental level between the religious and secular world view. While the religious world view is described by its adherents as a unique and closed frame of reference, the secular world view is open to universalistic frames of reference. From the latter point of view, there is no impermeable boundary between Jewish culture and other cultures, nor should there be. In fact, according to an expressly secular world view, there should be cross-fertilization between Israeli culture and the varied cultural foundations of modern society which both draw from and act back on particular cultures.

Paradoxically, the religious revival in Israel which stressed the uniqueness of Judaism as religious nationhood was, at least as far as its timing was concerned, similar to changes in the cultural climate of Christian and Moslem societies. The revival of religious fundamentalist movements and their increasing political involvement occurred in Israel at about the same time as it did among the Sunni and Shiite factions of the Moslem world and among the American Protestants. The Khomeini revolution in Iran was perhaps the most extreme manifestation of populist religious fundamentalism that spurned modern Western culture and which sought to impose conservative behavior and morals by means of the state. A similar fundamentalist awakening occurred in the Sunni Moslem countries, but even though the religious extremists did not seize power, their social, cultural, and political influence grew considerably.[114] The Christian variant of this fundamentalism trend was especially powerful in the "Bible Belt" states of the southern and midwestern states of the United States. Here the fundamentalist preachers called for a return to the "solid" values of patriotism and family virtue, bitterly opposed permissiveness and sought to desecularize agents of socialization such as the schools and the mass media. These fundamentalist surges, whether Jewish, Christian, or Moslem, had two things in common. First, they stressed a "return" to religion. And second, they sought to impose traditional values and behavior by political means.

The ideological changes that occurred in Israel in the status of religion revolved around the relation between religion and politics. This change occurred mainly in the Religious Zionist wing of the religious camp and can be described as an extension of the connection between religion and state. This connection, which was first established in the political system of the Yishuv and continued with the state, was characterized by the secular opponents of the religious parties as a "politicization of religion." This concept in Israel came to represent the use of political power by the religious parties to assure the cultural autonomy of the Orthodox sector and to impose Halachic norms in public life by legislative means. After the Six Day War, in addition to the politicization of religion, there emerged what may be called the "religionization of politics." The use of political power to advance the interests of the religious sector continued as before, but there was now a greater stress on the attribution of religious significance to issues of national policy which bear upon the condition of the collectivity rather than the religious needs of individuals. This was apparent, primarily but not exclusively, in relation to the future of the occupied territories. Indeed, within several years, a transformation occurred within the Religious Zionist camp that posed a potential threat to Israel's democratic rules of the game. This threat stemmed mainly from the belief that gradually took root in some parts of the Religious Zionist camp that in certain fundamental political issues not necessarily related to the state of religion in society, they consider themselves bound by Halacha which does not permit compromise, bargaining, or even compliance with decisions reached by majority rule.[115] This fundamental belief and its related absolutist imperatives on the operative level, encompassed types of policy issues that had not previously been regarded as subject to religious legitimation, even in the religious sector. The desire to seek Halachic guidance in making political decisions was not new in itself, particularly among the non-Zionist ultra-Orthodox whose political positions were dictated by its Council of Torah Sages. However, in these circles, which did not attribute religious significance to the state or to the conquests of the Six Day War, the rabbinical rulings on political matters usually concerned issues affecting the particularistic interests of the ultra-Orthodox. The National Religious Party (NRP), on the other hand, had usually refrained from requesting binding rulings on political issues from its rabbinical leaders. However, the NRP's growing tendency to resort to the Halacha in formulating its positions on political issues after the Six Day War was of more far-reaching significance since it was related to the search for signs of imminent religious redemption in the territorial gains made during the 1967 war in the historic Land of Israel. This created a situation in which not only did political positions receive religious sanction, but decisions of the legally constituted authorities incompatible with these positions were declared illegitimate in advance on religious-Halachic grounds. In other words, the "religionization" of politics—and its companion the "theologicization" of ideology—sought to usurp the autonomous authority of Israel's elected representatives to resolve policy questions according to the constitutional procedures of democracy.[116]

The awareness that Halachic rulings are considered by religious Jews superior to secular legislation was one of the factors that led the Israeli body politic to grant monopolistic status to religious law in the areas such as marriage and divorce. The fear of a conflict of authority that could result from the non-recognition by the religious of the decisions of the state courts in matters of personal status has thus prevented separation of religion and state. Yet, at the same time, there is not state religion in Israel. Other religions were also granted the same privileges as Judaism in the area of personal status. Thus, there was never any doubt that, on the whole, Israel is a state governed by law and not by rabbinic rulings. However, the prevailing perception in the Religious Zionist camp that the state is suffused with religious meaning, when combined with the reliance on Halachic rulings on national policy issues, opened up the possibility that acts of resistance to the decisions of the legally-constituted authorities could be legitimated by recourse to the dictates of a higher law.[117] An extreme expression of this approach appeared in the Jewish terrorist underground that operated in the occupied territories against Arab targets.

Starting from an ideological position attributing religious significance to the state, the members of the underground ended up paradoxically rejecting its very authority. In this respect, the fundamental position of many Religious Zionists turned out to be simply the other side of the ideological coin to the anti-Zionist ultra-Orthodox—both of them refused to adopt a position of unconditional commitment to the legal authority of the state. The former refused to do so as a result of the religious meaning it attributed to the state, while the refusal of the latter was anchored in its belief that the establishment of a Jewish state by a human rather than a divine hand had emptied it of religious significance. The fundamental ideological dispute between Religious Zionism and the anti-Zionist ultra-Orthodox, therefore, revolved around the question of whether the State of Israel had arisen as an act of providence or in contradiction to Divine Will. The fundamental ideological dispute between the religious and secular focused on the legitimacy of granting special status to those who sought transcendent religious sanction for social and political policy decisions. Thus, the ideological disputes over religion and state became linked to ideological conflicts over democracy.

Democracy as an Ideological Issue

The broad range of consensus in Israel on democratic norms and institutions—freedom of political association, a parliamentary regime, universal suffrage, and an independent judiciary—has held for a long time, at least in respect to declared ideological positions. Israel has thus been known for decades as the "bastion of democracy" in the Middle East. Nevertheless, the ideological commitment to democracy has not always been unconditional among all political groups, and consensus has not always prevailed concerning the specific norms implied by the broad concept of democracy. Actually, Israeli democracy, like the democracy of the Yishuv before it, has been anchored to a greater extent in arrangements of political convenience than in a fundamental commitment to the normative foundations of democracy. Expressions of conditional acceptance of democracy have appeared both during the Yishuv and since independence, on the right as well as the left, but most of all in the religious sector. The assumption that democracy is valid as long as the decisions made under its aegis do not contradict the Halacha is, to one extent or another, common to all the religious parties.[118]

Most of the problems of Israeli democracy can trace their origin to the circumstances in which the Yishuv emerged. The Yishuv was built by political movements, each of which demanded a high level of commitment to the movement's values from its members. These values were, in some cases, radically opposed to the status quo or to the values of other movements, thus creating appropriate conditions for the emergence of ideological fanaticism. Some of these movements tended to attribute absolute validity to their values while condemning the positions of their rivals as false and pernicious. However, in the absence of the means of coercion available to a sovereign state, the only way to maintain any institutionalized political life in the Yishuv was for the movement to be willing to support a pluralistic system based on compromise.

It can therefore be argued that the democracy of the Yishuv, which eventually gave rise to Israeli democracy, at least partially evinced reversal of the usual casual relationship between the development of democratic institutions and the development of an ideological commitment to democracy. Instead of democratic ideology shaping the institutional contours of a democratic political system, the democratic ideology of the Yishuv was shaped by its experience with certain democratic institutional arrangements. As a result, the ideological commitment to democracy focused mainly on the aspects of representation such as the multi-party structure, free elections, and the rule of the majority. Less attention, on both the fundamental and operative levels, was given to other components of democracy such as political tolerance, especially the recognition of the role of the opposition as a check against the abuse of political power and civil rights, both in the sense of equality before the law and protection of the individual from an arbitrary exercise of power.

The restricted perception of democracy that regarded political representation as its essence, while tending to downplay its other components, also took a dim view of the autonomy of the mass media and of freedom of information. The state communication media operated until the 1960s, for all practical purposes, as organs of the government and the independent non-party press often aroused the antagonism of the political establishment.[119] The capacity of the new media to mobilize public opinion and channel it in non-partisan directions was frequently regarded by the political establishment as usurping the legitimate functions of politicians. Furthermore, there was little understanding that freedom of expression may also imply minimizing restrictions on public access to information. This narrow perception of democracy was shaped by the notion that the party system was the only legitimate or authentic channel for political participation. Attitudes to the public's right to know were also influenced by the experience of most of Israel's leaders in clandestine or semi-clandestine activities before the establishment of the state, and by elitist tendencies that made access to sensitive information a reward to be enjoyed only by the elite inner circles.

The tendency to impose some sort of central control over freedom of information and, to a lesser extent, over freedom of expression, weakened over the years as Israel was more and more influenced by the democratic models of Britain and the United States. One of the first signs of this shift was in the Supreme Court decisions of 1953 in the appeal of the Communist newspapers Kol Ha'am and Al-Ittihad against the Interior Minister's decision to close the latter for publishing information seen as threatening to public security. The court limited the authority of the Interior Minister to inhibit freedom of expression, saying that this right is not only a means to an end but an end in itself. Subsequent social and political developments gradually reinforced this ruling. During the Lavon Affair of 1960-61, the "taboo" on criticizing the defense establishment, which was in large measure self-imposed out of concern for national security, was weakened. For the first time, an internal scandal in the defense establishment became the focus of public debate and criticism and the subject of a tug-of-war for public opinion. Moreover, the press coverage of the affair played a major role in influencing political developments that led to the resignation of Ben-Gurion from the premiership and the holding of early elections.[120]

Another development in the 1960s that enlarged the scope of freedom of expression was the establishment of the Broadcasting Authority on the model of the BBC by the government of Levi Eshkol which ended the direct supervision of radio and television by the government.[121] The public's involvement in criticism of the political system—not necessarily through party channels—expanded after the Yom Kippur War of 1973, as non-party protest movements formed to seek the ouster of those leaders held responsible for the blunders that led to the surprise at the outbreak of the war.[122] In the wake of these events, the news media gradually won increased acknowledgment of their right to have access to information and to disseminate it, thereby taking an active role in shaping public opinion.

The attitude from the days of the Yishuv that political representation through the party system is the sole authentic arena for the practice of democratic freedoms was reflected not only in the tendency to restrict freedom of expression and freedom of information. It was also manifested in criticism by politicians of the powers vested in statutory bodies whose legitimacy was not rooted in the party system, such as the Attorney-General, the State Comptroller, and the Governor of the Bank of Israel.[123] Reservations were sometimes voiced even about the role of the courts in imposing restrictions on government action. Such attitudes left little room for sensitivity to the rights of the individual, especially his or her right to protection from the arbitrary exercise of power by the state.[124] Indeed, this approach was apparent in many areas: The tendency of government agencies to ignore certain rights and rules of eligibility as long as individuals did not explicitly demand them; excessive use of powers granted by law to "protect the public," such as the right to hold suspects in custody while investigating whether charges should be pressed against them; and the resort to the powers provided under the emergency defense regulations when dealing with many matters affecting the Arab population, not only those concerning security.

All these tendencies were especially pronounced in the early years of the state as pre-state traditions tended to reinforce the somewhat authoritarian style of leadership characteristic of Ben-Gurion. His final departure from the premiership in 1963 and the selection of Eshkol to succeed him marked the start of a period of greater liberalization and less authoritarianism. The relaxation of press censorship and the establishment of an autonomous state broadcasting authority were expressions of this trend. Even more important was the dismantling of the military government from the Arab areas of the country and the continuation of the depoliticization of the security services which actually began in the last stage of Ben-Gurion's tenure. All in all, the general political climate gradually became more tolerant

The trend toward the ascendancy of political tolerance and the decline of ideological fundamentalism was reversed following the Six Day War. The revival of the debate on the territorial limits of Zionist aspirations and the friction that was generated in the direct contacts between the Jewish population and the Arabs of the occupied territories fueled a revival of fundamental ideological conflicts in Israel. The ideological and political polarization that emerged exposed, once again, the ambivalence to democracy among prominent ideological and political groups in Israel. ideological approaches advocating a conditional acceptance of democracy or the application of democratic norms to Jews alone—which were found only among small marginal groups before 1967—were now expressed not only by the overtly racist Kach movement, but also by the adherents of less marginal right-wing parties such as Tehiya. Such approaches were most apparent in groups that combined national fundamentalism with religious fundamentalism, such as Gush Emunim, which became the most prominent exponent of the conditional acceptance of democracy. The idea that the government of Israel has no right to yield any portion of Eretz Israel or to limit Jewish settlement in any part of the land at first gave rise to unauthorized settlement efforts by Gush Emunim and later provided the ideological justification for the Jewish terrorist underground in the territories. Warnings were also voiced among the religious settlers in the territories that any decision by the government to give up part of the territories to the Arabs and uproot Jewish settlements there might arouse armed resistance. The uprooting of Jewish settlements in the Yamit region of Sinai, following the peace treaty with Egypt, led to strong protests there by the proponents of Greater Israel and to several violent confrontations between protesters and soldiers, though no armed resistance or bloodshed occurred. However, the threat of armed resistance in the event of an Israeli withdrawal from the West Bank has been publicly discussed despite the precedent of Yamit since the latter region did not form a part of the heartland of historic Eretz Israel.[125]

Another manifestation of the conditional acceptance of democracy, whether for Halachic or ideological reasons, appeared in groups which sought to limit the application of democratic norms to Jews alone. The most extreme version of this approach was advocated by the Kach movement led by Rabbi Meir Kahane which rejected democracy altogether as contrary to Jewish tradition; advocated expulsion of the Arabs or, at the very least, strict separation between Jews and Arabs; and the establishment of a theocratic regime.[126]

Conceptions allowing for only a limited acceptance of democracy or rejecting it altogether appeared on the radical left as well as the radical right. However, in Israel after the Six Day War, such left-wing extremists were so few in number and politically marginal that they posed no real threat to the ability of the political system to function. The Communists, however, whose fundamental ideology does not posit an unconditional commitment to democracy in the framework of capitalist society, followed an operative approach based on strict observance of the rules of parliamentary democracy. Positions on the far left advocating the total rejection of the political system and its democratic rules of the game thus remained the province of small, transient groups such as Matzpen.[127] During the Lebanon War, however, groups on the left appeared which did not challenge the legitimacy of the democratic decisionmaking process, but still argued, in the tradition of civil disobedience, that the individual has the right to refuse to take part in carrying out government decisions if these violate the dictates of conscience, as long as they are willing to accept the legal consequences of their actions. Some of the proponents of this position were members of a group called Yesh Gvul (There is a limit), which defended the actions of those who refused to serve in the army in Lebanon or in the occupied territories while not denying the right of the authorities to try to punish them. Despite the stress here on refusal to serve as an act of individual conscience, this position was rejected by most of the critics of the war such as the spokesmen of Peace Now.[128]

The conditional acceptance and the ambivalent attitudes toward some of the components of democratic culture has affected the responses of the Israeli body politic on issues related to perceptions of democracy. Most of these issues concern one or more of three major dilemmas: an emphasis on representative democracy versus emphasis on participatory democracy, the rule of law and the rights of the individual versus considerations of raison d'etat, unconditional application of the freedom of political organization versus the imposition of limitations in this area (at least in regard to participation in elections) on political groups that challenge the normative foundations of the State of Israel, its democratic regime, or the consensus that it represents the "state of the Jewish people." Issues related to the first dilemma have become prominent with the emergence of extra-parliamentary politics since the Yom Kippur War of 1973, including the appearance of such movements as Peace Now and Gush Emunim. However, traces of this dilemma can also be found in debates concerning the role of an independent press and the public's right to know. The second dilemma is most apparent in issues related to national security. Indeed, some of the "affairs" that have shaken the Israeli political establishment, including the Lavon Affair in the 1960s and the General Security Service (Shin Bet) Affair in 1986-87, revolved around such issues. The third dilemma was referred to explicitly in the Supreme Court decision in the case of the ban on the radical Arab group El Ard, which claimed the right to take part in elections to the Knesset despite its platform denying the legitimacy of the State of Israel. Similar questions were raised twenty years later in regard to the Kach movement which challenged the foundations of Israel's democratic system, and the Progressive Movement for Peace, whose positions were interpreted as denying the claim of Israel to be the "state of the Jewish people." A decision of the Central Election Committee to ban the two lists was not upheld by the Supreme Court; the Knesset later amended the law in order to facilitate such a ban in the 1988 elections.

Ideology has thus played a dual role in the development of Israeli democracy as both a unifying and dividing factor. Ideological consensus, even if minimal in scope, has served both as a substitute for a common cultural tradition in promoting social cohesion, and as a point of departure for shaping Israel's rules of the political game. Under these circumstances, it is not surprising that the outbreak of fundamental ideological disputes after the 1967 war tended to erode both social cohesion and the effectiveness of Israel's democratic system.

4

Government and Politics: From a Dominant Center to a Dual Center

The Establishment of the State: The Strengthening of the Political Center

Israeli society inherited a tradition of political activity from the Yishuv that is not only intensive, but also tends to penetrate into spheres which, in other societies, are considered to be inappropriate for politics. The central forces in this comprehensive and intensive political activity were the political parties and movements. As a result, there was a far-reaching politicization of practically all spheres of life in the Yishuv. This was expressed not only in the staffing of public organizations in accordance with the balance of political power (the political "party key"), but also extended to activities such as providing employment, education, housing, culture and sports, all of which operated under the guidance or direction of political movements.[1] Despite the fact that a large part of these political activities was split among various sectors, with much of it conducted within the enclaves representing ideological subcultures, the Yishuv did not lack a political-communal center. The effectiveness of this center, in fact, led observers to describe the Yishuv as a "state in the making."

The establishment of the state led to the strengthening of the political center and the imposition of new burdens upon it. On the one hand, new needs emerged that increased the burden. On the other hand, the political center now had the means of compulsion of a sovereign state at its disposal which enabled it to mobilize resources—and not only to distribute them—and to impose its authority on various groups and sectors in society. This change meant additional power for the political center which thereby lessened the reliance on bargaining and compromise. It also became possible to involve fewer social sectors and political movements in the national leadership and in access to resources concomitant with such an involvement. During the War of Independence, the governmental coalition still included all the political elements that had been part of the Organized Yishuv with the addition of Agudat Israel which had previously remained outside. After the elections to the First Knesset, however, in early 1949, a narrow coalition was established comprising Mapai, the religious parties and the Progressive Party. Left out were Mapam, the main part of the left, and the General Zionists and Herut, the main parties of the right. The General Zionists joined the coalition in 1952, but Mapam did not join until 1955, at which point the General Zionists left. Thus, although Israel's parliamentary system was characterized by a narrower coalition than that which had led the Organized Yishuv, it was still larger than what was needed to create a "minimum winning coalition."[2] In all the periods prior to 1967, there were parties—such as Mapam prior to 1955 and the General Zionist thereafter—which were considered potential coalition partners, even though they were in opposition. The advent of the Six Day War led to the re-establishment of a broad coalition consisting of the parties that had shared power in the past, together with Herut which had in the past been manifestly excluded as a potential coalition partner according to Ben-Gurion's formula, "except Herut and the Communists."

Another aspect of the strengthening of the political center during the 1950s was the reduction in the quasi-consociational arrangements which conferred partial autonomy on political movement "enclaves," thereby permitting them to act as agents of the center in providing various services to their respective constituencies.[3] However, this policy was applied unevenly. For instance, although the school system became "nationalized," the system of independent "trends" in the school system was abolished only in respect to the secular trends, the "labor trend" and the "general trend" being merged to form a state secular school system. The state religious school system, however, was based in practice, if not necessarily in principle, on the pre-state Mizrahi trend. Thus, the quasi-consociational arrangements remained in force for the religious sector and, to a lesser extend, for the settlement movements. Furthermore, over the years, the government assumed responsibility for funding the independent school network of Agudat Israel thus creating a consociational pattern in which state resources are allocated to a non-governmental body so that it may provide a basic public service, in this case education, to a particular social sector.[4] Recognition of the partial autonomy of the religious sector, in general, and the ultra-Orthodox subculture, in particular, was not limited to the school system. It also included exemption from military service for women on the basis of a formal declaration that they are religiously observant, and a blanket exemption from regular army service granted to yeshive students.

In contrast, there was a real reduction in the extend of quasi-governmental services provided by the Histadrut which served as the institutional base of the secondary center of the Labor Movement. Even before the establishment of the state, the labor exchange of the Jewish Agency had removed the virtual monopoly held by the Histadrut in providing employment. After the establishment of the state, state labor exchanges were set up which operated under the Employment Service Law. In the area of social security, the role of the Histadrut was reduced following the enactment of the National Insurance Law[5] although the Histadrut continued to provide certain essential services to its members and to the members of its affiliates, the labor organization of the Mizrahi and Agudat Israel. The most prominent of these services is the health insurance provided by Kupat Holim of the Histadrut. Moreover, during the period of mass immigration, the Jewish Agency paid Kupat Holim to provide health services in the transit camps, thus making it easier for the Histadrut to mobilize the immigrants as new members. The Histadrut continued to provide social security services through its pension funds for wage-earners in the private and Histadrut sectors.[6] Thus Israel's welfare state came to be based on a division of labor or responsibility between government and non-governmental bodies, with the latter usually based on voluntary organizations established during the period of the Yishuv.

Another sector to be recognized as a distinct subculture was the Arab sector. Arabic is an official language of the State of Israel, and it is the primary language of instruction in the Arab schools. Moreover, the curriculum in the Arab schools differs from that in the Jewish state schools in that it includes Arabic culture and history. Neverthless, the Arab state schools do not enjoy the organizational autonomy conferred on the religious schools in the Jewish sector.

The reduction of the quasi-consociational arrangements based on ideological or cultural distinctions did not mean the end of the tradition of bargaining and compromise. Indeed, there was an increase in the use of the mechanisms of bargaining and compromise in the relations between the government and interest groups, especially in the economic sphere. The government's economic policy over the years has been determined to no small extent through negotiations between the government and associations representing economic or professional interests necessarily defined in ideological terms. Organizations representing employers, white-collar or blue-collar workers, or main branches in the economy cultivated direct channels of access to the government administration, thus bypassing party and parliamentary channels. These contacts became part of the pattern of activity that sociologists and political scientists call "corporatist politics." This pattern has been especially prominent in determining wage policy, which is usually formulated in national wage agreements negotiated by the government, employers' organizations, and the trade unit arm of the Histadrut.

These developments show that the political culture of Israel that was shaped after the establishment of the state was a product of the joint influence of the quasi-consociational tradition rooted in the Yishuv, the centralistic "statist" approach that was stressed in the early years of the state, and the corporatist arrangements that emerged as the economy developed and resources became dispersed among the three economic sectors — state, Histadrut, and private. The remnant of the quasi-consociational tradition is reflected mainly in arrangements granting partial autonomy in the provision of services on a particularistic basis to cultural, ideological or political enclaves. The statist approach is expressed in extensive government intervention in the economy and in the high degree of dependence of the public on government bureaucracy. The corporatist trend is expressed in institutionalized arrangements in which government and various social and economic interest groups make an effort to reach an acceptable policy through bargaining and compromise. No single one of these three patterns ever became completely dominant, but the relative importance of each has shifted in various periods. The early years of the state were marked by the emergence and strengthening of the statist pattern. The tendency to political centralization and the strengthening of state authority had several roots. First, the State of Israel was born during its War of Independence which demanded a near total mobilization of manpower and material resources for the war effort.[7] The pervasive sense of emergency that held sway then made it much easier for the new institutions of the state to enforce their domination over all groups in society and to intensively impose their authority over a broad range of activities. Second, the adoption of a universalistic legal system, a legacy of the British Mandate, worked to reduce the occurence of particularistic arrangements between the political center and groups and individuals that were common under the ambiguous rules of the game of the Organized Yishuv. Third, the rituals attached to sovereignty and its symbols, particularly the cultivation of David Ben-Gurion as a charismatic national leader, enhanced the identification of broad social groups with the new government.[8] Fourth, the consensus that emerged on the need to accept the authority of Israel's democratic regime removed the threat to the authority of the center that existed during the Yishuv from dissident groups which challenged or refused to accept the authority of the Organized Yishuv.[9] Fifth, the extensive needs of the new immigrants who arrived in the early years of the state for basic services provided by governmental and quasi-governmental bodies, such as the Jewish Agency, made them directly dependent on the state. Dependence of another sort was imposed on the Arab population by the military government. All these dependency relations and the extensive involvement of the government in the everyday life of a large part of the population considerably strengthened the power of state institutions.

The centralistic trend reached its apex in the early 1950s, but then weakened because the factors behind it gradually lost much of their force. The War of Independence was concluded in 1949 by the signing of armistice agreements that reduced the need for extensive mobilization. The universalist legal system became institutionalized. The commitment aroused by the rituals and symbols of sovereignty became routinized, thus reducing their mobilizing potential, and attitudes to national leaders, including Ben-Gurion, became more critical. Ethnic identities were less extensively articulated, which meant less pressure on the center. The long-term absorption of the mass immigration, and especially the improvement in its employment opportunities in the late 1950s and early 1960s, considerably reduced its dependence on public agencies. Portions of the particularistic political culture of the Yishuv remained, especially in the religious community and among the ultra-Orthodox in particular. Demands on the center from such peripheral groups increased as group identities became more articulated along with their associated interests. For example, the ultra-Orthodox community won considerable particularistic concessions such as exemption from army service for yeshiva students and full government support for its independent school system. These factors in the weakening of centralistic political trends were augmented by developments occuring in the early 1950s. The election results of 1951, which were seen as a backlash against the government's excessive control of the economy, led to the gradual abolition of the austerity measures such as rationing and administrative price controls.[10] The shortage of investment capital led to the formulation of a policy aimed at encouraging private investment and the expansion of the private sector. These developments explain the partial survival of consociational political patterns and the appearance of new patterns of bargaining and compromise characteristic of corporatist politics. The inevitable result of these trends was a decline in the mobilizing capacity of the political center.

The Legislative Authority, Judicial Authority, and Public Administration

The interrelations between state and society were thus changed by the transition from Yishuv to state and in the wake of developments after the establishment of the state. To the extent that it is possible to discuss the "state" as an entity under the Mandate, it was a rather weak body that had to reconcile itself to the existence of collective political entities that made up the Yishuv, and to a lesser extent, the organized Arab community. The establishment of Israel as a sovereign entity with many of the attributes of a nation-state strengthened the "statelike" qualities of the political system.[11] The statist ideology, the tendency to political centralization and the weakening of consociational arrangements reflected this trend. On the other hand, the legacy of the political culture of the Yishuv, the survival capacity of the sub-centers composed of party and movement enclaves, and the emergence of new particularistic interest groups, mainly in the economic sphere, hampered the further development of "statist" trends in the political system. Moreover, further erosion of state-centered politics occurred as a result of the increasing power of sectors and groups whose bargaining power vis a vis the state grew, because they were not subject to its direct supervision.

There is thus no clear-cut answer to the question as to the extent to which the political culture of the Yishuv survived. On the one hand, some aspects of politicization and excessive influence of political parties were preserved but, on the other, new patterns of relations between the government and the public which were not based on parties did emerge. This change came about mainly because of the need to adapt the political process to a government resting on a binding legal-constitutional base. These patterns were not anchored in the political system of the Yishuv, but rather in the Mandate. Since there was no orderly transfer of power between the Mandate and its successor, there was no possibility of preparing a constitution that would replace Mandatory law. The State of Israel had no choice but to pour the contents of the political system of the Yishuv into the only available legal vessel—the Mandatory legal framework which was still in force on May 14, 1948.[12] However, this did not completely solve the problem of defining the various authorities of the new sovereign state. Israel's Declaration of Independence stated that the People's Council, which had been set up before May 14th, would become the Provisional Council of State and would serve as the legislative authority until an elected constituent assembly was convened. As for the executive authority, the Declaration of Independence said that the executive arm of the People's Council would serve as the Provisional Government. These two bodies were more than simply extensions of national institutions of the Yishuv because they included representatives of groups that were not part of the Organized Yishuv.[13]

At this point, even before Israel possessed elected institutions, its political character as a parliamentary democracy had already been shaped. The Law and Administration Ordinance, the law that guided the arms of Israel's government in the period prior to the elections to the first Knesset, stated that the Provisional Government would act "in accordance with the policies to be determined by the Provisional Council of State." It was originally intended that these provisional bodies would govern until the election of a constituent assembly which would then establish a constitution for the new state. However, when the first elected legislative authority of the State of Israel convened in early 1949, it decided in its first session that it would act as a full-fledged parliament to be called the "First Knesset."[14] Moreover, in June 1950, the Knesset decided not to prepare a comprehensive constitution, but rather to pass a series of Basic Laws that would eventually serve as parts of a constitution.[15] The various branches of government were thus defined in the Basic Laws dealing with the presidency, the Knesset, the government, and the judiciary.[16] According to these laws, Israel's form of government is a parliamentary democracy in which the cabinet is responsible to the Knesset.

The authority granted to the Knesset by Israeli law is quite broad. In contrast to the limitations imposed on parliaments in most other democracies, there is no rigid constitution in Israel to prevent the

Knesset from changing practically any law by a simple majority,[17] An exception to this is the section of the Basic Law: Knesset, which defines the system of elections which can be changed only by vote of a majority (i.e., at least 61) of all 120 members of Knesset. There is no other parliamentary body in Israel besides the Knesset; no other branch of government is authorized to disperse the Knesset except the Knesset itself; and most important, the government or cabinet is responsible to the Knesset and must resign if it loses a vote of confidence in the Knesset. In addition, the Members of Knesset or MKs enjoy full immunity before the law in relation to any proposals or statements they make, whether written or oral, or in relation to any actions in the Knesset or outside it, if these were made within the framework of their duties as MKs or in support of these duties. Furthermore, MKs enjoy partial immunity from criminal prosecution, since criminal charges can be pressed against them only if the Knesset votes to strip them of their immunity in relation to a particular charge.[18]

However, the potential power of the Knesset does not give a true picture of its actual power which is restricted, in practice, by the power of the government and the power of the political parties. The relative weakness of the Knesset vis a vis the government and the parties is rooted in the ability of the parties to impose sanctions on MKs who violate party discipline, especially by denying them a place on the party's list of candidates at the next election.

The status of the parties is anchored in the system of proportional representation used in Israel. According to this system, the entire country comprises one electoral district, and each party that wins more than one percent of the vote is entitled to be represented in the Knesset in accordance with its share of the total vote.[19] The background to the adoption of this system is twofold: First, this system represents the political traditions of the Zionist Movement and the Yishuv, according to which political authority was accepted on a voluntary basis and second, this system embodies a tradition of strong ideological divisions that did not attribute much significance to the representation of local interests.

The proportional representation system enables and indeed encourages a multiplicity of parties. Thus, Israel has always been a multi-party democracy, in contrast to the English-speaking democracies which are, for the most part, two-party systems. As a result of this multi-party system, no one party has ever won an absolute majority in any of the twelve elections to the Knesset held during Israel's first forty years. Thus, all governments have been coalition governments. Nevertheless, despite the coalitionary nature of the governments and the fact that they were responsible to the Knesset, they have all been quite stable in that the number of coalition crises to actually force a government to resign has been relatively small. For Israel's first twenty-nine years, this relative stability was due to the presence of a dominant party with a pivotal position in the system—no government could be formed without it because neither the parties to its left nor to its right could form a majority on their own. On the other hand, any coalition made up of the right and left omitting the center party was inconceivable for ideological reasons. In the years that followed, no new dominant party emerged. However, the emergence of two large political blocs created a polarized pattern similar, in some ways, to a two-party political system.[20]

While the relations between the legislative and executive branches were influenced mainly by the political tradition of the Yishuv and the Zionist Movement, the relations between the executive and the judicial branches were shaped mainly by the British legal system. As a result, the judicial sphere, more than any other, remained immune to the influence of party politics. The pervasive politicization that characterizes most spheres of organized social activity in Israel stopped at the threshold of the legal system, which was guided mainly by professional norms. The relative autonomy of the legal system was assured by the influence of Israel's first Misnister of Justice, Pinhas Rosen. The courts, and particularly the Supreme Court sitting as the High Court of Justice, thus became the "watchdog" of the rule of law in Israel. The absence of a constitution and the special stature acquired over the years by the Supreme Court led it to take on the task, albeit with some degree of caution, of articulating judicial norms. This approach taken by the courts is often expressed in broad interpretations of legislative intent which amount to the creation of legal norms. For example, the principles of freedom of the press were articulated in the Supreme Court's decision on a petition brought by the Communist daily *Kol Ha'am*.[21] Likewise, in the case of Brother Daniel, the Supreme Court laid down the rule that a Jew who converts to another religion cannot enjoy the privileges extended to Jewish immigrants under the Law of Return. This rule was later adopted by the Knesset and included in the amendment made to the Law of Return in 1968. The Supreme Court occasionally criticizes the legislature while at the same time reluctantly declaring itself bound by existing law. For instance, in its decision in the Aharon Cohen espionage case, the Supreme Court stated that the law, as laid down by the Knesset, was unreasonable.[22]

This ruling, too, led to changes in the relevant laws. A Supreme Court decision that overturned a political decision was its ruling permitting television broadcasts on the Sabbath which had been banned in a coalition agreement.[23]

The most sensitive area in terms of the tension between observance of legal norms and policy dictated by raison d'etat is the sphere of security. The Supreme Court has always been extremely cautious when intervening in the considerations of the defense establishment. Nevertheless, the court has insisted on enforcing its right to criticize these considerations and even to reject them. Moreover, the very involvement of the court in matters concerning the occupied territories was the result of a far-reaching Supreme Court decision to allow Arab residents of the territories to seek redress for their grievances in the High Court of Justice even though Israeli law had not been imposed on them.[24] This decision, which was not part of Israel's obligations as an occupying power under international treaties, gave the judicial branch the authority to review the conduct of Israel's military government and civil administration in the territories. The tension between considerations of state security and norms of the rule of law is not confined to matters affecting the occupied territories. The Supreme Court has dealt with such problems in various contexts. One of most important of these cases concerned the attempt of the General Security Services (GSS) to cover up the killing of two terrorists taken prisoner after hijacking a bus in 1984. Though in this case the court did recognize the validity of the security considerations that guided the President in granting pardons, it left no doubt as to its right to review the legitimacy of these considerations.[25]

The tendency of the Supreme Court to render judgments in a broad range of areas does not extend to the sensitive area of judicial review[24] in which the court rules on the constitutionality of laws passed by the legislature. In Israeli law, the Basic Laws that were formulated as a basis for an eventual constitution, do not have preference over other laws. Furthermore, the Basic Laws themselves, with very few exceptions, may be changed like all other laws. One of these exceptions, which may be changed only by a vote of at least 61 out of 120 MKs, defines the nature of Israel's electoral system. The existence of this entrenched provision enabled the Supreme Court to overturn a law, passed by a simple majority in the Knesset, concerning the public financing of elections, which did not make provision for funding the election expenses of parties not previously represented in the Knesset. The petitioner to the High Court argued that the definition of the elections as "equal" applied not only to the right to vote, but also to the right to be elected. Thus, the law passed did not give an equal opportunity for new lists taking part in the elections. The court accepted this argument, but did not relate it to the question of whether it had the authority to hear petitions that sought to overturn acts of the legislature.[27] The court could have avoided ruling on this issue, which bordered on judicial review, because the Attorney General had refrained from arguing that the hearing on this petition exceeded the authority of the court. If neither side sought to raise this issue, then the court was free to ignore it. Thus, the question of whether Israeli courts should have the full or partial right of judicial review was left unresolved.

The judicial branch is not the only institutional framework that helps preserve the rule of law in Israel. The Attorney General has also become, to a considerable extent, a representative of a legal-professional approach to matters of state that involve both purely administrative as well as political aspects. However, a tradition has emerged in Israel—bolstered by the conclusions of a committee headed by a Supreme Court judge—that holds that the Attorney General should be guided by considerations of the rule of law rather than those of interests of state.[28] Paradoxically, despite the fact that decisions taken by various Attorney Generals have sometimes raised the ire of senior political leaders, over the years, governments have increasingly tended to place decisions which have sensitive personal or political implications in his hands. The politicians' tendency to evade personal responsibility for making difficult decisions collided in these cases with their desire to avoid the risks entailed in letting someone else make a decision which may not be to their liking. It is against this background that we may examine the tensions that have sometimes arisen between the Attorney General and the Prime Minister. For example, Attorney General Aharon Barak created personal difficulties for Prime Minister Yitzhak Rabin when he insisted on prosecuting Rabin for maintaining an illegal foreign currency account abroad, rather than allowing him the option of paying a fine. A major confrontation occured between Attorney General Yitzhak Zamir and the cabinet, including the Minister of Justice, when Zamir insisted on prosecuting the GSS (General Security Service) officials suspected of involvement in the killing of two captured terrorists and in obstructing an investigation into the affair. This affair ended with pardons granted to all the suspects by the President before the matter could go to trial following the replacement of the Attorney General.[29] While the areas subject to the jurisdiction of the courts have witnessed the growth of a tradition of universal legal norms that are equally binding on all citizens, a part of the legal system has remained outside the purview of the judiciary. The civil courts are not permitted to intervene in matters of personal status—i.e., marriage and divorce, which are under the sole jurisdiction of the religious courts run respectively by the Jews, Moslems, Christians, and Druze.

In addition to the permanent judicial bodies that form part of Israel's governmental structure, there exists also the quasi-judicial institution of the state commission of inquiry.[30] According to law, these commissions have the authority to summon witnesses and to question them under oath. Such commissions are usually appointed in the wake of serious malfunctions of governmental or other public bodies. Two of the most important commissions of inquiry were the commission headed by Supreme Court Justice Agranat which investigated the opening phases of the Yom Kippur War;[31] and the one headed by Supreme Court Justice Kahan which investigated the massacre at the Sabra and Shatila refugee camps in Beirut.[32] These commissions did not limit themselves to the factual determination of the events but also assigned personal or official responsibility for them at the ministerial or executive level. The recommendations of these commissions of inquiry led to the removal of Chief of Staff David Elazar and other officers in the wake of the Yom Kippur War, and to the removal from the position of Minister of Defense Ariel Sharon and several IDF officers in the case of the Sabra and Shatila affair. Another commission of inquiry of major importance was the one headed by Supreme Court Justice Beiski which investigated the bank share collapse of 1983. Its recommendations led to the resignations of four of the five heads of Israel's major banks.

The judiciary is not the only institutional framework that represents the principle of professional autonomy, in a partial sense at least, in its relations with the executive branch. The State Comptroller and the Governor of the Bank of Israel are assured by law of autonomy—full in the case of former and partial in the case of the latter—in the performance of their duties.[33] This autonomy, like the independence enjoyed by the legal system, has served as a barrier to excessive politicization in their areas of responsibility.

Not all attempts to depoliticize state functions by setting up authorities independent of the government have succeeded. For example, the Broadcasting Authority was set up as an independent body along the lines of the BBC, but it turned into a politically-competitive arena since its governing bodies were composed of representatives. selected according to a "party key."[34]

The problem of politicization has arisen not only in the context of statutory authorities independent of the executive branch with discretionary powers defined by law. This problem has also been a central source of concern in the development of public services in general, and the government civil service, in particular.[35] Recruitment to the government bureaucracy in its early stages was conducted, at least for key positions, mainly through political channels. As the civil service gradually became more professionalized, staffing and promotion based on the tradition of the party key became less prominent. This was not a linear trend, however, and certain reverses have occurred. The politicization which had tapered off in the 1960s and early 1970s got a new lease on life after 1977 when the Likud took over as the ruling party and received a further boost during the tenure of the "national unity government" when the Likud and the Alignment made formal agreements on how to "divide the spoils" concerning appointments to senior government posts. However, the politicization of the civil service in the late 1970s and 1980s differed from that of the 1950s in two ways. First, in the latter period the scope of politicization was narrower and penetrated only into senior levels. Second, politicization hardly affected the decisions made by lower level officials in their everyday contacts with the public. The tendency to exploit the public's dependence on the bureaucracy for purposes of political mobilization, which was common in the 1950s and 1960s, virtually disappeared during the two decades that followed.

The changes in the extent of politicization in the civil service did not affect the most important characteristic of the state bureaucracy—the broad sweep of its intervention and involvement in Israel's society and economy. The extent of the government's intervention in the economy can be described as a series of concentric circles. In the center lie the state-controlled industries and services where government involvement is naturally greatest, although differences exist between bodies run by ministries and those organized as government corporations which have somewhat more autonomy. The second circle contains the non-governmental public services such as those provided by the Jewish Agency and the Histadrut which are influenced by the government through corporatist arrangements. The third circle consists of the private sector of the economy. These bodies are not run by the government or public bureaucracy, but they are dependent on services provided by them and are subject to laws and regulations administered by the government. The fourth circle consists of the "underground economy" which operates, at least in part, outside the law and is thus not covered by government supervision.

Israel's administrative elite eventually became subject to tensions and cross-pressures resulting from the co-existence of a public bureaucracy with extensive influence over the economy together with a private sector operating according to capitalist principles of motivation and reward. On the one hand, the administrative elite was supposed to be committed to the ethos of a "service elite" responsible to the public for its actions, but on the other hand, as a status group, it maintained contacts with the economic elites of the private sector, whose level of material rewards reflected the profit-oriented ethos of capitalist society. The existence of shared social networks among the economic elites of the private sector, the administrative elite, and leading politicians, influenced the politicians as well as senior officials in the public sector. Since the success of private economic ventures often depended on having effective access to government offices, the use of political connections to obtain preferential access became widespread. This encouraged private businessmen to utilize the services of MKs as lawyers or economic consultants. The expansion of such services was not due just to the expertise of the MKs who provided them, but also to the possibility of using their influence on the government bureaucracy. The extensive dependence of the Israeli economy on the public bureaucracy, together with the development of a profit-motivated private sector that also served as a source of status, has inevitably led to an erosion of ethical standards in the civil service.

The Political Party Map

From the above analysis of the interrelations between the government and the public, the autonomy of the judicial system, and the characteristics of Israel's public administration, it is clear that each of these areas is closely connected with the status, influence, and scope of activities of political parties. In the 1950s, Israel was actually described as a "party state." However, although the institutional basis of the state has its roots in the Organized Yishuv, the establishment of the state made it necessary to redefine the institutional consensus linking the parties. Under these circumstances, it comes as no surprise that the study of politics in Israel has focused in the past and continues to focus, to a large extent, on political parties: the party map, inter-party coalitions, the functions of parties (especially their role expansion), organization and internal democracy, the social composition of the parties' electoral base of support, and the conduct of election campaigns.[36]

The party map in Israel is marked by several characteristics: first, a multiplicity of parties in the Knesset coming in all sizes—small, medium, and large—and ideological shadings, in addition to other lists that did not make it over the threshold of parliamentary representation; second, no one party has ever won an absolute majority of the vote in any election from 1949 to 1988; third, despite the absense of a majority party, until 1977, one party—Mapai and its successor, the Labor Party—always won considerably more votes than any other party; fourth, all parties have experienced splits and mergers, or have at least attempted to set up blocs with other parties in the Knesset; fifth, almost all the parties represented in the Knesset have gone through one or more election campaigns as part of a larger bloc with the result that party membership did not always coincide with the lists that competed in the elections.

The party map in a multi-party system has several implications for the formation and stability of governments. Viewed from this perspective, two periods can be distinguished: the period preceding the 1977 electoral upheaval and the period thereafter. What both periods have in common is a multiplicity of parties and ideological diversity. The main difference between the two periods relates to the shift from a party map characterized by a dominant party to a *polarized* party map. For twenty-nine years, from 1948 to 1977, Mapai, and later its successor, the Labor Party, was not only the largest party but also a pivotal party, without which it was impossible to form a ruling coalition. Mapai could therefore adopt a tough bargaining stance that gave it much room for maneuver in choosing its coalition partners. In contrast, after 1977 there were two large parties of approximately the same size, each of which formed blocs together with smaller parties. The smaller parties fell into three categories: satellite parties that could always be counted on to support one of the larger parties; parties that could hold the balance of power by switching their allegiance from one bloc to the other; and parties that would not be invited to join any coalition, but which could play a spoiler role in blocking coalitions not to their liking.

Studies of the party system prior to 1977 present several models which seek to explain the position of parties on the political map in terms of their importance for the coalition. Attempts have also been made to devise a research approach that would provide a systematic description of the map in terms of the tendencies of parties to join with others in coalitions or political blocs. The first and most simplistic model devised to describe the party system was based on "factional groupings" or "blocs." This model assigned parties to several main blocs marked by two characteristics: Votes tend to shift from one party to another within each grouping, so that the overall balance between the groupings remains stable, and all mergers and splits occur within the groupings, so that parties do not move from one grouping to another. The first characteristic was refuted by studies that showed that the electoral balance between the groupings was true only on an aggregate level. When the voting patterns of various social groups were examined, it was found that votes moving out of one grouping were offset by votes coming in from another.[37] Over the years, the aggregate electoral balance between the groupings changed as well, the center-right bloc growing at the expense of both the left and the religious blocs. The validity of the second characteristic ascribed to the groupings endured somewhat longer, but it also ceased to be relevant after 1977. For instance, part of the Rafi Party, which originated in the labor grouping, eventually found its way to the Likud. The Tehiya Party attracted voters which had previously been attached to three different groupings: labor, religious, and center-right.

While the model of the factional groupings touched only indirectly on the special position of the dominant party, other models dealt with this directly. The central question in this context was What permitted Mapai to act as a dominant party and to preserve this status? The most common explanation relates to Mapai's pivotal position in the system. According to this model, Mapai's dominant status was based not only on the fact that it was the largest party but also on its pivotal position on the ideological map. This position prevented the formation of a coalition based on a partnership between the parties to the right of Mapai and the parties to its left. Under the conditions prevailing until 1977, with the members elected to the Knesset arranged on an ideological spectrum from left to right, the median always fell within Mapai.[38] The terms left or right in this case refer less to formal ideological positions than to the self-image of parties which determined their willingness to take part in coalitions with others. Coalitions including Mapam and Achdut Ha'avodah on the one hand and Herut and the General Zionists (Liberals) on the other, without Mapai, were a political impossibility. The center-right bloc, even with the religious parties, did not have a majority in the Knesset until 1977; and the parties to the left of Mapai had even fewer seats.

The threat to Mapai's pivotal position came more from the right than the left. This was because the majority that Mapai could form with the parties to its left in order to block a coalition of right-wing parties, was smaller than the majority that Mapai could put together with parties to its right in order to block a left-wing coalition. Under these conditions, a significant shift of Mapai votes to the right or the defection of a group with rightist leanings from Mapai could permit the formation of a right-wing coalition without Mapai and thereby undermine its pivotal status. Indeed, in 1964 a group left Mapai, led by Ben-Gurion, Shimon Peres, Moshe Dayan, and Yosef Almogi, that sought to exploit this very weakness and become a new party holding the balance of power. This group, which became the Rafi Party, based its hopes on its ability to create a situation in which it would be possible to form a coalition without Mapai, which would then force Mapai to accept Rafi's terms for allowing Mapai to remain in power. However, in the 1965 elections, Mapai succeeded in preserving its pivotal position forcing Rafi to join the opposition to the right of Mapai. Most of Rafi's leaders, with the exception of Ben-Gurion, eventually found their way back to the dominant party when Mapai merged with Rafi and Achdut Ha'avodah in 1968 to form the Labor Party. Another attempt to take hold of the balance of power in parliamant by taking votes from Mapai was made in 1977 by the Democratic Movement for Change (DMC). The DMC failed, too, in this effort but for different reasons. While in 1965 the shift of Mapai votes to the right was too small to enable Rafi to assume a pivotal position, in 1977 the drop in Labor's electoral strength was so great that the Likud and the religious parties were able to form a majority on their own without the DMC. The DMC eventually joined the coalition formed by the Likud and the religious parties, but without the strong bargaining position of a pivotal party.[39] In 1977, Mapai/Labor lost its controlling position as a dominant party, a position it had enjoyed for close to thirty years.

Between 1948 and 1977, then, there was no change in the ruling party but there were changes in the ruling party's coalition partners. Mapai's pivotal position gave it the option of choosing its partners from among those parties which it considered worthy of participation in the coalition which meant all parties except for Herut and Maki. Mapai also had the option of choosing a limited number among a field of potential partners which made a broad coalition unnecessary and removed the need to make concessions to a wide range of partners. In this fashion, Mapai and Labor managed to maintain a majority position within the ruling coalition itself. The only attempt, made in 1961, by all of Mapai's potential partners to force it into a broad coalition failed. This tactical coalition of four parties broke up when Mapai succeeded in driving a wedge between several of its potential partners.[40]

The possibility for Mapai to choose among a field of potential coalition partners was also related to the existence of different lines of ideological division that partially overlapped for certain parties. These parties held similar positions on some issues, and opposing positions on others. This characteristic of Israel's political structure is part of the legacy of the Yishuv where each political grouping sought to organize independently in order to be able to express its views more independently on a variety of issues. This prevented the formation of a polarized structure along a single ideological axis. Mapai's status as a dominant party did not derive soley from its pivotal position, but also reflected its centrist location on most lines of ideological division. In addition, Mapai's traditional tendency to stress the operative rather than the fundamental elements of ideology made it easier for it to utilize its advantages as a pivotal party, as there were no rigid ideological constraints preventing it from making alliances with different partners.

The position of Mapai and the Labor Party in the party system until 1977 can also be described as a series of concentric circles. In this model, the dominant party is placed in the innermost circle, since it is the nucleus of any coalition. In the second circle come all the parties that have taken part in a coalition at any time up to 1977 even though none of them have been part of all governments. In the third circle are parties that never took part in a coalition and were never regarded by Mapai/Labor as potential partners. These are parties that, intentionally or not, found themselves in the situation known in Europe as an "opposition of principle." The concentric circle model lost much of its relevance even before Labor lost its position as the dominant party. In the period of uncertainty and tension preceding the outbreak of the 1967 war, two leaders of Gahal—a bloc comprising Herut and the Liberals and the forerunner of the Likud—were brought into the government; and in 1969 a coalition with a joint platform was set up that included the Alignment (Labor and Mapam), Gahal, the National Religious Party and the Independent Liberals. The formation of this coalition represented the conclusion of a process through which Herut gradually gained legitimacy as a partner in national governance. The process began when Herut was asked to join the coalition in the World Zionist Organization, continued when Herut organized its own faction in the Histadrut and gained momentum when it joined with the Liberals in the formation of Gahal, a step which, in retrospect, prepared the ground for Herut to join the cabinet in 1967 and 1969. This, in turn, prepared the way for the transfer of power in 1977 from the Labor Party to a coalition headed by the leader of Herut, Menachem Begin.[41]

The relation between the party map and the structure of the coalition in the period prior to 1977 can also be described in spatial terms of the proximity or distance between parties, with the time spent as a coalition partner and the willingness to form joint lists for the Knesset serving as the criteria of measurement. According to this approach, the parties are not mapped out a priori in accordance with ideological criteria, size, or pivotal position. Rather, this approach seeks to examine the validity of the other models in terms of the parties' actual behavior in respect to coalition formation. This examination of party behavior employing the tool of the mathematical Smallest Space Analysis (SSA) indeed showed that the resulting parties' order presented in the form of mapping in a two-dimensional space conforms with the assumptions of the models of a pivotal party, ideological blocks and concentric circles.

The overall power of Mapai and Labor until 1977 can therefore be explained on three levels: the electoral, the parliamentary, and the governmental. On the electoral plane, Mapai's power was based on its ability to continually attract at least one third of all votes in the various elections to the Knesset despite demographic, cultural, and ecomonic changes in the composition of the electorate.[42] This success can be explained by Mapai's characteristics as they are expressed in terms of its position among the parties. First, given the "party key" practices, Mapai's very size assured it control of considerable resources, which in itself influenced the distribution of the vote. However, its control of resources was not sufficient; to use these resources to its electoral advantage, Mapai required the development of mechanisms that would use these resources to acquire the support of groups and individuals. Mapai's broad range of activities and functions, which extended into areas outside the conventional boundaries of politics, created the mechanisms needed to translate its resources into votes. Mapai's control of a network of activists also helped Mapai maintain its dominant position from one election to the next.

In the parliamentary arena, Mapai's power was determined not only by its electoral strength, which determined its seats in proportion to its share of the vote, but also by its pivotal position on the left-right continuum. Mapai's bargaining position in parliament was translated into power in the governmental sphere since it enabled Mapai to assure itself a majority in the cabinet and to distribute portfolios in such a way that it kept the most important posts for itself. The probability that Mapai would enter into a coalition alliance with a given party was influenced not only by the number of issues in dispute between them, but also by the salience of these issues in a given period.

For example, the serious dispute between Mapai and Mapam over Israel's foreign policy orientation in the early 1950s—Mapam favored an overt pro-Soviet policy—prevented Mapam from joining the coalition during that time.[43]

The general recognition of Mapai's strength and of the lack of any possibility in the foreseeable future to displace it from power stimulated centripetal forces that generated mergers and joint electoral lists among various parties, in the hope that this would improve their prospects in the circle of potential coalition partners.In the left wing of the spectrum, this tendency was expressed in the formation of electoral "alignments" between Mapai and smaller parties, which led ultimately, in 1968, to the merger of Mapai, Achdut Ha'avodah and Rafi to produce the Labor Party. Centrifugal forces were also evident in the party system, but these were weaker and narrower in scope than the centripetal forces. The most prominent of these processes was Rafi's split from Mapai in 1964 which thrust it out of the inner circle and into the second circle of potential coalition partners. This split, led by Ben-Gurion, constituted a threat to the stability of the inner party structure held together by Mapai. The defection of a group of prominent Mapai figures, including its leader for several decades, and the establishment of a new party to the right of Mapai based on former Mapai voters, could have created a parliamentary majority to the right of Mapai for the first time. However, the failure to deny Mapai's pivotal position brought most of Rafi's leaders and activists, with the exception of Ben-Gurion himself, to give up their wanderings in the outer circle and to return to their political home when the Labor Party was formed. Nevertheless, the possibility of a defection of the right wing of Mapai under the popular leadership of Moshe Dayan continued to pose a threat to Mapai's pivotal position. This possibility enabled Dayan to impose some of his views on the rest of the party, such as the position formulated by Israel Galili on settlement in the occupied territories, which was intended to appease Dayan.[44]

Some of Mapai's most prominent characteristics enabled it to merge with Rafi and Achdut Ha'avodah to form the Labor Party and to form the alignment with Mapam. Mapai was a non-doctrinaire, heterogeneous party, non-selective in recruiting members and supporters, with a great capacity, due to its size and scope of functions, for mobilizing and allocating resources. Moreover, on the most salient issue of the late 1960s, the future of the occupied territories, Mapai did not maintain a uniform position. The "hawkish" Rafi and Achdut Ha'avodah and the "dovish" Mapam were opposed in their positions on the territories and the peace process, but each of them had potential allies within Mapai.[45]

The various explanations offered for party behavior and the formation of government coalitions in a dominant party system reflected both the advantages and disadvantages of the approach that assumes the autonomy of politics as a phenomenom in social science. The advantage of this approach is that it permits analysis at the level of parties as corporate actors and their leaders as representatives of the political elite. On the other hand, its explanatory power of political phenomena is limited because this approach does not systematically take into account the impact of demographic, cultural, or economic developments or the influence of external historical events such as wars or waves of immigration on the balance of power between parties. Indeed, voter preferences in Israel were changed by demographic, cultural, economic processes, by shifts in the stratification structure and by external developments such as the Six Day War and the Yom Kippur War. These changes took place gradually at first and were reflected in a decline in support for the parties of the Labor Movement. The process of change accelerated, however, in the elections of 1977, when the Alignment lost a third of its voters—partly directly to the Likud and partly to the Democratic Movement for Change (DMC), which was formed several months prior to the elections.[46] This massive electorial shift arose from several sources: a shift in the voting patterns of Afro-Asian Jews, particularly among the offspring of the immigrants of the 1950s; the increased share of Afro-Asian voters in the electorate; the persistence of a high degree of correspondence between ethnic origin and socio-economic status; a general hostility toward the government bureaucracy and the Histadrut; the impact of the Six Day War which led to ideological polarization due to an increase in fundamentalist nationalist sentiment, mainly among the younger generation of the Religious Zionist sector; and the Yom Kippur War, which eroded public confidence in the political establishment and the veteran leadership.

Virtually none of these processes of change were under the control of the political elites involved in the inter-party bargaining that determined the contours of the ruling coalitions up to 1977. However, the cumulative impact of these changes in the electoral sphere undermined the central factor that had maintained the rules of the game characterizing coalition politics up to 1977. These rules of the game stemmed from the existence of a dominant party. The voters in the 1977 elections, however, pulled the rug out from under these rules of the game by removing the dominant party's status as both the largest party and as a pivot.[47]

A Change of Ruling Parties and the Emergence of Political Polarization

The main difference between the pattern of inter-party politics before 1977 and afterward is that the dominant party structure gave way to the polarized situation of two large blocs competing for supremacy. Neither of these blocs—composed of the Likud and its satellites and Labor and its satellites — succeeded in winning a majority in the election of 1977, 1981, 1984, or 1988. Even in 1977, when the Likud came closest to the position of being independent of coalition partners, it still needed the support of the NRP, which clearly preferred this new alliance to its old partnership with Labor, in addition to the support of Agudat Israel and/or the DMC.

The election results in 1981 were more balanced, as a result of Labor managing to restore some of its lost support and the Likud had to negotiate a narrow coalition based on the support of the religious parties. The 1984 elections created a situation in which, with the help of its respective satellite parties, each of the large parties was in a position to block any coalition set up by its rival.[48] Thus, since neither Labor nor the Likud could form a coalition without the other, the only alternative to new elections was the establishment of a "national unity government." In this situation, each of the blocs had enough strength to force its rival into a broadly balanced coalition which included an agreement requiring rotation of the post of Prime Minister and an "inner" cabinet composed on a parity basis to deal with questions of defense and foreign affairs. The political stalemate created by the 1984 elections led to the emergence of a coalitionary structure new to the Israeli system and with no parallel in any other democratic country. The rotation of the premiership midway through the Knesset's term of office symbolizes the internal logic of this model which is based on a decision not to decide between alternative political and ideological approaches. No less important is the principle of mutual veto embodied in the overall coalition agreement and the formation of an inner cabinet composed of an equal number of representatives of the two large parties which, for the most part, stripped the full cabinet of its authority to shape policy in crucial areas.

A "national unity" government is not a common occurrence under conditions of political polarization. Only the combination of polarization and a balanced array of political forces could lead to such an arrangement. In other situations of political polarization, the main feature is a minimum winning coalition in parliament with a small majority. Thus, two alternative foci of power, comprising the two largest parties, emerge instead of a situation where a dominant party concentrates most of the power in its hands. The smaller parties are aligned in terms of their relations with the larger parties and their readiness to come to terms with the other partners in the coalition.

The political polarization created when the Labor Party lost its dominance occurred during a period when the political system was able to cope with a change of ruling parties without this leading to a breakdown of the democratic rules of the game. By the mid-1970s, Israel's parliamentary democracy was able to absorb this far-reaching change without it causing any major shocks to the system. This happened despite the fact that Labor was deposed by Herut, the Party that in the 1950s was deliberately excluded from power. The downfall of the dominant party in May 1977 did not even lead to an immediate intensification of political conflicts between the two large blocs. The norms of parliamentary democracy accepted by both parties seeking political supremacy had become part of the rules of the game accepted by all parties. Thus the change in the ruling party that occurred in 1977 did not imply change in the system.

Nevertheless, the Hebrew term used to describe this change, *mahapach* or "political upheaval," expressed the wiespread feeling that what had happened was more than just a change in the ruling party. Indeed, several factors could be discerned that later led to the intensification of political tensions. The first factor concerns the electoral base of both leading parties. The election results of 1977 reflected an increasing congruence between ethnic background and political preference. Most voters of European background, who are usually middle class, voted for the Alignment or the DMC while most voters of Afro-Asian background voted for the Likud. In the elections of 1981, following the breakup of the DMC, most of its supporters returned to the Labor-Alignment fold. The trend toward ethnic polarization in the electoral sphere reached new heights in the 1984 elections.[49] Even though the increasing overlap between ethnic origin and political affiliation did not lead to the Alignment or the Likud becoming homogeneous parties, it tended to increase the tensions between them. This was to be expected on the assumption that overlap, even partial, between social cleavages and ideological cleavages tends to intensify political conflicts.

The second factor in the intensification of political conflicts was the redistribution of political power on the party map as a whole. Prior to 1977, ideological polarization was prevented by the concentration of power in the hands of a party that was centrist in its ideological positions. Mapai, as a pragmatic party with a tendency to seek compromise, was positioned in the center of each major ideological spectrum: left-right, dove-hawk, secular-religious. After 1977, the national leadership was in the hands of Herut, which held positions close to the end of the spectrum, at least in respect of left-right and dove-hawk. Moreover, the very existence of two large blocs tended to increase the salience of their ideological differences, thus increasing their intensity. This could be expected on the basis of the premise that dichotomous conflicts tend to be more intense than non-dichotomous ones.

The third factor to contribute to the intensification of political conflicts concerned the leanings of most members of the elites in the spheres of culture, communications, economy, administration, and the military toward the pragmatic and moderate style cultivated over the years by Mapai and the Labor Party. In contrast, most of the supporters of the Likud were characterized by radical, populist, or fundamentalist tendencies and identified with nationalistic and traditionalistic stands. The political elite of the right, especially in Herut, thus faced the dilemma of whether to seek a common ground with the social elites by moderating its fundamentalist ideological positions and adopting a pragmatic approach, or whether to appeal directly to its mass base of support over the heads of the other elites by means of radical and populist positions. The path followed by Herut here has not been consistent. During the first government headed by Menachem Begin, Herut made an effort to appease the social and cultural elites as part of its broader effort to gain legitimacy as a ruling party. Manifestations of this effort included the co-option of former Labor leader Moshe Dayan to the cabinet as Foreign Minister, the efforts to bring the DMC into the coalition and the tendency to leave senior government officials appointed by Labor in their posts. Moreover, when the peace treaty with Egypt came up for ratification in the Knesset, Begin found himself in need of votes from the Alignment since some of his own party leaders opposed it. This approach was radically reversed prior to the elections of 1981 when Herut realized that it had not succeeded in winning the support of the elites, and that it had weakened its support among its mass constituency by adopting moderate, pragmatic positions and by following policies of budgetary restraint under Finance

Minister Yigal Horowitz. Herut dramatically switched its orientation during the 1981 election campaign for the Tenth Knesset. A permissive and wasteful economic policy that encouraged private consumption, the use of radical nationalistic rhetoric, the delegitimization of Herut's opponents by portraying them as lacking in credibility and the exploitation of ethnic resentment—all reinforced by anti-elitist sentiments—enabled the Likud to win back the support of its traditional constituency. On the other hand, these tendencies led to a deepening of the alienation between Herut and many of those who composed the elites or the "establishment." The political tension sparked by this approach persisted throughout the entire tenure of Begin's second government and was aggravated by the government's failures in Lebanon and in its economic policy. The outcome of the 1984 election, which forced both large parties to adopt the pragmatic course of sharing power in the national unity government, led at first to a mitigation of hostility between the two blocs as well as the alienation of the elites or a considerable part of them. This hostility reasserted itself, however, following the implementation of the rotation agreement in which Labor's Shimon Peres turned over the premiership to Likud leader Yitzhak Shamir.

This examination of the Likud's conduct as a ruling party does not provide a clear-cut answer to the question of whether it preferred to seek legitimacy for itself by cultivating a broad consensus, or whether it has sought to maintain supremacy by delegitimating its chief rival. The lack of a decisive approach on the Likud's part stimulated the growth of new political forces that served as radical right pressure groups on the Likud, mainly in relation to the Arab-Israeli conflict. Tehiya, Gush Emunim, and Meir Kahane's Kach party represent various degrees of the extremist reaction in the radical-nationalist wing of the political spectrum which is rooted in their anxiety over expressions of pragmatic moderation in the Likud, as reflected in the peace treaty with Egypt. These groups contain anti-democratic elements such as the Jewish terrorist group led by West Bank settlers and the theocratic and racist declarations of the Kach platform. Tehiya, formally not a party to such actions, adopted a permissive stance toward the Jewish terrorist group and did not dissociate itself from unauthorized and illegal reprisal actions launched against Arabs by the West Bank settlers.

The possiblity of periodic changes in the ruling party and the growth of political and ideological tensions represent two aspects of the problem of political stability in Israel in the context of the balance of power between parties. The elections of 1977 marked the turning point in respect of both aspects. The transfers of power from one ruling party to another that have occurred show that Israel's political system has formed a relatively stable set of rules of the game for its parliamentary democracy. In contrast, the aggravation of political and ideological tensions brought about by political polarization posed the threat of more intense conflicts between the major blocs, and the emergence of radical groups outside the party structure not always willing to be bound by the democratic rules of the game.

Party Politics, Corporatist Politics, and Extra-Parliamentary Politics

Israel's democracy has been described as a "party state" not only because of the role played by parties in the formation of government coalitions, but because of the role-expansion tendencies of Israeli political parties. This phenomenon has two aspects: the intensity of party activities and the broad range of areas in which they are involved. Here too changes have occurred in the four decades of Israel's statehood. The common denominator of most of these changes is a reduction in the scope of the functions performed by parties and in the extent of their involvement in people's lives. The reduction in the scope of party functions began gradually in the 1950s at the end of the period of mass immigration and speeded up in the period between the Yom Kippur War and 1977. Subsequently, there was something of a revival of party activity in the area of policy-making and in the distribution of positions in the public services. During the mass immigration of the 1950s, parties served as channels of political mobilization for the newcomers by virtue of their function as intermediaries between the public services—the government, Jewish Agency, and the Histadrut—and the public. In comparison with the period of the Yishuv, the role of parties as direct provider of public services such as education decreased after 1948, but their role expanded as channels of access to the government which became more important as a provider of services than both the Mandatory government and the national institutions of the Yishuv combined. The government's role in building the economic and public service infrastructure of the new state, in addition to its role in rural settlement, industrial development, housing, employment, and social welfare—not to mention the increase in the number of positions available in the government ministries themselves—created vast opportunities for political patronage and influence. the political parties exploited their access to officials in the government and public services in order to aid their members and supporters.

The parties that were best positioned to take advantage of the dependence of the new immigrants on the public services, in order to recruit them as members and voters, were those in the ruling coalition—primarily the dominant Mapai party and its perennial partner the NRP. In that period, the parties operated intensively in three different areas: in packing the public services with their members in order to pay political debts and to gain influence in the government bureaucracy; in representing the demands of interest groups and even individuals vis a vis the political center; and in involvement in everyday life through activities in the local community.

Party activity in all three areas tapered off over the years, but was revived in the area of "dividing the spoils" after 1977 with the resurgence of politicization in the public services. These changes in party activities from the early 1950s to the mid-1980s are related to a number of developments, some connected to the political system itself, others to social, economic, and cultural processes, and to external events such as wars.

The first major change was a reduction in the range of services provided directly by parties as part of the quasi-consociational arrangements of the Yishuv. This change stemmed from the transfer of responsibility for the provision of educational and social welfare services from political movements to the government.

While the first process reduced the areas of party activity, another change occurred during the period of mass immigration that temporarily increased the scope of party activity. As the emphasis in political mobilization shifted from ideological indoctrination to serving as an intermediary between the citizen and the government, considerable portions of the public found themselves dependent on parties. However, this dependence declined over the years with the emergence of full employment and the depoliticization of the civil service at the middle and lower levels.

The third change that influenced the role of parties was connected indirectly to the second. There was a significant decline in the ideological-educational work of parties and a significant weakening of the connection between actual party policies and the imperatives of their respective ideological traditions.

Relationships weakened between party leaders and their followers. This process is related to the bureaucratization of party activity and a shift from politics based on narrow social networks to mass politics, with leaders reaching their followers through the mass media rather than through direct contact.[50]

The reduction of ideological activity in the parties and the blurring of their programmatic distinctiveness through years of bargaining and compromise created a situation where, in most cases, ideological politics in its classic sense became the preserve of extra-parliamentary movements. Some of these movements such as Gush Emunim have comprehensive ideologies, while others such as Peace Now have single-issue ideologies. In either case, both types conduct their activities outside the established parties although members of parties can and have taken part in these activities. Peace Now arose as a movement drawing its members from several parties while Gush Emunim was initially formed within the Religious Zionist camp but some of its leaders and members later joined the Tehiya party.

The development of independent, non-party newspapers forced most party newspapers out of business and also made for broad awareness of controversial issues from a non-partisan perspective. This also had the result of reducing the salience of party activity in the public arena.

The most important factor in changing the functions of parties was that in several crucial areas of policy-making, especially economic affairs, the parties lost their starring role to other actors such as non-party or inter-party public bodies. This development, known as corporatist politics, is not unique to Israel, but it had far-reaching consequences there due to the very central role played by the government in the economy.

The most prominent example of corporatist politics are the agreements reached between the government, the Histadrut, and the employers' organization. The parties, whose main arena is the Knesset, have little influence on these arrangements. Even the government acts in this context as a party to the negotiations and not as a supreme authority that becomes involved only to bring the other sides to an agreement. Corporatist arrangements differ from the quasi-consociational arrangements that characterized the political system of the Yishuv in that the bodies involved in a corporatist agreement do not appear as representatives of diffuse, comprehensive ideological subcultures but as representatives of narrow social or economic interests. This situation also influences the level at which negotiations are conducted and the compromises worked out. The negotiations are not usually conducted by the party leaders who command broad authority in their movements but by those with executive responsibility such as the Finance Minister and his senior staff, the Secretary-General of the Histadrut or the head of its trade union department, or the heads of the Manufacturers' Association. It could be argued, in this case, that corporatist politics is simply a more developed stage of the politics of interest groups and pressure groups.

A major role in all corporatist arrangements is played by the Histadrut, the strongest and most comprehensive non-governmental body in Israel. The Histadrut's power has decreased compared to its position in the Yishuv and the early years of the state, because of the transfer of certain services to the government and to a decline in its economic role as entrepreneur and employer. Nevertheless, the Histadrut continues to be Israel's largest voluntary organization, with 1.5 million members in the mid-1980s. The Histadrut has a virtual monopoly among non-professional trade unions but a number of the professional unions are independent of the Histadrut—the secondary school teachers, doctors, engineers, and architects. The Histadrut also has a dominant role in health insurance and services and in pension funds. Moreover, in contrast to most trade union federations in other countries, the Histadrut is a centralistic organization whose governing bodies are composed of representatives of political parties. These governing bodies supervise the national trade unions in the various branches, and the dominant tendency is for them to sign national wage agreements that include all workers in a given branch, such as construction or metal-working. The tendency to follow centralistic corporatist patterns in labor relations is reinforced by the practice of including all wage-earners in the arrangement providing for cost-of-living increments, based on rises in the Consumer Price Index. This arrangement is maintained by the Histadrut, the employers' organization and the government, which appears not only as one of the country's biggest employers but also as the body responsible for formulating and implementing national economic policy.[51] The Histadrut has a dual status in these corporatist arrangements: it represents labor in the comprehensive agreements signed with employers and the government, but it must also balance internal conflicting interests between its role as trade union and as management and employer. The Histadrut's economic enterprises are grouped in the framework of Hevrat Ha'ovdim, a holding company subordinate to the Secretary-General of the Histadrut. Nevertheless, these enterprises maintain regular contacts with the Ministry of Finance, the Ministry of Trade and Industry, the Ministry of Agriculture, and the Bank of Israel, sometimes in conjunction with private sector companies in the same branch. The collective and cooperative settlements of the Labor Movement have a special status with the Histadrut. They are not part of Hevrat Ha'ovdim but are organized separately in the Agricultural Center. The cooperative enterprises of the Histadrut have a special status as well.

The position of the Histadrut as a party to corporatist arrangements in the economic sphere differs from that of the private sector in that the Histadrut is a political body whose leaders are elected as representatives of parties. As a result, influence by political parties over corporatist arrangements is exercised not only in the coalitionary or parliamentary arena, but also in the governing bodies of the Histadrut, its Central Committee and Executive. While no single party has ever held a majority in the Knesset, there has always been a majority grouping in control of the Histadrut, either Mapai or an alignment between Mapai and Achdut Ha'avodah or Mapam. Thus, even during the years of Likud rule in the government, the Alignment as an opposition party still had considerable influence over economic policy through the Histadrut's participation in corporatist arrangements.

The differences between the Histadrut and the private employers' organizations are not confined to the fact that the leaders of the former are elected on a political party basis while the latter are chosen on a nonparty basis. They also differ in the extent to which they are centralistically structured. In contrast to the Histadrut, which shapes uniform policies in its elected governing bodies, coordination between the employers' organizations is weak and they represent distinct and sometimes conflicting interests. During the heyday of Labor rule the corporatist format for formulating economic policy enabled the private sector to have direct access to economic decision makers without having to depend on the good offices of the middle class parties such as the General Zionists or their successors, the Liberals which were, most of the time, in opposition. When Labor went into opposition after 1977, the Histadrut found that it had a major interest in maintaining the corporatist system which allowed it to represent the workers directly vis a vis the government. As a result, the position of the leaders of the Histadrut in the Labor Party grew stronger when Labor was in opposition. During the tenure of the national unity government, the common party ties between the heads of Labor and the heads of the Histadrut made it easier for the Histadrut to accept the austerity program adopted when Labor leader Shimon Peres was Prime Minister.

Parliamentary politics has thus been bypassed or supplemented by corporatist and extra-parliamentary politics. Both of these alternatives to parliamentary politics worked to reinforce the decline in the functions of political parties. On the other hand, they differed considerably in the threat they posed to the democratic rules of the game. Corporatist politics tends to reduce the political expressions of tensions rooted in social and economic divisions. Extra-parliamentary politics, however, tends to aggravate political tensions rooted in ideological differences because of its affinity with the politics of extremism which, in turn, is fueled by ideological fundamentalism. Since ideological fundamentalism and political extremism propel their adherents to proclaim, at times, that they will not be bound under all circumstances to the democratic rules of the game, they may carry with them a possible threat to the rule of law.

Social Cleavages and Voting

Even though the perception of Israel as a party state has lost much of its validity, parties still perform major functions in two contexts. First, parties select and place people in political roles, primarily through the electoral process and appointments to senior administrative positions (which also involve political considerations). Second, parties serve as mechanisms of political mobilization, primarily through the act of voting. Voting in elections, as the broadest form of political participation, serves as a channel through which the social system influences the political system. Voting thus links the social map to the political map. During the period of the Yishuv, there was a close connection between social cleavages, mainly the socio-economic cleavage, and voting patterns.[52] Furthermore, the close correlation between class divisions and party divisions matched the common pattern of most European countries according to which wage-earners, especially blue-collar workers, tended to vote for left-wing parties, while the middle class tended to vote for parties of the center and right.[53] Nevertheless, even during the Yishuv, voting patterns did not always correspond to these tendencies. Religious Zionist voters, for example, sometimes voted for separate religious labor and middle class lists both affliated to the Mizrahi movement, and at other times, for a joint Religious Zionist list. Another exception concerns the wage-earners and manual laborers of Sephardic background who usually did not vote for the parties of the left but rather for the ethnic lists headed by the communal leaders or for the right-wing parties.[54]

These voting patterns changed after the establishment of the state. The Afro-Asian immigrants of the 1950s did not follow the pattern set by the veteran Sephardim who voted for ethnic or right-wing parties, but voted instead for Mapai or the NRP. Paradoxically, the ethnic parties of the Sephardim and the Yemenites gradually disappeared from the political map during the mass aliyah from Islamic countries. In the 1949 elections these parties received five seats in the Knesset, in 1951 they received three, and in 1955 neither reached even one per cent of the vote, the threshold for Knesset representation.[55]

It seemed, then, that during the 1950s a situation similar to continental European voting patterns was developing, with the "proletarian" vote going to left-wing parties and the "bourgeois" vote to the center and right-wing parties. However, developments in the late 1950s showed that this impression was misleading. The vote of the new immigrants for Mapai was not rooted in class consciousness, but was rather an expression of their identification with Mapai as the ruling party or their instrumental dependence on Mapai as the party controlling public absorption services.[54] When their dependence on the public services decreased as their employment prospects improved, as the public services became depoliticized and as the charisma of Mapai leader David Ben-Gurion waned, new voting patterns emerged. The Afro-Asian immigrants began to show a growing tendency to vote for Herut. This tendency was especially pronounced among the offspring of these immigrants as they reached voting age in the 1960s and 1970s.

The tendency of Afro-Asians to vote for Herut, and later Gahal, and the Likud in proportions exceeding their overall share of support, changed little during the late 1960s and early 1970s. The slight drop in support for Mapai and its various electoral alignments and the slight rise in support for Herut and the electoral blocs that it formed apparently reflected the increasing share of Afro-Asian voters in the electorate during that period. The dramatic intensification of the inclination of Afro-Asians to vote Likud occurred only in 1977 when the massive defection of such voters from the Alignment to the Likud transformed the party map. Simultaneously, a parallel defection of voters of European background from the alignment to the DMC occurred. In the 1981 elections, however, the Afro-Asian voters who had left the Alignment tended to remain with the Likud but most of the Western voters who had supported the DMC returned to the Alignment. The correlation between ethnic background and voting was highest in the elections of 1984, when seven out of every ten Likud voters were of Afro-Asian background, with the about same proportion holding for voters of European background and the Alignment.

The correlation between ethnic origin and voting also reflected the social class composition of the voters of these two parties. Afro-Asians are over-represented among wage-earners and manual laborers and among low-income and low-status groups, while the opposite is true for Europeans. Thus the situation prevailing in the 1950s reversed itself: during the 1980s, those of low socio-economic status tended to vote for the Likud, while those of high socio-economic status tended to vote for the Alignment.

Since there is a partial correspondence between ethnic background and social status, and between both of them and voting patterns, it is difficult to isolate the influence of either socio-economic or socio-cultural factors on voting. Nevertheless, there are indications that socio-cultural factors have a greater weight in Israel in influencing voting preferences than socio-economic factors. The socio-cultural factor of ethnic identity is correlated with voting preferences irrespective of social class. In other words, the tendency of Afro-Asians to give a greater share of their vote to the Likud and the tendency of Europeans to give a greater share of their vote to the Alignment hold in all education and income groups, albeit not to the same extent.[57] However, these correlations between ethnicity and voting do not point to a trend toward ethnic separatism, at least not in the political sphere.[58] This is indicated by the repeated failure of Afro-Asian ethnic lists to secure enough votes for representation in the Knesseet. Exceptions to this were Tami and Shas which drew their support mainly from religious or traditional voters, who, in addition to their feelings of socio-economic deprivation, also resented discrimination against them by the leadership of the established religious parties.

The correlation between ethnicity and voting cannot be understood in isolation from the sense of deprivation, whether socio-economic or socio-cultural, experienced by many Afro-Asians. The correlation between ethnic background and voting is found at all income and educational levels, but it is strongest at the lowest levels. Moreover, the tendency to "ethnic voting" is not equally pronounced among all groups or origin. Among Afro-Asians, the tendency to vote Likud is stronger among those from Morocco than among those from Iraq, while among the Europeans the tendency to vote for the Alignment is stronger among those from Poland than among those from Romania.[59]

The relation between country of origin and voting has been explained in various ways. The first explanation makes a direct link between voting and feelings of deprivation rooted in the connection between ethnicity and social class, and relates this to the partial integration of the Afro-Asian immigrants of the 1950s and their offspring in Israeli society. According to this approach, the correlation between voting and ethnic origin is explained largely as a reaction against the establishment. The emergence of a correlation between low status and Afro-Asian origin is sometimes viewed as the result of the absorption policies adopted in the 1950s by Mapai and its political allies which are depicted as elitist, paternalistic, and predominantly Ashkenazi. There are several versions of this charge leveled against the establishment. Some would go as far as to accuse the establishment then of taking deliberate steps to turn the Afro-Asian immigrants into "hewers of wood and drawers of water."[60] Another less extreme version attributes the failure of the establishment's absorption policies to its sense of cultural superiority over the newcomers, leading it to impose the dominant culture of the veteran population on them without allowing for any legitimate expressions of their Middle Eastern heritage.[61] A third version acknowledges the objective difficulties created by the mass immigration but blames the establishment for a lack of sensitivity to the unique absorption problems of the Afro-Asian immigrants which would have let the establishment to allocate resources differently in the 1950s.[62] Actually, all three versions of this explanation relate to the same basic phenomenon—the economic gap between the veterans and the newcomers that originated in the 1950s. The difference between them lies in how they explain this lack of equality. The political implications of each explanation also differ. While the first two versions place the blame directly on the dominant elites of the 1950s, Mapai and its allies, the third gives more weight to the conflicting interests of oldtimers and newcomers present in any immigrant society, which is not necessarily connected to the attitudes of the ruling elite.

The attempt to explain the correlation between ethnic background and socio-economic status as the result of absorption policies in the 1950s reflects a tendency to ignore certain objective factors that shaped these policies. First, there was the need to choose between an absorption policy that would provide better services in education, housing, and employment opportunities, but only for small numbers at a given time, and a policy that would enable the rapid absorption of greater numbers, but with inferior services. Second, absorption policies had to take into account the cultural backgrounds and educational levels of immigrants from countries or regions that had not yet experienced modernization. In addition, the search for someone to blame for the failure of the absorption process could also be motivated by a reluctance to face up to the failure of individuals to cope with the challenges, and the corresponding need to project responsibility for this failure on "society" or the "establishment."[63] None of these considerations, however, can explain away the powerful feelings of deprivation among the Afro-Asian immigrants and their offspring, with all the attendant political consequences.

A subjective sense of deprivation, felt even in the absence of actual experiences of discrimination, served as the basis for the political mobilization of Afro-Asian voters by the opposition. These feelings were cultivated by manipulative means by Herut, which presented itself as the only alternative to the dominant party since the early years of the state. This was done by manipulating the voters' devotion to their communities and religious traditions and the symbols of these attachments. The Mapai establishment was blamed as the source of all their problems, while Herut successfully presented itself as the patron of the oppressed and as the only party that could fulfill their aspirations for full integration into Israeli society. In this manner, a feeling of common political fate was formed between those who were political outcasts and those who felt themselves to be social outcasts. It is noteworthy that the ethnic protest against Mapai and the Afro-Asian support for the Herut reached their peak only many years after the initial phase of absorption. This delayed reaction can be attributed to the cumulative impact of repeated disappointment at failing to break the link between low status and ethnic origin.

The feelings of deprivation were thus articulated more in ethnic terms than in terms of social class. This can be explained by the cultural and conceptual framework brought to Israel by the Afro-Asian immigrants. Middle Eastern and North African Jewish culture tends to conceive society as divided primarily along ascriptive lines such as family, clan, community, or nationality, while social class divisions are seen as secondary. The images of a society divided along class lines—wage-earners vs. proprietors, manual workers vs. white-collar workers and low income vs. high income—was therefore alien to them. However, the tendency to express their feelings of deprivation in ethnic rather than class terms was based not only on their cultural background, but also on the socio-economic structure that they encountered in Israel. During the 1950s, the vast majority of the immigrants found work in the government and public sectors, and only a small portion were employed in the private sector where concepts of class struggle had any relevance. Thus, for most of the immigrants, the opposing side in conflicts over wages and working conditions was the veteran political establishment and not private employers. Thus, during the 1950s, conditions did not emerge in Israel for the development of a class consciousness of the type known in Europe or even in Yishuv. Furthermore, those who articulated a conception of the social order in terms of class struggle were identified by the immigrants as the bureaucratic-political elite, predominantly Ashkenazi, that controlled their livelihoods.

Another possible explanation for the tendency of Afro-Asian immigrants to express social protest by means of voting for Herut relates to several elements of their cultural heritage. The assumption underlying this explanation is that voting in elections can serve psychological-expressive needs that do not stem from instrumental considerations or from a desire to see a particular platform implemented. One student of voting patterns in Israel suggested in this context that one should distinguish among three types of voters: 1) the traditional voter who regularly supports the party that represents his or her image of the proper social order; 2) the rational voter who examines party platforms in light of his or her own interests and in light of his or her views on current affairs; 3) the charismatic voter who pays less attention to the substance of a party's positions, and is attracted more by symbols, slogans, and declarations which are seen as granting legitimacy to problematic elements in his or her individual or group identity. For the charismatic voter, participation in elections is primarily an expressive experience that fulfills a symbolic or psychological function.[64] These differences in the motivational basis of political participation can be related to differences in the cultural backgrounds of different groups. For example, a cultural tradition that stresses values of personal, group, or national honor, or that prefers immediate gratification to delayed gratification is compatible with expressive or charismatic voting. In contrast, a cultural outlook that stresses rational or instrumental considerations in the relation between means and ends, and which tends to accept delay of gratification in order to invest in future goals, is more compatible with rational voting. Traditional voting seems to involve both instrumental and expressive elements. The assumption made by certain sociologists that there is a significant correlation between pre-modern cultures and an expressive orientation to politics, and between modernity and an instrumental orientation to politics, has lost much of its validity over the years. Nevertheless, even if one cannot identify tradtional culture conclusively with an expressive and religious orientation and modern culture with an instrumental rational and secular orientation, one can still point to differences of emphasis related to them.[65] Moreover, experts in Islamic culture, especially, point to elements such as a keen stress on honor and on the desire for immediate gratification as important parts of this culture.[66] Even though such psychological-cultural analyses relate to the majority culture in Islamic countries, it may be assumed that the Jewish minority was also influenced by it.

According to the psycho-cultural explanation of the correlation between voting and ethnicity, these cultural emphases are connected to the messages and images transmitted by the Alignment and the Likud. The constructivist ideological tradition of the Alignment contains instrumental elements stressing delay of gratification; the party itself is bureaucratic, with a more institutionalized system of decision-making, and it has less of an emotional style than the Likud. The symbolic elements projected by the Alignment would thus not be very appealing to those steeped in a traditional culture. Herut, on the other hand, would be more appealing, with its ideological tradition stressing the symbols of collective identity and values of national and collective honor together with the rhetorical and declarative trappings associated with them. Herut projects an image that is more diffuse, more emotional, and with a less institutionalized system of decision-making. One of the characteristics of expressive politics is a tendency to personify ideologies or parties and to identify with a charismatic leader who embodies them. While party supporters of this type tend to glorify their leader, they also tend to reject their political rivals in personal terms, by attributing negative and even offensive traits to rival leaders. These tendencies burst forth in the election of 1981. Menachem Begin was hailed as a hero by his followers in his public appearances, while Shimon Peres was subjected to verbal abuse and violence.[67]

The third explanation for the tendency of Afro-Asian voters to support Herut and other radical nationalist parties is connected to their hawkish political views which, in turn, are rooted in their purported hostility to Arabs. Various studies of the relation between voting and political attitudes have indeed confirmed the correlation between Afro-Asian origin and hawkish views and between these and voting for the Likud.[68] This trend has sometimes been explained by factors that are not always mutually compatible. One common explanation attributes the hawkishness of the Afro-Asians to their collective experience of centuries of living under Moslem or Arab rule, which supposedly left the Jews with deep feelings of hostility and mistrust toward the Arabs. Another version of this argument does not relate to the actual experience of the Afro-Asians in Moslem or Arab countries, but to the image of this experience that has been conveyed to the generation raised in Israel. Another explanation based on the cultural background of the Afro-Asians holds that their hostility toward the Arabs is a reaction to their being stereotyped in Israel as similar to Arabs. Their hostile attitudes to the Arabs thus reflect an attempt to rid themselves of their "Arab-like" image, which is rooted in their physical appearance, patterns of behavior, and cultural tastes. The assumption underlying this explanation is that the Afro-Asians' desire to be fully integrated in the majority culture of Israeli society has led them to a demonstrative rejection of the Arabs.[69] This argument is compatible with familiar patterns of behavior among low-status ethnic groups in multi-ethnic societies. In such societies, low-status groups tend to project hostility toward groups with even lower status. Thus in the United States, blue-collar populations of Polish, Italian, or Irish background tend to show hostility toward blacks. The desire of lower-status groups to identify with higher status groups by distancing themselves from those at the bottom of the scale is reinforced in the cases of both Israel and the United States by the fact that members of the lowest groups rub shoulders at their places of work and compete with each other in the job market.[70]

The connection between the status anxiety of the Afro-Asians and their hostility toward Arabs serves as the point of departure for a more "instrumental" explanation of the tendency of Afro-Asians to vote Likud. According to this view, their vote for the Likud is instrumental rather than expressive, and is linked to the Likud's stand on the future of the occupied territories. The entry of the Arabs from the territories into low-status jobs in Israel following the Six Day War opened up opportunities for social mobility among the Afro-Asians, who had filled these positions in the occupational structure prior to 1967. The hawkish Afro-Asian position is therefore viewed as a response to their fear that the return of the territories would rob them of their mobility achievements and force them back into the lower levels of the status system.[71] The various explanations offered for the link between voting and ethnicity are, for the most part, hypotheses that are not easy to verify empirically. Some of these explanations are not mutually exclusive and therefore it seems most likely that the impact of several factors working in the same direction may be more powerful than any single cause.

In addition to the correlation between ethnic background and voting, there is also a connection between age and voting preference. The younger the voters, the less they tend to vote for the Alignment, and the more they tend to vote for the Likud or a right-wing party. This is true even when ethnicity is held constant. Thus the correlation between age and voting does not simply reflect the lower average age of Afro-Asian voters, indeed, it also holds for both ethnic groups. A striking expression of the connection between youth and voting was evident in the relatively large number of votes for right-wing parties returned by conscripted soldiers in the elections of 1981, and to a lesser extent in 1984.[72]

A correlation found in few elections between age and voting is not sufficient to determine whether this is an age-voting related trend or a generational phenomenon. An age-related trend would not be expected to persist throughout the voter's life; voting preferences would change, at least for some, with age. A generational trend, however, would be expected to have long-term influence, since it would be rooted in experiences shared by a generation in their formative period of political socialization. The actual nature of the phenomenon can be determined only by tracing the voting patterns of cohort groups over several successive elections.[73] However, in Israel there are indications that the correlation between age and voting is in part age-related and in part generational. The age-related voting tendencies can be explained, in part, by the impact of military service, while the generational trend can be explained by the conditions in which political socialization occurred after 1967. According to this view, the generation that reached maturity after 1967 has never known a reality other than the Greater Israel comprising pre-1967 Israel and the occupied territories, and tends to support the party that promises to maintain the territorial status quo seen by them as normal. Both the age-related and the generational explanations, it should be noted, stress the impact of the Arab-Israel conflict on the young. Thus young people and those who matured after 1967 tend to be more hawkish than older groups.

A third factor that influences voting, in addition to ethnic background and age, is education. The influence of education on voting tendencies is negligible among those with only elementary or secondary education, but is considerable among those with higher education. The latter tend to vote for the Alignment and the parties close to it to a greater extent than their average support in the entire population. The opposite holds true for the Likud. Both trends hold even when ethnic background is held constant, meaning that voters with higher education, of both European and Afro-Asian background tend to prefer the Alignment over the Likud. Indeed, the only group among the Afro-Asians where the Alignment leads the Likud is among those with higher education degrees.[74]

The correlation between voting and age and ethnicity influences the balance of electoral power between parties over time. To the extent that these correlations remain valid, demographic changes such as the reduction in the average age of the population and the rise in the share of Afro-Asian voters will tend to strengthen the bloc comprising the Likud and its allies. The demographic source of increased support for the Likud is the outcome of differences in family size among ethnic groups. Since these differences in family size are gradually disappearing, the trends which have increased the relative size of the Likud's electoral reservoir will also be of less importance in the future even if the correlation between voting and ethnicity continues to hold.[75] In contrast, the gap in family size between Jews and Arabs is narrowing more slowly than the gap between Jews of different ethnic backgrounds. As a result, an increase should be expected in the number of Arab voters who will support either Rakah or parties of the Alignment bloc. Another group with a demographic electoral advantage is the ultra-Orthodox who have very large families.

The connection between demographic changes and political power goes beyond the electoral sphere. Since differential birth rates for various groups may have far-reaching political implications, their potential impact has a bearing on political attitudes. For example, the high rate of natural increase of Arabs, particularly in the occupied territories, has been emphasized by the proponents of territorial compromise who warn that this demographic trend poses a serious threat to efforts to maintain a Jewish majority in Greater Israel. According to this assessment, retaining the occupied territories under Israeli control is incompatible with the concept of a Jewish democratic state. The same "demographic threat," as it is termed, has led some proponents of Greater Israel to look for radical solutions such as a transfer of all or part of the Arabs in the territories to other Arab lands. Another source of political concern rooted in demographic trends is the rapid growth of the non-Zionist ultra-Orthodox population which has created particularly acute problems in Jerusalem. Secular and traditional groups in Jerusalem have begun to voice concern over the possibility that the ultra-Orthodox will succeed in imposing their norms of conduct on other parts of the population through violence and other pressure tactics.

Elites, Ideology, and Political Mobilization

Political tensions are closely connected to the centrality of ideology in Israel's political system. Before the establishment of the state, ideology defined the boundaries of the Jewish political community in Palestine.

This resulted in a close correspondence between the political center of the Yishuv and of Israeli society thereafter, and the cultural center. To the extent, then, that a distinctive culture has developed in Israel, it is more an elitist product reflecting developments in the center than an expression of popular culture in the periphery. From a cultural perspective, the periphery was much more segmented than the center, a situation which intensified with the mass immigration of the 1950s. The political cleavages along national, ethnic and religious lines divided Israeli society into subcultures organized mainly on an ascriptive basis. In contrast, the ideological divisions were the result of deliberate action taken by the elite groups that occupied Israel's social and political center. Each of these elites had its own ideological constituency, a broad social sector that served as an intermediary between center and periphery. These sectors were composed mainly of immigrants from Europe who came to Palestine out of Zionist conviction, and their offspring and others who became part of this sector through intensive ideological indoctrination.

While these elites were bound by a common Zionist ideology, they were often riven by intense disputes over their specific ideological visions of the Jewish society of the future. Thus, among these elites and within the intermediate sectors, ideological and political conflicts occurred that, at times, strained the unity of the Yishuv and Israeli society. In the early years of the state, there was a slacking off in ideological activity which also reduced the political tensions stemming from ideological differences. The group consciousness rooted in the major cleavage divisions had not reached a level of articulation at that time that would have permitted broad and persistent political mobilization. Thus, for example, the national cleavage had a weak political expression due to the trauma of the Arab debacle of 1948 and the lack of Arab leadership on the national level. The considerable differences in ethnic background, length of residence, and socio-economic status between the new immigrants of the 1950s and the veteran population were seen as temporary and, in any case, the possibilities for political mobilization of the immigrants on this basis were limited because of their extensive dependence on the absorption authorities. The religious-secular cleavage was not afflicted with great tensions then since the acceptance of the principle of the status quo in religious affairs reduced the potential for conflict and prevented the formation of an explosive Kulturkampf atmosphere.

The conditions changed in all these areas during the 1960s and 1970s. The dormant conflicts in these three areas gradually emerged as a result of the rise of new elites in the townships and neighborhoods where most of the Afro-Asian immigrants of the 1950s were concentrated,[76] among the younger elements of the Religious Zionist sector, and among the younger educated Arabs. The rise of these elites was marked by an articulation of group identity by means of symbols and ideological concepts rooted in social cleavage divisions. As a result, the veteran elite in the center lost its primacy as a source of cultural and ideological inspiration. In addition, the dominant elites had lost their capacity for ideological and cultural innovation as a result of the need to focus on solving practical problems of the "here and now." Thus, much of the fundamental ideological activity had become an empty ritual. Ideological polarization within the center emerged after 1967 in addition to the ideological ferment and articulation that had begun in the periphery. This renewal of ideological concerns in the center was not stimulated by the Labor Movement elite that had been dominant for decades. This elite continued its search for pragmatic solutions beneath the protective covering of a broad ideological consensus. The new ideological militance came from groups on the fringes of the political and cultural center, such as the younger elements of the Religious Zionist sector and the nationalist right that formed Tehiya, and the radical fringe groups of the left. Some of the characteristic traits of the ideological revival on the right, including Herut, were the manipulation of mobilizing symbols; ethnocentricity and a sense of "blood and homeland"; demonizing the enemy and presenting political rivals as defeatists and even traitors.[77]

The ideological revival on the right was not matched by a corresponding attempt at ideological innovation on the left. The veteran cultural elites had, in effect, come to comprise a center stressing the consensus common to all of Israeli society which had made it easier for groups to cross the old ideological lines dividing right from left. Pressures for ideological polarization arose among the nationalist right, the Religious Zionist sector, and fringe groups on the left, much more than among the veteran elites of the Labor Party and its allies. The impact of these developments on Israeli political culture intensified with the rise of power of the formerly ideological "out-groups" in 1977 and with the hostility-laden election campaign waged by the Likud in 1981. These trends signaled the loss of cultural dominance by the veteran elites. As a result, the latter became partially alienated from the new center, a process that reached its apex in the political reaction to the Lebanon War in the early 1980s. Nevertheless, the political culture that had been nurtured by and within the Labor movement remained a source of inspiration for most of the non-political elites, primarily the academic, cultural, and communication elites and to a lesser extent, the economic,security, and administrative elites.

The takeover of the political center by groups representing nationalist, neo-traditional and ethnic subcultures, together with the sense of lost centrality that swept over the veteran elites, created a populist political configuration. Dissonance emerged between the ordering of groups on the scale of social status and their position on the center-periphery axis. The elites who had enjoyed high status as well as political dominance now found themselves with greatly reduced political power and without a platform from which they could exert ideological influence. Thus, the outcome of the electoral upheaval of 1977 was not the creation of a new dominant center by the right, but a split center in a polarized polity.

These sub-centers in the polarized polity did not serve, however, as a focal point for the formation of institutionalized subcultural enclaves as they did in the Yishuv. Actually, after the upheaval of 1977, the sub-center comprising the Labor bloc ceased to serve as a source of authority and political mobilization for broad segments of the public. In these circumstances it did not become an "opposition of principle" even during 1981-84 when the polarization in the system was deepened by Likud policies in the sphere of security (the Lebanon War) and the economy (the permissive approach of Finance Minister Aridor). This polarized situation, although failing to produce a sharp confrontation between left and right, did lead to a weakening of the capacity of the political system for decisive action because of the lack of consensus on central issues. The Likud government was unable to extricate itself from the Lebanese quagmire and was unable to cope with the economic crisis which culminated in the collapse of the share prices of Israel's leading banks. During this period, the political system showed clear-cut signs of becoming ungovernable. However, this process was arrested with the establishment of the national unity government in 1984. During the first two years of this government, the government's capacity to act decisively was restored sufficiently to permit a withdrawal from Lebanon and to introduce an economic policy of restraint which brought down inflation rates dramatically within several months. However, after the rotation of the premiership, when the unity government had to face dilemmas on issues where there was dissensus on the fundamental level, it was paralyzed as a result of the mutual veto possessed by the two large blocs.

The difficulties faced by the national center in regulating conflicts stemming from fundamental ideological disputes were reflected during the latter half of the unity government by the conduct of a dual foreign policy, with each part articulated by a leader of one of the blocs—Prime Minister Shamir for the Likud and Foreign Minister Peres for Labor. The problems of ungovernability and the difficulties in conflict regulation were not confined to constraints on action imposed by the mutual veto. They were also reflected in the inability of the government to impose its authority on the radical nationalist sub-center that emerged to the right of the Likud, whose core was the settlers in the West Bank and Gaza Strip. It may be concluded, then, that the political center which had emerged from a tradition of "authority without sovereignty" during the Yishuv, found it difficult, forty years after the establishment of the state, to exercise even that authority conferred by sovereign status.

5

Democracy and National Security in a Protracted Conflict

The Salience of the Security Factor

Yitzhak Rabin, one of Israel's leading political and military figures, once described Israel's security situation since its establishment as "dormant war" erupting every few years into active conflict.[1] Indeed, Israel has fought more wars (though short ones) than any other country since World War II; and the periods between have been marked by persistent limited conflicts including border clashes, terrorist strikes and reprisal raids. This situation has resulted in the issue of national security becoming central to Israeli society and having a major impact on values and institutions as well as on the everyday life of the people. Basic societal contours such as Israel's territorial and demographic boundaries gave have been shaped by two Arab-Israeli wars. The first overall military confrontation between Israel and the Arab states in 1948-49 concluded with the partition of Mandatory Palestine along lines determined mainly by the fighting. No less crucial was the demographic shift brought about by this war due to the exodus of the vast majority of the Arabs living within the boundaries of what became Israel, thus moving it closer to the ideal type of the nation-state. The second war to have a crucial impact on Israel was the Six Day War of June 1967 in which Israel conquered the rest of Mandatory Palestine west of the Jordan River, the Gaza Strip which had been under

Egyptian administration, the Sinai which was later returned to Egypt following the signing of a peace treaty, and the portion of Syria known as the Golan Heights. This territorial expansion entailed a reversal of the earlier trend limiting the number of Arabs under Israel's jurisdiction, and imposed Israeli rule on more than a million Arabs living mainly in the West Bank and Gaza Strip.

These post-1967 territorial and demographic changes have forced Israel to wrestle with the fundamental problems of defining its national and civic identity and the boundaries of the collectivity. The extended conflict has also affected the amount of resources devoted to national security with the share of the GNP allocated to defense steadily rising, reaching a peak in the wake of the Yom Kippur War of 1973.[2] By 1984, Israel had the highest per capita defense expenditure of any democratic state, and among the highest in the entire world. During the mid- and late 1970s and early 1980s, the national security effort consumed between a quarter an a third of Israel's GNP, a fifth of all resources at the disposal of the economy (including imported capital), about half of the government's budget, and a fourth of the country's labor force.[3]

In addition to the direct financial outlays for defense, another resource devoted to this end that has had crucial social implications is the time consumed in military activity by the average Israeli. The periods of compulsory military service and reserve duty required by law of most Israeli males between the ages of 18 and 55 can add up to between five and six years not counting the periods of special reserve duty during wartime or other emergencies. Another indicator of the centrality of national security in Israeli society is the salience of this area in mass communications. Studies conducted by Israeli researchers have established the high proportion taken up by items on the Arab-Israeli conflict and other security issues in the mass media; and other studies have demonstrated the impact of security events on national morale and the public's evaluation of the overall functioning of the government.[4] This salience in the area of mass communications is more than a mere reflection of the flow of security-related events. It can also be viewed as confirmation of the centrality of national security concerns in the public mind.

Beyond the political and ideological disputes in the area of national security, there has always been a broad consensus on the potential threat to Israel's existence posed by its conflict with the Arabs. This perceived existential dimension to the Arab-Israeli conflict has two facets: it entails a possible threat of genocide, or short of that, what has been called "politicide" (the destruction of a state);[5] and it has been widely viewed as a "given" fact of life that cannot be changed either by Israeli military successes or by diplomatic efforts initiated by Israel. The latter conception holds that Israel does not have the power to impose a military resolution to the conflict that would force the Arabs to accept Israel's coalitions for peace; nor can Israel possibly make the concessions sought by the Arabs as their condition for making peace. Parts of the Israeli public saw the Six Day War as providing an opportunity to break out of this situation claiming that peace should be offered in exchange for the return of captured territory. This perceived option undermined the prevailing national consensus based on the assumption that the Arab-Israeli conflict was an immutable fact of life and unrelated to Israel's willingness to make concessions. The dispute over the departure from this assumption intensified in the wake of the 1973 Yom Kippur War and again following the signing of the peace treaty with Egypt in 1979. This development constituted a challenge to the common belief that consensus made it easier for Israel to manage the protracted external conflict without compromising its democratic regime.

The 1948 war that gave birth to the State of Israel was concluded in armistice agreements that fell short of peace. Thus, the new state found itself in urgent need of conceptual and institutional guidelines that would enable it to stand up to protracted conflict. What emerged as Israel's national defense posture includes military-strategic aspects as well as social and institutional ones. The first aspect entails military planning and doctrine, the structure of the armed forces and its equipment, and its modes of organization, discipline, and combat. The second aspect entails mechanisms for mobilizing manpower and other resources for defense as well as patterns of interrelations between the military and civilian spheres.

The military and social aspects of national security are closely interrelated. From a strategic point of view, the Israel Defense Forces' wartime Order of Battle depends to a considerable extent on reserve forces, which provides an operative military solution to the problem of the demographic imbalance between Israel and the Arab states. At the same time, the Israeli system of reserve mobilization is also a social phenomenon that shapes civilian lifestyles and civilian-military relations.[6] The reserve service system entails both a partial militarization of civilian life and a partial "civilianization" of the military making for permeable boundaries between the two sectors.

Another example of the strong interconnection between the strategic and social aspects of national security is the dual nature of political and military control exercised over the military. Since Israel's military operations are usually defined as "limited war" or "peacetime military actions," a failure of military control of military operations can have far-reaching political consequences. By the same token, lack of clear political guidelines for military actions can create severe problems on the operational level. Israel's military history contains more than a few instances of poor operational control adversely affecting political control and vice versa.[7] Problems stemming from the political supervision of military operations came to the fore in the Yom Kippur War and the Lebanon War, and resulted in a sharpened public awareness of the mutual connections between strategic concepts and patterns of relations between the military and society at large. This issue sparked political controversies, stimulating protest movements and actions in the wake of the 1973 war and during the Lebanon involvement of 1982-84.[8]

The threat of a military confrontation with the Arabs was already present as a "strategic" problem and as a political issue during the period of the Yishuv. Violent clashes between Jewish settlers and Arabs, which began in the earliest stages of Zionist colonization, led eventually to the establishment of the Haganah, the underground self-defense organization subordinate to the political center of the Yishuv.[9] Over the years, the Haganah organized military frameworks and adopted patterns of action that reflected the social and political conditions in which it operated. For example, it set up militia forces based on part-time mobilization, and a fully mobilized strike force—the Palmach—that maintained itself by combining military training with work on collective agricultural settlements.[10] These bodies were run by a small professional cadre whose budget was covered by the officially recognized National Institutions even though these military frameworks were illegal. However, there were substantial differences between the nature of the conflict with the Arabs in the period of the Yishuv and the conflict as it developed with the establishment of the state. Before 1948, the conflict was between two ethnic-national communities living together in the same territory ruled by a foreign power. After 1948, at least until 1967, the conflict was primarily between states separated by territorial lines of demarcation. This transformation of the nature of the conflict resulted from two events that occurred on May 14, 1948: as Israel was established as a sovereign state, the military organization of the Yishuv that had fought with local Arab guerrilla forces from November 1947 was declared a regular army; and on the same day, the armies of Egypt, Jordan, Syria, Lebanon (and later Iraq) invaded the former territory of Mandatory Palestine.

Changes in the nature of the conflict also implied changes in the way it was conducted. Before independence, Jewish immigration and settlements were key instruments used by the Yishuv in its conflict with the local Arabs. These activities virtually ceased to have this function after 1948, although they continued to fulfill other functions. Militarily, the perception of the primary threat shifted from terrorist activities and guerilla warfare to a full-scale confrontation between regular armies of sovereign states. Following the 1967 war, however, the intercommunal dimension of the conflict returned, alongside the international dimension. The parts of Mandatory Palestine that until June 1967 had been under Jordanian or Egyptian control, and which were populated by over a million Palestinian Arabs, were now under Israeli control. The future of these areas, the West Bank and Gaza Strip, and their populations became a central issue of controversy in Israel involving opposing conceptions of the Arab-Israeli conflict and the national security priorities stemming from it.

An intercommunal conception of the conflict implies the lack of a territorial demarcation line separating the two communities which could prevent the friction resulting from daily, direct interaction between members of the two groups. Intercommunal conflict intensified with the renewal of Jewish settlement across the 1949 armistice lines. As in the days of the Mandate, these settlements served as a means of establishing a permanent Jewish presence in areas that some groups sought to incorporate into the state. Thus, settlement, once again, became an instrument in delineating the territorial boundaries of Zionist aspirations.[11]

A resurgence of the symbolic expressions of intercommunal conflict also occurred, especially among those espousing religious, theological, or historiosophical justifications for political claims.[12] These changes in the nature of the conflict after 1967 did not lead to any basic changes in Israel's national defense posture. Strategically speaking, the might of the regular armies of the Arab states continued to constitute the primary threat to Israel's national security. The threat posed by terrorism, which was related to the resurgence of the intercommunal conflict, remained secondary as it was not perceived as endangering Israel's very existence. This distinction was not new; already in the 1950s it had been determined that top priority in resource allocation should go to meeting the threat to the state's existence. This came to be defined as an issue of "basic security," while terror was assigned to the realm of "current security" problems. This distinction also influenced Israel's conception of what constituted a *casus belli*. An example of a basic threat to Israel's security and a valid reason to wage war would be the concentration of Arab forces along its borders, as along the border with Egypt just prior to June 6, 1967. Major problems of current security were usually dealt with by limited military initiatives such as the reprisal raids of the 1950s or the preventative and punitive actions along the Lebanese border during the 1970s.[13] The 1982 War in Lebanon was a partial exception to this generalization. The official justification for the war, to assure "Peace for the Galilee," was, as its formal name implies, rooted in current security concerns, and its military objective, the destruction of the terrorist infrastructure in Lebanon, was related more to the intercommunal conflict over the future of the occupied territories than to a threat by an Arab state. And indeed, the absence of a threat to Israel's existence in this war resulted in it being fought without a supporting national consensus.[14]

The strategic threat to Israel's basic security is rooted in three points of strategic vulnerability that are accepted as givens in Israel's security doctrine:

1) A lop-sided demographic advantage to the Arab states.
2) Vulnerable borders due to the lack of strategic depth.
3) The need to hold up under a protracted, violent conflict requiring extensive allocation of resources to national security.

Israel's response to the first source of weakness has been to adapt the concept of a "nation in arms" by developing a system of mobilization based on the maximum use of available manpower during wartime and military emergencies. The armed forces are based on a three-tiered structure: a professional cadre of career army personnel; a conscript force serving for three years; and a reserve force available for immediate call-up composed of men serving until age fifty five. The distinctive nature of the IDF and its mobilization system lies in this latter component element, which differs from reserve forces in most other countries in scope, state of readiness and the extent to which it meshes with the overall military structure. The proportion of career personnel, conscripts, and reserves varies from unit to unit. However, in contrast to most other armies, the IDF employs reservists in a wide range of military functions and at almost all levels of command. Israel's tank corps is composed mainly of reserve units, reserve pilots are expected to take part in aerial combat, reserve officers take charge of units up to and even beyond the division level, and it is common for regular army officers to serve under commanders drawn from the reserves.

This system of mobilization has far-reaching strategic implications: Israel cannot launch major war without first calling up the reserves thus depriving it of the option of strategic surprise. A war of attrition or form of prolonged warfare is difficult for Israel to handle and so conflicts may be intentionally escalated in order to force a conclusion, thus making it possible to release the reservists. By the same token, Israel cannot afford to call up the reserves for an extended period of time without coming to a decision on whether to go to war. Extensive reliance on reserves also makes it difficult to hold large, densely-populated captured areas, as in Lebanon for example. Finally, the key role played by reserve units and reserve commanders also makes it socially problematic for Israel to wage war without the backing of a national consensus.

As to the second source of strategic weakness—the lack of strategic depth—until the Six Day War, Israel had to accept its vulnerable borders as givens and plan accordingly. This led Israel to adopt the doctrine of the "pre-emptive strike."[15] This doctrine raises the question of when and under what conditions should Israel's deterrent power be viewed as having deteriorated to the extent that it is deemed necessary to launch an attack to pre-empt an anticipated enemy action. A partial answer to this question is provided by defining a number of vital interests which, if threatened, would constitute a *casus belli.* Such interests were defined in the early 1960s as the blocking of the Straits of Tiran, the massing of enemy forces along Israel's borders, the undermining of the status quo in Jordan, etc.[16] The assumption of this doctrine is that, given its vulnerable borders close to its population centers, Israel can hardly afford to absorb a full-scale enemy attack before moving to the offensive. After the Six Day War, the doctrine was replaced by the notion of "defensible borders" to enable Israel to absorb an enemy attack without the need for a pre-emptive strike.[17] This shift in concepts resulted in debates over strategy becoming enmemeshed in the ideological controversy over the future of the territories, with proponents of various positions drawing maps of "defensible borders" to suit their ideological predilections.[18] Each area conquered by Israel in the Six Day War—the Sinai Peninsula and Gaza, the Golan Heights, and the West Bank—was viewed from a different perspective in this debate. In respect of the Sinai Peninsula, the approach eventually adopted in the peace agreement with Egypt was that demilitarized buffer zones would provide Israel with adequate early warning in case of enemy attack. For the West Bank, however, where ideological, political, and strategic concerns were highly intermingled, such an arrangement was not considered appropriate or applicable and three different approaches emerged.

The first was embodied in the "Allon Plan" that guided the governments led by Labor-Alignment until 1977, even though it was never adopted as official policy.[19] The strategic concept here was that Israel should seek border changes, mainly in the sparsely-populated Jordan Rift Valley, that would allow it to control the axes linking the West Bank to the East Bank. The presence of Israeli forces in these parts of the West Bank would ensure that heavy weapons such as tanks, artillery and, above all, surface-to-air missiles that can cover Israel's airfields would be kept out of the remainder of the territory. The second approach is based on Israeli control of the mountain ridge running north-south through the heavily-populated heart of the West Bank, with all the social and political consequences implied in continued Israeli rule there.[20] The third approach, favored by only a small minority, calls for a return to the 1967 borders along with demilitarization of the West Bank, thus accepting the need to revert to the preemptive strike as a means of countering attempts to violate the area's demilitarized status. The controversy over the three approaches reflected the incursion of political and ideological considerations into the sphere of national security: No longer was it possible to achieve a consensus based soley on expert military judgments accepted by the entire defense establishment. A striking indication of this quandary was provided by the opposing report of the Chief of Staff and one of his predecessors in a case before the Supreme Court on whether the Gush Emunim settlement of Elon Moreh near Nablus was essential on security grounds. Chief of Staff Rafael Eitan testified that the settlement, built on land appropriated from Arabs on security grounds, was essential for national defense, while former Chief of Staff Haim Bar-Lev maintained that it had no security value. The Defense Minister at the time, Ezer Weizman, was also known to be opposed to the settlement.[21]

The third national security challenge faced by Israel has been adapting its civilian-military relations to the conditions of the protracted conflict. There are two facets to this challenge: Ensuring the optimal use of manpower and other resources for national security while maintaining a democratic regime and creating a system of control for the military appropriate to a prolonged state of emergency marked by occasional limited clashes in periods of "dormancy" and periodic eruption of full-scale war fought under international political constraints. These two facets of national security are intertwined. Israel's unique patterns of civilian-military relations have largely determined both the extent of national consensus on the allocation of resources to security needs, and the types of civilian control of the defense establishment. These characteristics—broad civilian participation in national security tasks, vague boundaries between military and political institutions, and social networks including members of both military and civilian elites—have encouraged intensive interaction between the military and civilian sectors.

The Conceptual Framework

The relations between the strategic aspects of national security and the social and political aspects of this area have been a source of tension in most democratic political systems. These aspects are related to different societal needs: The need for external security which, in societies subject to an acute military threat, is perceived as a basic existential need; and the need for a properly functioning democratic political system which usually reflects the desire of the population for optimal conditions of social welfare.[22] This tension can be expressed on three levels: values, institutions, and relations among elites.

On the value level there is a dual tension. The first is between a conflictual conception of international relations that generates feelings of pervasive threat and a cooperative conception that reduces the consciousness of an external threat and stresses the diplomatic and economic dimensions of international relations. The second is between an authoritarian-hierarchical conception and a democratic-egalitarian conception of governmental and social patterns and civil rights.[23]

On the institutional level, tension exists between the clear subordination of the security establishment, particularly the armed forces, to civilian political institutions, and the possibility of extensive autonomy for the security establishment.

On the level of relations among elites, tension exists between the military elite with its sense of mission as "defenders of the nation" stemming from its monopoly over the legitimate means of violence, and the political elites that restrict the military elite to the specific function of carrying out national security policy, as opposed to having a role in formulating that policy.[24]

The tension between the "civic" values of democratic societies and the "militaristic" values of authoritarian, hierarchical organizations trained in the use of violence is basically unavoidable. Democratic societies have dealt with this inherent tension in various ways. The alternatives in this context can be analyzed through the concepts of convergence and divergence of the civilian and military sectors or by means of the concepts of permeable or integral boundaries between the two sectors.[25] Actually, there is a connection between the problems of the closeness or distance between these elites and the nature of the boundaries between them. Integral boundaries are usually associated with a process of divergence between the two elites, while permeable boundaries tend to appear as value and social differences between the two elites diminish. We may therefore distinguish between two opposing trends that are embodied in two models representing extreme cases: the closed military "caste" and the nation in arms. The ideal type of military caste is based on the premise that the difference between the military and civilian sectors, especially in democratic societies, cannot be bridged. Thus, the military should be isolated as much as possible but it can be permitted to cultivate its own values within its own framework as long as it is prevented from influencing society as a whole. This model is usually based on a professional army without conscripts which poses no threat to the democratic political system as long as society faces no acute threat to its security and as long as resources are provided for limited military needs. It was Harold Lasswell who pointed out that under conditions of worsening international tensions and increasing allocations of resources for defense, this model could be transformed into what he called a "garrison state" ruled by the "experts in violence."[26]

The alternative model is based on a reduction in the social and value gaps between the civilian and military sectors combined with permeable boundaries between them that permit two-way influence.[27] Characteristic of this model is a pattern of military service based on a nucleus of professional soldiers that make up the permanent army, with the addition of conscripts and a comprehensive reserve force. A condition for the emergence of this model is a national consensus concerning the existence of a serious external threat to the state which, in turn, requires the allocation of considerable resources to security and the involvement of the military in processes of political decision-making.

These models represent two extreme ideal types that do not exist empirically in any democratic society. All democratic societies are actually found at some point on a continuum between these two extremes. For example, Great Britain is closer than other democracies to the end of the continuum represented by the military caste, while Israel comes closer than any other society to the model of a nation in arms.[28] Where democratic regimes are concerned, both models are based on the subordination of the military to the civilian authorities, but each implements this principle in a different way. In the model of the military caste, there are clear demarcation lines between the civilian sector and the military sector subordinate to it. In the model of the nation in arms, however, there are rules of the game that define the areas in which a convergence between the sectors occurs, and where it is legitimate for the army to be involved in civilian decision-making processes and those areas in which the permeable boundaries between the sectors are open to reciprocal influence. This model is therefore premised on an extensive and diverse range of contacts between the military and civilian sectors. Furthermore, this model tends to generate an intermediate sector for the military and civilian establishments where many of these contacts take place. An example of such a sector is provided by military industries in Israel which are subordinate to the Defense Ministry or, at least, guided by it.[29]

Neither ideal type model of military-society relations is able to resolve the tension between the opposing values of the two sectors, but the nature of the threat to democracy entailed in this tension is different in each case. When the military is segregated from society, it tends to cultivate its own values to the point where a military subculture crystallizes which, in extreme circumstances, can lead to the emergence of "putschist" tendencies. On the other hand, in the case of nation in arms with many points of contact between the two sectors, opportunities arise for the manipulation of civilian institutions by the security establishment, particularly the military, and vice versa.

Permeable Boundaries between Military and Civilian Sectors

In Israel the interaction between the military and civilian sectors takes place at multiple points of contact on both the individual and institutional levels.[30] The most important area of contact on the micro level is through compulsory service for men and women as conscripts and later for men and some young women as reservists. This has wide-ranging implications for the individual:

A. An Economic Burden. The three-year period of compulsory service for men and two years for women means delaying one's entry into the labor market or putting off acquiring higher education or professional skills. Periodic reserve duty can restrict employees' choice of job and chances of advancement, and for the self-employed it can hamper the management and profitability of a business.

B. Limits on Individual Freedom. As a reservist, the Israeli citizen is subject to military jurisdiction on matters connected with his military service—keeping of military secrets, the care of military property in his possession, etc., even when he or she is not on active duty. A reservist has to obtain permission from his unit in order to travel abroad and must always be available for mobilization at relatively short notice. In emergency call-ups, the reservist must report for duty immediately, irrespective of whatever hardship this may cause in his private or work life.

C. Risks and Rewards. Israelis doing military service may be exposed to physical danger during their compulsory service as well as during their later reserve duty. But military service also has its rewards. There are certain jobs open only to veterans. Certain welfare benefits are available only to veterans or their children, these being officially denied to Arab citizens of Israel who are not subject to the draft. Taking part in a national task of central importance in itself confers a degree of prestige on the participant. It also enhances status in other ways such as providing access to information, particularly of a classified nature. Officers are permitted to use both their rank and professional expertise as resources in the civilian labor market. Referring to or indicating one's rank in the reserves in certain social or public contexts is also an accepted way of enhancing one's civilian status. Military rank thus becomes a sort of professional title indicating one's status and abilities.

The interface between civilian and military life also influences the performance of military roles. The presence of conscripts and especially of reservists in military frameworks dictates their ambience to a large extent. The relationships between commanders and their subordinates have always been more flexible and less authoritarian in Israel than in most other armies. This is reflected both in patterns of discipline and in the symbolization of status and authority. Many military rituals and insignia are noted by their absence in the IDF, and those which are observed are usually treated as a mere formality. Attempts to introduce stricter observance of the externals of military discipline have met with a notable lack of success due mainly to the spillover effect of concessions made to reservists who are inclined to be more lax in appearance and behavior than conscripts. The permeable boundaries between military and civilian life are also manifested in the structure and life-style on IDF bases. With the exception of the Air Force, officers and their families do not live on the bases, and many of the enlisted men and women spend much of their free time in civilian surroundings. This is due to Israel's small size and the virtual absence of the barracks' subculture found in other armies. Consequently, not only conscripts but also professional soldiers are exposed to civilian influences through open social networks which provide for close uninterrupted relationships with civilian friends. At the highest levels this is reflected in close contacts between the military elite and civilian elites.[31] senior officers have an interest in cultivating ties with the civilian sector because of the prospect of a "second career" when they retire in their forties, as most do.[32] The partial "civilianization" of military life in Israel can thus be attributed to the fact that the IDF is less of an autarchic total institution than most other armies.

The permeable boundaries between civilian and military sectors exist at the institutional as well as the individual level, the former being of course, more important in terms of the overall relations between the military and society. In particular, it is at the institutional level that we must examine the question of how Israel's democratic political system has managed to function under conditions of a protracted violent conflict. The problem of how developed political systems are influenced by a high salience of national security concerns and high levels of resources mobilized for these ends has occupied political scientist and political sociologists since Harold Lasswell coined the term "garrison state." Lasswell argued that the growing importance of national security issues in an increasingly conflict-ridden world could lead to the ascendance of military values over civilian ones, and ultimately to a regime dominated by the "experts in violence." Israel's experience has not borne out this contention of a direct relationship between the increased salience of security concerns and a growing proportion of resources devoted to security, and the dominance of the military elite over civilian elites. In fact, following the Yom Kippur War, precisely the opposite occurred: The importance of security issues increased, along with an increase in resources allocated to this area—but the prestige of the military declined, along with its influence on national security policy. After 1973, the defense budget rose from an annual average of about 20 per cent of the GNP to an average of about 30 per cent. The war of attrition with Syria in 1974 led to an increase in reserve duty and to greater public concern with security. Nevertheless, public criticism of the army and particularly its senior commanders increased, reversing an earlier tendency to keep them relatively immune from public evaluation of their performance. Likewise, at this time, the patterns of civilian control of the military were redefined following the recommendations of a state commission of inquiry—the Agranat Commission—which had found some of the previous patterns seriously wanting.[33]

From the perspective of institutional analysis, it is possible to identify organizational patterns and modes of operation that permit a high level of involvement by the military in shaping policy in foreign affairs and defense:

A. Professional Expertise. The most salient expression of civilian reliance on the military is in expert input provided by the Chief of Staff and by general staff officers who are often invited to participate in cabinet sessions. The high priority assigned to military-strategic considerations in foreign polity decisions and the prevailing broad definition of the sphere of military professionalism in Israel has led to an extended role played by senior military officers as consultants and advisers to political decision-makers. Politically-minded Chiefs of Staff such as Moshe Dayan in the 1950s and Yitzhak Rabin in the 1960s often exploited their advisory role to promote their own military political and strategic views and, in some cases, to initiate certain policy decisions as well. It was Dayan who initiated the transformation of the Israeli polity of reprisals into a systematic strategy of controlled retaliation based on the utilization of the concept "military operations in peacetime" as a political instrument. Rabin served under Prime Minister and Minister of Defense Levi Eshkol whose dependence on Rabin's professional advice resulted in a considerable extension of the Chief of Staff's political role. Consequently, Rabin played a central role in the formulation of Israel's policy toward Syria when that country attempted to divert the sources of the Jordan River. Military advice also contributed to the failure of the 1971 negotiations on the possibility of an Israeli pullback from the Suez Canal to enable the reopening of the waterway to shipping. On the other hand, a positive military recommendation assured a majority in the cabinet of the national unity government in 1984 for a phased withdrawal of the IDF from southern Lebanon.

B. National Intelligence Evaluations. In Israel the Intelligence branch of the IDF is charged with making national intelligence estimate on the possibility of war. Other Israeli intelligence agencies—the Mossad, the General Security Services (Shin Bet Kaf) and the Research Department of the Foreign Ministry—are also involved, among other things, in intelligence-gathering, but only the IDF Intelligence Branch is responsible for analyzing and shaping the available information into a national intelligence estimate.[34] This military monopoly, which does not exist in other countries, was one of the factors that contributed to the intelligence failure prior to the Yom Kippur War. The Agranat Commission that investigated this failure thus recommended that other intelligence brances be strengthened, but this has been only partly implemented.[35]

C. Diplomats in Uniform. Since the few direct, public contacts that have taken place between Israel and the neighboring Arab states have usually been conducted in the context of armistice or cease-fire negotiations, these contacts have been handled by military men. During the 1950s, the IDF officers serving on the Mixed Armistice Commissions were thus subordinate to both the Foreign Ministry and the IDF General Staff which gave rise to constant conflicts of authority between the Foreign Minister and the Defense Minister and Chief of Staff—with the latter two coming out on top most of the time.[36] The negotiations which led to the signing of the first disengagement of forces agreement with Egypt after the 1973 war were also conducted by military men at Kilometer 101 on the road to Cairo. Four years later following Sadat's visit to Jerusalem, Israel was represented diplomatically in Egypt by a military mission for the first half of 1978. The role of diplomats in uniform in Israeli diplomacy, however, has not been confined to the context of Arab-Israeli relations. During the French-British-Israeli negotiations which led to the coordinated Sinai Campaign and Suez Operation, it was Israel's Chief of Staff, Dayan, who contrived the scheme for what came later to be known as the British-French-Israeli "collusion."

D. Military Government. Israel has imposed military government on two occasions: in Israel proper from 1948 to 1966, to administer predominantly Arab areas; and in the territories of the West Bank, Gaza Strip, and the Golan Heights captured in the Six Day War. The military government exercises both military and political functions. In this framework, day-to-day security is in the hands of the IDF, while overall policies are determined by the civilian head of the defense establishment, the Minister of Defense. These policies are influenced by the professional judgments of the IDF officers who actually run the military government.

E. Military Doctrines that Create Constraints for Political Decision-Makers. Implicit and explicit military doctrines and the planning based on them create constraints that cannot be ignored by civilian decision-makers. Though the IDF has never adopted a coherent body of operative prescriptions which can be labeled a military doctrine, its organizational structure, strength and modes of operation reflect the impact of a cluster of prevailing concepts which actually prescribes the general outline for military planning and training. In spite of its flexibility and non-binding nature, this cluster of concepts is sufficiently integral and effective to constitute a tacit military doctrine for the IDF. This tacit doctrine affects Israel's defense posture though its impact on military planning and strength. In this sense, it determines, to a considerable extent, the degree to which various strategic options are backed by military capabilities and thus serves to impose effective constraints on the discretion of the civilian decision-makers responsible for the formulation of national security policies.

The most salient example of the impact of tacit military doctrines on the range of options in political decision-making is that of the IDF's offensive doctrines on the eve of the Six Day War. Since the mid-1950s, the IDF command never made any serious effort to prepare for absorbing an enemy's first strike before "carrying the war into the enemy's territory." The underlying assumption of Israel's military thinking was that Israel would be able to pre-empt an enemy attack and strike first. The first strike doctrine was most apparent in the operational planning of the Israeli air force, whose command concentrated its efforts on developing a capability for destroying the enemy's air force on the ground in the first hours of the war. Thus, when the Egyptian army concentrated along the Israeli-Egyptian armistice line in a potentially offensive disposition, the need to pre-empt in order to secure military success became a major consideration in determining the Israeli response to the Egyptian threat. The government was under considerable pressure from the defense establishment to end the "waiting period" and prevent the enemy from taking the military initiative. It is noteworthy, however, that the offensive doctrine was not just a consequence of military operational and tactical preferences of the IDF command. It was rooted in the basic geographic and demographic conditions of Israel, which put Israel in an inferior position vis a vis its hostile Arab neighbors. The vulnerability of the core area of Israel to an enemy's surprise attack and the need to offset Arab quantitative superiority by reliance on the reserves, induced the IDF to prefer the offensive option with its first-strike consequences. The link between the doctrine and the conditions which are its source are also apparent in the 1967 crisis, since one of the main factors which led to the decision to implement the doctrine was the burden of full IDF mobilization on Israel's economy and society. The experience of the "waiting period" thus showed that, in the context of the Israeli defense posture of the 1960s, *casus mobili* is apt to become *casus belli.* This lesson, and that of the limited range of opinions in the absence of reliable first-strike absorption capability, led to a modification in Israel's strategic doctrine. The new concept of "defensible borders" has been introduced into Israeli strategic thinking in order to provide the IDF with the "strategic depth" necessary for the development of an "absorption capability."

F. Conceptions of the Operational Control in the IDF. Control of operations in the IDF is based on the principle of sticking to an objective rather than to a schematic plan and of decentralized decision-making, both of which grant broad discretionary authority to relatively low levels of command.[37] The resulting pattern of control rests on the options available and improvisations exercised in the field: The commander on the spot must report to his superiors on the steps taken to achieve the designated objective, but does not usually have to secure authorization for measures taken in response to situations unfolding on the battlefield. This doctrine of flexible command and "optional" control has suited the operational needs of the IDF, but has sometimes created political problems. For example, during the Sinai Campaign, the then Chief of Staff Moshe Dayan was furious with the head of the Southern Command, who threw an armored brigade into battle prior to the stage that had been agreed on with the British and French.[38] During the Six Day War, rapid developments in the battlefield thwarted plans made at the political level by Defense Minister Moshe Dayan for troop advances to stop 30 kilometers from the Suez Canal.[39]

G. Lack of Clarity in the Division of Authority between the Senior Political and Military Echelons. There is no "Commander in Chief of the armed forces" in Israel. Basic Law: the IDF of 1976 states that the supreme command over the IDF is vested in the government of Israel (i.e., the cabinet) as a collective body, and that the Minister to exercise this collective responsibility on behalf of the cabinet is the Minister of Defense.[40] Until this law was enacted, the IDF Ordinance of 1948 was in force which did not relate directly to this issue. Under these circumstances, the relations between the Prime Minister and the Chief of Staff were plagued by friction and misunderstandings which hampered civilian control of the armed forces. What is more, most Defense Ministers tended to view their role as representatives of the defense establishment vis a vis the political system rather than the other way around. The Agranat Commission thus found it necessary to note that the Defense Minister should not intervene in operational matters to the extent that he becomes a "superordinate Chief of Staff."[41]

The absence of a Commander in Chief and the unclear lines of authority between the Prime Minister, Defense Minister, and the Chief of Staff created favorable conditions for the General Staff to increase its influence over the cabinet. It should be emphasized, however, that the supreme authority of the cabinet over the military has never been challenged in Israel—even though its effectiveness has sometimes been eroded. Not all areas of national security are in the hands of the Defense Ministry and the IDF. At least two central areas, the development of a nuclear capability and the security services (the Shin Bet Kaf and the Mossad), are the responsibility of the Prime Minister.

The army's influence on decision-making has thus been subject to considerable fluctuations which, among other reasons, stemmed from the personal stature and experience of the various Prime Ministers and Chiefs of Staff. This follows the particularistic traditions of politics in Israel in which role definitions were flexible and, in practice, usually reflected the personality of the role occupants and their own conception of their positions. For example, when Moshe Dayan was Chief of Staff, he saw the Defense Minister's job as acting as the IDF's advocate vis a vis the political echelon; However, when he himself became Defense Minister, he sought to control the IDF as something of a "superordinate Chief of Staff." Yitzhak Rabin too, who served as Chief of Staff in the 1960s, Prime Minister in the 1970s and Defense Minister in the 1980s, acted according to different patterns of authority depending on which role he occupied. As Chief of Staff under Levi Eshkol, who served simultaneously as Defense Minister and Prime Minister, Rabin exercised a decisive influence on national security policy leading some to claim that he was in effect acting as Minister of Defense. As Prime Minister, he exercised his personal authority as a military man in sometimes opposing the expert judgments of the Defense Minister and Chief of Staff concerning military budgets and arms purchases.[42] As Defense Minister in the government of national unity, Rabin assumed the primary role in shaping national security policy, as both a leading political figure and a respected military authority. The pinnacle of influence as Defense Minister was reached by Ariel Sharon, who essentially initiated the Lebanon war and determined its contours by exploiting his superior military background over the members of the cabinet, including the Prime Minister, Menachem Begin.[43]

Indeed, Sharon's tenure as Defense Minister was especially controversial. He was accused of manipulating and deceiving the cabinet in order to win approval of his policies and also of blocking communication between the senior command and the government thereby making himself the exclusive political authority vis a vis the military.

H. The Military as a Political Group. The exertion of pressure by the military on security policy formation is facilitated by the military's institutional role in the formation of national security policy, the high accessibility of politicians to senior military officers due to the social linkages of these elites, and the military's capacity to influence public opinion via the channels of communication at its disposal—the IDF spokesman's office, the IDF radio station, a newsweekly and and control of press censorship. In the history of civilian-military relations in Israel, there is at least one example of the systematic use of these facilities for the purpose of manipulating the civilian decision-making bodies into adopting a military strategy advocated by the Chief of Staff. During 1944-5, Chief of Staff Dayan effectively utilized all the political resources available to the General Staff in order to induce Prime Minister Sharett to adopt a tough policy of retaliation in response to terrorist infiltration along Israel's borders with Egypt and Jordan. Another example of pressure-group-like behavior of men in uniform was the lobbying by members of the General Staff for an immediate pre-emptive strike in May 1967. Military leaders did not suffice then with advising the cabinet through formal channels, but used their connections with politicians to persuade them of the necessity of going to war.[44]

The Role-Expansion of the Military

The unofficial rules governing the relationship between the civilian and military spheres that developed over the years allowed the military to acquire a legitimate right to function in certain civilian areas, as opposed to others which were off limits. Military involvement was recognized as legitimate in the broadly-defined areas of national security which included most aspects of foreign policy as well. On the other hand, internal affairs such as social welfare policy and the workings of Israel's democratic regime were treated as distinctly civilian spheres. However, the question as to what should be included or excluded from the broad area of national security was left open. Issues such as the military censorship of the news media occasionally emerged that could be viewed as both military and a political matter. The tendency to expand the sphere of legitimate national security concerns did not necessarily emanate from the military men. On the contrary, debates on such issues were usually conducted within the civilian sector.

The compliance with the rules of the game by the civilian and military elites alike was rooted in a broad consensus which viewed Israel as a society whose existence was constantly subject to an acute military threat. The subordination of foreign affairs to national security stems from this fundamental perception. The prevalent foreign affairs outlook among the elites and the general public alike is rooted in a national security approach that gives priority to strategic considerations over diplomatic ones. Violence is seen as a legitimate means in international relations in the context of a protracted conflict. This conflict-related outlook also influences internal affairs associated with the communal division between Arabs and Jews, as in the case of the military government imposed over predominantly Arab areas within Israel from 1948 to 1966. On the other hand, with few exceptions, the military elite has internalized democratic values and norms, and has not exhibited authoritarian leanings in the realms of domestic politics, government and public administration, freedom of speech and cultural expression, civil rights, and the right of labor to organize and strike. To the extent that proposals to restrict these rights have arisen, it has been from radical groups on the fringe of the political map and not from the ranks of the military.

The trends of militarization of the civilian sector and the "civilianization" of the military can be examined also from the perspective of the concept of the "military mind."[45] The characteristics of the military mind fall into two categories. The first category concerns the utility or desirability of violence as a mean to attain goals in international relations. The second concerns authoritarian values and the symbolic importance attached to the hierarchical structure of the military. These categories are not necessarily found together to the same degree in all cases. Israel provides a case where, as we have noted, there is a consensus between the military and the civilian elites on the legitimacy of employing violence in international conflicts on the one hand, and on the need to restrict the authoritarian dimensions of military life and to prevent them from spilling over into the civilian sector, on the other. The shared dominant approach is thus "civilian" where politics is concerned and "military" where national security is at stake. There is, however, evidence indicating that the tendency to "civilianize" the military has declined over the years, and there are indications that authoritarian influences are gaining strength, at least as far as the organization of the military itself is concerned.[46]

In the wake of the 1973 war, there has been a major expansion of the economic role of the defense establishment. These trends are expressed not only in the portion of the GNP devoted to defense. Especially important in this context is the expansion of Israel's military-industrial complex, which includes the IDF, the civilian arms of the Defense Ministry, and public and private firms in the civilian sector. All sectors of the economy are thus represented in the military-industrial complex, and there are no clear rules about the respective responsibility of each sector in the development and production of weapons and supplies. Thus, military aircraft and the Gabriel sea-to-sea missile are produced by the Israel Aircraft Industries which is a government corporation. Several types of weapons and ammunition are produced by the Military Industries, an auxiliary to the Ministry of Defense. Another ministry unit, Rafael (the Weapons Development Authority), is responsible for the development and production of sophisticated weapons system. The IDF Armored Corps, however, has overall responsiblity for the production of Israel's first domestically-produced tank, the Merkava, although some of its systems are produced by various public and private firms. Private and non-governmental public firms, such as those owned by Histadrut are also involved in arms production. Thus, mortars are produced by Soltam, a subsidiary of the Histadrut holding company Hevrat Ha'ovdim, while some electronic equipment is manufactured by firms with joint public and private ownership.[47] The growing demand of the military has made the defense industries into Israel's largest industrial branch. This branch includes 43 percent of all government corporation employees, 50 percent of those in the Histadrut sector, and 10 percent of the private sector—altogether 25 percent of those employed in industry. Defense production plays an especially prominent role in large corporations. Seven of the twenty large corporations in Israel are dependent, to a large extent, on defense orders.[48] In addition, the army purchases vast quantities of non-military products such as food, clothing, and construction materials in the civilian market, making it the biggest single consumer in the entire economy.

The very existence of a military-industrial complex influences the composition of the elites. Civilian firms in both the private and the public sector that conduct extensive defense business employ a large number of retired senior officers who are responsible for maintaining their firm's connections with the defense establishment. Retired senior officers are also heavily involved in the export of the Israeli-made weapons and security services, an area that comprises about a quarter of Israel's total exports.[49]

Israel's military industries have passed through several stages of development. At the outset, their job was to supply rather elementary types of weapons and ammunition to the IDF. Nevertheless, even at that time, in the 1950s, the military industry was developing unique types of arms, most of them light weapons, some of which, such as the Uzi submachine gun and later the Galil assault rifle, became sought-after items in the international arms markets. In the second stage of their development, the military industries established Rafael, the Weapons Development Authority, and the Israel Aircraft Industries (IAI) to develop new weapons ordered by the IDF. Later, these bodies began to establish their own weapons development programs. These developments and the rapid growth of the IAI, which became Israel's largest industrial firm, endowed the military industries with greater autonomy vis a vis their main client, the IDF. The initiative taken in weapons development by the defense industries was particularly important in the IAI's effort at developing an Israeli-made fighter plane. This process began with the introduction of improvements into existing fighter aircraft, took a step forward with the production of the Kfir fighter plane based on the French Mirage, and culminated with the development of the Lavi fighter. The Lavi began as a relatively inexpensive fighter for specific and limited tasks, but later developed into a much more sophisticated aircraft. At that stage, the IAI became a pressure group representing independent business and employment interests. The IAI's attempts to further these interests, especially through its campaign to continue the development of the Lavi, led eventually to an open clash of interests between the needs of the IDF as defined by the General Staff, and those of the IAI. This happened when the development and production of the Lavi became much more expensive than alternative ready-made fighter planes that could be purchased directly from the United States.

In this context it became evident that the government, in particular the Defense Minister and the Finance Minister, had failed to develop effective procedures for supervising the independent research and development efforts of the military industries with the result that hundreds of millions of dollars had been spent on projects that had no economic or military justification.

In contrast to the economic role-expansion of the defense establishment after the 1973 war, the monopoly previously held by the IDF in certain areas of intelligence and strategic planning decreased. The Agranat Commission investigating the intelligence failures prior to the war recommended that the civilian intelligence arms be strengthened, especially the Research Department of the Foreign Ministry—a recommendation that has been only partially implemented.[50]

No less important was the emergence of a flourishing public debate on national security issues. Universities established research institutes for strategic studies that have since branched out in various directions, and public discussion of security issues increased, even touching on technical military matters. In the press and in accademic symposia, the military was frequently criticized in various areas: organization, discipline, military operations, and the conceptual basis of planning and the future development of the armed forces.

In other areas, the role expansion of the military was subject to alternating growth and contraction, as in the educational activities of the IDF where such fluctuations were often due to the personal predilections of the Defense Ministers and Chiefs of Staff. Sometimes the same Chief of Staff would seek to expand the cultural and educational role of the army in some areas and reduce it in others. Chief of Staff Rafael Eitan, for example, considerably expanded the army's attempts to rehabilitate and educate so-called marginal youth, many of whom had previously been rejected on educational and moral grounds as unfit for military service.[51] However, Eitan also cut back on cultural activities and entertainment organized by the army, ordering the disbaning of the various military entertainment troupes which had previously played a leading role in the area of Israeli popular culture. The educational activity of the IDF outside its ranks was also reduced, primarily following the contraction in the activities of the para-military training unit for teenagers known as the Gadna. During the 1950s and 1960s, the Gadna served, in many ways, as a substitute for the political youth movements that were influential in pre-state days, but later it transferred part of its functions to the Ministry of Education and Culture, and virtually ceased activities among youths from the better-off segments of the population.[52]

A politically sensitive area of contact between the military and civilian sectors is mass communications. In the 1950s and 1960s, the dominant trend for the military was role expansion. The army radio station Galei Zahal, the IDF weekly Bamahaneh, the professional military journals and Defense Ministry publishing house, the army spokesman's activities, and the appearance of army song and dance troupes before civilian audiences—all these expressed the military's ventures into the communications field, many of which were aimed at civilians. During the 1970s and 1980s, role expansion in this area ceased and the weight of these endeavors in relation to their civilian counterparts dropped.

The trend of role contraction can be explained by budgetary constraints as well as by the decline in the military's prestige and an erosion of the national consensus on security matters. The erosion of the consensus on security issues aroused a special sensitivity to the messages conveyed by the army through the communications media under its control. One result of this was the increased vagueness of the messages themselves.

The diminished consensus on national security and the emergence of critical public debate on military and security affairs were also related to the reduced influence of the defense establishment over communications through military censorship. The basic rules of the game governing censorship in Israel recognize the legitimacy of such intervention where security is concerned, but reject it when it comes to political matters. These rules of the game are accepted by the defense establishment and the press despite the fact that the original laws establishing censorship, carried over from the British Mandate, permit the imposition of censorship on many matters liable to affect public security, which includes political matters, too. Despite the basic agreement on the operating principles of military censorship, which is staffed by IDF officers, many disputes have occurred between the censor and the press over matters that the former sees as security and the latter sees as basically political. During the 1960s, the censor blocked publication of the details of a botched intelligence and sabotage operation in Egypt in 1954 that later gave rise to the prolonged political crisis known as the Lavon Affair. The political debate over the Lavon Affair that was conducted in the press was thus resorted to code-words and euphemisms such as the "security mishap" to refer to the failed operation itself, and to terms such as "the third man" and "the senior officer" to refer to protagonists in the original events. An absurd situation resulted: The political system was thrown into severe crisis over the political recriminations resulting from the original operation, the government fell, and new elections had to be held, while the public was not even presented with an official version of what the crisis was all about. While the foreign press published details of the operation, the Israeli media were prevented from quoting these sources, as they are usually allowed to do even in sensitive security matters.[53] The loosening of censorship restrictions during the late 1960s, 1970s, and 1980s was an outcome of the emergence of a more active press which increasingly challenged decisions of the censor.[54]

These disputes between the censor and the media were, in most cases, resolved by the censor backing down under pressure from the press. The censor eventually had to accept the fact that the press had become less susceptible to regimentation and less prone to self-censorship. This trend was reflected in a decline in the status of the Editors' Committee of Daily Newspapers which in the 1950s and 1960s, had become a channel of the defense establishment for setting informal guidelines on how to treat new stories on sensitive issues and for voluntarily imposing restrictions going beyond those required by formal military censorship.[55] The critical stance of the press and its willingness to flout censorship restrictions reached a new plateau during the war in Lebanon as military correspondents took the lead in criticizing the aims of the war and the manner in which it was conducted.

Changes have thus occurred, over the years, in the extent to which the fragmented boundaries between the military and civilian spheres have permitted one sphere to influence the other. Some sectors of this boundary have become more permeable and thus more open to influence from the other side, while others have become less so. At any rate, over the years, there has been an increase in the number and variety of the points of contact between the two spheres as a result of the growth in resources devoted to national security and to the diversification of the activities of the defense establishment. These processes have occurred within the framework of rules of the game that are accepted, for the most part, by the civilian and military elites and by public opinion. The system of norms that have emerged in this sphere can be described as Israel's dominant pattern of the civilian-military relations that has not been seriously opposed for many years. Only with the erosion of the national security consensus and the declining prestige of the military following the Yom Kippur War and the Lebanon War, have voices been heard challenging some or all of these norms. One expression of this trend has been the demand to tighten formal civilian control of the defense establishment. A prominent advocate of this approach was a former Chief of Staff, Yigael Yadin who became a political figure in the 1970s. Yadin's outlook influenced the recommendations of the Agranat Commission of which he was a member, which in turn led the Knesset to pass the Basic Law: The Army.[56] Others proposed the establishment of a national security council which would have the power to examine and review decisions made by the military professionals. However, this proposal met with opposition based on the claim that such a body would only cause additional complications without solving the basic problems in the relations between the military and civilian spheres.[57] In contrast to the large number of those who sought to reform the dominant pattern of civilian-military relations, very few sought to attack the fundamentals of this normative system.

One goal of the system was to reduce the impact of the prolonged conflict on the functioning of social and political institutions and the daily life of the individual. This was achieved by shaping institutional mechanisms for making orderly transitions from routine situations to emergencies and back again without creating serious disruptions. This type of arrangement has been called an "interrupted system" by an Israeli sociologist who has studied the macro and micro patterns of adjustments to this situation.[58] Israeli society has institutionalized arrangements for suspending social roles and activities when priorities suddenly change in times of emergency as the dormant conflict erupts into war. This phenomenon goes beyond mobilizing the manpower and the other resources technically necessary for conducting a war. Not only does the military sphere expand and the civilian sphere contract, but the civilian sphere changes its patterns of operation for the duration without losing the capacity to return to routine functioning once the emergency has passed.

There are two types of transition mechanisms from routine to emergency situations: special logistical arrangements take effect to allow the continued functioning of services, commerce, and industry for the duration; and the system of social status is adapted to the changed value and esteem attached to various roles and activities. While it is taken for granted that the arrangements of the first type are temporary, those of the second type pose a different problem. Here the concern is to prevent the crystallization of a temporary societal order of priorities and the institutionalization of the status hierarchy related to it. The logic of the "interrupted system" achieves this by giving temporary preference to those contributing to the collective effort, by means of various forms of status-enhancement, without legitimating them as permanent status components. This applies mainly to those whose wartime roles depart from their everyday activities. As for professional soldiers, especially the senior officers, the enhanced reputations they may attain because of their wartime performance tend to become a permanent component of their social status.

The logic of the interrupted system implies that along with mechanisms restricting the security establishment during the periods between emergencies, there are also mechanisms, for defining the timing and conditions under which priority is suddenly given to security considerations. The mechanisms for this demarcation of institutional activities and time contribute to the ability of Israel society to function normally under conditions of a protracted conflict. Normal functioning in periods when the conflict is dormant is based on carefully distinguishing security activities from other spheres. While in wartime security encompasses far more activities, this expansion is understood to be temporary.

Politics and the Military

The influences flowing through the permeable institutional boundaries between the military and political spheres did not move in one direction only. While the involvement of the army in shaping defense policy implies a certain degree of militarization of civilian instiututions, the impact of party politics on military affairs can be looked upon as a component of the partial civilianization of the military. An awareness of the danger of politicization of the army is reflected in The Israel Defense Forces Ordinance, one of the first laws passed by the provisional government. This law specifies that in the oath of allegiance to the IFD, the loyalty of the recruit will be affirmed to "the State of Israel, its laws, and to its legitimate authorities."[59] The stress of the "legitimate authorities" was intended to block partisan political interference in the army stemming from the strong loyalties to parties and movements that military men still carried with them from the time of the Yishuv when virtually all areas of public life, and especially the area of security, were highly politicized. The attempts to remove partisan influences from the IDF brought about two major political crises during the first few months of the state's existence: The sinking of the arms ship Altalena and the disbanding of the Palmach. Just after the establishment of the state, following months of difficult negotiations, an agreement was reached for intergrating the forces of the IZL

(Irgun Zvai Leumi), the right-wing dissident underground group, into the IDF. However, IZL members were allowed to preserve the frameworks of their underground units in the IDF instead of being required to join as individuals. Thus, when the arms ship Altalena, which had been organized by agents of the IZL in Europe and dispatched from France, arrived in Israel, the IZL leaders demanded that some of the arms be allocated to IZL battalions in the IDF with the rest to be divided up as the IDF saw fit. The rejection of this demand, which was incompatible with the concept of a unified depoliticized army, led to an armed clash between the IZL and units of the IDF loyal to the government, first near the village of Kfar Vitkin and later, off the coast of Tel Aviv. Eventually, Ben-Gurion ordered an IDF artillery unit to open fire on the ship, which caused it to burn and sink. This demonstration of fierce determination to prevent, at all costs, any expression of political autonomy within the IDF secured the integrity of the IDF as a unified army. The Altalena affair reflected the concern of Ben-Gurion and his government with politicization of the IDF by incorporating formerly independent bodies into its ranks. This was perceived as particularly threatening where the bodies concerned—the IZL and the LHI—had a long tradition of rejecting the authority of the Organized Yishuv.

The second crisis involving partisan influences in the IDF differed considerably from the Altalena affair, and focused on Ben-Gurion's decision to disband the Palmach, a prestigious military unit that had been an integral part of the Haganah, the organization from which the IDF itself sprang. In this respect, the Palmach had been subject to the authority of the Organized Yishuv, and continued to accept without question the authority of the Israeli government and the IDF command. Nevertheless, the Palmach enjoyed organizational autonomy within the IDF that was manifested in an separate command and staff structure that handled training, supply, and manpower.[60] Moreover, many Palmach members were close to the kibbutz movements, especially to the Kibbutz Hameuchad organization which was led by a left-wing faction of the Labor Movement known as Achdut Ha'avodah. The latter had once been a faction in Ben-Gurion's party Mapai, but later broke away and merged with another left-wing group, Hashomer Hatzair to form a new party called Mapam. The Palmach thus appeared to be providing Mapam—Mapai's main rival in the Labor Movement—with a channel of influence to the younger generation.

Politically, then, the Palmach was a thorn in the side of Ben-Gurion and his party. In addition, the ideological arguments advanced by those who sought to retain the Palmach's partial autonomy clashed with Ben-Gurion's concepts of statehood (mamlachtiut) that adamantly upheld the need for a depoliticized army. While Ben-Gurion justified the disbanding of the Palmach's seperate command in terms of the need to depoliticize the army, his left-wing opponents sought to prevent or, at least, to delay this step by pointing to the unique character of the Palmach as a volunteer force inspired by Labor Zionist values.[61] The decision to disband the Palmach was, at least on the ideological plane, a crucial step toward a unitary army cleansed of particularistic political attachments. The controversy surrounding Ben-Gurion's action was conducted within the bounds of democratic rules of the game, and the Palmach accepted the inevitable once the decision of the cabinet had been ratified by the Provisional Council of State.

The elimination of military units with particularistic allegiances to political movements did not mean the end of politicization in the IDF. Ben-Gurion himself applied political criteria in the promotion of senior officers. For example, the advancement of officers with IZL or LHI backgrounds was severely restricted, as was the advancement of Palmach veterans (especially those identified with Mapam, albeit to a lesser extent). In any case, the disbanding of the Palmach and the surrounding controversy had led to a wave of resignations of officers identified with Mapam, including some of the most outstanding commanders of the War of Independence. Ben-Gurion himself contributed to this process when he removed several senior officers from their posts, including the former commander of the Palmach himself, Yigal Allon, who was replaced by Moshe Dayan as commander of the Southern Command.[62]

Another expression of politics in the army was the participation of officers on active duty in party activities. An extreme manifestation of this was the appearance of several senior officers as candidates in the elections to the first Knesset in 1949.[63] Yigal Allon, Moshe Carmel, and Shimon Avidan appeared on Mapam's list of candidates for the Knesset, and Moshe Dayan had a place on the Mapai list. This was seen to be justified because the elections were held before the major demobilization took place, and the senior officers who stood as candidates were regarded as only serving for the duration of the war and not as military professionals. This phenomenon did not, however, recur, and was indeed prohibited by the Basic Law: Knesset. Nevertheless, General Staff rules still permit officers to be inactive members of political parties.

Most parties, especially the Labor movement parties and kibbutz movements, actively seek to cultivate ties with their members serving as career officers. The settlement movements have set up special offices to handle this task, and the parties periodically organize what are described as "informational" meetings for their members in the officers' corps.[64] These considerations were seen as unavoidable given the close involvement of the army in shaping foreign and defense policy. In this context, party ties could still play a role in promotions, but often more important was the social or ideological background shared by senior officers and decision-makers that predisposed them to similar views on matters of national security.

It is in this context that we should understand the emergence, in the 1960s, of two schools of thought in the area of national security, both of which included politicians as well as military men. The first group was the "Ben-Gurion school" whose most prominent members were Moshe Dayan and Shimon Peres. The second was composed of those with Achdut Ha'avodah backgrounds, led by Israel Galili and Yigal Allon. Among the senior officers on active duty, the Ben-Gurion group included the Chiefs of Staff from the late 1950s and early 1960s, Chaim Laskov and Zvi Tsur, while the second group included the Chiefs of Staff who served after them, Yitzhak Rabin, Chaim Bar-Lev, and David Elazar.

Beyond the personal and political elements that divided these schools, there were also differing conceptions of national security, particularly on the question of Israel's nuclear option.[65] While the Ben-Gurion school favored investing heavily in creating an infrastructure that could one day enable Israel to produce nuclear weapons, the other school sought to rely on conventional forces combined with the strategy of "pre-emptive attack." In the international arena, Dayan and Peres sought to cultivate alliances with European countries, primarily France, while the other group gave priority to developing political and defense ties with the United States. During the 1970s, the conceptual differences between the two groups became blurred, but the personal and political networks underlying them continued to function.

Another manifestation of close ties between senior officers and the political establishment was the "recruitment" of senior officers for top party and government positions upon their leaving the military. This began in the 1950s with men such as Dayan, Allon, and Moshe Carmel and, after a hiatus, resumed following the Six Day War which brought considerable public acclaim to a number of generals. After 1967, the parties began to compete with each other in attracting senior officers to their ranks. Even parties that had not done this in the past began to assign top political positions for senior officers to take over as soon as they had doffed their uniforms. Perhaps the most blatant case in the years following the Six Day War was the appointment of Ezer Weizman, a former Air Force commander and IDF Chief of Operations to a ministerial post by Herut less than twenty-four hours after he had officially left the army.

The tendency for parties at both ends of the political spectrum to put up former senior officers as candidates for the Knesset indicates that even parties outside the mainstream saw this as a means of acquiring wider legitimacy and attracting voters, the halo provided by the IDF being used to symbolize their commitment to the security of Israel. The presence of reserve officers at practically all points of the political map indicates that the officer corps does not form a caste with a uniform political and ideological outlook. While the political deployment of reserve officers has not been an exact reflection of civilian political preferences, they have also not been bunched at either end of the spectrum. Most of them have gravitated to the two large parties, with an edge here to Labor.[66] Only the religious parties lack reserve officers among their leaders.

The political activity of some of the senior officers recruited to leadership positions created problems of a constitutional nature. Some of these ex-commanders continued to hold senior reserve positions that could be activated in wartime. In the Yom Kippur War, for example, Ariel Sharon commanded a division that played a crucial part in the fighting along the Suez Canal, while Chaim Bar-Lev, a former Chief of Staff and then Minister of Trade and Industry, was called on while the war was still in progress to take command of the fighting on the Egyptian front. Bar-Lev's position as a leader of the ruling Labor Alignment and Sharon's position as a leader of the opposition Likud bloc generated mutual suspicion and distrust which were aggravated by Sharon's tendency to take independent initiatives on the battlefield and by his outspoken comments on the war, made mainly to foreign journalists, while the fighting was still going on. In his characteristically belligerent style, Sharon accused his superiors of showing political and personal bias in their decisions during the fighting, in particular those which affected the tasks assigned to his forces. For his part, Sharon was accused of insubordination, making unwarranted charges of politicization against his superiors, and of maintaining personal contact during the fighting with the leader of the opposition,

Menachem Begin.[67] The suspicions that each side was using their military exploits to reap political gains led eventually to a decision not to give wartime reserve appointments to senior officers-turned-politicians.[68]

Reserve officers played central roles not only in established political parties but also in the extra-parliamentary protest movements of the 1970s, particularly those which arose in the wake of the Yom Kippur War. Senior officers, however, played only a minor role in the protest movements aroused by the war in Lebanon. Nevertheless, the leaders and members of these movements made frequent references to the fact that they served in the reserves. One of the groups to emerge during the war in Lebanon, for example, was called "Soldiers Against Silence." It should be noted that the dovish Peace Now Movement that arose in 1977 as a major political-ideological pressure group stemmed from an open letter sent by reserve officers to Prime Minister Menachem Begin urging him to seize the opportunity for a peace initiative. The stress on their military background as this letter was undoubtedly intended to show that their willingness to make concessions for the sake of peace did not mean that they were turning their backs on Israel's national security needs.

The involvement of the military in political decision-making and the connection between political parties and military men comprise the two main institutional aspects of the permeable boundaries between the military and civilian spheres. Sometimes these tendencies interact with each other, with interesting results. The political roles attained by former senior officers meant that they could influence political decisions by means of the doctrines and expertise acquired by them in the IDF. However, their political roles could also enable the political system to reduce its dependence on the professional expertise provided by the Chief of Staff and his aides.

The legitimation of military involvement in political decision-making and the civilian influences on the military establishmenthave also had an impact on the relations between the military and civilian elites. Students of the relations between these elites have referred to them as a "partnership."[69] This term, however, can have different meanings. Some of its possible meanings do not apply to Israel in particular, but rather to trends in civilian-military relations in democratic countries since World War II. Students of civilian military relations maintain that the conduct of modern warfare, as well as the role of the military in peacetime, requires close formal and informal contacts between the military elite and groups and individuals in the political elite which lead to a "convergence" between the two elites.[70]

The processes of convergence between the military and political elites have led students of the military and politics in democratic societies to pose sharper questions concerning the nature of the military profession itself. One of the difficulties in attempting to define the specific characteristics of the military profession has arisen in examining the differing social and organizaional contexts in which the professional officer corps functions. The characteristics of a professional officer corps whose subordinates are conscripts differ from those of an officer corps whose subordinates are also professional soldiers. There is also a difference between countries which have active reserve forces that include officers who are not career soldiers, and those countries where career officers have a monopoly in the sphere of military command.

One of the sources of variation in the characteristics of the military profession is the range of functions that the military fulfills in each case. This is, of course, related to the issue of the role expansion of the military. The more the roles of the military extend beyond the narrow functions of combat or preparedness for combat, the more points of contact there are between the military and civilian sectors, and the smaller the gap between the characteristics of military professionals and their civilian counterparts. An organizational factor that shapes the characteristics of the military elite is the framework in which the officer corps receives its basic military training. The basic difference here is between those countries with military academies whose graduates become commissioned officers without first serving as enlisted men, and those countries where those who achieve officer status must come up through the ranks. In countries with military academies, the tendency is to stress the uniqueness of the military profession, including its diffuse cultural dimensions, while in other countries, the specific instrumental components of the military profession are stressed. The distinction between a more technocratic image of the military profession and a diffuse cultural image is also related to the question of the social background of the officer corps. The difference here is between an officer corps with a homogeneous social and cultural background and one with a heterogeneous background and between similar socialization experiences prior to the army related to different class and subcultural backgrounds.

Modern armies take in professionals at their top ranks whose training removes them considerably from the image of the traditional "man of war."[71] The expansion of their contacts with civilian elites has usually reduced the traditional gap between them in terms of perceptions and attitudes: the gap between the narrow professional military outlook and the broader view of the international system characteristic of civilian decision-makers; the gap between the military's demands for greater resources for its needs, and the civilian concern for economic and social welfare; and the gap between the authoritarian approach of the professional military and the democratic values of the political elites.

Israel stands out among western countries in the scope and intensity of the partnership between the political and the military elites mainly because of the circumstances that have made Israel into a nation-in-arms. This confers a more central social status and a greater involvement in political affairs on the Israeli military than on their Western counterparts. At the same time, Israeli civilian leaders are more involved in national security affairs through their service in the military reserves and through their contacts with the military elite in shared social networks. These networks are not limited to formal contacts between military men on active duty and senior politicians and administrators which take place by virtue of their official posts. The networks also include contacts between officers and reservists in their units as well as informal contacts with neighbors and common circles of friends. The practice of officers leaving military service at a relatively young age (forty-five to fifty) to start a second career is also an important factor working against any tendencies of the military to self-segregation. The expectations that they will retire from the service and start a second career leads many military men to cultivate social ties outside the army. One result of these contacts and expectations is that in the final phase of their military career, when they have reached top positions in the army, military men begin to adopt civilian perspectives on many matters, at least to some extent. Officers who leave the regular army at a relatively young age continue to maintain social contacts with their comrades still on active duty, and to take up new positions as commanders in the reserves. These criss-crossing social networks operate to close gaps and to increase the resemblance between civilian and military elites. They also facilitate the exchange of information and help cultivate mutual understanding by generating common conceptions and terminology.

The partnership between the civilian and military elites does not mean that the boundaries between the two sectors are ignored. The partnership is based on rules of the game, most of them informal, that define the legitimate areas of military involvement in civilian affairs, as well as the areas of professional military autonomy where civilian elements have only marginal influence.

Although Israel has been immersed in a prolonged violent conflict, it does not behave like a society under siege. Its democratic government and routine civilian life are a far cry from the type of "siege mentality" bred by living under a constant state of emergency. Israel has not turned into a garrison state, a modern Sparta ruled by specialists in violence whose entire way of life is subordinated to meeting the challenge of an external threat. Thus, the dilemma facing Israel is how to maintain democratic rules of the game, especially civilian control of the military, in a society that lives in constant awareness of a threat to its existence?

It can be argued that the partial involvement of the military in areas of national security officially under civilian control has, paradoxically, made it possible for Israel to preserve its democratic regime and its civilian way of life. The tendency of the civilian and military spheres to develop a resemblance to one another—through the partial militarization of civilian activities and the limited "civilianization" of the military—has prevented the military from becoming a separate caste which feels itself alienated from, and in conflict with, the values represented by the civilian elites. As a result, Israel's susceptibility to a military coup and to the ascendancy of the specialists in violence over the civilian sector has been low. However, the very characteristics that have made a military coup a remote possibility in Israel have made its political decision-making instruments open to manipulation by the defense establishment or portions of it. The ill-defined mechanisms of control, the contradictions between the drive to impose political controls on military activities and the army's professional stress on operative flexibility, the long-standing practice of involving senior officers in policy-making—all these have created possibilities for military leaders and the defense establishment to exercise unwarranted influence on decisions taken by the political echelon. The results of such manipulation, as the war in Lebanon shows, can not only undermine proper governmental processes but can also erode the national consensus, at least in those cases where military escalation is the product of manipulation.

Another threat to the rules of the game that have enabled Israel to maintain its democratic regime during a prolonged external conflict, is rooted in the rising cost, in both human and material terms, of the national security effort in the years following the Yom Kippur War. The rules of the game were developed in the 1950s and 1960s, when the collective security effort did not impose especially heavy burdens in casualties, morale, or material resources. Both the Sinai Campaign and the Six Day War claimed relatively few casualties, did not exact an inordinate cost, and were short in duration. In the 1970s and 1980s, however, the cost of national security greatly increased, both during wartime and the periods in between, in terms of material resources, casualties, and prolonged emergency mobilizations. Thus, the longer periods of reserve duty imposed following the wars of the 1970s and 1980s have been one factor in motivating young people to go abroad for extended periods of time and even to leave Israel altogether. The rising cost of national security has also increased the influence of the military-industrial complex on policy-making, thus imposing other constraints, not directly related to security, on the political leadership.

A third factor that threatens the rules of the game is the weakening of the national consensus concerning the nature of the Arab-Israeli conflict and its possible solutions. The fundamental ideological disputes over Israel's central national goals assumed significance in the wake of the Six Day War. This has led to a political polarization which could seriously impair the effective functioning of Israel's democracy, making it more difficult to mobilize the resources necessary to maintain current level of security and to ensure public readiness to abide unconditionally by authoritative policy decisions in matters of national security.

6

Israel at Forty: Utopia Impaired

The Waning of a Vision

The story of Israeli society is one of flawed fulfillment. Israel's development has been accompanied by high expectations for the achievement of collective goals which were inspired by an ideology shared by the vast majority of the population and the dominant elites. While some of these collective goals, at the outset, entailed a strong utopian component, others could not be achieved without mobilizing considerable resources or without the readiness of the population to delay gratification of certain group demands and individual needs. Under such circumstances, the social system became overburdened with competing collective tasks and conflicting group demands, and the need to deal with these tasks and demands influenced the institutional structure of Israel and the rules of the game of its democratic system. Most of the institutional patterns and the main political rules of the game were already shaped in Israel's first decade.[1]

In those years, Israeli society underwent a far-reaching transformation in a relatively short time as part of its transition from a minority community in a binational territory to a sovereign state. Additional transformations occurred in the wake of the Six Day War of 1967 when the State of Israel, which had started out as a nation-state was forced by the demographic implications of territorial expansion to confront, once ıin, some of the problems of the conflict between national communities that had characterized the period of the Mandate. These two transformations—the transition from a binational society to a close approximation of a nation-state, and the shift back to a conflict between communities within the territory controlled by the state—came about as a result of wars, the War of Independence in 1948 and the Six Day War of 1967.

The state that arose amidst the fighting in the War of Independence was not identical, neither in its territorial boundaries nor in the composition of its population, to the Organized Yishuv whose national institutions had functioned as an "authority without sovereignty." The new territorial boundaries of Israel were shaped by the lines of deployment of its military forces. The Israeli army had to meet the challenge of an invasion by the armies of the neighboring Arab states and the conflict between communities became a conflict between states. Israel did not conform to the model of a nation-state because of the presence of a minority which was Israeli in citizenship but Arab in ethnic-national identity and because of the special attachments between Israel and the Diaspora. However, the exodus of most of the Arab population from the territory taken over by Israel during the War of Independence and the increase in the political and demographic importance of Israel for the Jewish people as a result of the mass immigration brought Israel considerably closer to the conditions of an integral nation-state with overlaps between territorial boundaries, citizenship, and ethnic-national identity. The presence of an Arab minority created some ambiguity with regard to defining the nature of Israeli identity which gave rise to discrimination on a particularistic ethnic-national basis between Jews and Arabs through the segregation of the latter under the military government. But on the other hand, Arabs were granted political rights that expressed the universalist component of the Israeli identity. This component became even more prominent with the dismantling of the military government, an act reflecting the desire to base the attachment of Israel's Arab citizens to the state on consensus instead of coercion, as with the state's Jewish citizens. The fact that most of the Jewish population came to accept, at least de facto, that the territorial aspirations of Zionism were to be realized in only a portion of historic Eretz Israel, also reflected the trend to prefer a more ethnically and nationally homogeneous state over expanding the borders set by the 1949 armistice agreements.

These trends changed considerably in the wake of the Six Day War. The transformation brought about by the war created a distinction between two sets of territorial boundaries—the boundary of sovereignty and the boundary of control—and between two populations, the citizens of Israel, Arabs and Jews alike, versus the Arabs in the occupied territories who were either citizens of another state or stateless. The problem of dual territorial boundaries was exacerbated by the political aspirations of part of the Jewish population to convert the boundary of control into the boundary of sovereignty. These aspirations created several kinds of partial interpenetration between the occupied territories and the State of Israel resulting from the establishment of Jewish settlements in the territories, from Arabs from the territories working in Israel and Israeli investment in the territories, and from a partial application of Israeli law in the areas controlled by the military government. Under these conditions, the relations between the Arabs of the occupied territories and Israel became problematic. These Arabs did not become full members of the Israeli collectivity, but came to comprise a part of its periphery. Thus, a dual set of legal and political norms emerged in relation to the two populations living under Israeli control: a legitimate authority that rests on consensus, versus control based on coercion; and a population with full political rights, versus a population under foreign rule. In other words, the dual boundaries of the Israeli collectivity created the potential basis for a binational state in terms of the composition of its population and the pattern of conflict developing between two ethnic-national communities, with all that this implies—mutual hostility, terrorism and oppressive steps to counteract it, and the use of coercive state powers to control the minority population.[2]

Not all the transformations that have taken place in Israel have stemmed from such drastic turning points as wars. The cohesion of Israeli society has also been influenced by the need to maintain a balance between the requirements of security, immigrant absorption and economic development, the amount of resources available for collective needs and the ability to utilize them. The extent to which resources are utilized is influenced by the mobilizing capacity of the collectivity, whether by coercive means, which are naturally limited in a democratic regime, or by appealing to the commitment of groups and individuals to the collectivity. In this respect, the mobilizing capacity of the system based on commitment has weakened considerably, at least in comparison to the voluntary mobilization patterns common in the Yishuv. The center no longer represents a coalition of secondary centers comprising organized political movements. These movements took part in building the institutions of the Organized Yishuv and were thus usually readily available for mobilization. The government of the new state replaced this approach by reliance on state authority proclaiming that it was responsible for all citizens. The population within Israel's borders now included the Arab minority, peripheral groups that had been outside or on the fringe of the Organized Yishuv, and the newcomers who arrived in the mass immigration of the 1950s. These immigrants were alien to the political culture of the veteran establishment and thus less responsive to mobilization by the means of association with the voluntary frameworks of the period of the Yishuv. Nevertheless, the political stability of the system was not impaired. Stability was preserved on the one hand, by extensive import of resources from abroad, used simultaneously for immigrant absorption, economic growth, and raising the standard of living; and by a partial adaptation of the system to the new conditions. This was accomplished by developing patterns of mobilization and allocation of resources based on the fact that the new peripheral groups were dependent on the bureaucracy and on a paternalistic approach adopted toward them by the center.

During the first stage of the transformation, two patterns of center-periphery relations operated simultaneously. Within what was known as the First Israel, the older norms of participation still held, but the center had to offer more tangible material rewards to maintain the same levels of participation. In any case, the same particularistic channels of access to the center still held for many individuals and groups. For the Second Israel, however, new rules of allocation and mobilization were applied. The dependence of the newcomers on the absorption frameworks became the dominant mode of political mobilization. In addition, the integration of the newcomers into national tasks, such as the settlement of border regions, was usually facilitated by their lack of resources which gave them no option but to go where the authorities sent them. This sort of participation required neither high motivation nor great rewards. Thus, the Second Israel was placed in a distinctly peripheral role: not much was expected of them, nor was much given to them, at least, compared to the benefits enjoyed by the First Israel. This does not mean that the establishment denied the periphery a minimal standard of living or essential services. These were furnished but at a lower standard than those that were available to the First Israel. Many of the newcomers found their only employment, at first, in public works projects and when they eventually joined the regular labor force, their opportunities were usually limited to low-status and low-paying jobs. Thus, a high correlation came to be established between the status of new immigrant and membership in a low socio-economic stratum, bereft of prestige or access to power.[3]

Ironically, many of these newcomers shunted into manual jobs or onto border settlements filled roles which were considered to be the embodiment of the "pioneering spirit" in the days of the Yishuv and which were, then, a source of widespread esteem. The immigrants did not derive any prestige or other special rewards from these roles because they had been recruited by bureaucratic instead of voluntary channels and because they lacked the commitment to the values or ideologies of the pioneering political movements. The patterns of absorption in the early 1950s which practically guaranteed that most immigrants would receive housing, education, and jobs of a "peripheral" nature were, in a large measure, a reflection of the meager resources at the center's disposal. The authorities faced the dilemma of providing rapid absorption for many immigrants at a low standard, or working at a slower pace, offering higher standards for a few—and chose the former. While the process of mass absorption of immigrants in the 1950s was impressive in both its pace and dimensions, it nevertheless left painful scars that continued to be felt in the social and political spheres.

Social problems were aggravated by the impact of the process of immigrant absorption on the social cleavage structure. A partial correspondence emerged between the class cleavage and the ethnic cleavage, and between this combination and the division between oldtimers and newcomers. The overlap between the class cleavage, which pertains to the stratification structure, and the ethnic cleavage which, among other things, determines the central or peripheral qualities attributed to various groups of origin, aggravated the tensions stemming from the absorption process. These tensions had social and political manifestations. The social tensions appeared sporadically with long periods of dormancy punctuated by outbursts such as the protests of Waddi Salib in 1959, the Black Panthers in the early 1970s, and the election disturbances of 1981. The electoral expression of the ethnic division was more persistent than the extra-parliamentay protests, gradually producing an ethnic polarization. This did not take the form of a massive shift to ethnic parties, but rather in a tendency for immigrants of North Africa and Middle Eastern origin to vote for the Likud and the parties akin to it and for Ashkenazim to vote for the Alignment and its satellite parties. This type of voting pattern implies that the correlation between ethnic origin and political preference did not usually reflect a trend to ethnic separatism, but rather a desire for integration that was not being fulfilled quickly enough. In other words, the imbalance between the slow progress of social mobility in the stratification sphere and the aspirations for improving a group's collective position on the center-periphery axis in the political sphere were expressed by transferring support from the political parties of the establishment to those perceived as anti-establishment. At any rate, the feeling of being shunted to the periphery, the outbursts of protest, and the shifts in political affiliation led to a decrease in social commitment for collective tasks, except during wartime.[4]

Not all of the changes in the attitudes to the national center are the result of developments stemming from the mass immigration of the 1950s. A decrease in social commitment was also quite apparent among the veteran population, including the elites among this group, some of whom found it difficult to adjust to the social and institutional changes that occurred following the establishment of the state. The problems of adapting patterns of govenment to the needs of a sovereign state whose authority does not rest on the voluntary commitment of the population was expressed in the controversy over the concept of statism. The most forceful proponent of the statist approach to public affairs was David Ben-Gurion, who sought to reduce the autonomy of the movement fiefdoms that performed quasi-governmental functions during the Yishuv. The disbanding of the dissident military undergrounds, the creation of a state school system, and the first steps taken toward depoliticizing of the civil service embodied the new statist political norms that Ben-Gurion sought to introduce. On the other hand, the continued existence of the health services affiliated to political movements, the preservation of the Religious Zionist school system as a part of the state network, the state support to the independent schools of Agudat Israel, the imposition of military government on most of the Arabs, and most of all, the primacy accorded to the interests of the political establishment over the rights of the individual—all these reflected the perpetuation of the particularistic traditions of the pre-state days that often conflicted with the principle of equality before the law.[5]

The problems of adaptation to the conditions of a sovereign state were exacerbated by the results of the Six Day War in 1967. While still heavily involved in shaping a new society out of the masses of immigrants and building new institutions, Israel was forced to deal with new problems stemming from the reappearance of the intercommunal conflict between Jews and Arabs that had largely disappeared with the establishment of the state. While the War of

Independence converted the struggle for supremacy in Palestine from a communal to an international conflict, the Six Day War partially reintroduced the communal dimensions.[6] When the military government over the Arabs of Israel was abolished in 1966, it appeared as if the legacy of the communal conflict between Arabs and Jews would no longer trouble Israel's political and security establishment. However, less than a year later, Israel found itself drawn into a new version of the Jewish-Arab conflict unfolding within a single political-territorial unit, the ideological, social, and political implications of which were far greater than those connected to the status of Israel's Arabs after 1948. On the ideological plane, the operative consensus on the territorial limits of Zionist aspirations, which had been tacitly established after 1948, now broke down, since it was never grounded in a consensus on the fundamental level. When the political controversy over the partition of Palestine resumed after the 1967 war, an ideological clash emerged between the positions calling for the incorporation of the territories captured into Greater Israel on the one hand and on the other for a territorial compromise aimed at preserving the "democratic, Jewish" character of the state. Each of the political positions to emerge from this controversy—annexation of the territories, giving up all or part of the territories, functional compromise, expelling the Arabs, or maintaining the status quo—had different implications for the boundaries of the collectivity and the nature of its identity. The renewed debate of these issues brought the ideological polarization on the fundamental level out into the open. This, in turn, undermined the delicate pragmatic modus vivendi which had enabled Arabs and Jews, the secular and the religious, and ideological diehards of various stripes to co-exist fairly peacefully within one system. The polarization worsened after the Yom Kippur War of 1973 in the wake of the international peace initiatives stimulated by that conflict. It became progressively more difficult to maintain political stability in Israel because of a growing fundamental ideological militancy and to the weakening of political and strategic posture which prevailed from 1967 to late 1973.[7]

On the social plane, a profound change swept over the labor market as tens of thousands of workers from the occupied territories took over many of the low-status, low-paying jobs in Israel's economy. On the political level, a governmental dualism set in where one population was governed by one set of norms, and the other population by another set. The territory under Israeli sovereignty was governed by the law and administration of a democratic state, while the occupied territories were ruled by a military government that left its subjects without political rights. Finally, in the security sphere, new problems of current security arose of protecting the daily life of civilians from terrorist attacks or other outbreaks of violence. For the second time in thirty years, Israel was forced to deal with changing norms and institutions stimulated by external historical events.

Besides these problems of adaptation arising from changing historical events, other problems emerged as a result of more gradual social changes. However, these social changes, too, occurred with greater intensity than similar processes in societies less preoccupied with collective tasks. The need to make adjustments to rapidly changing historical circumstances hampered Israeli institutions by inducing two kinds of functional incompatibility: between sub-systems and the comprehensive societal system, and between various sub-systems. An example of the first kind of functional incompatibility is provided by the practice of deficit budgeting to raise the standard of living which, in terms of societal needs, made it more difficult to attain the goal of economic solvency. Likewise, social welfare policy sought to improve the quality of life, but thereby reduced the amount of resources available for stimulating economic growth. Another contradiction appeared in the sphere of education and culture. Here a marked dissonance emerged between the goal of integrating the newcomers into a unitary cultural system over the years, and pluralistic trends which accepted the autonomy of subcultures, based for the most part, on ethnic background, in order to mitigate short-term social tensions.

Functional incompatibilities of the second type, between various sub-systems, are more numerous and include those of a fundamental nature as well as those of mainly operative-technical significance. A fundamental contradiction appears in the disparity between the Jewish-Zionist identity of the State of Israel and its civil-democratic nature. A less critical example are the functional contradictions between social justice and economic considerations in the shaping of economic policy. The use of wage incentives to increase output does not always square with the declared aim of reducing income gaps between groups. The incompatibilities between sub-systems are sometimes expressed as conflicts between groups representing different interests, such as producers vs. consumers, periphery vs. center, employers vs. employees, and bureaucracy vs. its constituents.

Conflict Regulation in an Overburdened System

A major share of the functional problems of the political system can be explained by the marked imbalance between the level of resources at the system's disposal and the large number of specific goals imposed on it. Specifically, the concept of an overburdened system refers to the imbalance created when the system's capacity to mobilize instrumental resources and normative commitments lags behind the concrete demands placed on the political center. This condition makes it difficult to deal simultaneously with a wide range of goals and needs on which there is a broad consensus. Moshe Dayan referred to this problem in the early 1970s as the difficulty of raising two banners at once, the "banner of security" and the "banner of social welfare."

Many of the major problems of Israel society are related to the overburdened nature of the system. In the economic sphere, inflation and the balance of payments deficit reflect the failure to balance demands to raise living standards and social welfare benefits, provide adequate defense and promote economic growth with the resources at the disposal of the system. In the area of security, the strain on the country's resources is expressed in the high cost in life and money exacted by successive wars, and in the extensive periods of military reserve duty, particularly during wartime and the periods of increased tensions thereafter. In the political sphere, the "ungovernable" tendencies of the system reflect its overburdened condition which stem from its inability to meet contradictory political demands rooted in opposing fundamental ideological positions. This is reflected for example in failures to cope with the challenges to state authority posed by Jewish settlers in the occupied territories. Opposing demands, even ideological ones, are not in themselves an indication of an overburdened condition as long as the political regulatory mechanisms can deal with them through bargaining and compromise or by means of majority vote. These mechanisms, however, are stymied by political polarization on the fundamental level, in which groups are not prepared to accept the decision of established political institutions. In such a situation, regulatory mechanisms cannot deal effectively with cross-pressures. The absence of consensus thus means that unresolved political conflicts accumulate, thus increasing the burden on the system. Another source of political overburdening stems from the appearance of new issues requiring national attention that cannot be dealt with on the basis of the center's past experience. In the social sphere, overburdening appears in the attempts of the system to reduce socio-cultural gaps between groups. A constant dilemma here has been whether to concentrate resources on those who are most able to make the best use of them, or to spread them more widely and thinly to provide small improvements for a larger number. Since formal equality in resource allocation often works against the disadvantaged, reducing social gaps may require proportionately larger investments among society's weakest elements. This, however, means denying certain opportunities to groups with elite potential whose achievements, in many ways, determine the quality of life in society as a whole. These issues, which are related to resource allocation and distributive justice, usually arise in connection with social cleavage divisions.

The crystallization of Israeli society into a cohesive social and political system has involved dealing with tensions and conflicts emanating from social cleavage divisions. As in other societies, the relation between the cleavages and the overall social structure can be delineated and analyzed in terms of a group's respective positions on the status hierarchy and on the center-periphery axis. In mapping a group's overall social position in terms of these two coordinates, we should take into account that they are not completely independent, and that a group's position on the center-periphery axis may be influenced by its position in the stratification structure, and vice versa. However, a group's social position is not determined solely by this factor since the nature of the relationship between the status hierarchy and the center-periphery axis varies between one type of society and another. In pre-modern societies, in which there is little differentiation between property, political power, and social status, the overlap between these two dimensions does not in itself serve as a source of social instability. The stability of such societies is undermined, among other things, by a change in one of the dimensions, as when a new status group emerges which lacks political power. In contrast, in a society such as Israel's, in which there is considerable differentiation between political power, property, and status, the existence of a group's consciousness of its deprived position in both dimensions can generate more intense social protest than if the deprivation were to exist in only one dimension. For that reason, alleviating feelings of deprivation in one dimension, for example, by enhancing a group's centrality in society, can compensate groups at the bottom of the status hierarchy for their persistent social distress. In the modern socio-political lexicon, this phenomenon is known as populism, a phenomenon which characterized Israeli society while the Likud was in power. During this period, there was no change in the stratification structure, but the Afro-Asians' feeling of centrality in society did improve. The stratification gap between the Afro-Asians and the Ashkenazim was not reduced, but the former were compensated for this by the feeling of power that they derived from their political identification with the Likud.[8]

The drive to dominate the political center is not the only possible response from social groups in a peripheral position. To the extent that these groups were alienated from the dominant values of Israeli society, without there being any chance of their values taking over and becoming dominant, they tended to withdraw from society at large and create enclaves where their own culture would reign supreme. Such segregation could be voluntary, as in the case of the ultra-Orthodox during the period of the Yishuv or later, in the state, or it could occur as in the case of the Arab population because a group's ethnic-national identity closed off the option of full integration in society. Although groups such as the ultra-Orthodox would occasionally express a total rejection of society's dominant values, they had limited impact on the intensification of political conflicts. This was because their ideological positions were not usually translated into political action. The segregation practiced by or imposed on these he other groups. This happened with the ultra-Orthodox community as portions of it increased their involvement in political affairs with the aim of putting their stamp on the general culture and way of life. Expressions of protest also increased among Israeli Arabs following the abolition of the military government in 1966 and the end of the ghetto-like conditions imposed on them. Along with the centripetal forces that brought groups in the periphery closer to the political center, centrifugal forces generated by the various social cleavages were also at work. Moreover, there are indications that conflicts based on some of the cleavages have intensified, thus putting an additional burden on the conflict-regulating mechanisms. The experience of Israel has borne out some basic propositions concerning the intensity of social conflicts and the possibility of bridging the social differences from which these conflicts stem. The experience of Israeli society has indicated that social class cleavages are easier to regulate through bargaining and compromise over the allocation of resources, compared to primordial cleavages rooted in different conceptions of collective identity and different belief systems.[9]

Thus, dealing with the national cleavage dividing Jews and Arabs, which is also a religious and linguistic cleavate, is a most difficult task. Nevertheless, certain regulatory mechanisms were applied in order to cope this cleavage, too. The most prominent mechanism is the legitimacy accorded to ecological and cultural separation on the part of Israel's Arab population.[10] This has created a cultural and social enclave for the Arab population where it can cultivate some of its collective symbols, especially its linguistic autonomy. In addition, the universal

p in the Israeli policy have partially compensated ir peripheral position from an ethnic-national per- over, Israeli Arabs themselves tend to stress univer- ples, especially when seeking judicial remedies to certain r rough the High Court of Justice, which is expected to safe equality before the law. These mechanisms are effective with Israeli Arabs. With regard to the Arabs in the occupied territories, the tension inherent in the national cleavage is exacerbated by the lack of civil rights for this population and by uncertainty concerning the future disposition of the territories. Furthermore, because the confrontation with the Arabs of the territories has also influenced Arab-Jewish relations in Israel proper, the national cleavage has, since 1967, become more difficult to regulate and moderate in practically any context.

The cleavage between the religious and the secular sectors is rooted in beliefs of primordial origin. This primordial distinction, however, applies more to differences between Jews and non-Jews, while the distinction between secular and religious Jews is not usually charged with primordial sentiments since, according to the Halacha, a Jew is still a Jew, even if he has strayed from the faith. The main issue dividing religious and secular Jews concerns the relation between the authority of the state vs. the authority of the Halacha. From the secular viewpoint, this dispute is seen as ideological in nature, while the religious see it as a matter of faith that cannot be compromised. This difference in the basic perception of the nature of the conflict by both parties to it is a factor in intensifying the secular-religious conflict and encumbering its regulation. Actually, this conflict was regulated, to an extent, through pragmatic, ad hoc arrangements that circumvented the problem of authority and deferring confrontation to an indeterminate future date. However, such pragmatic arrangements proved to be vulnerable to social changes that created situations that could not be dealt with by the original solution. As a result, the polarization between the religious and secular intensified, thus weakening the position of moderate forces in both camps attempting to bridge the differences.[11]

The conflicts stemming from the ethnic cleavage have appeared sporadically over the years in varying degrees of intensity, but significant enclaves of ethnic subcultures have not emerged. During the early years of the state, the political establishment tended to ignore the problems stemming from ethnic differences but a different approach was later adopted. This approach was based on the assumption that, in order to reach a state of full integration—embodied in the concept of the ingathering of the exiles—policies in the political, educational, and social spheres had to take into account the distinct characteristics of ethnic groups. These characteristics included specific cultural patterns that could be woven into the common cultural fabric without changing its basic modernizing orientation; and cultural and social handicaps, including demographic characteristics such as large family size, that could be overcome by various compensatory mechanisms. This change in approach stimulated more sophisticated strategies for regulating the ethnic conflict but did not resolve the basic problem of the considerable overlap between geographic-cultural origin and social class that continued to generate ethnic tensions.[12]

The social class cleavage that became less polarized over the years, mainly as a result of economic growth which stimulated greater upward mobility and created a multi-tiered stratification structure with most of the population, concentrated in the middle status and income levels. As a result, the conflicts stemming from the social class cleavage became less intense. Unlike some of the social conflicts, ideological conflicts has become more salient in the seventies and eighties, the fundamental ideological cleavage concerning Israeli identity and the territorial boundaries of Eretz Israel became more polarized after the 1967 war. This war raised fundamental issues that had previously been circumvented or postponed which made it easier to regulate these conflicts. These conflicts stemmed from the opposition between a humanistic approach that perceived the state in civic terms, and the ethnocentric approach that defined the state as primarily an ethnic-national entity. The tensions generated by social and ideological cleavages pushed the political center more deeply into an overburdened condition.[13]

Israeli society's ability to cope with its overburdened condition, to a large extent, determined its ability to realize its collective ideological aspirations. Such collective goals can be attained either through the availability of vast resources or through a high level of commitment, with people willing to defer gratification of individual needs and demands. If the supply of resources is limited or if a low level of social commitment blocks belt-tightening efforts, then the realization of collective goals will be hampered in both scope and thoroughness. It should be noted, however, that the objective gap between the scope of demands and the supply of resources does not, by itself, determine the functional capacity of the center; there also has to be a degree of awareness of such a gap. For example, low levels of expectations from the center tend to reduce the pressure on it. It is also known that deprived groups tend to articulate and press their demands only when their situation begins to improve. The immigrants of the 1950s, for example, had a much higher threshold of suffering while languishing in the tent camps and shanty towns of that time, than both they and their children showed in the period of relative prosperity in the late 1960s and 1970s. The threshold of the veterans also dropped relative to the period of the Yishuv and even to the years of austerity in the early 1950s.

Israel's sensitivity to casualties in its wars provides another example. In the 1948 War of Independence, Israel lost about one percent of its population without this undermining national morale while during the Yom Kippur War of 1973, the level of casualties became a major source of dissatisfaction despite the fact that they comprised only about .01 percent of the population. In the Lebanon War, when the concensus on the need to fight was much less firm compared with the other wars, a level of casualties at one-fifth the 1973 level stimulated serious controversy.[14] Another example of the role of subjective attitudes in determining the level of pressure on the center is to be found in processes of political exchange according to which parties are willing to trade concessions in areas of peripheral importance to them in return for gains in areas of more central concern. In such cases, despite the fact that the supply of resources available for distribution is objectively limited, both sides to the deal are satisfied because they have gained in areas of greater subjective utility in return for concessions in areas of lesser subjective utility. Such an exchange relationship bound Mapai (later Labor) with the religious Zionist Mizrahi Party from the mid-1930s to the mid-1970s. Mapai yielded to the Mizrahi (later the National Religious Party) on issues concerning religion and state in return for support on its positions on social and foreign policy issues. This "historic partnership," as it was called, broke up once Labor had lost its dominant position, while in the Religious Zionist camp, a tendency emerged to broaden the range of issues on which the party formulated distinct ideological positions, especially with regard to the future of the occupied territories. Broadening the range of issues on which the NRP presented political demands purportedly grounded in the Halacha thus reduced the room for bargaining between the two parties since the number of issues on which the religious parties were ready to compromise declined.[15]

This overburdening, which has both impaired Israel's ability to fully carry out the collective tasks it set for itself and limited the center's ability to respond fully to the demands of the periphery, has not threatened the basic stability of the political system. Stability has been maintained because of several major factors that have compensated for the system's overburdened condition. The most important of these have been the funds donated by world Jewry or provided as grants from the United States or as reparations payments from West Germany. These resources have enabled Israel to work toward the achievement of most of its collective goals while simultaneously raising the standard of living. In other words, the importation of capital has made it possible for the center to distribute resources over and above those extracted from the population. The inflow of resources has also shaped the subjective perceptions of political actors. An expansionist as opposed to a restrictive orientation has tended to prevail, political actors being aware that some group demands can be met without taking resources away from others, and certain obligations can be undertaken simultaneously. Thus, despite the fact that the supply of resources has been limited in relation to demands, the struggle over distribution has not been conducted in the pressured atmosphere of a zero sum game. Moreover, various indexing arrangements for salaries and savings have neutralized most of the social impact of inflation and have prevented the sharp fluctuations in income distribution that often accompany it.

In addition to the resource mobilization measures that have mitigated pressures on the center, overburdening has also been reduced by political mechanisms. For example, some of the pressure originating in the drive for the resolution of fundamental ideological conflicts has been deflected by a pragmatic approach offering solutions in ambiguous formulations, political inconsistencies, and avoiding decisions on controversial issues. The decision in the early 1950s not to adopt a full-fledged constitution is a primary example of this approach which, in this case, sought to avoid a confrontation over the overall status of religious law in Israel. The tendency to seek flexible solutions to problems reflects the incremental approach to problem-solving that guided the gradualist nation-building strategy of the ruling Labor movement elite both before and after the establishment of the state.

The Weakening of Social Cohesion

The supply of resources available to the center in later years was certainly greater than during the period of the Yishuv or the early years of the state due to extensive American aid and the resources provided by economic growth in Israel itself.[16] Nevertheless, the awareness of being overburdened became stronger in later years, due mainly to the erosion of society's willingness to sacrifice for collective goals except in periods of acute national emergency.

The drop in level of commitment can be viewed from the perspective of social integration and disintegration. From this perspective, we may conclude that there has been a decline in the level of social cohesion. This has occurred despite the increase in attachment to the center on the part of peripheral groups with a history of separatism. This centripetal process includes the ultra-Orthodox Agudat Israel, the Communists and, to a certain extent, parts of the Arab population.

This centripetal process did not make a significant contribution to political integration because it was manifested mainly on the instrumental plane as a means to obtain greater material resources from the center and did not involve any significant increase in these groups unconditional normative commitment to the collective. Indeed, the expectation of material rewards from the center had been one of the main factors motivating groups to participate in the Organized Yishuv during the pre-state period. However, after 1948, peripheral groups who adopted similar attitude toward the state were not inclined to increase their involvement in normative terms as well, although such a shift was expected of them by the political establishment. The trend of increasing pressure on the center for material rewards without a corresponding willingness to contribute to the attainment of collective goals has become more prevalent, thus considerably undermining social solidarity. Nevertheless, it should be noted that the overall willingness to serve national goals has been and still is higher in Israel than in most other democratic societies. The Israeli public is subjected to a tax burden that has few peers or precedents. Even more striking is the readiness to accept compulsory military service and subsequent reserve duty that keep men in uniform for a longer period than in any other democratic country. Many recruits volunteer for elite combat units that require greater effort and in some cases longer periods of service. Moreover, some political groups have increased their involvement in the center in both the instrumental and normative dimensions, the most prominent being the younger generation of the Religious Zionist sector, and especially its offshoots, Gush Emunim. On the other hand, with the transfer of power in the center in 1977 from the Labor Movement to the Likud, several movements that formerly held leading positions experienced a decline in their own self-perception of centrality. This applies mainly to the kibbutz movement which formerly regarded itself as a vanguard always ready to contribute in the collective effort. This change is, of course, related to a transformation in the ideological content of national goals as defined by the politically-dominant groups.

The transformations brought about by the establishment of the state have not only broadened the scope of communications between center and periphery, but have also changed the patterns of relations between the political establishment and the citizenry. During the period of the Yishuv and in the early years of the state, exchange relationships between the political center and its "clients" were mediated by parties and other organizations acting as sub-centers. The transfer of functions from these frameworks to the government, where access is based on universalistic principles, reduced the importance of the sub-centers controlled by political parties as mediating bodies. This development created conditions for direct contact between the citizens and the political establishment, but it also entailed the "atomization" of the citizenry and its conversion from an organized public into a mass. A public is characterized more by its reliance on institutional channels for routine political activity, while a mass is an amorphous body available for populistic mobilization and manipulation by charismatic leaders.[17]

Populistic political appeals have had a disintegrative impact by undermining the status of societal elites. This overall process has impinged negatively upon elites in two ways. Some of these elites filled positions in the mediating bodies which were superceded and made redundant by the state. In addition, the populistic mobilization tended to either disregard or ridicule certain components of elite status such as education and cultural accomplishments. Conditions are thus created where low-status groups play a central role in the political arena. This trend contributes in turn, to the alienation of elites still holding leading positions in the areas of public administration, higher education, and mass communication and to a consequent weakening of their motivation to take an active part in preserving and creating cultural traditions.[18] Populistic trends pose a threat to social solidarity in Israel because of the elitist nature of the dominant culture which is a reflection of the centrality of ideological creativity in the shaping of Israeli culture. Cultural creativity drew its inspiration to a greater extent from developments in the center than it did from folk traditions and popular culture in the periphery. Moreover, the periphery was much more fragmented than the center, a condition which increased with the mass immigration of the 1950s. The fragmentation of the periphery into subcultures followed the main lines of social cleavage:

nic, and religious. These subcultural divisions were largely ...criptive, whereas the realm of ideology shared by the elites were shaped by their own creative efforts. These elites interacted with broad ideologically-oriented constituencies that stood between center and periphery. This sector was composed of European-born veterans whose immigration had been ideologically motivated, together with the native-born of European background whose education was permeated by ideological themes. However, this sector was internally divided along political lines and the political struggles that occurred within it also weakened social cohesion especially in the period of the Yishuv when only part of the Jewish population was affiliated to the Organized Yishuv. In the early years of the state, ideological intensity waned and with it, the political tensions that it generated. Moreover, the group consciousness accompanying the various social cleavages was weakly articulated and not politically significant at that time.

The differences in ethnic background and social status between the immigrants of the 1950s and the veteran population were perceived as a temporary condition. Moreover, political mobilization seeking to exploit these differences was not a practical possibility because of the near total dependence of the immigrants on the public absorption frameworks. The secular-religious conflict was not a source of great tension because of the agreement within the ruling elites that a status quo in religious affairs should be maintained and to the decision to put off indefinitely the formulation of the constitution. The national cleavage between Jews and Arabs became dormant politically because of the "paralysis" that descended on Israeli Arabs resulting from their traumatic defeat in 1948 and the weakness of their political leadership.

All these conditions changed during the 1960s and 1970s, and the dormant conflicts of the 1950s gradually resurfaced. This was due to the emergence of a more militant leadership in the disadvantaged development towns and urban neighborhoods where most of the immigrants of the 1950s had been concentrated; to the appearance of a stratum of Arab intellectuals who began articulating an Arab political consciousness based on national lines; and to the emergence of new religious elites, particularly in the Religious Zionist sector that increased tensions over national issues with religious connotations. These developments led to the demise of the primacy of the old elites as a source of ideological and cultural inspiration. The capacity of the veteran elites for ideological and cultural innovation declined as they became increasingly preoccupied with immediate practical problems, while resorting to fundamental ideology mainly as a form of political ritual.

In addition to these trends, many of which stem from demographic changes, an increasing ideological polarization in the center occurred following the Six Day War. The locus of ideological creativity in the 1970s and 1980s shifted away from the groups that were dominant in the Yishuv and in the early years of the state. These groups, led by the Labor movement elite, kept their eyes focused on day-to-day problems while attempting to keep the political consensus intact. The spokesmen of the newer ideological militancy were groups that had been active in the past on the fringes of the political center and stemmed, for the most part, from the Religious Zionist sector and the radical nationalist right. The symbols these elites cultivated as a basis of their appeal were ethnocentric, contained a strong emphasis on historical rights to territory, and tended to demonize Israel's enemies and to cast their political rivals in the role of defeatists or worse. Two developments in the political sphere—the attempts to articulate group identities based on social cleavages and the renewed salience of ideological conflicts among the elites over issues of central national importance—gradually strengthened the right wing of Israel's party system which led to the political upheaval of 1977 that ended the long dominance of the Labor movement. Nevertheless, this shift did not lead to the rise of a new dominant elite since the array of political forces comprising the two large parties and their allies was more balanced than in the earlier periods of Labor dominance. The system soon became polarized between two large political camps of approximately equal strength, a trend reinforced by the 1984 and 1988 elections. Since neither large party was strong enough to form a ruling coalition of its own, they both had to settle for joint rule in a grand coalition called the National Unity Government.

The experience of the National Unity coalition demonstrated how weakened social and political cohesion can affect the performance of the government, thus raising the issue of the center's capacity to govern. On the one hand, this government was able to exercise its capacity to govern in those areas where it rested on a broad consensus: It brought a dangerous inflationary spiral to a halt and extricated Israel from the military-political morass of Lebanon. On the other hand, however, it slipped into a state of paralysis in the political-diplomatic sphere because of the mutual veto power held by each of the political-ideological blocs where disputes of a fundamental ideological nature were concerned.

Values and Institutional Dilemmas

Forty years after its establishment, Israel stands out as a success story where the overall performance of the national center is concerned, but it also appears as a case of failure and frustration when one examines the gap between aspirations and actual achievements. At any rate, looking at both the encouraging and the discouraging aspects of Israel's experience, it is clear that the latter have stood out more prominently the further Israel has traveled from what was initially perceived as the crowning point of its success story—the Six Day War. In historical perspective, the reversal of the success story image that began after the first two decades of statehood can be seen as the result of the inevitable gap between the ideological drive with its utopian overtones, and the imperfect and incomplete reality. This crisis of ideological vision exposed the lack of consensus concerning the substance of that vision beyond the basic element of the re-establishment of Jewish sovereignty in the Land of Israel. From one direction, the crisis created conditions for the rise of the adherents of the Messianic variant of the Zionist utopia, who, driven by their transcendent faith, sought to replace this-worldy criterion of action with divine imperatives. The rise of the Messianic strain of Zionism, which had a dominant influence on Gush Emunim, was accompanied by a religious interpretation of the Six Day War that saw it as the "beginning of Israel's redemption." The carriers of this ideological vision saw themselves as constrained by the Halacha to seek the realization of the ideal of Greater Israel as part of their three fundamental principles of the Jewish people, the Torah, and the Land of Israel. By doing this they put themselves outside the framework of the rules of the game of Israeli democracy which cannot accept the view that the fundamental question of determining Israel's borders cannot be resolved by decisions made by the secular political authorities.

From another direction, there was a growing sense of disillusionment among the adherents of the Zionist social utopia who had sought to create an exemplary society in Israel based on values of cooperation and equality. Since the socialist strain of Zionism adopted a constructivist and pragmatic approach, the test of concrete, practical achievement was central to its outlook and to its conception of the social order. Thus, once it became apparent that reality did not measure up to Zionist aspirations because of the drastic decline in aliyah and the slowdown in economic growth, and that socialist aspirations are in decline because of Israel's development as a Western consumer society, this strain of Zionism lost much of its destinctiveness. On the surface, it would seem that the only ideological current to benefit politically from these developments would be that represented by the Likud. This ideological current has attempted to blend "bourgeois" economic liberalism, which was the hallmark of the Liberal Party until the establishment of the Likud, with the radical nationalism and expansionist drive of Herut. However, this ideological grouping has also suffered from its internal contradictions. Tension was created between the liberal tradition upholding a free economy based on the profit motive, and the populistic strain in Herut that required state intervention in the economy to allocate the resources needed to meet the welfare demands of the lower socio-economic strata. This contradiction led the political carriers of this ideological blend to adopt an economic policy based on an illusion of prosperity created by exploiting the country's foreign currency resources that did not necessitate any change in the class structure. This led, in turn, to a severe economic crisis the symptoms of which were runaway inflation and a widening gap in the balance of payments. Furthermore, since this ideological approach had to devise some solution to what is known as the "demographic problem," the Likud grasped onto the prospect of a mass aliyah in the future that would somehow assure a firm Jewish majority in Greater Israel, without being able to point to any reasonable indication that this would indeed materialize.

The gap between utopian visions and mundane reality experienced by all of the main ideological currents contributed to the fading of Israel's image as a success story. This process had two aspects. First, the feeling of disappointment with Israeli society experienced primarily by the elites led to a slackening of their social and political activity. And the second, rifts appeared in the national consensus with regard to the central goals of the collectivity. The political system thus became increasingly polarized. The feelings of unease with the new realities of post-1967 Israel assumed different forms among different groups within the elite. On the one hand, new elites sprang up, mainly in the Religious Zionist camp, that moved from pragmatic realism to Messianic or quasi-Messianic idealism, and which sought to liberate collective action from the constraints of mundane limitations. On the other hand, the veteran elites that had dominated the system during Israel's first two decades lost their self-confidence and their sense of assuredness that Israeli society was developing in a direction that conformed with their most basic beliefs and values. A malaise set in among these elites and their social constituency. This was first reflected in the works of authors, poets, and playwriters of the generation that grew up with the state, and later, to an even greater extent, among the older cultural and political elites. These elites which had formed the cultural center during Israel's first decades, and who drew their inspiration from the legacy of the Yishuv, felt increasingly alienated from the prevailing currents of thought in the late 1970s and early 1980s. Their unease at these trends was reinforced by their resentment at having been displaced from prominence as a result of the political upheaval of 1977. They increasingly viewed their displacement as an act of collective ingratitude and saw the emerging combination of strident populism, militant nationalism, ethnocentric separatism, and religious fundamentalism as a threat to the basic values of Israeli society, if not to its very existence.[19]

These differences in the reactions of various elite groups to developments after 1967, and even more so after 1977, reflected the second aspect of the gap between utopian aspirations and reality. The controversies that arose in the wake of the crisis of national consensus—which went beyond disputes over means of implementation—revealed value dilemmas concerning the nature of Israeli society. These dilemmas could not be circumvented with interim or ad hoc solutions that had previously been tolerated by the proponents of the various ideologies.

Several such dilemmas became increasingly salient as Israel passed through the Six Day War, the Yom Kippur War, and the political upheaval of 1977. The first value dilemma pits an ethnocentric nationalism propped up by religious sentiments, antagonistic to the outside world and assertive of exclusive national rights, against a secular-humanist nationalist outlook rooted in a universal process of national self-determination. The latter is thus more receptive to the demands of other nations for recognition of their collective aspirations.[20]

The second dilemma derives to a considerable extent from the first, but the emphasis shifts from orientations to external groups to the problem of ethnic-national heterogeneity among the citizens of Israel. This dilemma pits a Jewish definition of Israel against a civil definition, which corresponds to the distinction sometimes made between Israel as a "Jewish state" or Israel as a "state of the Jews." Is the State of Israel indeed primarily a state belonging to the Jewish people, with non-Jews relagated to the status of second-class citizens; or is Israel a civil political entity with a Jewish majority, which, due to the state's

democratic nature, takes the lead in shaping the cultura
in accordance with its national aspirations? It is not easy to
distinctions between ideological groups based on their
regarding this dilemma. This is because the goal of maintaining J
political autonomy is shared by the Zionist ideological curre
accepted by most of the Jewish population. The adherents of the civil definition of statehood thus seek to overcome this dilemma by means of a geographical partition that would maintain the Jewish character of Israel by assuring Jewish demographic preponderance in the area remaining under Israeli sovereignty.[21]

The third value dilemma is between a collective sense of mission that subordinates the resources available in the present to future societal needs, and a normalizing trend that seeks to maximize the quality of life in the present without regard to collective goals of the future. In practice, this dilemma is not completely dichotomous, since the pragmatic constructivist approach is future-oriented to a certain extent, and in a gradual, incremental fashion has sought the golden mean between meeting the needs of the present and investing for the future. The constructivist approach therefore contains an active future-orientated element lacking in the normalizing approach. However, neither of these approaches has recourse to a transcendental source of legitimation that propels the Messianic strain among the radical mission-oriented groups.[22]

Subordination to a transcendental source of legitimation usually entails only conditional acceptance of democratic principles since such an approach demands a commitment to a source of authority that is absolute and unchallengeable. Such a commitment, thus, naturally supercedes any commitment to democratic rules of the game. Extreme mission-oriented approaches not rooted in religious beliefs may also encourage an absolute commitment to specific ideological goals that can occasionally override the authority of democratic rules of the game. Accordingly, the claim that the government of Israel has no authority to make a decision ceding part of Eretz Israel to another state has found support among the proponents of Greater Israel whose ideals are rooted in Halacha, and among the radical secular nationalists who share the same goals.[23]

The fourth value dilemma is between collectivism and individualism in relation to the confrontation between social mobilization for collective goals and the protection of individual rights and freedom of choice. This dilemma is connected to the one mentioned above in that a radical mission-oriented approach usually tends to resort to coercive means that constrain individual freedom of choice. The collectivist approach also tends to delegitimate individuals and groups whose preferences conflict with the goals derived from the essence of the collective identity which are thus perceived as absolute imperatives.

The fourth dilemma is related to the issues of civil rights and the rule of law as part of the democratic way of life.[24] This connection arises in the choices that must be made between compulsion, majority rule, and compromise in relations between the government and individuals and groups, and in inter-group relations. The choice here is not only between democracy and dictatorship, but also between a democratic "tyranny of the majority" and a democracy based on bargaining and compromise. Democracy based on a strict interpretation of majority rules does not usually recognize the autonomy of secondary centers, whether these are corporatist frameworks such as trade unions, communities based on national, ethnic, or religious membership, or ideological subcultures.

These value dilemmas reflect the various controversies dividing society. These controversies do not relate only to national policy decisions since there is also a reciprocal influence between these controversies and the patterns of performance of the Israeli government. In this context we may point to several institutional dilemmas reflecting contradictory trends in Israel's political and administrative culture. These contradictory trends developed as part of the tension between the administrative legacy of the period of the Yishuv and the requirements of statehood, further complicated by the emergence of an overburdened policy.

The first institutional dilemma—which is related to the value dilemmas of collectivism vs. individualism and mission orientation vs. pragmatism—places the desire for a high level of social mobilization over demands to give preference to the needs of the present over the needs of the future, and preference to individual and group interests over the interests of the collectivity. This dilemma is related to two of the most prominent factors contributing to the overburdened condition of the Israeli government. The first factor is the decline in the level of commitment of groups and individuals to the collectivity which hampers voluntary political mobilization; the second factor is the competition between the parties in promising benefits to their supporters, which usually reaches a frenzied level during general election campaigns.[25]

The second institutional dilemma is between centralization and decentralization. This dilemma concerns mainly organizational issues but is, nevertheless, indirectly connected to the value dilemmas of collectivism vs. individualism and mission orientation vs. pragmatism. A centralized form of government is generally considered more effective for the implementation of collective goals. However, the liberal school of economics holds that even where collective goals are concerned, too much centralization gives rise to bureaucratic role expansion and waste of resources.

The third institutional dilemma is the most important because it relates to the question of distributive justice. This dilemma appears on the abstract level as the choice between universalism based on general normative principles and particularism based, in its most extreme form, on decisions made ad hoc and ad hominem. On the operative level, this dilemma affects the degree of flexibility in the system. A particularistic system is of course more flexible than one based on universalism because allows for improvised responses to a wide variety of problems and phenomena. A universalistic system, however, provides greater accountability and is less vulnerable to arbitrariness and corruption. The institutional dilemma is indirectly related to the value dilemma between the conception of Israel as a civil as opposed to a Jewish entity since the application of universal rules to all citizens would not leave room for legal discrimination on as ethnic-national bases.

The choices posed by these institutional dilemmas stood out clearly during the early period of the state while its patterns of institutional functioning were being shaped. The organizational and political culture that emerged over the years eventually reduced the sharpness of the conflicts stemming from these dilemmas. This is not true, however, of the value dilemmas. The wars of 1967, 1973, and 1982, together with the political upheaval of 1977, intensified the conflicts stemming from the positions taken by those on the opposite sides of the value dilemmas. The regulation mechanisms that had previously avoided dealing with the roots of conflicts—such as ad hoc decisions that avoided long-term policy commitments ("pragmatic incrementalism") and vague formulations that permitted cooperation between adherents of opposing ideological views ("constructive ambiguity")[26] —were no longer effective for resolving explicit differences on the fundamental level. As a result, radical fundamentalist outlook gained ascendancy and led to ideological and political polarization that undermined the national consensus.

The value and institutional dilemmas confronting Israeli society and its elites are not confined to the realm of abstractions. These dilemmas relate to central—and very real—political issues and are

eans of the various positions taken in the contro-
-Jewish relations, religion and state, and social justice
In the sphere of Arab-Jewish relations, the major
cerns the future status of the two national groups in
the territory under Israeli control. There are four ways in which the relations between the two groups can be resolved: by living separately alongside one another, which should require a repartition of Eretz Israel; by one side dominating the other, which would mean continuing the Jewish-controlled status quo in the occupied territories or annexation without extending political rights to the Arabs; by one replacing the other, which would mean the expulsion of the Arabs from the territories; or both living together in a binational state and society with full political rights granted to the Arabs. The choice made among these political alternatives will determine the future shape of Israel's system. Will it be a democratic Jewish entity approximating the model of a nation-state; a binational democratic state; a non-democratic Jewish state in terms of political participation, but a binational state in terms of the composition of its population; or a state that has been "cleansed" of Arabs but lack any internal or international legitimacy?

In the sphere of relations between religion and state, the main question is whether the theocratic tendency contained in the lack of separation between religion and state will be ascendant; or whether a secular, pluralistic system will be established that allows the secular population to be free of religious coercion, and assures legal equality not only for all religions, but also for all streams within Judaism. In the Socio-economic sphere, there are two main questions: Will the tripartite nature of the economy, with its attendant corporatist structures, be preserved as the basis for ecomenic policy-making? Will the mechanisms of Israel's welfare state be expanded or reduced? With regard to the political regime, the questions are whether Israeli democracy can deal with the challenge posed by the conditional acceptance of democracy by fundamentalist ideological groups; and whether freedom of expression and association and the legal mechanisms protecting the individual from the arbitrary exercises of power will be preserved.

The common denominator to the questions in all four of these areas is whether the status quo in each area which, in any case, rests partially on inertia, will continue to exist, or whether emerging trends and forces will bring new patterns into being. The status quo in each area is reflected in the following patterns: Jewish domination of Arabs in the sphere of ethnic-national relations; lack of separation of religion and state, albeit without an official state religion; a multi-sector corporatist economy co-existing with a welfare state; and unconditional acceptance of democracy within the sphere of Israeli sovereignty, but not within the areas under Israel's control beyond its sovereign borders. In all these spheres, most political initiatives during the 1980s have emerged mainly from the right wing of the political spectrum. These pressures have been reflected in demands to annex the occupied territories without granting political rights to the Arabs, or even in demands to expel the Arabs; in a willingness to make legal and political concessions to the organized ultra-Orthodox community; in a tendency to reduce the resources allocated for social welfare; and in a greater intolerance of differing views on Arab-Jewish relations and on the fundamental controversy over the territorial boundaries of Zionist aspirations. These trends have been perceived as negative and disturbing mainly by the elites on the center and the left-wing of the political spectrum. But these elites failed to agree on their own alternative to the status quo, let alone to articulate it.

The unease felt by these elites, together with the shattered national consensus, have resulted in a change in how Israel is perceived both by its own citizens and by other nations. There has been a tendency to retreat from the pretentious goal of being a "light unto the nations," but the problems generated by the overburdened policy—stemming from the tensions and gaps between ideal and reality—have not enabled Israel to withdraw into routine concerns of a Jewish, democratic nation-state attempting to live a "normal" collective existence. In light of the weakening of the resolve to pursue the ambitious goals that guided Israel in its earlier years, the question must be asked whether Israel has become a flawed utopia that has reached a cul de sac, trapped by contradictions that cannot be resolved; or whether it is an innovative social, cultural, and political enterprise that is still in the process of developing? Any answer to this value-laden question must itself reflect certain value preferences. One can attempt to answer it by extrapolating existing trends. But such an answer, especially in a country subject to so many external influences, is liable to miss the mark. It thus seems that social scientists should avoid making the transition from analyzing the past and present to forecasting the future. This latter task is better left to prophets, utopian ideologists, and aspiring politicians.

Appendixes

1. Results of Elections to the Knesset by Main Lists, 1949-1984
2. Knesset Members by Main Lists, 1949-1984
3. Legend to Appendixes 1 and 2
4. Results of Elections to the Histadrut Conventions (Main Lists)

Appendix 1
Results of Elections to the Knesset by Main Lists, 1949-1984

	KNESSET										
	XI 7/23/84	X 6/30/81	IX 5/17/77	VIII 12/31/73	VII 10/28/69	VI 11/2/65	V 8/15/61	IV 11/3/59	III 7/26/55	II 7/30/51	I 1/21/49
Eligible Voters (Absolute Numbers)											
	2,654,613	2,490,014	2,236,293	2,037,478	1,748,710	1,499,709	1,271,285	1,218,483	1,057,795	924,885	506,567
Voted	2,091,402	1,954,609	1,771,726	1,601,098	1,427,981	1,244,706	1,037,030	994,306	876,085	695,007	440,095
Percent voters	78.8	78.5	79.2	78.6	81.7	83.0	81.6	81.6	82.8	75.1	86.9
Valid votes— Total	2,073,321	1,937,366	1,747,820	1,566,855	1,367,743	1,206,728	1,006,964	969,337	853,219	687,492	434,684
List Symbol*											
AMT	724,074	708,536	430,023	621,183	632,035	—	—	—	—	—	—
AT	—	—	—	—	—	443,379	—	—	—	—	—
KA	—	—	—	—	—	95,323	—	—	—	—	—
M	—	—	—	—	—	—	79,985	75,654	62,469	(a)86,401	(a)64,018
A	—	—	—	—	—	—	349,330	370,585	274,735	256,456	155,274
TW	—	—	—	—	—	—	66,170	58,043	69,475	(a) —	(a) —
Minorities' lists connected with Alignment[b]	—	—	(c)24,185	48,961	47,989	45,430	35,376	37,722	37,777	32,228	13,413
B	73,530	95,232	160,787	130,349	133,238	107,966	98,786	95,581	77,936	(d)56,730	(e)52,982
G	36,079	73,312	58,652		44,002	39,795	37,178			13,799	
				60,012				45,569	39,836		
D	—	17,090	23,571		24,968	22,066	19,428			11,194	—
NJ	31,103	44,466	—	—	—	—	—	—	—	—	—
SHAS	63,605	—	—	—	—	—	—	—	—	—	—
AD	33,287	—	—	—	—	—	—	—	—	—	—
HN	54,747	29,837	—	—	—	—	—	—	—	—	—
JB (Dash)	—	—	202,265	—	—	—	—	—	—	—	—
T (Yahad)	46,302	—	—	—	—	—	—	—	—	—	—

T (Free Center)	—	—	—	16,393	—	—	—	—	—	—	—
MHL[f]	661,302	718,941	583,968	—	—	—	—	—	—	—	—
TH	83,037	44,700	—	—	—	—	—	—	—	—	—
JS (Ometz)	23,845	—	—	—	—	—	—	—	—	—	—
TLM	—	30,600	—	—	—	—	—	—	—	—	—
KN	—	—	33,947	—	—	—	—	—	—	—	—
HLTAM[f]	—	—	—473,309	—	—	—	—	—	—	—	
HL	—	—	—	—	296,294	256,957	—	—	—	—	—
AM	—	—	—	—	42,654	—	—	—	—	—	—
H	—	—	—	—	—	—	138,599	130,515	107,190	45,651	49,782
L[g]	—	—	—	—	—	—	[h]137,255	59,700	87,099	111,394	22,661
LA[i]	—	11,764	20,384	56,560	43,933	45,299 [h]	—	44,889	37,661	22,171	17,786
RZ	49,698	27,921	20,621	35,023	—	—	—	—	—	—	—
S-Shelli	—	8,691	27,281	—	—	—	—	—	—	—	—
KN	—	—	—	22,147	—	—	—	—	—	—	—
K	—	—	—	—	15,712	13,617	42,111	27,374	38,492	27,334	15,148
S (Haolam Haze)	—	—	—	10,469	16,853	14,124	—	—	—	—	—
P	38,012	—	—	—	—	—	—	—	—	—	—
W[k]	69,815	64,918	80,118	53,353	38,827	27,413	—	—	—	—	—
Other Minorities' lists	—	22,490	6,780	3,269	—	—	3,896	8,469	4,484	—	—
PS	2,430	10,823	35,049	—	—	—	—	—	—	—	—
Kach	25,907	5,128	4,396	—	—	—	—	—	—	—	—
Other lists	56,548	24,061	35,793	52,220	14,845	15,369	3,181	21,422	16,133	24,380	43,620
Percentages											
Valid Votes— Total	100.0	100.0	100.0	100.0	100.0	100.0	100.0	100.0	100.0	100.0	100.0
AMT	34.9	36.6	24.6	39.6	46.2	—	—	—	—	—	—
AT	—	—	—	—	—	36.7	—	—	—	—	—
KA	—	—	—	—	—	7.9	—	—	—	—	—

Appendix 1 (cont'd)
Results of Elections to the Knesset by Main Lists, 1949-1984

	KNESSET										
	XI 7/23/84	X 6/30/81	IX 5/17/77	VIII 12/31/73	VII 10/28/69	VI 11/2/65	V 8/15/61	IV 11/3/59	III 7/26/55	II 7/30/51	I 1/21/49
M	—	—	—	—	—	6.6	7.5	7.2	7.3	(a)12.5	a)00.0
A	—	—	—	—	—	—	34.7	38.2	32.2	37.3	00.0
TW	—	—	—	—	—	—	6.0	6.0	8.1	(a) —	(a) —
Minorities lists connected with											
Alignment[b]	—	—	(c)1.4	3.1	3.5	3.3	3.5	3.9	3.3	1.1	0.0
B	3.5	4.9	9.2	8.3	9.8	8.9	9.8	9.9	9.1	(d)8.3	0.0
G	1.7	3.7	3.4		3.2	3.3	3.7			2.0	0.0
				3.8				4.7	4.7		
D	—	0.9	1.3		1.8	1.8	1.9			1.6	0.0
NJ	1.5	2.3	—	—	—	—	—	—	—	—	—
Shas	3.1	—	—	—	—	—	—	—	—	—	—
AD	1.6	—	—	—	—	—	—	—	—	—	—
HN	2.6	1.5	—	—	—	—	—	—	—	—	—
JS (Dash)	—	—	11.6	—	—	—	—	—	—	—	—
T (Yahad)	2.2	—	—	—	—	—	—	—	—	—	—
T (Free Center)	—	—	—	—	1.2	—	—	—	—	—	—
MHL[f]	31.9	37.1	33.4	—	—	—	—	—	—	—	—
TH	4.0	2.3	—	—	—	—	—	—	—	—	—
JS (Ometz)	1.2	—	—	—	—	—	—	—	—	—	—
TLM	—	1.6	—	—	—	—	—	—	—	—	—
KN	—	—	1.9	—	—	—	—	—	—	—	—
HLTAM[f]	—	—	—	30.2	—	—	—	—	—	—	—
HL	—	—	—	—	21.7	21.3	—	—	—	—	—
AM	—	—	—	—	3.1	—	—	—	—	—	—
H	—	—	—	—	—	—	13.8	13.5	12.6	6.6	11.5

L[g]	—	—	—	—	—	—	[h]13.6	6.2	10.2	16.2	5.2
LA[i]	—	0.6	1.2	3.6	3.2	3.8	[h] —	4.6	4.4	3.2	4.1
RZ	2.4	1,4	1.2	2.2	—	—	—	—	—	—	—
S-Shelli[j]	—	0.4	1.6	—	—	—	—	—	—	—	—
KN	—	—	—	1.4	—	—	—	—	—	—	—
K	—	—	—	—	1.2	1.1	4.2	2.8	4.5	4.0	3.5
S (Haolam Haze)	—	—	—	0.7	1.2	1.2	—	—	—	—	—
P	1.8	—	—	—	—	—	—	—	—	—	—
W[k]	3.4	3.4	4.6	3.4	2.8	2.3	—	—	—	—	—
Other Minorities lists	—	1.1	0.4	0.2	0.0	0.5	0.4	0.8	1.6	3.6	—
FS	0.1	0.6	2.0	—	—	—	—	—	—	—	—
Kach	1.2	0.3	0.3	—	—	—	—	—	—	—	—
Other lists	2.7	1.6	2.2	3.3	1.1	1.3	0.3	2.2	1.9	3.6	10.1

(a) Achdut Ha'avodah (Unity of Labor) is included in United Workers' Party (MAPAM).
(b) Includes lists which had been connected with Labor parties prior to the establishment of Alignment.
(c) Name of lists United Arab List (IM) connected with the Alignment.
(d) Includes Misrahi and HaPoel HaMisrahi.
(e) United Religious Front.
(f) MHL includes: GAHAL and LAAM, Free Center, and State List.
(g) Until the fourth Knesset, the name of the list had been: General Zionists(Z).
(h) The Progressive Party is included in the Liberal Party (P).
(i) Until the fourth Knesset, the name of the list had been: Progressive Party. In the eleventh Knesset included in Alignment.
(j) Shelli includes Moqed (KW) and Haolam Haze (S).
(k) Until eighth Knesset, name: New Communist Party (RAKAH); from ninth: Democratic List for Peace and Equality (RAKAH), Blcak Panters and Jewish and Arab Circles.

Source: Central Bureau of Statistics, Results of Election to the Eleventh Knesset 7/23/84. Special Series No. 1975, Jerusalem, 19?????

Appendix 2
Knesset Members, by Main Lists, 1949-1984

	KNESSET										
	XI 8/23/84	X 6/30/81	IX 5/17/77	VIII 12/31/73	VII 10/28/69	VI 11/2/65	V 7/15/61	IV 11/3/59	III 7/26/55	II 7/30/51	I 1/21/49
Total	120	120	120	120	120	120	120	120	120	120	120
List Symbol											
AMT	44	47	32	51	56	—	—	—	—	—	—
AT	—	—	—	—	—	45	—	—	—	—	—
KA	—	—	—	—	—	10	—	—	—	—	—
M	—	—	—	—	—	8	9	9	9	(a)15	(a)19
A	—	—	—	—	—	—	42	47	40	45	46
TW	—	—	—	—	—	—	8	7	10	(a) —	(a) —
Minorities lists connected with											
Alignment[b]	—	—	(o)1	3	4	4	4	5	5	5	2
B	4	6	12	10	12	11	12	12	11	(d)10	—
G	2	4	4		4	4	4			3	(e)16
				5				6	6		
D	—	—	1		2	2	2			2	—
NJ	1	3	—	—	—	—	—	—	—	—	—
SHAS	4	—	—	—	—	—	—	—	—	—	—
AD	2	—	—	—	—	—	—	—	—	—	—
HN	3	2	—	—	—	—	—	—	—	—	—
JS (DASH)	—	—	15	—	—	—	—	—	—	—	—
T (Yahad)	3	—	—	—	—	—	—	—	—	—	—

T (Free Center)	—	—	—	—	2	—	—	—	—	—	—
MHL[f]	41	48	43	—	—	—	—	—	—	—	—
TH	5	3	—	—	—	—	—	—	—	—	—
JS (Ometz)	1	—	—	—	—	—	—	—	—	—	—
TLM	—	2	—	—	—	—	—	—	—	—	—
KN	—	—	2	—	—	—	—	—	—	—	—
HLTAM[f]	—	—	—	39	—	—	—	—	—	—	—
HL	—	—	—	—	26	26	—	—	—	—	—
AM	—	—	—	—	4	—	—	—	—	—	—
H	—	—	—	—	—	—	17	17	15	8	14
L[g]	—	—	—	—	—	—	[h]17	8	13	20	7
LA[i]	—	—	1	4	4	5	[h] —	6	5	4	5
RZ	3	1	1	3	—	—	—	—	—	—	—
S-Shelli[j]	—	—	2	—	—	—	—	—	—	—	—
KN	—	—	—	1	—	—	—	—	—	—	—
K	—	—	—	—	1	1	5	3	6	5	4
S (Haolam Haze)	—	—	—	—	2	1	—	—	—	—	—
P	2	—	—	—	—	—	—	—	—	—	—
W[k]	4	4	5	4	3	3	—	—	—	—	—
Other Minorities' lists											
PS	—	—	1	—	—	—	—	—	—	—	—
Kach	1	—	—	—	—	—	—	—	—	—	—
Other lists	—	—	—	—	—	—	—	—	—	3	7

(a)-(k) See notes to Table 1.
The data relates to distribution of mandates according to the election results. Changes in party affiliations between elections are not presented.
Source: see Appendix 1

Appendix 3
Legend to Appendixes 1 and 2

Symbol	*Name of List*
AMT	Alignment—Israel Labor Party and United Workers' Party
AT	Alignment—Israel Labor Party and Unity of Labor
KA	Israel Workers' List (RAFI)
M	United Workers' Party (MAPAM)
A	Israel Labor Party (MAPAI)
TW	Unity of Labor
	Minorities' lists connected with Alignment
B	National Religious Front, Mizrahi and Mizrahi Workers
G	Agudat Yisrael (Orthodox religious)
D	Agudat Yisrael Workers
NJ	Israel Tradition Movement (TAMI)
SHAS	Association of Sefardi Observants of the Torah
AD	Morasha, Matzad, Agudat Yisrael Workers
HN	Change—Center Party
	Democratic Movement for Change (DASH)
T	Yahad—Movement for National Unity
T	Free Center
MHL	Likud (Gahal)
Th	Resurrection
JS	Ometz—for Recovery of the Economy
TLM	Movement for State Renewal (KEN)
KN	Shlomzion—Realization of Zionism Movement
HLTAM	Likud
HL	Herut—Liberal Front (GAHAL)
AM	State List
H	Freedom Party
L	Liberal Party
LA	Independent Liberals
RZ	Citizens' Rights Movement
S	Shelli
KN	Moqed (Tekhelet-Adom-Movement)
K	Israel Communist Party
S	Haolam Haze
P	Progressive List for Peach
W	Democratic List for Peace and Equality—The Israel Communist Party (RAKAH), Black Panthers and Jewish and Arabic Circles
	Other minorities' lists
FS	Flatto-Sharon—Development and Peace
Kach	Kach Movement founded by Rabbi Meir Kahane
	Other lists

Appendix 4
Results of Elections to the Histadrut Conventions (Main Lists)

7th convention 1949	*8th convention 1956*	*9th convention 1960*	*10th convention 1966*	*11th convention 1969*
Mapai 57.1	Mapai 57.7	Mapai 55.4	Alignment[1] 50.9	Alignment[4] 62.1
			Rafi[2] 12.1	
Mapam 34.4	Mapam 12.5	Mapam 13.9	Mapam 14.5	
	Achdut Ha'avodah 14.6	Achdut Ha'avodah 17.0		
Haoved Hatzioni 3.8	Haoved Hatzioni 5.3	Haoved Hatzioni 5.8	Haoved Hatzioni 4.4	Liberal Labor Movement 5.7
	General Zionists 3.8	General Zionists 3.5	Gahal[3] 15.2	Gahal 16.9
Other Lists 4.7	Other Lists 6.1	Other Lists 4.4	Other Lists 6.9	Other Lists 15.3
100.0%	100.0%	100.0%	100.0%	100.0%

12th convention 1974	*13th convention 1977*	*14th convention 1981*	*15th convention 1985*
Alignment 58.3	Alignment 55.3	Alignment 63.1	Alignment 66.7
Liberal Labor Movement 5.8	LA + RZ[6] 1.3	LA 1.8	LA —
Likud[5] 22.7	Likud 28.2	Likud 26.8	Likud 21.4
Other Lists 13.2	Other Lists 15.2	Other Lists 8.3	Other Lists 11.9
100.0%	100.0%	100.0%	100.0%

[1] Mapai + Achdut Ha'avodah
[2] Israel Worker's List
[3] Herut — Liberal Front
[4] Mapai + Achdut Ha'avodah—Mapam
[5] Gahal + other small parties
[6] Independent Liberal + Citizens' Rights Movement
Source: Histadrut Publications

Notes

Chapter One

1. For other ideological and political solutions wee S. Etinger, *History of the Jewish People—Modern Times*, A. Malamat, H. Tadmor, M. Stern, S. Safrai, H.H. Ben-Sasson and S. Etinger (eds.), *History of the Jewish People*, Tel Aviv, Dvir, 1969, Vol. 3 (Hebrew); Part 2, Ch.4-5; S. Dubnov,*Letters on Old and New Judaism*, Tel Aviv, Dvir, 1937, pp.52-62, 73-82 (Hebrew); J. Frankel, *Prophecy and Politics: Socialism, Nationalism and the Russian Jews*, Cambridge, Cambridge University Press, 198l.

2. On Zionism as an ideological and social movement see W. Laqueur, *A History of Zionism*, London, Weidenfeld and Nicolson, 1972; B. Halpern, *The Idea of the Jewish State*, Cambridge, Harvard University Press, 1961; A. Hertzberg (ed.), *The Zionist Idea—A Historical Analysis and Reader*, New York, Atheneum 1970; S.N. Eisenstadt, *The Transformation of Israeli Society*, London, Weidenfeld and Nicolson, 1985, Ch.5; D. Vital, *The Origins of Zionism*, Oxford, Oxford University Press, 1975; S. Avineri, *Varieties of Zionist Thought*, Tel Aviv, Am Oved, 1980 (Hebrew).

3. D. Horowitz and M. Lissak, *Origins of the Israeli Polity*, Chicago and London, The Chicago University Press, 1978, Ch. 8.

4. The area of Israel following the 1949 Armistice agreement was 20,770 square kilometers. The area controlled by Israel after 1967 extended to 89,959 kilometers. The area of the West Bank, the Gaza Strip and the Golan Heights (not including the Sinai peninsula, which was returned to Egypt according to the 1979 Peace Treaty) is 7,391 square kilometers. The population of Israel on the eve of the 1967 war was 2,800,000. The population of the occupied territories in 1967 were 603,400 in the West Bank and 394,000 in the Gaza Strip and the northern part of Sinai. See Central Bureau of Statistics, *Statistical Abstract of Israel 1969*, No. 20, Jerusalem, 1969, pp.3, 20 (Hebrew); and *Census of Population*, Jerusalem, 1967, 1968, pp. 9, 15 (Hebrew).

5. B. Kimmerling, "Between the Primordial and the Civil Definitions of the Collective Identity: Eretz Israel or the State of Israel" in E. Cohen, M. Lissak, and U. Almagor (eds.), *Comparative Social Dynamics—Essays in Honor of S.N.*

Eisenstadt, Boulder and London, Westview Press, 1985, pp. 263-83; E. Cohen, "Ethnicity and Legitimation in Contemporary Israel," *The Jerusalem Quarterly,* No.28, Summer 1983, pp. 111-24; S.N. Herman, *Israelis and Jews: The Continuity of Identity,* New York, Random House, 1970; S. Smooha, "Existing and Alternative Policy Toward the Arabs in Israel" *Megamot,* Vol. 26, No. 1, September 1980, pp. 7-36 (Hebrew). Also, Horowitz and Lissak, *op.cit.,* pp. 1-2.

6. Palestine Royal Commission Report, London, July 1937, *Cmd. 5478* Ch. 14/5.

7. D. Horowitz, "The Yishuv and Israeli Society-Continuity and Change," in *State, Government and International Relations,* No. 21, Spring 1983, pp. 32-36 (Hebrew).

8. The Jewish Agency derived its legal authority from Article 4 of the Mandate: "An appropriate Jewish Agency shall be recognized as a public body for the purpose of advising and cooperating with the Administration of Palestine in such economic, social and other matters as may affect the establishment of the Jewish National Home and the interests of the Jewish population in Palestine." *Palestine Royal Commission Report,* Cmd. 5479 (July 1927), Ch. 5, p. 35.

9. Y. Porath, *The Emergence of the Palestinian—Arab National Movement, 1918-1929,* London, Frank Cass, 1974, Ch. 2;*The Palestinian-Arab National Movement 1929-1939—From Riots to Rebellion,* London, Frank Cass, 1977, Ch. 10.

10. The Declaration of Independence has been published in State of Israel, *Iton Rasmi,* (Official Gazette), No. 1, 1948 (Hebrew).

11. W. Connor, "The Politics of Ethno-nationalism," *Journal of International Affairs,* Vol. 27, No. 1, 1973, pp. 1-21; K.W. Deutsch, *Nationalism and Social Communication,* Cambridge, MIT Press, 1953, Ch. 2; C. Geertz, "The Integrative Revolution, Primordial Sentiments and Civil Politics in New Nations," in C. Geertz (ed.), *Old Societies and New States,* Glencoe and New York, The Free Press, 1963, pp. 105-57.

12. G. Sheffer, "A New Field of Study: Modern Diasporas in International Politics," in G. Sheffer (ed.), *Modern Diasporas in International Politics,* St. Martin's Press, 1986, pp. 1-16; W. Connor, "The Impact of Homelands Upon Diasporas," in G. Sheffer (ed.), *ibid.*

13. On primordial sentiments see, C. Geertz, *The Interpretation of Cultures,* New York, Basic Books, 1973, pp. 259-67; C. Geertz, " The Integrative Revolution, Primordial Sentiments and Civil Politics in New Nations," *op. cit.,*

14. See The Flag and National Emblem Law 8, *LSI,* (The Laws of the State of Israel), May 1949, p. 37 (Hebrew).

15. The Law of Return 51 *LSI,* July 1950, p. 159 (Hebrew). The law was mended twice in 1954 and 1970. See 163, *LSI,* August 1954, p. 174 and 586,*LSI,* March 1970, p. 34 (Hebrew).

16. G. Ben Dor, "The Military in the Politics of Integration and Innovation: The Case of the Druse Minority in Israel," *Asian and African Studies,* Vol. 9, No. 3, 1973, pp. 339-70.

17. Security Service Law 296 *LSI,* 9/24/1959, p. 286 (Hebrew).

18. See "Basic Law—The Knesset," 244, *LSI,* February 1958, p. 69 (Hebrew).

19. The legal origin of religious jurisdiction in matters of personal status can be traced to the Mandatory period, see*The Palestine Order in Council 1922,* Drayton, *Laws of Palestine* 3, p. 2569. The Israeli legislation made only a few changes in this established tradition. The Israeli laws applying to jurisdiction in matters of personal status of Jews are the "Jurisdiction of Rabbinical Courts Law" and the "Law of Rabbinical Courts Judges" (Dayanim), see Jurisdiction of Rabbinical Courts—Marriage and Divorce Law 200, *LSI,* March 1956, p. 40 (Hebrew). With regard to the Moslems, "The Law of the Qaddis," 399, *LSI,* May 1961, p. 118 (Hebrew); and with regard to the Druzes, the "Law of Druzen Courts," 430,*LSI,* June 1964, p. 141 (Hebrew). The law which applies to Christians has not been changed from the Mandatory law.

20. C.S. Liebman and E. Don-Yehiya, *Civil Religion in Israel,* Berkeley, University of California Press, 1983; A. Rubinstein, *Constitutional Law of Israel,* Jerusalem and Tel Aviv, Schocken, 1974, pp. 133-62 (Hebrew).

21. B. Kimmerling, "Between the Primordial . . . " in Cohen et al. (eds.), *op.cit.,* pp.263-83.

22. M. Benvenisti, *The West Bank and Gaza Data Base Project,* Interim Report No. 1. Jerusalem, 1982, pp. 33-42.

23. Horowitz and Lissak, *op.cit.,* Ch. 6; S.N. Eisenstadt, *Israeli Society,* New York, Basic Books, 1967, Ch. 3; S. Etinger, *History of The Jewish People, op.cit.,* Part 2, Ch. 6.

24. D. Ben-Gurion, "Uniqueness and Mission," State of Israel, *Government Yearbook, 1951,* pp. 22-25 (Hebrew); T. Segev, *1949-The First Israelis,* Tel Aviv—Jerusalem, Domino, 1984, pp. 105-22 (Hebrew).

25. For the ideological-political debate on the future of the "territories" see, for example, Y. Harkaby, *Fateful Decisions,* Tel Aviv, Am Oved, 1986, Ch. 1 (Hebrew); Y. Beilin, *The Price of Unity,* Tel Aviv, Revivim, 1985, Chs. 1-4 (Hebrew); A. Eliav, *Glory in the Land of the Living,* Tel Aviv, Am Oved, 1972 (Hebrew); T. Raanan, *Gush Emunim,* Tel Aviv, Sifriat Hapoalim, 1980, pp. 75-101 (Hebrew).

26. Horowitz and Lissak, *op. cit.*, Ch. 6.

27. Eisenstadt, *The Transformation, op.cit.*, Chs. 15-18.

28. S.N. Eisenstadt, *Revolution and the Transformation of Societies, A Comparative Study of Civilizations*, New York, The Free Press, 1978, Ch. 8; A. Inkeles, *Social Change in Soviet Russia*, Cambridge, MIT Press, 1968, Chs. 1-3.

29. On institution building in the Yishuv see Horowitz and Lassak, *op. cit.*, Chs. 2, 4, 7.

30. D. Bell, *The End of Ideology, On the Exhaustion of Political Ideas in the Fifties*, Glencoe, Ill., The Free Press, 1960.

31. B. Akzin and Y. Dror, *Israel: High-Pressure Planning*, Syracuse, 1966, pp. 7-14; N. Yanai, *Split at the Top*, Tel Aviv, A. Levin-Epstein, 1969, pp. 77-140 (Hebrew).

32. A. Oz, *Under this Blazing Light*, Tel Aviv, Am Oved, 1979, p. 92.

33. The phrase is attributed to the Zionist English author Israel Zangwill, See, A. Elon, *The Israelis: Founders and Sons*, New York and London, Holt, Rinehart and Winston, 1971, p. 149.

34. For a discussion of this phenomenon see E. Shils, "Comparative Study of the New Nations" in C. Geertz (ed.), *Old Societies and New States, op. cit.*, pp. 1-26.

35. Eisenstadt, *Israeli Society, op. cit.*, pp. 3-5.

36. S. Deshen and M. Shoked (eds.), *Jews of the Middle East: Anthropological Perspectives on Past and Present*, Jerusalem and Tel Aviv, Schocken, 1948, pp. 11-26 (Hebrew); H.E. Goldberg, "Historical and Cultural Dimensions of Ethnic Phenomena in Israel," in A. Weingrod (ed.), *Studies in Israeli Ethnicity: After the Ingathering*, New York, Gordon and Beach, 1985, pp. 179-200; S. Smooha, *Israel, Pluralism and Conflict*, London, Routledge and Kegan Paul, 1978; M. Friedman, *Society and Religion, the Non-Zionist Orthodox in Eretz-Israel 1918-1936*, Jerusalem, Yad Yitzak Ben Zvi, 1977, Chs. 2-3 (Hebrew).

37. Eisenstadt, *The Absorption of Immigrants, op. cit.*, Chs. 4-6; R. Bar-Yosef, "The Moroccans: Background to the Problem" in S.N. Eisenstadt, R. Bar-Yosef, and C. Adler (eds.), *Integration and Development in Israel*, Jerusalem, Israel University Press, 1970, pp. 419-28; A. Weingrod, "Moroccan Jewry in Transition," *Megamot*, 10, No. 3 (1960), pp. 193-208 (Hebrew).

38. M. Lissak, *Social Mobility in Israel Society*, Jerusalem, Israel University Press, 1969, Ch. 5; Smooha, *Israel: Pluralism, op. cit.*, Ch. 7; H. Herzog, "Ethnicity as a Negotiated Issue in the Israeli Political Order: The Ethnic Lists; to the Delegates' Assembly and the Knesset (1920-1977)" in A. Weingrod (ed.), *Studies*

in Israeli Ethnicity—After the Ingathering, op. cit., pp.159-78; Y. Peres, "Horizontal Integration and Vertical Differetiation Among Jewish Ethnicities in Israel" in Weingrod (ed.), *ibid.*, pp. 39-56.

39. M. Lissak, "Political-Social Map Overlap,"*The Jerusalem Quarterly*, No. 38, 1986, pp. 28-42.

40. Poless, "Historical Orientation of Religious Revival," *Ha'aretz*, 11/22/1957 (Hebrew); U. Simon, "The Israeli-Jewish Consciousness, A Turning Point in Hebrew Education?," *Ha'aretz*, 12/10/1957 (Hebrew); B. Evron, "The Jewish Consciousness—A Symptom of Value Confusion," *Ha'aretz*, 10/25/1957 (Hebrew).

41. See, for example, M. Shoked and S. Deshen, *The Generation of Transition: Continuity and Change Among North African Immigrants in Israel*, Jerusalem, Yad Yitzhak Ben Zvi, 1977, Ch. 9 (Hebrew); Y. Bilu, "Traditional Medicine Among North African Jews in Israel" in S. Deshen and M. Shoked (eds.), *The Jews of the Middle East, op. cit.*, pp. 166-75 (Hebrew).

42. S.N. Eisenstadt, "Traditional and Modern Social Values and Economic Development," *Annals of the American Academy of Political and Social Sciences*, No. 305, 1956, pp. 145-56; "Some New Looks at the Problem of Relations Between Traditional Societies and Modernization," *Economic Development and Cultural Change*, 16, No. 3 (1968), pp. 436-450; M. Lissak, *Military Roles in Modernization: Civil-Military Relations in Thailand and Burma*, Beverly Hills and London, Sage Publications, 1976, Ch. 2; E. Sivan, *Radical Islam: Medieval Theology and Modern Politics*, Tel Aviv, Am Oved, 1985 (Hebrew).

43. In 1985 the population of Israel was about 4,250,000. See State of Israel, *Statistical Abstract of Israel No. 36*, 1985, p. 32 (Hebrew).

44. A. Shalev, "The Arms Race in the Middle East in the 1980s," in Z. Lanir (ed.), *Israeli Security Planning in the 1980s—Its Politics and Economics*, Tel Aviv, Misrad Habitahon and Tel Aviv University, 1985, pp. 15-30 (Hebrew); The International Institute for Strategic Studies, *The Military Balance 1985-1986*, London, 1985, p. 77.

45. Israel was party to five major wars: the War of Independence (1948-1949); the Sinai Campaign (1956); the Six Day War (1967); the Yom Kippur War of 1973; and the Lebanon War (1982-1983)—this without taking into account the 1969-1970 war of attrition with Egypt and the 1978 Litani Operation in Lebanon.

46. S. Aronson, *Conflict and Bargaining in the Middle East*, Baltimore, Johns Hopkins University Press, 1978, pp. 25-54; Y. Evron, "Israel and the Atom" The Uses and Misuses of Ambiguity, 1957-1967," *Orbis*, 17, No. 4, 1974, pp. 1326-43; S. Feldman, *Israel Nuclear Deterrence: A Strategy for the 1980s*, New York, Columbia University Press, 1982.

47. U.O. Schmelz and S. Dellapergola, "World Jewish Population," *American Jewish Year Book*, 1982, pp. 277-290.

48. The sum total of United States foreign aid since the end of the Second World War is $250 billion. Through 1984 Israel had received about 10% of this total, i.e., about $25 billion. See A. Razin, " The Honey and the Sting: The Impact of Aid to Israel" in Z. Ofer and A. Kober, *The Price of Power*, Tel Aviv, Maarachot, 1984, p. 48 (Hebrew).

49. On military aid to Israel see A. Razin, *op. cit.*, p. 49; N. Hassid and Y. Leser, "Defence and the National Pie" in Z. Ofer and A. Kober (eds.), *op. cit.*, pp.33-47.

50. D. Horowitz, *The Enigma of Economic Growth: A Case Study of Israel*, New York, Praeger, 1972, Chs. 3-4; N. Halevi and R. Klinov, *The Economic Development of Israel*, New York, Praeger, 1968, Chs. 2, 10; H. Barkai, *The Formative Years of the Israeli Economy*, Jerusalem, 1983, Ch. 4 (Hebrew).

51. C.S. Liebman, "In Search of Status: The Israeli Government and the Zionist Movement", *Forum*, 1978, pp.28-29, pp. 38-56; G. Sheffer, "The Uncertain Future of American Jewry-Israel Relations," *The Jerusalem Quarterly*, No. 32, 1984, pp. 65-80; S.N. Eisenstadt, *The Transformation, op.cit.*, Ch. 16.

52. G. Shimoni, *Jews and Zionism: The South African Experience, 1910-1967*, Capetown, Oxford University Press, 1980.

53. F.E. Shinar, *The Burden of Necessity and Emotions: Israel-Germany Relations, 1950-1966*, Jerusalem, Schoken, 1967, pp.28-42 (Hebrew).

54. S.N. Eisenstadt, *The Transformation of Israel Society, op. cit.*, pp. 476-88; S.M. Cohen, *Attitudes of American Jews Toward Israel and Israelis*, Institute of American Jewish-Israeli Relations, The American Jewish Committee, September 1983; G. Sheffer, "The Uncertain Future of American Jewry-Israel Relations," *op. cit.*, pp. 65-80.

55. S. Dellapergola, "Aliya and Other Jewish Migrations: Toward an Integrated Perspective," in U. Schmeiz and G. Nathan (eds.), *Studies in the Population of Israel in Honor of Roberto Bachi, Scripta Hierosolymitana* XXX, Jerusalem, Magnes Press, 1986, pp. 172-209.

56. G. Schoken, "A New Look at Zionism: A Success of Failure?" *Ha'aretz*, 9/10/1980 (Hebrew).

57. S. Dellapergola, *ibid.*; Z. Rabi, "Demographic Development in Israel," *Ha'aretz*, 11/1/1983 (Hebrew); "The Emigration from Israel—1948-1977," *Revaon Le Kalkala*, 99 (1978), pp. 348-58 (Hebrew).

58. About the Ethiopian Jews see S. Newman, "Ethiopian Jewish Absorption and the Israeli Response: A Two-Way Process," *Israel Social Science Research*,

3, No. 1-2, pp. 104-11; Jeff Halpar, "The Absorption of Ethiopian Immigrants: A Return to the Fifties," *Israel Social Science Research*, 3, No. 1-2, pp. 112-39.

59. With regard to the Security Service Law, see Chapter 5.

60. For more details, see Chapter 5, pp. 213-21.

61. For more details, see Chapter 5, pp. 196, 213-21.

62. D. Horowitz, "Dual Authority Politics," *Comparative Politics*, Vol. No. 14, April 1982, pp. 329-336.

63. H. Lasswell, "The Garrison State," *The American Journal of Sociology*, 46, No. 4 (1941), pp. 455-62.

64. M. Lissak, "Paradoxes of Israeli Civil-Military Relations," in M. Lissak (ed.), *Israeli Society and Its Defense Establishment*, London, Cass, 1948, pp.1-12; Y. Peri, *Between Battles and Ballots, Israeli Military in Politics*, Cambridge, Cambridge University Press, 1983; D. Horowitz, "The Israeli Defense Forces: A Civilianized Military in a Partially Militarized Society" in R. Kolkowicz and A. Korbonski (eds.,), *Soldiers, Peasants and Bureaucrats*, London, G. Allen, 1982, pp. 77-105; D. Horowitz and B. Kimmerling, "Some Social Implications of Military Service and the Reserve System in Israel," *Archives Europeennes de Sociologie*, XV, 1974, pp. 262-76; B. Kimmerling, "Determination of the Boundaries and Frameworks of Conscription: Two Dimensions of Civil-Military Relations in Israel," *Studies in Comparative International Development*, XIV, No. 1, 1979, pp. 22-41.

65. M. Lissak, "Boundaries and Institutional Linkages Between Elites: Some Illustrations From Civil-Military Relations in Israel," in G. Moore (ed.), *Research in Politics and Society*, Vol. 1: *Studies of the Structure of National Elite Groups*, 1985, pp. 129-48; D. Horowitz, "The Israel Defense Forces . . . ," *op. cit.*.

66. R. Rose, "The Nature of the Challenge," in R. Rose (ed.), *The Challenge to Governance: Studies in Overloaded Politics*, Beverly Hills and London, Sage Publications, 1980, pp. 5-29.

67. J. Habib, "Redistribution Through National Insurance in Israel by Income and Demographic Groups," *Bitachon Sociali*, No. 9-10, 1975, pp. 87-114 (Hebrew)' A. Doron, N. Shamai, and Y. Tamir, "Income Maintainance, Policy From the Viewpoint of the Family—A Comparative Study of Eight Countries," *Bitachon Sociali*, No. 24, 1983, pp. 56-76 (Hebrew).

68. For this concept see, for example, H. Daalder, "The Consociational Democracy Theme," *World Politics*, 26, No. 4, 1974, pp. 604-27; A. Lijphart, "Consociational Democracy," *World Politics*, 21, No. 2, 1969, pp. 207-25.

69. B. Kimmerling, "Determination of the Boundaries . . .," *op.cit.*

70. I. Galnoor, *Steering the Polity: Communication and Politics in Israel*, Beverly

Hills and London, Sage Publications, 1982, pp. 53-97; Horowitz and Lissak, *Origins of Israel Polity, op. cit.*, Ch. 8.

71. S. Gazit, *The Stick and the Carrot, The Israeli Administration of Judea and Samaria*, Tel Aviv, Zmora Bitan, 1985 (Hebrew).

72. For an example of the use of the term "laboratory" in regard to Israel, see M. Bernstein, "Israel's Capacity to Govern," *World Politics*, Vol. 11, No. 3, 1959, pp. 399-417; for an example of an application of the metaphor in ideological writings, see Z. Jabotinsky *The Road to the State*, Jerusalem, 1953, pp.173-74 (Hebrew).

73. For a theoretical discussion of the implications of non-congruence of state and ethno-national community, see, W. Connor, "Nation-Building and Nation-Destroying" in *World Politics*, Vol. 24, No. 3, 1972, pp. 319-355.

74. See D. Horowitz, "Incomplete Association," in *Politica*, No. 17, October 1987, pp. 34-37 (Hebrew).

75. E. Shils, *Center and Periphery—Essays in Macrosociology*, Chicago, University of Chicago Press, 1975, pp. 3-16.

76. For the concept of sub-center see Horowitz and Lissak, *Origins of the Israeli Polity, op. cit.*, pp. 47-50.

77. For a theoretical discussion, see D. Horowitz, "Dual Authority Politics," *op.cit.*, pp. 330-336.

78. D. Easton, *The Political System: An Inquiry into the State of Political Science*, New York, A. Knopf, 1953, Ch. 1.

79. T. Parsons, *Structure and Process in Modern Societies*, Glencoe, Ill., The Free Press, 1960, Ch. 5.

80. See, for example, D. Kavanagh, "Political Behavior and Political Participation," in P. Geraint (ed.), *Participation in Politics*, Manchester, Manchester University Press, 1973, pp. 102-123.

81. See Horowitz, Lissak *op. cit.*, pp. 11-12; Horowitz, "Dual Authority . . ." *op.cit.*, pp. 329-336.

82. The terms "centrifugal and centripretal" are referred to in A. Sartori, "European Political Parties: The Case of Polarized Pluralism," in J. Lapalombara and M. Weiner (eds.), *Political Parties and Political Development*, London, Princeton University Press, 1966, pp. 137-176. See also Horowitz and Lissak, *op. cit.*, pp. 40-41.

83. H.H. Gerth and C. Wright Mills (eds.), *From Marx Weber: Essays in Sociology*, London, Kegan Paul, Trench Trubner and Co., 1947, Ch. 7.

84. On the notion of cleavages, see S.M. Lipset and S. Rokkan, "Cleavages, Structures, Party Systems and Voter Alignments: An Introduction" in S.N. Lipset and S. Rokkan, (eds.), *Party Systems and Voter Alignments*, New York, The Free Press, 1967, pp. 1-64.

On the notion of "pluralism," see M.G. Smith, "Institutional and Political Conditions of Pluralism" in L. Kuper and M.G. Smith (eds.), *Pluralism in Africa*, Berkeley, University of California Press, 1964, pp.29-67; M.G. Smith, "Some Developments in the Analytic Framework of Pluralism," in L. Kuper and M.G. Smith (eds.), *op. cit.*, pp. 415-448; L. Kuper, *Plural Societies, Perspectives and Problems*, in L. Kuper and M.G. Smith (eds.), *op. cit.*, pp.1-2.

For an analysis of the literature on "pluralism", see S. Smooha, *Israel: Pluralism and Conflict*, London, Routledge and Kegan Paul, 1972, Ch. 2.

85. M. Daalder, "The Consociational Democracy Theme" *World Politics*, Vol. 26, No. 4, July 1974, pp. 606, 612-614; E. Nordlinger, "Conflict Regulation in Divided Societies." Occasional papers, Center for International Affairs, Harvard University, 1972, p. 116; R.M. Williams, Jr.,*American Society*, New York, A. Knopf, 1952, p.53; J. Galtung, "Rank and Social Integration: A Multidimensional Approach" in J. Berger, M. Zelditch, Jr., and B. Anderson, *Sociological Theories in Progress*, Boston, Houghton Mifflin Company, 1966, Vol. 1, pp. 145-198.

86. See E. Gutmann, "Parties and Camps—Stability and Change" in M. Lissak and E. Gutmann (eds.), *The Israeli Political System*, Tel Aviv, Am Oved, 1977, pp. 155-156 (Hebrew).

87. G.M. Smith, *The Plural Society in the British West Indies*, Berkeley, University of California Press, 1965, p. 80; M. Lissak, *Social Mobility in Israeli Society*, Jerusalem, Israel University Press, 1969, pp. 1-6.

88. M. Seliger, "Fundamental and Operative Ideology: The Two Principle Dimensions of Political Argumentation," *Policy Sciences*, Vol. 1, 1970, p. 325. See also Horowitz, Lissak, *op. cit.*, pp.120-121.

89. See below Chapter 3, pp. 98-113.

90. R. Dahrendorf, *Class and Class Conflict in Industrial Society*, Stanford, Stanford University Press, 1959; S.M. Lipset, *Political Man*, New York, Doubleday, 1960, pp. 64-71; E.A. Nordlinger, *Conflict Regulation in Divided Societies*, Cambridge, Center for International Affairs, Harvard University. Occasional papers, No. 29, January 1972.

91. See below Chapter 4, pp. 176-181.

92. For the meaning of these terms see: A.R. Luckham, "A Comparative Typology of Civil-Military Relations," *Government and Opposition*, Vol. 6, 1971, pp. 17-20.

93. D. Rapoport, "A Comparative Theory of Military and Political Types" in S. Huntington (ed.), *Changing Patterns of Military Politics*, New York, The Free Press, 1962.

94. See Note 64.

95. On the concept of "role expansion" of the military (particularly in the context of modernization) see: M. Lissak, *Military Roles in Modernization*, Beverly Hills and London, Sage Publications, 1976, Ch. 1.

96. The various concepts in this respect are discussed in R.A. Alford and R. Friedland, *Powers of Theory: Capitalism, the State and Democracy*, Cambridge, Cambridge University Press, 1985, pp. 35-58.

97. B. Barry, "Political Accommodation and Consociational Democracy," *British Journal of Political Science*, Vol. 5, Part 4, October 1975, pp. 477-506.

98. For a presentation of the "autonomy of elites" approach, see G. Lowell Field and John Higley, *Elitism*, London, Routledge and Kegan Paul, 1980.

For a criticism of this approach, see P.Y. Medding, "Patterns of Elite Consensus and Elite Competitions: A Model and a Case Study" in H.D. Clarke and M.M. Czudnowski (eds.), *Political Elites in Anglo-American Democracies*, Northern Illinois University Press, 1987, pp. 17-43.

99. On the controversy between the "functionalist" and "conflict" approaches, see S.N. Eisenstadt with M. Curelaru, *The Forms of Sociology—Paradigms and Crises*, New York, John Wiley and Sons, Ch. 8; M.M. Poloma, *Contemporary Sociological Theory*, New York, Macmillan Publishing Co., pp. 15-30, 65-90; D. Lockwood, "Some Remarks on the Social System" in N.J. Demerpath and R.A. Peterson (eds.), *System, Change and Conflict*, New York, The Free Press, 1967, pp. 281-291.

Chapter Two

1. See E. Gutmann, "Parties and Camps—Stability and Change," in: M. Lissak, E. Gutmann, (eds.), *The Israeli Political System*, Tel Aviv, Am Oved, 1977, p. 155 (Hebrew).

2. A study of a sample of 1% of the Jewish population indicates that about 18% of the children born in the years 1981-1985 were born to "mixed" couples in terms of European versus Asian-African country of origin. (Source of data: Professor D. Friedlander of the Department of Demography, The Hebrew University of Jerusalem.)

3. The proposition that cross cutting cleavages tends to mitigate conflicts while overlapping cleavages tends to reinforce them has been endorsed by many sociologists and political scientists including G. Almond, L. Coser, S.M.

Lipset, A. Lijphart, J. Steiner. See G. Almond, "Comparative Political Systems," *Journal of Politics*, Vol. 18, No. 3, (August 1956), pp. 398-405; L. Coser, *The Functions of Social Conflict*, Glencoe, Ill., The Free Press, 1956, pp. 78-79; S.M. Lipset, *Political Man: The Social Bases of Politics*, Garden City, NY, Doubleday, 1960, p. 77; A. Lijphart, "Cultural Diversity and Theories of Political Integration," *Canadian Journal of Political Science*, Vol. 4, No. 1, March 1971, pp. 3-6; J. Steiner, *Amicable Agreement Versus Majority Rule: Conflict Resolution in Switzerland*, Chapel Hill, University of North Carolina Press, p. 49. For criticism of the proposition see: B. Barry, "Review Article: Political Accommodation and Consociational Democracy," *British Journal of Political Science*, Vol. 5, Part 4, October 1975; E. Nordlinger, *Conflict Regulation in Divided Societies*, Cambridge, Harvard University Press, Occasional Papers in International Affairs, 1972.

4. On the concept of "unbalanced status," see G.E. Lenski, "Status Crystalization, A Non-Vertical Dimension of Social Status," in *American Sociological Review*, Vol. 19, No. 4, August 1954, pp. 405-413; H.M. Blalock, Jr., "Status Inconsistency and Interaction: Some Alternative Models," *American Journal of Sociology*, Vol. 73, No. 3, November 1967, pp. 305-316; K. Hope, "Models of Status Inconsistency and Social-Mobility Effects," *American Sociological Review*, Vol. 40, No. 3, June 1975, pp. 322-344; M. Lissak, "Stratification Models and Mobility Aspirations: Sources of Mobility Aspirations," *Megamot*, Vol. 15, No. 1, January 1967, pp. 66-82 (Hebrew).

5. On the concept of "distributive justice," see J. Rawls, "Distributive Justice," in P. Laslett and W.G. Runciman (eds.), *Philosophy, Politics and Society*, Oxford, Basil Blackwell, pp. 58-82, 1967.

6. On ethnicity in the Jewish community in Palestine under the Mandate, see M. Lissak, "The Ethnic Problem and Ethnic Organizations in the Jewish Community in Palestine," *Jerusalem Quarterly*, No. 44, 1987, pp. 18-38 (Hebrew).

7. At the end of the 1948 war there were about 160,000 Arabs in Israel, see C. Kaymen, "After the Disaster: The Arabs in Israel 1948-1952," in *Machbarot Lemechkar Velebikoret*, No. 10, December 1984, pp. 7-16 (Hebrew); see also B. Kimmerling, *Zionism and Territory: The Socio-Territorial Dimensions of Zionist Politics*, Berkeley, Institute of International Studies, University of California, 1983, pp. 121-130; G. Kassaifi, "Demographic Characteristics of the Palestinian People," in K. Nakleh and E. Zureik (eds.), *The Sociology of the Palestinians*, London, Croom and Helm, 1980, Table 1.3, p. 20.

8. This approach was expressed in David Ben-Gurion's formula, "Palestine is assigned for the Jewish People and the Arabs living there," D. Ben-Gurion, *We and Our Neighbors*, Tel Aviv, Davar, 1931, p. 188 (Hebrew); For an analysis of manifestations of this approach see: Y. Gorny, *The Arab Question and the Jewish Problem*, Tel Aviv, Am Oved, 1986, pp.167-168 (Hebrew).

9. For the official Hebrew version of the Camp David Accords, see The

Government of Israel Information Service (M. Medzini ed.), *Collection of Documents Concerning the History of the State,* Jerusalem, Ministry of Defense Publications, 1982, p. 346 (Hebrew).

10. See Kaymen, *op.cit.,* pp. 63-65.

11. On the notion of "a split labor market," see E. Bonacich, "A Theory of Ethnic Antagonism: The Split Labor Market," *American Sociological Review,* Vol. 37, No. 5, October 5, 1972, pp. 547-559; S. Olzak, "Contemporary Ethnic Mobilization," *Annual Review of Sociology,* Vol. 9, 1983, pp. 355-74.

12. The awareness that the military government is instrumental for the regulation of the labor market was manifested in an article of Maj. General (Res.) Prof. Y. Ratner who was involved in policy making in this area as a chairman of a committee which examined the effectiveness of the Military Government. See Y. Ratner, "The Military Government," *Mibefnim,* Vol. 19, pp. 49-52 (Hebrew).

13. 80% of the Arab population in the '50s were living in villages. Among the minority who lived in towns were many who were unemployed. See Kaymen, *op. cit.,* p. 58.

14. On the use of the Military Government as a means of political control, see I. Lustick, *Arabs in a Jewish State,* Austin and London, University of Texas Press, 1980, Chs. 3, 4, 5.

15. See: Lustick, *op. cit.,* Ch. 6; J.M. Landau, *The Arabs in Israel: A Political Study,* London, Oxford University Press, 1970, Ch. 5.

16. The Communists's share of the Arab Vote in the '60s was about a quarter of the total Arab vote. See Lustick, *op. cit.,* p. 331.

17. See A. Liskovsky, "Resident Absentees in Israel," *Hamizrach Hachadash,* Vol. 10, No. 3 (39), 1960, pp. 186-192 (Hebrew).

18. See G. Ben Dor, "Military in the Politics of Integration and Innovation: The Case of the Druze Minority in Israel," *Asian and African Studies,* Vol. 9, No. 33, 1973, pp. 339-370; G. Ben Dor, *The Druze in Israel: A Political Study,* Jerusalem, The Magnes Press 1979, pp. 133-140.

19. See *Divrei Haknesset,* (The Knesset Proceedings), November 2, 1962, pp. 1315-1339, 1360-1365; February 20, 1963, pp. 1207-1244; November 11, 1966, p. 228 (the Government's statement on the abolition of the Military Government) (Hebrew).

20. In 1978 there were 2,000 Arab students studying in Israeli universities compared with 286 in 1966, see E. Rekhes, "The Educated," in A. Layish (ed.), *The Arabs in Israel: Continuity and Change,* Jerusalem, The Magnes Press, 1981, p. 181 (Hebrew).

21. See HC (High Court of Justice) 253/264, *Piski-din* (Court's Judgment), Vol. 18, p. 637 (Hebrew), for a description of the El Ard Affair and its background; see Landau, *op. cit.*, Ch. 4.

22. See S. Smooha, "Arabs an Jews in Israel: Minority-Majority Group Relations," *Megamot*, Vol. 22, No. 4, September 1976, pp. 410-412 (Hebrew); S. Smooha, "Existing and Alternative Policy Toward the Arabs in Israel," *Megamot*, Vol. 26, No. 1, September 1980, pp. 30-32 (Hebrew); H. Rouhana, in: A. Arian and M. Shamir (eds.), *Elections in Israel 1984*, New Brunswick, NJ, Transaction Books, 1986, pp. 127-147.

23. The distribution of the Arab votes in 1984 was: 34% Hadash (Communists allied groups); 23% Labor; 12% Progressive Movement for Peace; 25% other parties, *Yediot Aharonot*, December 15, 1987 (Hebrew).

24. On the occupational structure of the Israeli Arab population, see E. Schmelz, "Labor Force," in Layish (ed.), *op. cit.*, Tables 10 and 15 (Hebrew); for data on the occupations of Arabs from the occupied territories working in Israel see M. Benvenisti, *1986 Report: Demographic, Economic, Legal, Social and Political Development in the West Bank*, Jerusalem, American Enterprise Institute, The West Bank Data Base, 1986, pp. 11-14.

25. On the integration of Arab professionals in the Israeli economy, see E. Rekhes, in Layish (ed.), *op. cit.*, pp. 183-184 (Hebrew).

26. The number of students in the West Bank universities increased from 1,086 in 1974-75 to 7,487 in 1981-82. An estimate for 1985-86 is more than 10,000. The number of West Bank students studying abroad in 1983 was 7,800, M. Benvenisti, *The West Bank Handbook*, Jerusalem, Jerusalem Post, 1986, pp. 212-214.

27. *ibid.*, pp. 172-176.

28. The percentage of Jewish children under the age of fifteen in the entire area under Israeli control ("Greater Israel") dropped from 53.7% in 1982 to 52.9% in 1984, Benvenisti "1986 Report . . ." *op.cit.*, p. 4; According to a demographic forecast based on existing trends the share of Jews in the entire population of "Greater Israel" in the year 2,000 will be 57-59% compared with 63% in 1986.

29. See public opinion poll reported in Y. Peres, "The Stalemate," *Politica*, No. 18, December 1987, pp. 21-22 (Hebrew). M. Zemach, *Through Israeli Eyes*, New York, The American Jewish Committee, 1987, pp. 29-37.

30. See Declaration of the Extension of The Jerusalem Municipal Area, *Kovetz Hatakanot* (State of Israel Regulations) 2065, June 28, 1967, p. 2694 (Hebrew); This declaration did not, however, imply a full annexation of East Jerusalem to the State of Israel. Jerusalem was actually annexed to Israel only in

1980, see Basic Law—Jerusalem Capital of Israel 980, *LSI* (Laws of Israel), August 1980, p. 186 (Hebrew); On the background to the 1967 decision, see S. Gazit, *The Stick and the Carrot: The Israeli Administration in Judea and Samaria,* Tel Aviv, Zmora Bitan Publishers, 1985, p. 222 (Hebrew).

31. In 1985 Israel controlled 52% of the West Bank's Land; see Benvenisti, *1986 Report . . . op. cit.,* pp. 25-32.

32. On the "open bridges" policy, see Gazit, *op. cit.,* pp. 204-221.

33. 45% of the export of the West Bank but only 2% of the imports is transported via the "open bridges", Benvenisti, *1986 Report . . . op. cit.,* p. 6; about 300,000 West Bank people a year cross the bridges to Jordan and about 100,000 visitors from the Arab countries cross the bridges to the West Bank every year.

34. See Gazit, *op. cit.,* pp. 252-258.

35. On the effect of employment of workers from the occupied territories on occupational mobility in Israel see N. Lewin-Epstein and M. Semyonov, "Ethnic Group Mobility in the Israeli Labor Market," *American Sociological Review,* Vol. 51, No. June 1986, pp. 342-351; J.S. Migdal, *Palestinian Society and Politics,* Princeton, Princeton University Press, 1980, Ch. 5.

36. See M. Negbi, *Chains of Injustice.* Jerusalem: Kana Publishers, 1982, p. 12 (Hebrew); Benvenisti, *The West Bank Handbook, op. cit.,* pp. 105-106.

37. The inclination to use the powers of the military authorities in a manipulative manner is reflected in a document stipulating "Operative Principles for the Administrated Territories" issued on October 13, 1967, see Appendix 5, in Gazit, *op. cit.,* pp. 356-358 (Hebrew).

38. See P. Albeck, *Land in Judea and Samaria,* Tel Aviv, Chamber of Lawyers, 1985, pp. 12-16 (Hebrew); Benvenisti, *West Bank Handbook, op. cit.*p. 139.

39. The question of violations of the law by Israeli settlers in the West Bank and the ensuing problems of law enforcement are referred to in an official Ministry of Justice document known as, "The Karp Report," Government of Israel, Ministry of Justice, *Report of the Follow Up Team on Investigations of Suspicions Regarding Israelis in Judea and Samaria,* May 1982 (Hebrew); for details on the activities of the "Jewish underground," see The Jerusalem District Court, State of Israel versus Menachem Livni et al, *Criminal Case* 203/84 (Hebrew).

40. On the underground plan to destroy the Dome of the Rock as seen by one of plotters, see H. Segal, *Dear Brothers,* Keter Publications, 1987, Chs. 5, 12.

41. The position of the lobby for the release of the Underground prisoners is manifested in Rabbi I. Ariel's article in *Nekuda,* No. 73, July 25, 1984 (Hebrew).

42. See M. Maoz, *Palestinian Leadership on the West Bank*, Tel Aviv, Reshafim, Ch. 5 (Hebrew); Gazit, *op. cit.*, pp. 331-333.

43. See Maoz, *op. cit.*, Chs. 6 and 7.

44. See Y. Ben-Meir and P. Kedem, "Index of Religiosity of the Jewish Population in Israel," *Megamot*, Vol. 24, No. 3, February 1979, pp. 353-362 (Hebrew).

45. The religious parties' share of the vote fluctuated between 15.4% in 1961 (the 5th Knesset) and 8.9% in 1984 (the 11th Knesset).

46. For a survey of the various religious educational institutions see: M. Barlev, "Jewish Religious Education in Israel: Between Religious Activity and Educational Activity" in M. Barlev (ed.),*Religious Education in Israeli Society: A Reader*, Jerusalem, Department of Sociology and Social Anthropology and the School of Education at the Hebrew University of Jerusalem, 1986, pp. 3-28 (Hebrew).

47. See Ben-Meir and Kedem, *op. cit.*, pp. 357-362.

48. On patterns of ecological segregation of the ultra-Orthodox Jew in Jerusalem, see J. Shilhav and M. Friedman, *Growth an Segregation—The ultra-Orthodox Community of Jerusalem*, Jerusalem, The Jerusalem Institute for Israel Studies, 1985, pp. 25-58 (Hebrew).

49. See Shilhav and Friedman, *opo. cit.*, pp. 6-26.

50. On the circumstances that led to the establishment of Shas, see R. Kislev, "A Party of One Rabbi," *Haaretz*, December 18, 1987.

51. See "Anatomy and Pathology Law" 134 *LSI*, September 4, 1953, p.162 (Hebrew).

52. For comparisons of the policies of Agudat Israel and the National Religious Party, see E. Don-Yehiya, "The Politics of the Religious Parties in Israel," and G. Goldberg, "The Religious Parties in Opposition 1965-1977" in: S.V. Lehman-Wilzig and B. Susser (ed.), *Public Life in Israel and the Diaspora*, Ramat Gan, Bar Ilan University Press, 1981, pp. 110-137 and 146-150.

53. On the voting patterns of religious Jews, see A. Arian, *The Choosing People*, Ramat Gan, Massada, 1973, pp. 66-69 (Hebrew); see also the analysis of the voting pattern of the ultra—Orthodox in Shilhav and Friedman, *op. cit.*, pp. 25-34.

54. The autonomy of the religious state education is based on a coalition agreement between Mapai and the Zionist religious parties of January 1953, see Barlev, *op. cit.*, p. 78. The agreement paved the way to the acceptance of the "State Education Law" 1953, 131 *LSI*, August 1953, p. 137 (Hebrew).

55. See Jurisdiction of Rabbinical Courts—Marriage and Divorce Law, 134, *LSI*, August 1953, p. 68 (Hebrew).

56. For a description of these processes see: G. Aran, "The Beginning of the Road From Religious Zionism to Zionist Religion," *Studies in Contemporary Jewry*, Vol. 2, Jerusalem and Bloomington, Indiana University Press, 1985, pp. 402-428.

57. The rise of a new generation of young religious political activists and the changes in the National Religious Party are examined in M. Friedman, "The National Religious Party in Crisis," *State, Government and International Relations*, No. 19-20, Spring 1982, pp. 115-120 (Hebrew); E. Don-Yehiya, "Stability and Change in a 'Camp Party': The NRP and the Youth Revolution," *State, Government and International Relations*, No. 14, 1980, pp. 34-43 (Hebrew); E. Sprinzak, "Gush Emunim: The Iceberg Model of Political Extremism," *State, Government and International Relations*, No. 17, Spring 1981, pp. 37-42 (Hebrew).

58. See Palestine Order in Council 1922, in: R.H. Drayton, *Laws of Palestine*, III, pp.25-69.

59. See HC 72/62—"Oswald Rufeisen versus The Minister of Interior," *Piskei Din* (Courts' Judgments), Vol. 16, p. 2428 (Hebrew).

60. See HC 58/68—"Benjamin Shalit in his Name and in the Names of his Children, Oren and Galia, Versus The Minister of Interior and Registration Officer, Haifa District," *Piskei Din* (Courts' Judgments), Vol. 23, II, p. 477 (Hebrew).

61. The commitment to maintain the status quo is included in a letter of D. Ben-Gurion, Y.L. Fishman, and Y. Gruenbaum on behalf of the Jewish Agency Executive sent to Agudat Israel on June 19, 1947. See: Y. Galnoor, D. Avnon, and M. Biton (eds.), *Government of Israel: Book of Sources*, Vol. 2, Jerusalem, Akademon, 1984, pp. 559-561 (Hebrew); for an examination of the implications of the status quo agreement, see C.S. Liebman and E. Don-Yehiya, *Religion and Politics in Israel*, Bloomington, Indiana University Press, 1984, Ch. 3.

62. See, for example, the correlation between the religious background of youngsters and negative attitudes toward Arabs' civil rights as demonstrated in Dahaf Research Institute, *Political Attitudes among Youth: Public Opinion Survey Findings*, Tel Aviv, September 1987, pp. 22-53 (Hebrew).

63. See Y. Harkabi, *Fateful Decisions*, Tel Aviv, Am Oved, 1986, pp. 207-221 (Hebrew); A. Rubinstein, *From Herzl to Gush Emunim*, Jerusalem and Tel Aviv, Schocken, 1980, pp. 111-133 (Hebrew).

64. See I. Shelah, *Patterns of Cross-Community Marriages in Israel, 1952-1968*, Jerusalem, The Hebrew University of Jerusalem, The Center for Documentation and Research on Israeli Society, October 1973 (Hebrew); State of Israel, Central Bureau of Statistics, *The Israel Statistical Yearbook*, No. 38, 1987, Table 7/III, p. 105 (Hebrew).

65. On the role of ethnic synagogues see: S. Deshen, "Patterns of Change of a Religious Tradition: The Ethnic Community Synagogue," in *The Integration of Immigrants from Different Countries of Origin in Israel*, Jerusalem, The Magnes Press, 1969, pp. 66-73 (Hebrew); M. Shokeid, "Precepts versus Tradition: Religious Trends among Middle Eastern Jews," *Megamot*, Vol. 28, No. 2-3, March 1984, pp. 250-264 (Hebrew).

66. The meaning of the concept of "ethnicity" in the Israeli context is a controversial point among sociologists in Israel. Some of the aspects of this controversy were triggered by the publication of E. Ben-Rafael, *The Emergence of Ethnicity: Cultural Groups and Social Conflict in Israel*, Westport, Conn. and London, Greenwood Press, 1982; The author's approach was challenged by S. Smooha in "A Critique of an Updated Establishmentarian Formulation of the Cultural Perspective in the Sociology of Ethnic Relations in Israel," *Megamot*, Vol. 29, No. 1, February 1985, pp. 57-72 (Hebrew); E. Ben-Rafael responding in: "Ethnicity—Theory and Myth," *Megamot*, Vol. 29, No. 2, August 1985, pp. 190-204 (Hebrew); A more specific aspect of ethnicity discussed by social scientists concerns its political implications, see H. Herzog, *Political Ethnicity: Image versus Reality*, Yad Tabenkin, Hakibbutz Hamuchad, 1986 (Hebrew); H. Ayalon, E. Ben-Rafael and S. Sharot, "Ethnicity and Politics: Neglected Aspects," *Megamot*, Vol. 30, No. 3, August 1987, pp. 332-384 (Hebrew); As to the problems of ethnic consciousness, see H. Goldberg, "Historical and Cultural Dimensions of Ethnic Phenomena in Israel," in A. Weingrod, *Studies in Israeli Ethnicity*, New York, Gordon and Breach, Science Publishers, 1985, pp. 179-200; See also S. Deshen, M. Shokeid, "Introduction: The Study of Jews of the Middle East in Israeli Society" in S. Deshen and M. Shokeid (eds.), *Jews of the Middle East*, Jerusalem and Tel Aviv, Schocken, 1984 (Hebrew).

67. See M. Lissak, "The Ethnic Problem and Ethnic Organization in the Jewish Community," *op. cit.*

68. See H. Goldberg, "The Mimouna Festivity in Morocco" in Deshen and Shokeid, *op. cit.*, pp. 106-117 (Hebrew); Y. Ben-Ami, "The Mimouna Festivity of the North African Jews," in: Yeda Am (Folklore), Vol. 17, No. 39-40, pp. 36-44 (Hebrew); J. Halper and H. Abramovitz, "The Saharana Festivity in Kurdistan and Israel," in: Deshen and Shokeid, *op. cit.*, pp. 260-270 (Hebrew).

69. See, for example, M. Abitbol, "The Political System's Impact on the Study of The Eastern Jewish Heritage," in N. Cohen and O. Ahimeir (eds.), *New Directions in the Study of Ethnic Communities*, Jerusalem, The Jerusalem Institute for Israel Studies, 1984, pp. 67-70 (Hebrew).

70. The impact of the ethnic vote in Israeli elections is discussed from different points of view in Y. Peres and S. Shemer, "The Ethnic Vote in the Elections to the Tenth Knesset," *Megamot*, Vol. 28, No. 2-3, March 1984, pp. 323-327 (Hebrew); A. Diskin, "The Jewish Ethnic Vote: The Demographic Myth," *The Jerusalem Quarterly*, No. 35, Spring 1985, pp. 53-60. It is worth noting

that the disagreement between the authors of the two articles concerns forecasts regarding the impact of the ethnic vote in the future rather than the role they played in the past.

71. See M. Lissak, "Continuity and Change in the Voting Patterns of Oriental Jews," in A. Arian (ed.), *The 1969 Israeli Elections*, Jerusalem, Jerusalem Academic Press, 1972, pp. 264-277.

72. See Herzog, *op. cit.*, pp. 170, 181.

73. See B. Gill, *30 Years of Immigration to Eretz Israel—1919-1949*, Jerusalem, The Jewish Agency, 1950, Table 4 (Hebrew).

74. See W. Preuss, "The Occupational Structure and Work Conditions of Jewish Oriental Workers," *Hameshek Hashitufi*, (The Cooperative Economy), August 24, 1939, pp. 219-224 (Hebrew).

75. M. Sicrom, *Immigration to Israel, 1948-1953*, Jerusalem, Falk Institute and the Central Bureau of Statistics, Special Series No. 60, Ch. 9.

76. See H. Darin-Drabkin, *Housing and Immigrant Absorption in Israel 1948-1949*, Tel Aviv: Gadish Books, 1955, p. 120 (Hebrew).

77. See M. Lissak, "Immigrants' Images: Stereotypes and Stigmatization in the Period of Mass Immigration to Israel in the Fifties," in: *Kathedra*, No. 43, March 1987, pp. 138-139 (Hebrew).

78. See, for example, A. Simon, "The Structure of Elementary Education in an Immigrants' Town," *Megamot*, Vol. 3, No. 3, July 1953, pp. 387-389 (Hebrew).

79. See S.N. Eisenstadt, "Immigration Absorption, Integration of Immigrants from Different Countries of Origin and the Transformation of Israeli Society," in *The Integration of Immigrants from Different Countries of Origin in Israel*, Jerusalem, The Magnes Press, 1969, pp. 6-13 (Hebrew).

80. On the immigration from Germany in the Thirties, see M. Geter, "The Immigration from Germany 1933-1939: Social-Economic Absorption versus Social-Cultural Absorption," *Kathedra*, No. 12, July 1979, pp. 125-147 (Hebrew); G. Schocken, "The German Jews in Israel," *Haaretz*, June 19, 1979 (Hebrew).

81. D. McClelland, *The Achieving Society*, Princeton, Van Nostrand, 1961, Ch. 2.

82. For expressions of this approach, see S. Svirski, "The Orientals and Ashkenazim in Israel," Haifa, *Madhbanolt Lemehkar Velebikoret*, Haifa, 1981, pp. 324-329 (Hebrew).

83. See M. Lissak, "Immigrants' Images . . .," *op. cit.*, pp. 144.

84. On factors which affect the use of leisure time in Israel, see E. Katz and M. Gurevitch, *Leisure Culture in Israel*, Tel Aviv, 1973, pp. 101-103 (Hebrew).

85. See S.N. Eisenstadt, *Israeli Society*, Jerusalem, The Magnes Press, 1967, pp. 151-156 (Hebrew).

86. On the Waddi Salib affair, see Government of Israel *Report of Commission of Inquiry on the July 9, 1959 events in Waddi Salib (Haifa)*, presented to the Government of Israel on August 8, 1959 (Hebrew); On the "Black Panthers" see E. Cohen, "The Black Panthers and Israeli Society," *Jewish Journal of Sociology*, Vol. 14, No. 1, June 1972, pp. 93-109. See also, E. Etzioni-Halevy, "Patterns of Conflict Generation and Conflict Absorption: The Cases of Israeli Labor and Ethnic Conflicts," in E. Krausz, (ed.), *Studies of Israeli Society*, Vol. 1, New Brunswick and London, Transaction Books, 1980, pp. 231-254.

88. See Government of Israel, The National Insurance Institute, *Annual Survey*, Jerusalem, 1981, pp. 183-198 (Hebrew).

89. See M. Shamir and A. Arian, "Ethnic Vote in Israel's 1981 Elections," *State, Government and International Relations*, No. 19-20, Spring 1982, pp. 88-104 (Hebrew); A. Arian, "Competitiveness and Polarization: Elections 1981," *The Jerusalem Quarterly*, No. 21, 1981, pp. 3-27; A. Diskin, "The Jewish Ethnic Vote: The Demographic Myth," *op. cit.*, pp. 63-60.

90. See C. Adler, "School Integration and Developments in the Israeli Educational System," in Y. Amir, S. Sharan, and R. Ben-Ari, *School Desegregation*, Tel Aviv, Am Oved, 1985, pp. 48-54 (Hebrew); T.R. Horowitz, "An Awareness Without Legitimation: The Israeli Educational Response to Cultural Differences," *Journal of Educational Policy*, Vol. 3, No. 1, 1988, pp. 1-8.

91. See M. Smilansky, "The Educational System's response to Problems of the Culturally Disadvantaged," in: C. Ormian (ed.), *Education in Israel*, Jerusalem, Keter Publications, 1973, p. 122 (Hebrew).

92. Two volumes contain the results of much of the research on Israel's school integration policy and its implementation: Y. Amir, S. Sharan and R. Ben-Ari, *op. cit.*; M. Chen, C. Adler, and Z. Klein (eds.), special issue on "School Integration in Israel," *Megamot*, Vol. 23, No. 3-4, December 1977 (Hebrew).

93. See Y. Nahon, *Trends in the Occupational Status—the Ethnic Dimension*, Jerusalem, The Jerusalem Institute for Israel Studies, 1984, pp. 30-47, 93-96 (Hebrew). V. Kraus and D. Weintraub, "Community Structure and the Status Attainment Process of the Jewish Population in Israel," *Zeitschrift fur Soziologie*, Vol. 10, No. 4, October 1981, pp. 364-378.

94. See Y. Nahon, *Patterns of Educational Expansion and the Structure of Occupational Opportunities—The Ethnic Dimension*, Jerusalem, The Jerusalem Institute for Israel Studies, 1987, pp. 61-87 (Hebrew).

95. *Ibid.*, pp. 23-26.

96. Nahon, *Trends in Occupational Status, op. cit.*, pp. 61-81.

97. See E. Yaar, "Differences in Ethnic Patterns of Socio-economic Achievement in Israel: A Neglected Aspect of Structural Inquiry," *Megamot*, Vol. 29, No. 4, 1986, pp. 343-412 (Hebrew).

98. For data on socio-economic disparities in Israeli Society, see F. Ginor, *Socio-economic disparities in Israel*, Tel Aviv, Tel Aviv University and Transaction, 1979, Chs. 6-8; G. Hanoch, "Income Differentiation in Israel," in The Falk Institute, *5th Report 1959-1960*, Jerusalem, 1961.

99. C. Arlozoroff, "The Class Struggle in the Eretz Israel Reality," in: C. Arlozoroff, *Writings and Biographical Episodes*, Tel Aviv, Am Oved, 1958, pp. 54-63 (Hebrew).

100. Y. Yoran, "An Economy in a Structural Transition: The Israeli Economy after the Oil Crisis and the Yom Kippur War," *The Economic Quarterly*, Vol. 37, No. 131, 1987, pp. 841-845 (Hebrew).

101. On the expansion of the civil service after the establishment of the State, see D. Arian, "The First Five Years of the Israeli Civil Service," in R. Bachi (ed.), *Studies in Economic and Social Sciences*, Jerusalem, The Magnes Press, 1956, Vol. 3, p. 356; On the growth of the bureaucratic echelon of the Israeli military, see E. Wald, *The Curse of the Broken Tools*, Jerusalem and Tel Aviv, Schocken, 1987, pp. 149-159 (Hebrew).

102. See A. Doron, "The Welfare State: Issues of Rationing and Allocation of Resources," *Social Security*, No. 24, February 1983, pp. 5-15 (Hebrew); J. Habib, "Redistribution of Income through the National Insurance," *Social Security*, No. 9-10, December 1975, pp. 98-114 (Hebrew).

103. On Project Renewal, see M. Hill and N. Karmon, *Project Renewal—an Israeli Experiment in the Neighborhood Rehabilitation*, Haifa, The S. Neeman Institute, The Haifa Technion, June 1979, Publication No. 100/79/02.

104. The implications of the order of priorities in welfare policy for the integration of ethnic groups was referred to by the Waddi Salib Commission of Inquiry, see Government of Israel, *Report of Commission of Inquiry on the July 9, 1959* events in Waddi Salib, pp. 20-21 (Hebrew); See also the report of the commission on "youth in distress" appointed by the Prime Minister after the Black Panthers demonstrations, Israel Prime Minister's Office, *Prime Minister's Commission on Youth in Distress*, Jerusalem, May 1984, Vol. 1, Appendix 1 (Hebrew).

105. See, for example, S. Hershkovitz, *Social Diversity in Israel: The Spatial Pattern*, Jerusalem, The Jerusalem Institute for Israel Studies, 1984 (Hebrew).

106. The compostion and features of the elites of the Jewish community in Palestine are examined in M. Lissak, *The Elites of the Jewish Community in Palestine*, Tel Aviv, Am Oved, 1981, pp. 15-26, 36-44 (Hebrew).

107. See *Ibid.*, pp. 60-80.

108. See D. Miron, "From Creators and Builders to Dwellers," *Igra: Almanac for Literature and Art*, No. 2, 1985-'86, pp. 94-106 (Hebrew).

109. See Lissak, "The Elites . . .," *op. cit.*, pp. 45-60; E. Gutmann and J.M. Landau, "The Israeli Political Elite: Features and Compostition," in M. Lissak and E. Gutmann (eds.), *The Political System of Israel*, Tel Avev, Am Oved, 1974, pp. 195-197, 212-219 (Hebrew).

110. On the reorganization of the IDF after the 1948 war, see E. Luttwak and D. Horowitz, *The Israeli Army*, New York, Harper and Row, 1975, pp. 71-103; On Reorganization of the civil service see: D. Arian, *Op. cit.*, pp. 304-347 (Hebrew). On the reorganization of Higher Education, see D. Shimshoni, *Israeli Democracy: The Middle of the Journey*, New York, The Free Press, 1982, pp. 352-362.

111. See Y. Shapiro, *An Elite Without Successors: Generations of Political Leaders in Israel*, Tel Aviv, Sifriat Poalim, 1984, pp. 128-149 (Hebrew).

112. See S. Sandler, "The National Religious Party: Toward a New Role in Israel's Political System?" in S.N. Lehman-Wilzig and B. Susser (eds.), *Public Life in Israel and Diaspora, op. cit.*, pp. 158-170.

113. On conflicts between government and the press see: M. Negbi, *Paper Tiger: The Struggle for Press Freedom in Israel*, Tel Aviv, Sifriat Poalim, 1985 (Hebrew).

Chapter Three

1. The Zionist inspiration of the founding fathers of Israel is reflected in Israel's *Declaration of Independence* which referred to the Zionist Congress in 1897 and to Theodor Herzl's vision of a Jewish State.

2. See A. Oz, *Under this Blazing Light*, Sifriat Poalim, 1979, p. 92 (Hebrew).

3. See Amendment No. 9, The Knesset—Basic Law, 1155 LSI, August 7, 1985, p. 106 (Hebrew).

4. D. Horowitz, M. Lissak, *Origins of the Israeli Polity*, Chicago, The Chicago University Press, 1978, Ch. 6.

5. For a definition of ideology, see M. Seliger, "Fundamental and Operative Ideology: The Two Principal Dimensions of Political Argumentation," *Policy Sciences*, Vol. 1, (1970), p. 325. Seliger defines ideology as a set of ". . . ideas by which men posit, explain, and justify ends and means of organized human action with the aim to preserve, amend, uproot, or rebuild a given reality."

6. See F.R. Kluckhon, "Dominant and Variant Value Orientation," in C. Kluckhon and H.A. Murray (eds.), *Personality in Nature, Society and Culture,* New York, A. Knopf, 1953, pp. 349-350.

7. See: D. Ben-Gurion, *Vision and Method,* Tel Aviv, (no date), Ayanot Press, p. 43 (Hebrew).

8. On the Canaanites, see Y. Shavit, *From Hebrew to Canaanite: Aspects in the History, Ideology and Utopia of the "Hebrew Renaissance"—from Radical Zionism to Anti-Zionism,* Jerusalem, Domino Press, 1984 (Hebrew).

9. The theoretical rationale of the distinction between Tradition and Traditionalism is presented in E. Shills, "Tradition and Liberty: Antinomy and Interdependence," *Ethics,* Vol. 48, No. 3, 1958, pp. 160-163.

10. See N. Lamm, "The Ideology of Neturei Karta According to the Satmar Version," *Tradition,* Vol. 13, No. 1, pp. 38-53.

11. The most distinguished exponent of this approach was Rabbi A.I. Kook. For citations from his writings manifesting this approach see A. Hertzberg, *The Zionist Idea,* Jerusalem, Keter Publications, 1970, p. 329 (Hebrew); Rabbi Kook's approach was shared by his son Rabbi Z.J. Kook whose views that inspired Gush Emunim are examined in G. Aran, *From Religious Zionism to a Zionist Religion: the Origins and Culture of Gush Emunim—A Messianic Movement in Modern Israel,* Jerusalem, Ph.D. Thesis, The Hebrew University of Jerusalem, 1987, pp. 240-251 (Hebrew).

12. See Y. Drori, "Middle Class Political Organization in Eretz Israel," *Kathedra,* No. 44, June 1987, pp. 116-125 (Hebrew).

13. The confusion regarding the foundations of socialist ideology in both the international and the Israeli context is demonstrated in the contributions of some of the labor movement leaders such as M. Sharett and P. Lavon and of leading Israeli intellectuals to a book published following a symposium on the changing meaning of socialism, Min Hayesod Publication No. 2, *Capitalism and Socialism,* Tel Aviv, Kadima Press, 1963. (Particularly relevant in this context is Y. Yagol's article "The Liberation of Mapai from the Ideological Burden of the Past," p. 178) (Hebrew); see also G. Yatziv, *The Heart of the Matter,* Tel Aviv, Adam, 198, pp. 132-144 (Hebrew).

14. See D. Ben-Gurion, *Memiors,* Vol. 1, Tel Aviv, Am Oved, 1971, pp. 475-480 (Hebrew).

15. See Z. Jobotinsky, "On the Evacuation Plan," *Speeches 1927-1940,* Jerusalem, E. Jabotinsky, 1948, pp. 195-212 (Hebrew).

16. See Jabotinsky speech in the seventeenth Zionist Congress in Jabotinsky, "Speeches . . ." *op. cit.,* pp. 122, 131 (Hebrew).

17. See Y. Gorny, *Achdut Ha'avodah 1919-1930: The Ideological Principles and the Political System,* Tel Aviv, Tel Aviv University Press and Hakibbutz Hameuchad, 1973, pp. 23-28 (Hebrew).

18. See M. Lissak, "Immigration Policy in the Fifties: Organizational Aspects and their Political Implications" in A. Shinan (ed.), *Emigration and Settlement in Jewish and General History,* Jerusalem, The Zalman Shazar Center, 1982, pp.255-261 (Hebrew); T. Segev, *1949—The First Israelis,* Jerusalem, The Domino Press, 1984, pp. 142-149 (Hebrew).

19. See, for example, D. Ben-Gurion, "Uniqueness and Mission," in *Government of Israel Yearbook,* Jerusalem, 1951, p. 25 (Hebrew).

20. On the circumstances in which the Peace Now movement came into being, see M. Bar-On, *Peace Now: The Portrait of a Movement,* Tel Aviv, Hakibbutz Hameuchad, 1985 (Hebrew).

21. David Ben-Gurion expressed this view in a speech delivered to the opening session of the Rehovot Conference on the Economic and Social Development of Developing Countries; see David Horowitz, *In the Heart of Events,* Ramat Gan, Massada, 1975, p. 41 (Hebrew).

22. For Arlozoroff's condemnation of "heroic economics," see C. Arlozoroff, *Selected Writings and Memoir,* Tel Aviv, Am Oved and The Zionist Library, 1968, p. 39 (Hebrew).

23. See David Horowitz, "In The Heart . . ." *op. cit.,* p. 41 (Hebrew).

24. See A. Shapira, *The Futile Struggle: The Jewish Labor Controversy 1929-1939,* Tel Aviv, Tel Aviv University and Hakibbutz Hameuchad, 1977, pp. 103-110 (Hebrew).

25. A poetic expression of Greenberg's views can be found in his book of poems: U.Z. Greenberg, *The Book of Denunciation and Faith,* Jerusalem and Tel Aviv, Sadan, 1937 (Hebrew).

26. See D. Ben-Gurion, *The Restored State of Israel,* Vol. 1, Tel Aviv, Am Oved, p. 65 (Hebrew).

27. See D. Ben-Gurion, *op. cit.,* p. 68 (Hebrew).

28. See A. Eban, *Life Story,* Tel Aviv, Sifriat Maariv, Vol. 1, 1978, pp. 71-84 (Hebrew).

29. See David Horowitz "In the Heart . . ." *op. cit.,* pp. 115-130 (Hebrew); The Falk Institute, The Hebrew University of Jerusalem, 1983, Ch. 3 (Hebrew).

30. See Barkai *op. cit.,* p. 42 (Hebrew).

31. See Segev *op. cit.,* pp. 153-154 (Hebrew).

32. On the Labor Brigade of the 1920s, see E. Margalit, *Kibbutz, Society and Politics*, Tel Aviv, Am Oved, 1980, (Hebrew); A. Shapira, "The Dream and Disillusion: The Political Development of the Labor Brigade," *Baderech*, December 1968, August 1969 (Hebrew).

33. See A. Eliav, *The Short Cut*, Tel Aviv, Am Oved, 1985, Ch. 25 (Hebrew).

34. See B.Z. Fishler, "Language Instruction in the Period of Mass Immigration," in M. Naor (ed.), *Immigrants and Maabarot: 1948-1952*, Jerusalem, Yad Ben Zvi, 1987, pp. 145-156 (Hebrew).

35. See Jerusalem—Capital of Israel 1980: Basic Law, 980 *LSI*, August 5, 1980, p. 186 (Hebrew).

36. See Ramat Hagolan Law 1980, 1034 *LSI*, December 5, 1981 (Hebrew).

37. See Y. Harkabi, *Fateful Decisions*, Tel Aviv, Am Oved, 1986, p. 261 (Hebrew); E. Sprinzak, *Every Man Whatever is Right in his Own Eyes: Illegalism in Israeli Society*, Tel Aviv, Sifriat Poalim, 1986, pp. 121-145 (Hebrew); M. Negbi, "The Boundaries of Disobedience," *Politica*, No. 7, April 1986, pp. 4-5 (Hebrew).

38. See Harkabi, "Fateful . . .," *op. cit.*, pp. 234-242 (Hebrew).

39. See Z. Jabotinsky, *The Idea of Betar*, Tel Aviv, A. Betar Publication, 1934, pp. 18-19 (Hebrew).

40. The quotation is from LHI's anthem "Unknown Soldiers" (Hebrew). The author is the founder and first commander of LHI, Avraham Stern (Yair).

41. See Y. Shavit, *Revisionism in Zionism*, Tel Aviv, Yariv and Hadar, 1978, Ch. 5 (Hebrew).

42. Y. Drori, *op. cit.*, pp. 116-125 (Hebrew).

43. Z. Jabotinsky, *Towards a State*, Jerusalem, Jabotinsky Press, 1953, p. 74 (Hebrew).

44. See B. Kimmerling, *The Interrupted System: Israeli Civilians in War and Routine Times*, New Brunswick and Oxford, Transaction Books, 1985, pp.163-164.

45. On the effects of societal changes on the kibbutzim in the '50s and early '60s, see Y. Garber-Talmon, *The Individual and Society in the Kibbutz*, Jerusalem, The Magnes Press, 1970, pp. 223-263 (Hebrew).

46. See B. Kimmerling, "The Israeli Civil Guard," in L.A. Zurcher and G. Harries-Jenkins (eds.), *Supplementary Military Force; Reserves, Militias, Auxiliaries*, Beverly Hills and London: Sage Publications, 1978, pp. 107-125.

47. This saying is attributed to the English-Jewish novelist Israel Zangwill (1864-1926). Quoted in A. Elon, *The Israelis: Founders and Sons*, New York, Chicago, San Francisco, Holt, Rinehart and Winston, 1971, p. 149.

48. See HCJ (High Court of Justice) 253/64, *Piskei Din* (Courts' Judgments), No. 18, p. 637 (Hebrew).

49. For a comprehensive examination of the various positions on the "Arab Question" in the Yishuv, see Y. Gorny, *The Arab Question and the Jewish Problem,* Tel Aviv, Am Oved, 1985 (Hebrew).

50. See A.D.S. Smith, *Nationalism in the Twentieth Century,* Oxford, Martin Robertson, Ch. 4.

51. See Gorny, "The Arab Question . . ." *op. cit.,* pp. 19-108 (Hebrew).

52. See J. Katz, *Between Jews and Gentiles,* Jerusalem, Bialik Institute, 1960, pp. 17-57 (Hebrew).

53. See Harkabi, "Fateful Decisions . . ." *op. cit.,* pp. 211, 225 (Hebrew).

54. See B. Kimmerling, "Between the Primordial and the Civil Definitions of the Collective Identity: Eretz Israel as the State of Israel," in E. Cohen, M. Lissak, and U. Almagor (eds.), *Comparative Social Dynamics,* Essays in Honor of S.N. Eisenstadt, Boulder and London, Westview Press, 198 pp. 262-283; E. Cohen, "Ethnicity and Legitimation in Contemporary Israel," *The Jerusalem Quarterly,* No. 28, Summer 1983, pp. 111-124.

55. See S. Avineri, "Ideology and Israel's Foreign Policy," *Jerusalem Quarterly,* no. 37, 1968, p. 4-8.

56. See The analysis of the platform of the Greater Israel Movement, in D. Miron, "An Israeli Document," *Politica,* a special appendix of the August 1987 issue, No. 16, pp. 31-44 (Hebrew).

57. See S. Avineri, "A Right and an Attachment," *Maariv,* June 5, 1973 (Hebrew).

58. See A. Eliav, *Glory in the Land of the Living,* Tel-Aviv, 1972 (Hebrew).

59. See D. Schueftan, *A Jordanian Option,* Ef-al, Yad Tabenkin and Hikibbutz Hameuchad, Ch. 17 (Hebrew).

60. See Z. Schiff and E. Yaari, *A War of Deception,* Jerusalem and Tel-Aviv, Schocken, 1984, pp. 37, 241 (Hebrew).

61. See Schueftan, *op. cit.,* pp. 336-338 (Hebrew).

62. See B. Kimmerling, "A Paradigm for the Analysis of the Relationship between the State of Israel and American Jewry,"in *Yahadut Zemanenu — Comtemporary Jewry,* No. 4, 1977, pp. 15-21, (Hebrew); S.M. Cohen, *Attitudes of American Jews Toward Israel and Israelis,* Institute on American Jewish-Israeli Relations, The American Jewish Committee, September 1983; G. Sheffer, "The Uncertain Future of American Jewry — Israel Relations," The Jerusalem Quarterly, No. 32, Summer 1984, pp. 66-80.

63. See D. Ben-Gurion, "The Glory of Israel" in Government of Israel Yearbook 1954, pp. 37-43 (Hebrew).

64. See Kimmerling, "A paradigm..." *op. cit.*, pp. 3-6, (Hebrew); for a criticism of the prevailing pattern of Israel-Diaspora relations, see A.B. Yehoshua, *Between Right and Right*, Jerusalem and Tel Aviv, Schocken, 1984, pp. 27-74 (Hebrew).

65. U. Schmelz, "Evolution and Projection of World Jewish Population," *Yahadut Zemanenu — Contemporary Jewry*, No. 1, 1984, pp. 301-318, (Hebrew).

66. On the various Zionist approaches to Jewish Nationalism, see S. Avineri, *Varieties of Zionist Thought*, Tel Aviv, Am Oved, 1980 (Hebrew).

67. See Y. Gorny, *Partnership and Conflict*, Tel-Aviv, The Institute for the Study of Zionism, Tel Aviv University, 1976 (Hebrew).

68. Y. Shapiro, "The Weizmann-Brandeis conflict," *Zionism*, Vol. 3, 1974, pp. 258-272 (Hebrew); A. Gal, "Brandeis' View on the Upbuilding of Palestine," *Zionism*, Vol. 6, 1981, pp. 97-146, (Hebrew); P. STrum, *Louis D. Brandeis: Justice for the People*, Cambridge, and London, Harvard University Press, 1984, pp. 266-290.

69. See Shavit, "Revisionism...," *op. cit.*, pp. 164-180 (Hebrew).

70. See E. Margalit, *Anatomy of the Left*, Jerusalem, The Hebrew University of Jerusalem and the I.L. Peretz Press, 1976, pp. 103-105 (Hebrew).

71. See "The London Conference Raport," *Haolam (The World)*, August 16, 1920 (Hebrew).

72. See D. Ben-Gurion, *From Class to Nation*, Tel-Aviv, Davar, 1935, pp. 254 (Hebrew).

73. See N.T. Gross and J. Metzer, "Public Finance in the Jewish Economy in interwar Palestine," *Research in Economic History*, Vo. 3, 1978, pp. 87-160.

74. See Y. Gelber, "Zionist Policy and the Transfer Agreement 1933," *Yalkut Moreshet*, No. 18, February 1974, pp. 97-151.

75. A. Minz, "Military-Industrial Linkages in Israel," *Armed Forces and Society*, Fall 1985, Vol. 12, No. 1, pp. 11-12.

76. On capital investment in Israel in the 1950s, see D. Patinkin, "Israel's Economy in the First Decade," in The Falk Institute, *4th Report 1957-1958*, Jerusalem, The Falk Institute, 1959, pp. 73-82 (Hebrew).

77. See D. Horowitz, "Between Pioneer Society and ' Like All Other Nations'," *Moland*, No. 146-147, October 1960, pp. 427-429 (Hebrew).

78. See D. Worowitz, "Mapam Comes Back Home," *Molad*, No. 113-114, December 1957, pp. 571-580 (Hebrew).

79. See E. Margalist, *Hashomer Hatzair: From Youth Community to Revolutionary Marxism 1913-1936,* Tel Aviv, Tel Aviv University and Hakibbutz Hameuchad, 1971, pp. 136-139 (Hebrew).

80. See Y. Ben-Aharon, "His Personality and Thought," and D. Rudner, "On His Zionist Political Thought," in A. Pialkov and Y. Rabinowitz, (eds.), *Yitzhak Tabenkin — His Life Story and Deeds,* Yad Tabenkin, Hakibbutz Hameuchad, 1982, pp. 205-208 and 320-324.

81. See C. Gvati, *A Century of Jewish Settlement,* Tel Aviv, Hakibbutz Hameuchad, 1981, pp. 137-138 (Hebrew).

82. See A. Doron, *the Struggle for National Insurance 1948-1953,* Jerusalem, The Baerwald School of Social Work, The Hebrew University of Jerusalem, 1975 (Hebrew); A. Doron, "National Insurance in Israel — Patterns of Structure and Change," *State, Government and International Relations,* No. 13, Winter 1979, pp. 63-81 (Hebrew).

83. See E. Kleiman, "The Histadrut Economy in Israel in Search of Criteria," *The Jerusalem Quarterly,* No. 41, Winter 1987, pp. 84-89; E. Kleiman, "From Cooperative to Industrial Empire: The Story of Solel Boneh," *Midstream,* March 1964, pp. 26-51.

84. See A. Daniel, "Cooperation Between Histadrut Capital, State Capital and Private Ownership," *The Economic Quarterly,* No. 76, November 1972, pp. 338-345 (Hebrew).

85. On the opposition of the left to the abolition of the Labor Stream in Education, see A. Zisling, "The State Education Law," *Mibefnim,* Vol. 17, No. 1-2, November 1953, pp. 29-33, (Hebrew); M. Yaari, *The Trials of Our Generation,* Tel Aviv, Sifriat Poalim, 1953, pp. 143-149 (Hebrew).

86. See P. Lavon, "Beyond the Barriers," and Z. Goldberg, "Democracy in Israel," in *From the Foundations: A collection of Essays,* Tel Aviv, Amikam, 1962, pp. 55-93 and 220-229 (Hebrew).

87. See Y. Reshef and M. Netzer, "The Forum opf the thirteen Works Committees," *The Economic Quarterly,* No. 126, April 1983, pp. 532-541, (Hebrew); Y. Yishi, *Interest Groups in Israel,* Tel Aviv and Jerusalem, Am Oved and The Eshkol Institute — the Hebrew University of Jerusalem, 1987, p. 102 (Hebrew).

88. E. Rosenstein, "Workers' Participation in Management: Problematic Issues in the Israeli System," *Industrial Relations Journal,* Vol. 8, No. 2, pp. 55-69; M. Rosner and J.R. Blasi, "Theories of Participatory Democracy and the Kibbutz," in E. Cohen, M. Lissak and U. Almagor (eds.), *Comparative Social Dynamics — Essays in Honor of S.N. Eisenstadt,* Boulder, Westview Press, 1984, pp. 295-314.

89. See D. Horowitz, "Between Pioneer Society...," *op. cit.*, pp. 416-418 (Hebrew).

90. The most comprehensive work that applies the concept of civil religion to the case of Israel is C. Liebman and E. Don Yehiya, *Civil Religion in Israel*, Berkeley, University of California Press, 1983.

91. On the concept of presentation of the self see: E. Goffman, *The Presentation of Self in Everyday Life*, Garden City, NY, Doubleday Anchor Books, 1959.

92. See C. Adler and Y. Peres, "The Youth Movement and the 'Salon' Peer Group: A Comparative Analysis of Cultural Patterns," in S.N. Eisenstadt (ed.) et.al., *Education and Society in Israel*, Jerusalem, Akademon, 1968, pp. 361-381 (Hebrew).

93. See D. Miron, "From Creators and Builders to Homeless Persons," in *Igra*, No. 2, a yearbook published by Keter Publications, 1985-1986, pp. 104-106, (Hebrew); G. Shaked, *Hebrew Narrative Fiction 1880-1980*, Jerusalem, Hakibbutz Hameuchad and Keter Publications, 1983, Vol. 2, pp. 287-300 (Hebrew); A. Cordova and H. Herzog, "The Cultural Endeavor of the Labor Movement Between Intelligentsia and Intellectuals," *YIVO Annual of Jewish Science*, Vol. 17, 1972, pp. 247-252.

94. See E. Schweid, *The World of A.D. Gordon*, Tel Aviv, Am Oved, 1970, Ch. 6 (Hebrew).

95. See R. Kahane, "Attitudes of the Dominant Ideology in the Yishuv Period towards Science, Scientists and Professionals," in S.N. Eisenstadt (ed.) et. at., *Strata in Israel*, Jerusalem, Akademon, 1968, pp. 181-236 (Hebrew).

96. See A. Shapira, *Berl Katznelson: A Biography*, Am Oved, 1980, p. 309 (Hebrew).

97. See H. Lavski, "The First Days of Brit Shalom and the German Zionists," in *Yahadut Zemanenu: Contemporary Jewry*, No. 4, 1987, pp. 110-121 (Hebrew); A. Kedar, "The Views of Brit Shalom," in B.Z. Yehoshua and A. Kedar, (eds.), *Ideology and Zionist Policy*, Jerusalem, The Zalman Shazar Center, 1978, pp. 97-114 (Hebrew).

98. See S.N. Eisenstadt, *Israeli Society: Background Development Problems*, Jerusalem, The Magnes Press, 1966, pp. 151-163 (Hebrew).

99. See S. Reshef, "Ben Gurion and State Education," *Kathedra*, No. 43, March 1987, pp. 91-114 (Hebrew).

100. See S.N. Goldthorpe, "Class, Status and Party in Modern Britain: Some Recent Interpretations, Marxist and Marxisant," *Archives Europeennes de Sociologie*, Tome XIII, No. 2, 1972, p. 348.

101. See Y. Yishai, *Interest Groups in Israel, op. cit.,* pp. 127 1987, (Hebrew).

102. See A. Arian, *The Choosing People,* Ramat Gan, Massada, 1973, pp. 48-49 (Hebrew).

103. See Y. Yagol, "The Strength of Socialism in Israel," in *Capitalism and Socialism,* Tel-Aviv, Min Hayessod, 1963, p. 178 (Hebrew).

104. See M. McLuhan, and Q. Fiore, *War and Peace in the Global Village,* New York, Bantam Books, 1968.

105. See Shavit, "Revisionism. . .," *op. cit.,* pp. 241-253 (Hebrew).

106. A. Arian, "The Israeli Electorate, 1977," in A. Arian (ed.), *The Elections in Israel, 1977,* Jerusalem, Jerusalem Academic Press, 1980, pp. 253-278.

107. On the circumstances in which the issue of dual identity evolved see Y. Katz, *Out of the Ghetto,* New York, Schocken Books, 1978, Ch. 12; S. Ettinger, *History of the Jewish People,* Vol. 3, Tel Aviv, Dvir, 1969, Ch. 9 (Hebrew).

108. See C. Liebman and E. Don-Yehiya, *Religion and Politics in Israel,* Bloomington, Indiana University Press, 1984, Ch. 5.

109. See HCJ 76/62, O. Rufeisen versus the Minister of Interior, *Piskei Din* (Judgments), Vol. 16, p. 2428 (Hebrew).

110. On the history of the "Who is a Jew?" controversy, see M. Samet, "Who is a Jew 1958-1977," *The Jerusalem Quarterly,* No. 36, Summer 1985, pp. 88-108.

111. A.F. Kleinberger, *Society, Schools and Progress in Israel,* Oxford, Pergamon Press, 1969, pp. 323-330.

112. See J. Aviad, *Return to Judaism,* Chicago, The University of Chicago Press, 1983.

113. See Leibman and Don-Yehiya, "Religion and Politics. . .," *op. cit.,* Ch. 5.

114. See E. Sivan, *Radical Islam, Medieval Theology and Modern Politics,* Tel Aviv, Am Oved, 1985 (Hebrew).

115. This attitude is expressed in an article by one of the initiators of the underground activities in the settlers' journal, Y. Etzion, "I considered myself obliged to prepare an operation in order to purify the Temple Mountain," *Nekuda,* No. 88, June 6, 1985, pp. 24-25 (Hebrew); for an examination of the implications of such attitude, see Sprinzak, *op. cit.,* Ch. 8 (Hebrew).

116. See G. Aran, "The Beginnings of the Road from Religious Zionism to Zionist Religion," *Studies in Contemporary Jewry,* Vol. 2, Jerusalem and Bloomington, Indiana University Press, 1985, pp. 402-428.

117. See Sprinzak, *op. cit.*, pp. 140-141 (Hebrew)

118. See S.Z. Abramov, *Perpetual Dilemma — Jewish Religion in a Jewish State,* London, Associate University Press, 1976, pp. 128-134.

119. For a discussion and criticism of the treatment of the press by Israeli decision-makers, see M. Negbi, *Paper Tiger: The Struggle for Press Freedom,* Tel Aviv, Sifriat Poalim, 1985 (Hebrew); See also D. Goren, *Freedom of the Press and National Security,* Jerusalem, Magnes Press, 1976, Ch. 3 (Hebrew).

120. On the Lavon Affair, see E. Hassin and D. Horowitz, *The Affair,* Tel Aviv, Am Hassefer, 1961, (Hebrew); N. Yanai, *Political Crises in Israel,* Jerusalem, Keter Publications, 1982, pp. 99-184 (Hebrew).

121. See Z. Gil, *The House of Precious Stones: Case History of Israeli Television,* Tel Aviv, Sifriat Poalim (Hebrew).

122. On the post Yom Kippur War protest movement, see reports and interviews with activists in *Haaretz,* April 15, 1974 and April 17, 1974 (Hebrew); *Yediot Aharonot,* April 16, 1974, (Hebrew); for a detailed description and an analysis, see G. Barzilai, *Democracy in War: Attitudes, Reactions and Political Participation of the Israeli Public in Processes of Decision-Making,* Ph.D. Thesis submitted to the Hebrew University of Jerusalem, 1987, pp. 168-176 (Hebrew).

123. The status of the Attorney General is examined from the viewpoint of its critics in Y. Guttman, *The Attorney General versus the Government,* Jerusalem, Idanim, 1981 (Hebrew).

124. See M. Negbi, *Above the Law: The Constitutional Crisis in Israel,* Tel Aviv, Am Oved, 1987, pp. 47-98, (Hebrew); R. Gavison, *Civil Rights and Democracy,* Jerusalem, The Israeli Association for Civil Rights, 1985 (Hebrew).

125. On the confrontation in Yamit between the settlers and the Army see G. Aran, *Eretz Israel: Between Politics and Religion,* Jerusalem, The Jerusalem Institute for Israel Studies (Hebrew).

126. See G. Shafir and Y. Peled, "'Thorns in your Eyes'; the Socio-economic Characteristics of the Sources of Electoral Support of Rabbi Kahane," *State, Government and International Relations,* No. 25, Spring 1986, pp. 115-130 (Hebrew).

127. See N. Yuval-Davis, *"Matzpen—the Israeli Socialist Organization,* Jerusalem, The Hebrew University of Jerusalem, Deparment of Sociology, 1977 (Hebrew).

128. The positions of the *Yesh Gvul* movement are presented in a collection of essays: Y. and D. Menuchin (eds.), *The Limits of Obedience,* Tel Aviv, the Yesh Gvul Movement and Siman Kria Books, 1985 (Hebrew).

Chapter Four

1. On the political party key and its role in the politics of the Yishuv, see D. Horowitz, M. Lissak, *Origins of the Israeli Polity: Palestine under the Mandate,* Chicago, The University of Chicago Press, 1978, pp. 179, 182-183, 203, 210, 225; I. Galnoor, *Steering the Polity: Communication and Politics in Israel,* Beverly Hills and London, Sage Publications, 1982, Ch. 7.

2. On the notion of "minimal winning coalition," see W. Riker, *The Theory of Political Coalitions,* New Haven, Yale University Press, 1962, pp. 81-89; W.A. Gamson, "A Theory of Coalition Formation," *AMerican Sociological Review,* Vol. 26, June 1961, pp. 373-383.

3. For a discussion on the applicability of the consociational model to the case of Israel, see E. Gutmann, "Parties and Camps — Stability and Change," in M. Lissak and E. Gutmann (eds.), *The Israeli Political System,* Tel Aviv, Am Oved, 1977, pp. 155-170 (Hebrew).

4. On the support of rabbinical education by the state and the mode of its allocation, see *State Controller Report,* No. 33, 1983, pp. 217-221 (Hebrew).

5. The National Insurance system is based on the National Insurance Law, 1953, LSI November 1953, pp. 6-31 (Hebrew).

6. See M. Sarnat, *Saving and Investment Through Retirement Funds in Israel,* Jerusalem, The Falk Institute, 1966, Ch. 5 (Hebrew).

7. On the mobilization of resources for the war effort in 1948, see H. Barkai, *The Formative Years of the Israeli Economy,* Jerusalem, The Falk Institute, December 1983, pp. 29-30, (Hebrew); Y. Greenberg, "The Sources for the Financing of the War of Independence," in M. Naor (ed.), *The First Year of Independence 1948-1949,* Jerusalem, Yad Ben Zvi, 1988 (Hebrew).

8. See D. Handelman, and L. Shamgar-Handelman, "Shaping Time: The Choice of the National Emblem in Israel," in E. Ohnuki-Ticracy (ed.), *Symbolism and History,* (forthcoming).

9. See Horowitz, Lissak, *op. cit.,* pp. 188-189.

10. See Barkai, *op. cit.,* pp. 38-90.

11. The treatment of the state as a variable suggested in an essay by J.P. Nettle published in 1968 gave rise to the use of the notion of "stateness"; see J.P. Nettle, "The State as a Conceptual Variable," *World Politics,* Vol. 20, No. 4, July 1968, pp. 559-592.

12. See Law and Administration Ordinance 1948, *Iton Rishmi* (official Gazette), 1948, Appendix 1, Article 11 (Hebrew).

13. On the process of transition to the status of a sovereign state, see Z. Sharef, *Three Days,* Tel Aviv, Am Oved, 1959, pp. 38-58 (Hebrew).

14. See S. Sager, *The Parliamentary System of Israel,* Syracuse, Syracuse University Press, 1985, pp. 34-36.

15. For the Knesset decision of June 13, 1950 which is known as "the Harari's compromise," see *Divrei Hanesset,* (Knesset Proceedings), June 13, 1950 (Hebrew).

16. The Basic Laws enacted by the Knesset since the 1950 decision are: *Basic Law: The Knesset, 244 LSI,* February 12, 1958, pp. 69-71 (Hebrew); *"Basic Law: The President" LSI,* June 16, 1964, pp. 118-121, (Hebrew); *"Basic Law: The Government,"* 540, *LSI,* August 13, 1968, pp. 226-231 (Hebrew); *"Basic Law: the State Economy,"* 777, *LSI,* July 21, 1976, p. 206 (Hebrew); *"Basic Law: Jerusalem,"* Capital of Israel" 980 *LSI,* p. 186, (Hebrew); *"Basic Law: The Judiciary,"* 1100 *LSI* February 28, 1984, pp. 78-81 (Hebrew).

17. A majority of sixty-one members of the Knesset is required in order to change the election system in Israel as defined in Article 4 of "Basic Law: The Knesset" *op. cit.* (Hebrew).

18. See Article 42a of "Basic Law: The Knesset," *op. cit.,* (Hebrew).

19. For the details of the debate in Israel on the election system, see A. Brichta, *Democracy and Elections,* Tel Aviv, Am Oved, 1977, Chs. 1-4 (Hebrew).

20. On the fall of the dominant party in 1977, see D. Horowitz "More than a Change of Government," *The Jerusalem Quarterly,* No. 5, Fall 1975, pp. 3-20 and A. Arian "The Passing of Dominance": *The Jerusalem Quarterly,* No. 5, Fall 1977, pp. 13-32; Y. Shapiro, "The End of the Dominant Party System," in: A. Arian (ed.), *The Elections in Israel 1977,* Jerusalem, Academic Press, 1980, pp. 23-38.

21. See Judgment of HCJ 73/53, 87/53 — Kol Ha'am Ltd. and the El-itichad Newspaper versus the Minister of Interior, *Piskei Din Shel Beit Hamishpat Haelion,* No. 13, 1953, p. 423 (Hebrew).

22. See HCJ Judgment 23/62: Attorney General versus Aaron Cohen, *Piskei Din,* No. 16, 1962, pp. 2257-2259 (Hebrew).

23. See HCJ Judgment 287/69 "Simcha Miron versus The Minister of Labor, The Broadcasting Authority and the Minister of Post," *Piskei Din,* Vol. 27, Part 1, p. 337 (Hebrew).

24. See A. Rubinstein, "The Changing Status of the Territories," *Iyunei Mishpat,* Vol. 11, No. 3, October 1986, p. 439 (Hebrew).

25. See M. Negbi, *Above the Law: The Constitutional Crisis in Israel,* Tel Aviv, Am Oved, 1987, pp. 117-126 (Hebrew).

26. See M. Shamgar, "On the Written Constitution," *Israel Law Review*, Vol. 4, No. 4, October 1974, pp. 467-476; M. Shamgar, "Legislation, Judiciary and Civil Rights," *Hapraklit*, Vol. 37, No. 1-2, October 1986, pp. 5-12 (Hebrew).

27. See HCJ Judgment 89/69: A.A. Bergman versus the Minister of Finance and the State Controller, *Piskei Din*, Vol. 23, Part 1, p. 693 (Hebrew); See also HCJ Judgment 231/73: A.A. Bergman versus the Minister of Finance, *Piskei Din*, Vol. 27, Part 2, p. 785 (Hebrew).

28. See Y. Gutman, *The Attorney General versus the Government*, Jerusalem, Idanim, 1981, (Hebrew).

29. See M. Negbi, "Above the Law. . .," *op. cit.*, pp. 9-24, 99-126 (Hebrew).

30. See Commissions of Inquiry Law 1969, 548 *LSI*, January 1, 1969, p. 28 (Hebrew).

31. The Commission of Inquiry on the Yom Kippur War (the Agranat Commission) was appointed by the Israeli Government on November 18, 1973. For the published part of its report, see *The Agranat Commission Report*, Tel Aviv, Am Oved, 1975 (Hebrew).

32. The Commission of Inquiry on the Sabra and Shatila massacre (the Kahan Commission) was appointed by the Israeli Government on August 28, 1982. It recommended the removal of the Minister of Defense Ariel Sharon from his office.

33. The functions of the State Controller are defined in "The State Controller Law 1958," 248 *LSI*, February 19, 1958, p. 92 (Hebrew); The functions and powers of the Governor oaf the Bank of Israel are defined in "The Bank of Israel Law 1954," 164 *LSI*, August 3, 1954, p. 192 (Hebrew).

34. See "The Broadcasting Authority Law 1965," 451 *LSI*, March 17, 1965, p. 106 (Hebrew).

35. See I. Galnoor, *Steering the Polity: Communication an Politics in Israel*, Tel Aviv, Am Oved, 1985, pp. 184-202 (Hebrew).

36. Various aspects of the Israeli Political party system are dealt with in the following works. These are only a sample of the numerous publications in political science and political sociology that refer to the subject. See B. Akzin, "The Role of Parties in Israeli Democracy," *The Journal of Politics*, Vol. 17, No. 4, November 1955, pp. 507-545; A. Arian, "The passing of Dominance," *The Jerusalem Quarterly*, No. 5, Fall 1977, pp. 20-32; A. Arian and M. Shamir, "The Primary Political Functions of the Left-Right Continuum," *Comparative Politics*, Vol. 15, No. 2, January 1973, pp. 139-158; M.J. Aronoff, "The Decline of the Israeli Labor Party: Causes and Significance," in H.R. Penniman, (ed.), *Israel at the Polls: the Knesset Elections of 1977*, Washington D.C., American Enterprise Institute for

Public Policy Research, 1979, pp. 115-146; S. Aronson and N. Yanai, "Critical Aspects of the Elections and their Implication," in D. Caspi, A. Diskin, and E. Gutmann (eds.), *The Roots of Begin's Success: The 1981 Elections*, London, Croom Helm, 1983, pp. 11-42; Y. Azmon, "The 1981 Elections and the Changing Fortunes of the Israeli Labor Party," *Government and Oppostition*, Vol. 16, No. 4, Autumn 1981, pp. 432-446; D. Caspi, "Following the Race Propaganda and Electoral Decision," in D. Caspi, A. Diskin, and E. Gutmann (eds.), *op. cit.*, pp. 245-272; I. Galnoor, *Steering the Polity: Communication and Politics In Israel*, Beverly Hills and London, Sage Publications, 1982; H. Herzog, "Ethnic Political Identity: The Ethnic Lists to the Delegates' Assembly and the Knesset 1920-1977, Ph.D. Theses, Tel Aviv University, 1981; C. Liebman and E. Don-Yehiya, *Piety and Politics, Religion and Politics in Israel*, Bloomington, Indiana University Press, 1984; P. Medding, *Mapai in Israel*, Cambridge, Cambridge University Press, 1972; O. Seliktar, "Acquiring Partisan Preferences in a Plural Society: the Case of Israel," *Plural Societies*, Vol. 11, No. 4, Winter, 1980, pp. 3-20; D. Shimshoni, *Israeli Democracy: The Middle of the Journey*, New York, Free Press, 1981; E. Sprinzak, "Extreme Politics in Israel," *The Jerusalem Quarterly*, No. 5, Fall 1977, pp. 33-47; S. Weiss, "Results of Local Elections" in A. Arian, (ed.), *The Elections in Israel 1969*, Jerusalem Academic Press, 1972, pp. 96-108; Y. Yishai, "Israel Right-Wing Jewish Proletariat," *The Jewish Journal of Sociology*, Vol. 24, No. 2, 1982, pp. 87-97.

37. See A. Diskin, "Polarization and Volatility in the Election for the Tenth Knesset," *State, Government and International Relations*, No. 19-20, 1982, pp. 44-62 (Hebrew).

38. See A. Diskin, "The Competitive Multi-Party System of Israel 1949-1973," Jerusalem, Ph.D. Theses Presented to the Hebrew University of Jerusalem, 1976, pp. 143-175 (Hebrew).

39. On the rise and fall of the DMC, see A. Rubinstein, *A Certain Political Experience*, Tel Aviv, Idanim, 1982 (Hebrew); N. Urieli an A. Barzilai, *The Rise and Fall of the Democratic Movement for Change*, Tel Aviv, Reshafim, 1982 (Hebrew).

40. The "Club of the Four," after the 1961 election included the Liberal Party, The National Religious Party, Achdut Ha'avodah and Mapam. The Club disintegrated following the defection of the NRP which reached a separate agreement with Mapai.

41. See Horowitz, "More Than a Change . . .," *op. cit.*, pp. 3-19.

42. For election results, see Appendix No. 1-2.

43. See U. Bialer, "Ben-Gurion and Israel's Foreign Policy Orientation 1948-1956," *Kathedra*, No. 43, March 1987, pp. 145-174 (Hebrew).

44. See Y. Beilin, *The Cost of Unity: The Labor Party before the Yom Kippur War*, Tel Aviv, Revivim, 1985, Appendix on pp. 244-247 (Hebrew).

45. See *Ibid,* Chs. 2-5 (Hebrew).

46. See Appendix No. 1-2.

47. See I. Galnoor, "Transformation in the Israeli Political System Since the Yom Kippur War," in Arian (ed.), *The Election in Israel 1977, op. cit.,* pp. 119-148.

48. The stalemate was a consequence of the emergence of two balanced "blocking groupings" consisting of sixty Knesset Members each: The grouping that blocked the formation of a Likud-led government included the Labor Party, Mapam, Ratz (The Civil Rights Movement), Hadash (a Communist-led list), Yahad (Ezer Weizman's list), The Progressive Movement for Peace, Ometz (Yigal Horowitz). The grouping that blocked the formation of a Labor-led coalition included the Likud, Tehiya, Shas, Agudat Israel, The National Religious Party, Kach (Rabbi Kahane), and Tami.

49. See M. Shamir and A. Arian, "The Ethnic Vote in Israel's 1981 Elections," *State, Government and International Relations,* No. 19-20, Spring 1982, pp. 88-104 (Hebrew); Y. Peres and S. Shemer, "The Ethnic Factor in the Elections to the Tenth Knesset," *Megamot,* Vol. 28, No. 2-3, March 1984, pp. 316-331 (Hebrew).

50. See Galnoor, "Steering the Polity . . .," *op. cit.,* Ch. 7.

51. See M. Shalev, "The Political Economy of Labor Party Dominance and Decline in Israel," in T.J. Pempel (ed,), *Democratic Oddities: One-Party Dominance in Comparative Perspective,* Ithaca, Cornell University Press, 1988.

52. See M. Lissak, "Political-Social Map Overlap," *The Jerusalem Quarterly,* No. 38, 1986, pp. 28-42.

53. For comparison with European countries, see P.H. Merkl, "The Sociology of European Countries, Members, Voters and Social Groups," in P.H. Merkl (ed.), *Western European Party Systems,* New York, The Free Press, 1980, Ch. 25.

54. See H. Herzog, *Political Ethnicity: the Image and Reality,* Yad Tabenkin and Hakibbutz Hameuchad, 1986, Chs. 1-3 (Hebrew).

55. See Herzog, "Political Ethnicity . . .," *op. cit.,* pp. 3-4 (Hebrew); M. Lissak, "Continuity and Change in the Voting Pattern of Oriental Jews," in A. Arian (ed.), *The Elections in Israel 1969,* Jerusalem, Academic Press, 1972, pp. 264-277.

56. For explanations of the voting behavior of the immigrants of the Fifties, see G. Yatziv, *The Heart of the Matter: Essays on Socialism and Democracy in Israel,* Tel Aviv, Adam, 1986, pp. 145-149 (Hebrew); Lissak "Continuity and Change . . .," *op. cit.,* pp. 264-27.

57. For discussions of ethnicity, attitudes, and voting in the 1973, 1977, and

1984 elections, see Y. Peres and E. Yuchtman-Yaar, "Predicting and Explaining Voters' Behavior in Israel," in A. Arian (ed.), *The Elections in Israel 1973*, Jerusalem, Academic Press, 1975, pp. 189-303; Y. Yishai, "Israel's Right-Wing Jewish Proletariat," *The Jewish Journal of Sociology*, Vol. 24, No. 2, pp. 87-97; O. Seliktar, "Ethnic Stratification and Foreign Policy: The Attitudes of Oriental Jews Toward the Arab-Israeli Conflict,"*Middle East Journal*, Vol. 38, No. 1, Winter 1984, pp. 34-60; Shamir and Arian, *op. cit.*, pp. 88-104 (Hebrew); H. Ayalon, E. Ben Rafael and S. Sharot, "Ethnicity and Politics—Neglected Aspects," *Megamot*, Vol. 30, No. 3, August 1987, pp. 332-338 (Hebrew).

58. See Herzog, "Political Ethnicity . . .," *op. cit.* (Hebrew).

59. See Ayalon, Ben-Rafael, Sharot, *op. cit.* (Hebrew).

60. See, for example, S. Swirski, *Orientals and Ashkenazim in Israel: The Ethnic Division of Labor*, Haifa, Machbarot Lemechkar Ulebikoret, 1981 (Hebrew).

61. See S. Smooha, *Pluralism and Conflict*, London, Routledge and Kegan Paul, 1978, Ch. 9; D. Bernstein "Immigrant Transit Camps: The Formation of Dependent Relations in Israeli Society," *Ethnic and Racial Studies*, Vol. 4, No. 1, January 1981, pp. 26-43; M. Lissak, "Images of Immigrants: Stereotypes and Stigmatization in the Period of Mass Immigration in Israel in the 1950s," *Kathedra*, No. 43, March 1987, pp. 125-144 (Hebrew).

62. See S.N. Eisenstadt, *The Absorption of Immigrants*, London, Routledge and Kegan Paul, 1954.

63. See K. Frankenstein, *Poverty, Disturbedness, Primitiveness*, Jerusalem, The Szold Institute, 1957 (Hebrew).

64. See G. Yatziv, *The Social Class Base of Political Party Affiliation*, Jerusalem, The Hebrew University of Jerusalem, The Department of Sociology, 1979, pp. 29-38 (Hebrew).

65. See, for example, M.C. Hudson, "Islam and Political Development," in J.L. Eposito (ed.), *Islam and Development: Religion and Socio-Political Change*, Syracuse University Press, 1980, pp. 1-24; E. Sivan, *Radical Islam, Medieval Theology and Modern Politics*, New Haven and London, Yale Universtiy Press, 1985.

66. See, for example, *Temperament and Character of the Arabs*, New York, Twayne Publishers, 1960, pp. 34-39.

67. See A. Oz, *A Journey in Israel Autumn 1982*, Tel Aviv, Am Oved, 1983, pp. 24-42 (Hebrew).

68. See Shamir and Arian, *op. cit.*, pp. 96-102 (Hebrew).

69. See K. Benyamini, "On Political Tolerance," *Psychology and Consultation*

in Education, 1986, pp. 38-41 (Hebrew); M. Zemach, *Attitudes of the Jewish Majority in Israel toward the Arab Minority,* Jerusalem, The Van Leer Institute, 1980 (Hebrew).

70. On antagonism between ethnic groups in "split" labor markets, see E. Bonacich, "A Theory of Ethnic Antagonism: The Split Labor Market," *American Sociological Review,* Vol. 37, October 1972, pp. 547-559; S. Cummings, "White Ethnic Social Prejudice and Labor Market Segmentation, *American Journal of Sociology,* Vol. 85, No. 4, 1980, pp. 938-950.

71. See G. Shafir and Y. Peled, "'Thorns in your Eyes' the Socio-Economic Characteristics of the Sources of Electoral Support of Rabbi Kahane," *State, Government and International Relations,* No. 25, Spring 1986, pp. 115-130 (Hebrew).

72. See I. Galnoor, "The Soldiers' vote in the Seeking of a Leader," *Haaretz,* September 2, 1984 (Hebrew); I. Galnoor, "A Tendency toward Radicalization," *Haaretz,* September 6, 1984 (Hebrew).

73. See Y. Shapiro, *An Elite Without Successors: Generations of Political Leaders in Israel,* Tel Aviv, Sifriat Poalim, 1984, Ch. 4 (Hebrew).

74. See A. Diskin, *Elections and Voters in Israel,* Tel Aviv, Am Oved, 1988 (Hebrew).

75. *Ibid.*

76 See S. Hasson, *The Protest of the Second Generation: Urban Social Movement in Jerusalem,* Jerusalem, The Jerusalem Institute for Israel Studies, 1987 (Hebrew).

77. See N. Greetz, "The Few Against the Many: Rhetoric and Structure in Menachem Begin's Election Speeches," *Siman Kria,* No. 16-17, April 1983, pp. 106-126 (Hebrew).

Chapter Five

1. See Y. Rabin's lecture in *Academy in Memory of Yitzhak Sadeh,* September 21, 1967 (Hebrew).

2. In the post-1973 War period security expenditures amounted to 37-38% of the G.N.P. according to one estimate. See H. Barkai, *The Cost of Security in Retrospect,* Jerusalem, The Falk Institute, 1980, graph 2 (Hebrew); and 34% according to another estimate, E. Berglas, *Defense and the Economy: The Israeli Experience,* Jerusalem, The Falk Institute, 1983, p. 52; Israel's security budget and its economic effects are also discussed by several contributors to Z. Offer and A. Kober (eds.), *The Cost of Power,* Tel Aviv, Maarachot, 1984 (Hebrew); P. Zuzman, "Why is the Burden of Security so Heavy?" pp. 17-26; N. Hassid and Y. Lesser, "Security and the National Cake," p. 34; A. Noybach, "The Burden of Security

in the Economy of the State," pp. 161-184; D. Kochav, "Economy and Security," pp. 201-205.

3. See A. Mintz, "The Military-Industrial Complex," in M. Lissak (ed.), *Israeli Society and its Defense Establishment*, London, Frank Cass, 1984, pp. 110-111; A. Mintz, "Military-Industrial Linkages in Israel," *Armed Forces and Society*, Vol. 12, No. 1, Fall 1985, pp. 9-28.

4. See R. Stone, *Social Change in Israel: Attitudes and Events*, New York, Praeger, 1982, Chs. 7-8.

5. See Y. Harkabi, *Between Israel and the Arabs*, Tel Aviv, Maarachot, 1968, p. 11 (Hebrew).

6. D. Horowitz and B. Kimmerling, "Some Social Implications of Military Service and Reserve System in Israel," *European Journal of Sociology*, Vol. 15, No. 2, 1974, pp. 265-271.

7. See D. Horowitz, "The Control of Limited Military Operations: The Israeli Experience," in Y. Evron (ed.), *International Violence: Terrorism, Surprise and Control*, Jerusalem, The Hebrew University, The Leonard Davis Institute for International Relations, 1979, pp. 258-276.

8. See D. Horowitz, "Israel's War in Lebanon: New Patterns of Strategic Thinking and Civilian-Military Relations," in M. Lissak (ed.),*Israeli Society and its Defense Establishment, op. cit.*, pp. 95-97.

9. See Y. Slutzky, *History of the Haganah*, Tel Aviv, Maarachot, 1964, Vol. 1, Part 2, pp. 639-670 (Hebrew).

10. See M. Pail, *The Emergence of Zahal*, Tel Aviv, Zmora-Bitan-Modan, 1979, Chs. 9-11 (Hebrew).

11. See B. Kimmerling, *Zionism and Territory: The Socio-Territorial Dimensions of Zionist Politics*, Berkeley, University of California, Institute of International Studies, 1983, Ch. 6.

12. See Z. Raanan, *Gush Emunim*, Tel Aviv, Sifriat Poalim, 1980 (Hebrew); G. Aran, *From Religious Zionism to a Zionist Religion: The Origins and Culture of Gush Emunim—a Messianic Movement in Modern Israel*, Ph.D. dissertation, The Hebrew University of Jerusalem (Hebrew); E. Sprinzak, "Gush Emunim: The Iceberg Model of Political Extremism," in: *State, Government and International Relations*, No. 17, 1981, pp. 22-49 (Hebrew); G. Aran, "Mystic-Messianic Interpretations of Modern Israeli History: The Six Day War and its Aftermath," *Studies in Contemporary Jewry*, Vol. V,

13. See D. Horowitz, "The Control of Limited Military Operations," *op. cit.*, p. 259; B.M. Blechman, "The Impact of Israeli Reprisals on the Behavior of the

Bordering Arab Nations Directed at Israel," *Journal of Conflict Resolution*, Vol. XVI, No. 2, June 1972, pp. 155-181.

14. See Z. Schiff, E. Yaari, *War of Deception*, Jerusalem and Tel Aviv, Schocken, 1984, pp. 380-388 (Hebrew); D. Horowitz, "Israel's War in Lebanon," *op.cit.*

15. See I. Allon, *A Curtain of Sand*, Tel Aviv, Hakibbutz Hameuchad, 1968 (third printing), pp. 67-69 (Hebrew); D. Horowitz, *Israel's Concept of Defensible Borders*, Jerusalem, The Leonard Davis Institute for International Relations, The Hebrew University of Jerusalem, 1975, pp. 5-13; M. Handel, *Israel's Political-Military Doctrine*, Cambridge, Harvard University Center for International Affairs, Occasional Papers, 1973, pp. 1-36.

16. See I. Allon, "An Interim Assessment Between Two Wars," in *Mollad*, No. 29-30, October 1982-December 1983, pp. 502-503 (Hebrew); S. Peres, "The Time Dimension," *Maarachot*, No. 146, September 1962, pp. 3-5 (Hebrew).

17. See D. Horowitz, "Israel's Concept . . .," *op. cit.*, pp. 13-41.

18. See I. Allon, "Israel: The Case for Defensible Borders," *Foreign Affairs*, Vol. 55, No. 1, October 1976, pp. 38-53; A. Shalev, *The West Bank: Line of Defense*, Tel Aviv, Hakibbutz Hameuchad, 1982, pp. 104-153 (Hebrew); M. Dayan, *A New Map—New Relations*, Tel Aviv, Shikmona, 1969, pp. 30-31 (Hebrew); D. Horowitz, "The Israel Concept . . .," *op. cit.*, pp. 15-30.

19. See Y. Cohen, *The Allon Plan*, Tel Aviv, Hakibbutz Hameuchad, 1972 (Hebrew).

20. See Y. Erez and A. Kfir, *Talks with Moshe Dayan*, Tel Aviv, Massada 19, p. 27.

21. See Z. Schiff, "Whose Professional Opinion Prevails?" in *Haaretz*, June 24, 1979.

22. On the tension between national security and welfare needs in modern Western societies, see G. Harries-Jenkins (ed.), *Armed Forces and the Welfare Societies: The Challenge of the 1980s*, London, Macmillan, 1982.

23. On the tension between civilian control of the armed forces and their professional autonomy in developed and developing countries, see B. Abrahmsson, *Military Professionalism and Political Power*, Beverly Hills and London, Sage Publications, 1972, pp. 151-163; S.P. Huntington, *The Soldier and the State*, Cambridge, Vintage Books, 1975; S.P. Huntington, *Political Order in Changing Societies*, New Haven and London, Yale University Press, 1968, Ch. 4; S.E. Finer, *The Man of the Horseback: The Role of the Military in Politics*, London, Penguin 1976 (second edition), Chs. 1-3, M. Janowitz, *Military Institutions and Coercion in Developing Nations*, Chicago and London, The University of Chicago Press, 1977,

Chs. 1-3; A. Perlmutter, *The Military and Politics in Modern Times*, New Haven and London, Yale University Press, 1977; M. Lissak, *Military Roles in Modernization: Civil-Military Relations in Thailand and Burma*, Beverly Hills and London, Sage Publications, 1976, Ch. 1.

24. On the relations between military elites and the political echelon, see M. Janowitz, "Military Elites and the Study of War," *Journal of Conflict Resolution*, Vol. 1, March 1957, pp. 9-18; M. Janowitz, "Military Institutions . . ." *op. cit.*, pp. 183-201; M. Lissak, "Military Roles . . ." *op. cit.*, pp. 25-38.

25. On the meaning of the terms "convergence" and "divergence" in this context, see M. Lissak, "Convergence and Structural Linkages Between Armed Forces and Society," in M.L. Martin and E. Stern-MacCrate(eds.), *The Military, Militarism and the Polity: Essays in Honor of Morris Janowitz*, The Free Press, 1984, pp. 50-62; for a typology of boundaries between military and civilian institutions, see A.R. Luckham, "A Comparative Typology of Civil-Military Relations," *Government and Opposition*, Vol. 6, No. 1, Winter 1971, pp. 5-25.

26. H. Lasswell, "The Garrison State," *The American Journal of Sociology*, Vol. 46, No. 4, January 1941, pp. 455-458.

27. See M. Lissak, "Convergence and Structural Linkages . . .," *op. cit.*

28. See D.C. Rapaport, "A Comparative Theory of Military and Political Types," in S.P. Huntington (ed.), *Changing Patterns of Military Politics*, New York, The Free Press, 1962, pp. 79-101.

29. On the role of the Israeli aviation industry in this context, see A. Mintz, "The Military-Industrial Comples . . .," *op. cit.*, pp. 103-127 and A. Mintz, "Military-Industrial Linkages . . .," *op. cit.*, pp. 9-28.

30. See, for example, M. Lissak, "Convergence and Structural Linkages, Between Armed Forces and Society," *op. cit.*, pp. 50-62; M. Lissak, "Boundaries and Institutional Linkages Between Elites: Some Illustrations from Civil Military Relations in Israel," in G. Moore, (ed.), *Research in Politics and Society*, A Research Annual, Vol. 1, 1985, pp. 129-148.

31. *Ibid.*

32. Y. Peri and M. Lissak, "Retired Officers in Israel and the Emergence of a New Elite," in G. Harries-Jenkins and J. Van Doorn (eds.), *The Military and the Problem of Legitimacy*, Beverly Hills and London, Sage Publications, 1976, pp. 175-192.

33. See *The Agranat Commission Report*, Tel Aviv, Am Oved, 1975, pp. 25-33 (Hebrew).

34. D. Horowitz, "The Israel Defense Forces: A Civilianized Military in a Partially Militarized Society," in R. Kolkowicz and A. Korbonski (eds.), *Soldiers,*

Peasants and Bureaucrats, London, George Allen and Unwin, 1982, p. 192.

35. See *The Agranat Commission Report, op. cit.*, pp. 28-33.

36. D. Horowitz, "The Israel Defense Forces: A Civilianized Military in a Partially Militarized Society," *op. cit.*, p. 92.

37. See D. Horowitz, "Flexible Responsiveness and Military Strategy: The Case of the Israeli Army," *Policy Sciences*, Vol. 1, 1970, pp. 194-196.

38. See E. Luttwak and D. Horowitz, *The Israeli Army*, London, Allen Lane, 1975, pp. 151-153.

39. See H. Benjamini, "The Six Day War, Israel, 1967: Decisions, Coalitions, Consequences: A Sociological View," in M. Lissak (ed.), *Israeli Society and its Defense Establishment, op. cit.*, 1984, pp. 64-82.

40. "Basic Law: The Army" stipulates that the Chief of Staff, Who is the "superior echelon of the army," is "subject to the authority of the Government." He is appointed by the Government according to a recommendation of the Minister of Defense. 806*LSI*, April 9, 1976, p. 138 (Hebrew); for interpretation fo the legal implications of the Law, see S. Shetreet, "Israeli Democracy in a State of War," in *The Monthly Survey*, August-September 1984, pp. 46-56 (Hebrew).

41. See *The Agranat Commission . . . .," op. cit.*, p. 26 (Hebrew).

42. See Y. Rabin, *Service Book*, Tel Aviv, Maariv, 1979, pp. 234-238 (Hebrew).

43. On Sharon's role in the initiation and conduct of the Lebanon War, see Z. Schiff, E. Yaari, *War of Deception, op. cit.*, pp. 21-39; S. Shiffer, *Snowball: the Story Behind the Lebanon War*, Tel Aviv, Yediot Aharonot-Idanim, 1984, pp. 11-20, 62-120 (Hebrew); A. Naor, *Cabinet at War: The Functioning of the Israeli Cabinet During the Lebanon War, 1982*, Tel Aviv, Lahav, 1986, pp. 25-139 (Hebrew).

44. See, for example, E. Weizman, *On Eagle's Wings*, Tel Aviv, Maariv, 1975, p. 264 (Hebrew).

45. See S.P. Huntington, *The Soldier and the State, op. cit.*, p. 61; B. Abrahmsson, *Military Professionalization and Political Power*, Beverly Hills and London, Sage Publications, 1972; W. Eckhardt and A.G. Newcomb, "Militarism, Personality and Other Social Attitudes," *Journal of Conflict Resolutions*, Vol. 13, 1969, pp. 210-219, W. Eckhardt, "The Factor of Militarism," *Journal of Peace Research*, Vol. 2, 1969, pp. 123-132.

46. See M. Lissak, *Military Roles in Modernization, op. cit.*, Ch. 7.

47. See A. Mintz, "The Military-Industrial Complex." *op. cit.*, pp. 114-119.

48. See *Ibid.*, p.14.

49. See *Ibid.*, p.112.

50. See *The Agranat Commission . . . .," op. cit.*, pp. 25-33 (Hebrew).

51. See M. Gal, "Integration of Soldiers of Weak Population Groups in the IDF: Survey of Considerations," *Maarachot*, No. 238, July 1982, pp. 36-44 (Hebrew).

52. On the "Gadna," see V. Azarya, "Israeli Armed Forces," in M. Janowitz and S.D. Westbrood (eds.), *Civic Education in the Military*, Beverly Hills and London, Sage Publications, 1983, pp. 115-116.

53. There are several books on the Lavon Affair. For a book which describes both the affair itself and the political developments that ensued from it, see E. Hassin and D. Horowitz, *The Affair*, Tel Aviv, Am Hassefer, 1961 (Hebrew); for a different evaluation of the affair, see H. Eshed, *Who Gave the Order?*, Tel Aviv, Idanim, 1979 (Hebrew).

54. On the role of the military censorship in Israel, see D. Goren, *The Press in a Besieged Society*, Jerusalem, Magnes, 1975 (Hebrew); R. Kahane and S. Kna'an, *The Behavior of the Press in Security Emergency Situations and its Influence on Public Support of Government*, Jerusalem, The Hebrew University, 1973, pp. 29-32 (Hebrew); M. Negbi, *A Paper Tiger: The Struggle for Freedom of the Press in Israel*, Tel Aviv, Sifriat Hapoalim, 1985, Ch. 3 (Hebrew).

55. On the Editors' Committee see Goren, *op. cit.*, p. 202; Kahane and Kna'an, *op. cit.*, p.53.

56. See S. Shetreet, *op. cit.*, p. 49; Y. Peri, *Between Battles and Ballots: Israel Military in Politics*, Cambridge University Press, 1983, pp. 132-133.

57. See, for example, Maj. General (Res.) M. Peled, "Days on the Brink," *Maariv*, May 16, 1969 (Hebrew); See also the reminiscences of Brig. General I. Lior, Aide-de-Camp to Prime Ministers L. Eshkol and G. Meir in E. Haber, *Today War will Break Out*, Tel Aviv, Idanim, 1987, Ch. 12 (Hebrew).

58. See B. Kimmerling, *The Interrupted System: Israeli Civilians in War and Routine Times*, New Brunswick and Oxford, Transaction Books, 1985, p. 3.

59. See *Official Gazette 1948*, Appendix A, p. 9 (Hebrew).

60. See M. Pail, *op. cit.*, Ch. 11.

61. See A. Shapira, *The Army Controversy, 1948: Ben-Gurion's Struggle for Control*, Tel Aviv, Hakibbutz Hameuchad, 1985, pp. 50-57 (Hebrew); Y. Gelber, *The Dissolution of the Palmach*, Tel Aviv, Schocken, 1986, pp. 225-226 (Hebrew).

62. See Peri, *op. cit.*, pp. 61-64.

63. *Ibid.*, p. 60.

64. *Ibid.*, pp. 64-67.

65. Israel's nuclear capability has been dealt with in many books and articles, most of which ignore the domestic political and organizational implications of the issue. This does not apply to the few works on the subject by Israeli scholars who, unlike their non-Israeli colleagues, were sensitive to this context as well. See, for example, S. Aronson, *Conflict and Bargaining in the Middle East*, Baltimore, Johns Hopkins University Press, 1978, pp. 25-54; S. Feldman, *Israel's Nuclear Deterrence: A Strategy for the 1980s*, New York, Columbia University Press, 1982; Y. Evron, "Israel and the Atom: The Uses and Misuses of Ambiguity," *Orbis*, Vol. 17, No. 4, Winter 1974, pp. 1326-1343; Y. Evron, "The Relevance and Irrelevance of Nuclear Options in Conventional Wars: The 1973 October War," *The Jerusalem Journal of International Relations*, Vol. 7, No. 1-2, 1983, pp. 00.

66. Y. Peri and M. Lissak, *op. cit.*, pp. 188-190.

67. See Interview with Sharon, *New York Times*, November 1, 1973; See also H. Bartov, *Dado: 48 Years Plus 20 Days*, Tel Aviv, Maariv, Vol. 2, p. 313 (Hebrew).

68. See editorial on Sharon's position in the IDF reserves in *Haaretz*, December 17, 1974.

69. See Y. Peri, "Political-Military Partnership in Israel," *International Political Science Review*, Vol. 2, No. 3, 1981, pp. 303-315.

70. See Sam C. Sarkesian, "Military Professionalism and Civil-Military Relations in the West," *International Political Science Review*, Vol. 2, No. 3, 1981, pp. 283-298; M. Janowitz, "Armed Forces in Western Europe: Uniformity and Diversity," *Archives Europeenes de Sociologie*, Vol. 6, 1965, pp. 225-237; J. Van Doorn, *The Soldier and Social Change*, Beverly Hills and London, Sage Publications, 1975, pp. 98-100; C.C. Moskos, "Armed Forces and American Society: Convergence or Divergence?" in C.C. Moskos (ed.), *Public Opinion and the Military Establishment*, Beverly Hills and London, Sage Publications, 1971, pp. 271-294.

71. See A.D. Biderman and L. Sharp, "The Convergence of Military and Civilian Occupational Structures," *American Journal of Sociology*, Vol. 73, No. 4, 1968, pp. 381-399; K. Lang, "Technology and Career Management in the Military Establishment," in M. Janowitz (ed.), *The New Military*, New York, Russell Sage Foundation, 1964, p. 39-82; M.D. Feld, "Military Self-Image in a Technological Environment," in M. Janowitz (ed.), *The New Military, op. cit.*, pp. 159-194.

Chapter Six

1. See above, Chapter. 4, pp. 151-167.

2. See B. Kimmerling, *Zionism and Territory: The Socio-Territorial Dimension of Zionist Politics*, Berkley, University of California, Institute of International Studies, 1983, Chs. 7-8.

3. See above, Chapter 2, pp. 69-73.

4. See above, Chapter. 4, pp. 181-189.

5. See D. Horowitz and M. Lassak, *Origins of Israeli Polity*, Chicago, University of Chicago Press, 1978, Ch. 8.

6. See above, Chapter 5, pp. 195-203.

7. See above, Chapter 3, pp. 113-123.

8. See above, Chapters 2, pp. 64-83 and 4, pp. 181-189.

9. See above, Chapters 2, pp. 83-92 and 3, pp. 116-151.

10. See above, Chapter 2, pp. 36-45.

11. See above, Chapters 2, pp. 51-64 and 3, pp. 138-144.

12. See above, Chapter 2, pp. 64-83.

13. See above, Chapter 2, pp. 32-36.

14. See B. Kimmerling, *The Interrupted System: Israeli Civilians in War and Routine Times*, New Brunswick, NJ, Transaction Books, 1985, pp. 147-158.

15. See above, Chapter 3, pp. 138-144.

16. See above, Chapter 4, pp. 176-181.

17. On the concept of mass politics, see R. Kornhouser, *The Politics of Mass Society*, Glencoe, Ill., Free Press, 1959.

18. See above, Chapter 2, pp. 92-97.

19. See above, Chapter 2, pp. 92-97 and 4, pp. 190-194.

20. For expressions of a secular humanistic approach to nationalism in the Israeli context, see A. Oz, *A Journey in Israel, Autumn 1982*, Tel Aviv, Am Oved, 1983, pp. 100-122 (Hebrew); S. Aloni, "From Birth to Death," *Politica*, No. 17, October 1987, pp. 11-14 (Hebrew). For an expression of a religious version of the humanistic approach to nationalism, see S.H. Bergman, "An Israeli Synthesis of Humanism and Religion," in E. Ben Ezer, *Unease in Zion*, Tel Aviv, Am Oved,

1986, pp. 45-83 (Hebrew). Some of the most radical manifestations of religious ethnocentrism are cited, analyzed, and criticized in Y. Harkabi, *Fateful Decisions*, Tel Aviv, Am Oved, 1986, pp. 207-226 (Hebrew).

21. See, for example, J. Agasse, *Religion and Nationality: Toward Israeli National Identity*, Tel Aviv, Papyrus Publishing House, 1984, Part 3 (Hebrew).

22. See Harkabi, *Fateful Decisions, op. cit.*, pp. 204-211 (Hebrew); G. Aran, "The Beginning of the Road: from Religious Zionism to Zionist Religion," *Studies in Contemporary Jewry*, Vol. 2, Jerusalem and Bloomington, Indiana University Press, 1985.

23. See D. Miron, "An Israeli Document," a special appendix to the monthly issue of *Politika*, No. 16, August 1987 (Hebrew).

24. See above, Chapter 4, pp. 00.

25. See Y. Ben-Porath, "Years of Plenty and Years of Famine: A Political-Business Cycle," *Kyklon*, Vol. 28, No. 2, 1975, pp. 400-403.

26. The term "constructive ambiguity" was originally used in the context of the American mediation between Israel and Egypt in the '70s, apparently by Secretary of State Kissinger. It is, however, applicable to other contexts as well.

Glossary

Agudat Israel: Literally "Federation of Israel." A non-Zionist Orthodox party founded in 1912 in Eastern Europe. It was the strongest political party among the Orthodox communities in Eastern Europe until World War II. Its members in Palestine did not participate in Knesset Israel.

Achdut Ha'avodah: Literally "Unity of Labor." A Socialist-Zionist party founded in 1919. In the 1920s it was the largest party within the Labor movement. In 1930 it merged with Hapoel Hatzair to form a new party—Mapai.

Aliyah: Literally "going-up." The term used to describe Jewish immigration to Israel.

Ashkenazim: A term referring to Jews of European origin not including the Balkans or Spain.

DMC: Acronym for Democratic Movement for Change. A political party established in 1976 and dissolved following defections and splits in early 1980s.

Edah Hacherdit: An ultra-Orthodox Anti-Zionist Jewish faction. It maintains a separate communal-religious organization.

Gahal: Acronym for Herut Liberal bloc. Established in 1965. It was replaced in 1973 by a broader political bloc—the Likud.

Gush Emunim: Literally the "Bloc of the Faithful." An ideological-political movement established formally after the 1973 war. Consisted mainly of young Mafdal activists, committed to the idea of Greater Israel. Members of Gush Emunim are the dominant group among the West Bank settlers.

Habad: A Hassidic community, followers of the Rabbi of Lubavitch.

Haganah: Literally "defense." A paramilitary organization founded in 1920, supervised by the Histadrut during the 1920s and by the Jewish Agency and the Va'ad Haleumi since 1930. Its forces were the backbone of Jewish defense during the Arab revolt in 1936-39 and carried the main burden of the War of Independence.

Hakibbutz Ha'artzi: A federation of kibbutzim, founded in 1927 by kibbutzim whose members belonged to Hashomer Hatzair youth movement. It later affiliated to the Hashomer Hatzair political party and the Mapam party.

Hakibbutz Hameuchad: Literally "Federation of United Kibbutzim—founded in 1927 by kibbutzim affiliated with Achdut Ha'avodah party. In 1930 it became associated with Mapai. Split after the establishment of the state, following an earlier split between Mapai and Hatnua Le'Achut Ha'avodah in 1944.

Halacha: The full body of Jewish religious laws. Also known as Rabbinical Law.

Hashomer Hatzaer: Literally "The Young Guardsman." Originally a youth movement which became a political party in 1946. In 1948 it became part of the Mapam party. Its main political base was the kibbutz movement—the kibbutz Ha'artzi.

Herut: Literally "Freedom." A right-wing nationalist political party in Israel. Founded by the former leaders of IZL after the establishment of the state of Israel in 1948.

Hevrat Ha'ovdim: Literally "The Workers' Association." An umbrella organization which controls all the Histradrut economic enterprises.

Histadrut: Acronym for Histadrut Klalit Shel Ha'ovdim Ha'ivrim Be'eretz Israel (The General Federation of Jewish Workers in the Land of Israel). Founded in 1920. Combined of a trade union movement, a network of economic enterprises owned by its members and a provider of social services. Since 1920s about 70-75 percent of the hired workers are members of the Histadrut.

IDF: Acronym for Israel Defense Forces.

Irgun Zvai Leumi—IZL: Literally "National Military Organization." A right-wing, paramilitary organization founded in 1931. The IZL was loosely associated with the Revisionist movement and did not abide by the authority of the Jewish Agency. During the years 1944-47 it conducted guerilla warfare against British rule in Palestine.

Kach: An extreme right-wing party led by Rabbi Meir Kahane. Its platform calls for the deportation of the Arab population from both Israel and the occupied territories.

Kibbutz, Kevutza: Plural—kibbutzim. A communal settlement based on a collective ownership of the means of production.

Knesset: Literally "Assembly." The official name of the Israel parliament.

Labor Alignment: In Hebrew "Ma'arach." A coalition list and a parliamentary bloc established in 1965. Initially composed of Mapai and Achdut Ha'avodah. Later after the merger of Mapai, Achdut Ha'avodah, and Rafi into the Labor party, the Alignment included the Labor party and Mapam.

Likud: Literally "unity." A coalition list and parliamentary bloc composed of Herut, the Liberals, and additional small parties. Founded in 1973.

Liberals: The main partner of Herut in the Likud.

Lohamei Herut Israel—LHI: Literally "Fighters for the Freedom of Israel." A paramilitary organization that seceded from the IZL in 1940. Used terrorist tactics in the struggle against British rule in Palestine.

Mafdal: Acronym for Miflaga Dadit Leumit. (National Religious Party). A Zionist religious party. Participated in almost all the coalition governments in Israel.

Mapai: Acronym for Mifleget Poalei Eretz Israel (The Workers Party of the Land of Israel). Founded in 1930 following the merger of Achdut Ha'avodah and Hapoel Hatzair. It was the majority party in the Histadrut and the strongest party in the governing coalition in the World Zionist Organization and later in the government of Israel.

Mapam: Acronym for Mifleget Poalim Meuchedet (United Workers Party). A left-wing Zionist party established in 1948 following the merger of Hatnua Le'Achdut Ha'avodah and Hashomer Hatzair, which split again in 1954. Since then the name has been used by the former Hashomer Hatzair.

Moshav: Plural—Moshavim. A cooperative smallholders' settlement based on self-labor.

Neturei Karta: An extreme ultra-Orthodox and anti—Zionist group that seceded from the Edah Haredit.

Palmach: Acronym for Plugot Machatz. Literally "Striking Units." The commando force of the Haganah.

PLO: Acronym for Palestine Liberation Oranization.

Rafi: Acronym for Reshimat Poalei Israel (Israeli Workers' List). A faction led by David Ben-Gurion which split from Mapai in 1965. Its majority merged again with Mapai with the establishment of the Labor party in 1968.

Rakach: Acronym for Reshima Comonistit Hadasha (New Communist List). Established in 1965 following a split in the Communist Party. Rakach remained the only Communist party after the dissolution of Maki. Supported mainly by Arab voters.

Sephardim: Originally a term that referred to Jews of Spanish origin. Later used in reference to the entire Jewish communities of the Middle East, North Africa, and the Balkans.

Takam: Acronym for Ha'tenua Hakibbutzit Hameucheded (The United Kibbutz Movement). A federation of Kibbutzim affiliated with the Labor party established in 1980 following a merger of Hakibbutz Hameuchad and Hever Ha'kvutzot Ve Hakibbutzim.

Tami: A small predominantly religious party established in 1981, following a split in Mafdal. The bulk of its supporters are Sephardic Jews.

Tehiya: Literally "Revival." An extreme nationalist party which split from the Likud in protest against the peace treaty between Israel and Egypt.

Yishuv: Short for Ha'Yishuv Ha-yehudi—the Jewish Community in Palestine. Organized Yishuv—a term used to describe political movements and individuals who were affiliated to the institutional framework of the Jewish community in Palestine.

Shas: A small ultra-Orthodox religious party that seceded from Agudat Israel in 1984. Supported mainly by Sephardic Jews.

Selected Bibliography

M. Abitbol, "The Political System's Impact on the Study of the Eastern Jewish Heritage," in N. Cohen and O. Ahimeir (eds.), *New Directions in the Study of Ethnic Communities*, Jerusalem: The Jerusalem Institute for Israel Studies, 1984, pp. 67-70 (Hebrew).

B. Abrahmsson, *Military Professionalism and Political Power*, Beverly Hills and London: Sage Publications, 1972.

S.Z. Abramov, *Perpetual Dilemma—Jewish Religion in a Jewish State*, London: Associate University Press, 1976.

C. Adler and Y. Peres, "The Youth Movement and the 'Salon' Peer Group: A Comparative Analysis of Cultural Patterns," in S.N. Eisenstadt et al. (eds.), *Education and Society in Israel*, Jerusalem: Akademon, 1968, pp. 361-381 (Hebrew).

C. Adler, "School Integration and Developments in the Israeli Educational System," in Y. Amir, S. Sharan, and R. Ben-Ari, *School Desegregation*, Tel Aviv: Am Oved, 1985 (Hebrew).

J. Agassi, *Religion and Nationality: Towards Israeli National Identity*, Tel Aviv: Papyrus Publishing House, 1984 (Hebrew).

B. Akzin and Y. Dror, *Israel, High-Pressure Planning*, Syracuse: 1966.

B. Akzin, "The Role of Parties in Israeli Democracy," in S.N. Eisenstadt et al. (eds.), *Integration and Development in Israel*, Jerusalem: Israel University Press, 1970, pp. 4-46.

P. Albech, *Land in Judea and Samaria*, Tel Aviv: Chamber of Lawyers, 1985 (Hebrew).

R.A. Alford and R. Friedland, *Powers of Theory: Capitalism, the State and Democracy*, Cambridge: Cambridge University Press, 1985.

I. Allon, *A Curtain of Sand*, Tel Aviv: Hakibbutz Hameuchad, 1968 (Hebrew).

I. Allon, "Israel: the Case for Defensible Borders," *Foreign Affairs*, Vol. 55, No. 1, October 1976, pp. 38-53.

I. Allon, "An Interim Assessment Between Two Wars," in *Mollad,* No. 29-30, October 1982, December 1983, pp. 502-503 (Hebrew).

S. Aloni, "From Birth to Death," *Politica,* No. 17, October 1987, pp. 11-14 (Hebrew).

G. Aran, "The Beginning of the Road from Religious Zionism to Zionist Religion," *Studies in Contemporary Jewry,* Vol. 2, Jerusalem and Bloomington: Indiana University Press, 1985, pp. 402-428.

G. Aran, *Eretz Israel: Between Politics and Religion,* Jerusalem: The Jerusalem Institute for Israel Studies, 1985 (Hebrew).

G. Aran, *From Religious Zionism to a Zionist Religion: the Origins and Culture of Gush Emunim—A Messianic Movement in Modern Israel,* Jerusalem: Ph.D. Thesis, The Hebrew University of Jerusalem, 1987 (Hebrew).

G. Aran, "Mystic-Messianic Interpretation of Modern Israeli History: The Six Day War and its Aftermath," *Studies in Contemporary Jewry,* Vol. V, 1987, pp. 263-275.

A. Arian, *The Choosing People,* Ramat Gan: Massada, 1973 (Hebrew).

A. Arian and M. Shamir, "The Primary Political Functions of the Left-Right Continuum," *Comparative Politics,* Vol. 15, No. 2, January 1973, pp. 139-158.

A. Arian, "The Passing of Dominance," *The Jerusalem Quarterly,* No. 5, Fall 1977, pp. 13-32.

A. Arian, "The Israeli Electorate 1977," in A. Arian (ed.), *The Elections in Israel 1977,* Jerusalem: Jerusalem Academic Press, 1980, pp. 253-278.

A. Arian, "Competitiveness and Polarization: Elections 1981," *The Jerusalem Quarterly,* No. 21, 1981, pp. 3-27.

A. Arian and M. Shamir (eds.), *Elections in Israel 1984,* New Brunswick, NJ: Transaction Books, 1986, pp. 127-147.

D. Arian, "The First Five Years of the Israel Civil Service," in R. Bachi (ed.), *Studies in Economic and Social Sciences,* Jerusalem: The Magnes Press, 1956, pp. 340-377.

C. Arlozoroff, "The Class Struggle in Eretz Israel Reality," in C. Arlozoroff, *Writings and Biographical Episodes,* Tel Aviv: Am Oved, 1958, pp. 54-63 (Hebrew).

C. Arlozoroff, *Selected Writings and Memoir,* Tel Aviv: Am Oved and The Zionist Library, 1968 (Hebrew).

M.J. Aronoff, "The Decline of the Israeli Labor Party: Causes and Significance," in H.R. Penniman (ed.), *Israel at the Polls: The Knesset Elections of 1977,*

Washington, D.C.: American Enterprise Institute for Public Policy Research, 1979, pp. 115-146.

S. Aronson, *Conflict and Bargaining in the Middle East,* Baltimore: Johns Hopkins University Press, 1977.

S. Aronson and N. Yanai, "Critical Aspects of the Elections and their Implications," in D. Caspi, A. Diskin, and E. Gutmann (eds.), *The Roots of Begin's Success: The 1981 Elections,* London: Croom Helm, 1983, pp. 11-42.

J. Aviad, *Return to Judaism,* Chicago: The University of Chicago Press, 1983.

S. Avineri, "Ideology and Israeli Foreign Policy," *The Jerusalem Quarterly,* No. 37, 1969, pp. 4-8.

S. Avineri, *Varieties of Zionist Thought,* Tel Aviv: Am Oved, 1980 (Hebrew).

H. Ayalon, E. Ben Rafael, and S. Sharot, "Ethnicity and Politics: Neglected Aspects," *Megamot,* Vol. 30, No. 3, August 1987, pp. 332-384 (Hebrew).

V. Azarya, "Israeli Armed Forces," in M. Janowitz and S.D. Westbrook (eds.), *Civic Education in the Military,* Beverly Hills and London: Sage Publications, 1983, pp. 99-128.

Y. Azmon, "The 1981 Elections and the Changing Fortunes of the Israeli Labor Party," *Government and Opposition,* Vol. 16, No. 4, Autumn 1981, pp. 432-446.

H. Barkai, *The Cost of Security in Retrospective,* Jerusalem: The Falk Institute, 1980, (Hebrew).

H. Barkai, *The Formative Years of the Israeli Economy,* Jerusalem: The Falk Institute, The Hebrew University of Jerusalem, 1983 (Hebrew).

M. Barlev, "Jewish Religious Education in Israel: Between Religious Activity and Educational Activity," in M. Barlev (ed.), *Religious Education in Israeli Society: A Reader,* Jerusalem: Department of Sociology and School of Education at The Hebrew University of Jerusalem, 1986, pp. 3-28 (Hebrew).

H. Bartov, *Dado: 48 Years Plus 20 Days,* Tel Aviv: Maariv, Vol. 2, p. 313 (Hebrew).

R. Bar-Yosef, "The Moroccans: Background to the Problem," in S.N. Eisenstadt, R. Bar-Yosef and C. Adler (eds.), *Integration and Development in Israel,* Jerusalem: Israel University Press, 1970, pp. 419-28.

B. Barry, "Political Accommodation and Consociational Democracy," *British Journal of Political Science,* Vol. 5, Part 4, October 1975, pp. 477-506.

G. Barzilai, *Democracy in War: Attitudes, Reactions and Political Participation of the Israeli Public in Processes of Decision Making,* Ph.D. Thesis, submitted to The Hebrew University of Jerusalem, 1987 (Hebrew).

Y. Beilin, *The Price of Unity: The Labor Party Before the Yom Kippur War,* Tel Aviv: Revivim, 1985 (Hebrew).

D. Bell, *The End of Ideology, On the Exhaustion of Political Ideas in the Fifties,* Glencoe, Ill.: The Free Press, 1960.

Y. Ben-Aharon, "His Personality and Thought," in A. Piallov and Y. Rabinowitz (eds.), *Yitzhak Tabenkin—His Life Story and Deeds,* Yad Tabenkin, Hakibbutz Hameuchad, 1982, pp. 205-208 (Hebrew).

Y. Ben-Ami, "The 'Mimona' Festivity of the North African Jews," in *Yeda Am* (Folklore), Vol. 17, No. 39-40, pp. 36-44 (Hebrew).

G. Ben-Dor, "The Military in the Politics of Integration and Innovation: The Case of the Druze Minority in Israel," *Asian and African Studies,* Vol. 9, No. 3, 1973, pp. 339-70.

G. Ben-Dor, *The Druze in Israel: A Political Study,* Jerusalem: The Magnes Press, 1979.

D. Ben-Gurion, *We and Our Neighbors,* Tel Aviv: Davar, 1931 (Hebrew).

D. Ben-Gurion, *From Class to Nation,* Tel Aviv: Davar, 1934 (Hebrew).

D. Ben-Gurion, "Uniqueness and Mission," State of Israel, *Government Yearbook 1951,* pp. 22-25 (Hebrew).

D. Ben-Gurion, "The Glory of Israel," in *Government of Israel Yearbook 1954,* pp. 37-43 (Hebrew).

D. Ben-Gurion, *The Reborn State of Israel,* Tel Aviv: Am Oved, 1969 (Hebrew).

D. Ben-Gurion, *Memories,* Tel Aviv: Am Oved, 1970 (Hebrew).

D. Ben-Gurion, *Vision and Method,* Tel Aviv: Mayanot Press, (no date) (Hebrew).

Y. Ben-Meir and P. Kedem, "Index of Religiosity of the Jewish Population in Israel," *Megamot,* Vol. 24, No. 3, February 1979, pp. 353-362 (Hebrew).

Y. Ben-Porath, "Years of Plenty and Years of Famine: A Political-Business Cycle," *Kyklon,* Vol. 28, No. 2, 1975, pp. 400-403.

E. Ben-Rafael, *The Emergence of Ethnicity: Cultural Groups and Social Conflict in Israel,* Westport, Conn. and London: Greenwood Press, 1982.

E. Ben-Rafael, "Ethnicity—Theory and Myth," *Megamot,* Vol. 29, No. 2, August 1985, pp. 190-204 (Hebrew).

H. Benjamini, "The Six-Day War, Israel, 1967: Decisions, Coalitions, Consequences: A Sociological View," in M. Lissak (ed.), *Israeli Society and its Defense Establishment,* London: Frank Cass, 1984, pp. 64-82.

M. Benvenisti, *The West Bank and Gaza Data Base Project,* Interim Report No. 1, Jerusalem: 1982, pp. 33-42.

M. Benvenisti, *The West Bank Handbook,* Jerusalem: Jerusalem Post, 1986, pp. 212-214.

M. Benvenisti, *1986 Report: Demographic, Economic, Legal, Social and Political Development in the West Bank,* Jerusalem: American Enterprise Institute, The West Bank Data Base, 1986, pp. 11-14.

K. Benyamini, "On Political Tolerance," *Psychology and Consultation in Education,* 1986, pp. 38-41 (Hebrew).

E. Berglas, *Defense and the Economy: The Israeli Experience,* Jerusalem: The Falk Institute, 1983.

S.H. Bergman, "An Israeli Synthesis of Humanism and Religion," in E. Ben-Ezer, *Unease in Zion,* Tel Aviv: Am Oved, 1986, pp. 45-83 (Hebrew).

M. Bernstein, "Israel Capacity to Govern," *World Politics,* Vol. 11, No. 3, 1959, pp. 399-417.

D. Bernstein, "Immigrant Transit Camps: The Formation of Dependent Relations in Israeli Society," *Ethnic and Racial Studies,* Vol. 4, No. 1, January 1981, pp. 26-43.

U. Bialer, "Ben-Gurion and Israel's Foreign Policy Orientation 1948-1956," *Kathedra,* No. 43, March 1987, pp. 145-174.

A.D. Biderman and L. Sharp, "The Convergence of Military and Civilian Occupational Structures," *American Journal of Sociology,* Vol. 73, No. 4, 1968, pp. 381-399.

Y. Bilu, "Traditional Medicine Among North African Jews in Israel," in S. Deshen and M. Shoked (eds.), *The Jews of the Middle East,* Jerusalem and Tel Aviv: Schocken, 1984, pp. 166-75 (Hebrew).

H.M. Blaloch, Jr., "Status Inconsistency and Interaction: Some Alternative Models," *American Journal of Sociology,* Vol. 73, No. 3, November 1967, pp. 305-316.

B.M. Blechman, "The Impact of Israeli Reprisals on the Behavior of the Bordering Arab Nations Directed at Israel," *Journal of Conflict Resolution,* Vol. XVI, No. 2, June 1972, pp. 155-181.

E. Bonacich, "A Theory of Ethnic Antagonism: The Split Labor Market," *American Sociological Review,* Vol. 37, No. 5, 1972, pp. 547-559.

A. Brichta, *Democracy and Elections,* Tel Aviv: Am Oved, 1977 (Hebrew).

D. Caspi, "Following the Race Propaganda and Electoral Decision," in D. Caspi, A. Diskin, and E. Gutmann (eds.), *The Roots of Begin's Success: The 1981 Elections,* London: Croom Helm, 1983, pp. 245-272.

M. Chen, C. Adler, and Z. Klein, (eds.), "School Integration in Israel," *Megamot,* Vol. 23, No. 3-4, December 1977 (Hebrew).

E. Cohen, "The 'Black Panthers' and Israeli Society," *Jewish Journal of Sociology,* Vol. 14, No. 1, June 1972, pp. 93-109.

E. Cohen, "Ethnicity and Legitimization in Contemporary Israel," *The Jerusalem Quarterly,* No. 28, Summer 1983, pp. 111-124.

E. Cohen, M. Lissak, and U. Almagor (eds.), *Comparative Social Dynamics—Essays in Honor of S.N. Eisenstadt,* Boulder and London: Westview Press, 1985.

S.M. Cohen, *Attitudes of American Jews Towards Israel and Israelis,* Institute of American Jewish-Israeli Relations, The American-Jewish Committee, September 1983.

Y. Cohen, *The Allon Plan,* Tel Aviv: Hakibbutz Hameuchad, 1972.

W. Connor, "Nation Building and Nation Destroying," *World Politics,* Vol. 24, No. 3, 1972, pp. 319-355.

W. Connor, "The Politics of Ethno-nationalism." *Journal of International Affairs,* Vol. 27, No. 1, 1973, pp. 1-21.

W. Connor, "The Impact of Homelands Upon Diasporas," in G. Sheffer (ed.), *Modern Diasporas in International Politics,* London: St. Martin's Press, 1986.

A. Cordova and H. Herzog, "The Cultural Endeavor of the Labor Movement Between Intelligentsia and Intellectuals," *YiVo, Annual of Jewish Science,* Vol. 17, 1972, pp. 247-252.

L. Coser, *The Functions of Social Conflict,* Glencoe, Ill.: The Free Press, 1956.

S. Cummings, "White Ethnic Social Prejudice and Labor Market Segmentation," *American Journal of Sociology,* Vol. 85, No. 4, 1980, pp. 938-950.

M. Daalder, "The Consociational Democracy Theme," *World Politics,* Vol. 26, No. 4, July 1974, pp. 609-621.

R. Dahrendorf, *Class and Class Conflict in Industrial Society,* Stanford: Stanford University Press, 1959.

A. Daniel, "Cooperation Between Histadrut Capital and Private Ownership," *The Economic Quarterly,* No. 76, November 1972, pp. 338-345 (Hebrew).

H. Darin-Orabkin, *Housing and Immigrant Absorption in Israel 1948-49,* Tel Aviv: Gadish Books, 1955 (Hebrew).

M. Dayan, *A New Map—New Relations,* Tel Aviv: Shikmona, 1969 (Hebrew).

S. Dellapergola, "Aliya and Other Jewish Migrations: Toward an Integrated Perspective," in U.O. Schmelz and G. Nathan (eds.), *Studies in the Population of Israel in Honor of Roberto Bachi, Scripta Hierosolymitana XXX,* Jerusalem: Magnes Press, 1986, pp. 172-209.

S. Deshen, "Patterns of Change of a Religious Tradition: The Ethnic Community Synagogue," in *The Integration of Immigrants from Different Countries of Origin in Israel,* Jerusalem: Magnes Press, 1969, pp. 66-73 (Hebrew).

S. Deshen, *Immigrant Voters in Israel,* Manchester: Manchester University Press, 1970.

S. Deshen and M. Shokeid (eds.), *Jews of the Middle East: Anthropological Perspectives on Past and Present,* Jerusalem and Tel Aviv: Schocken, 1984 (Hebrew).

S. Deshen and M. Shokeid, "Introduction: The Study of Jews of the Middle East in Israeli Society," in S. Deshen and M. Shokeid (eds.), *Jews of the Middle East,* Jerusalem and Tel Aviv: Schocken, 1984 (Hebrew).

K.W. Deutsch, *Nationalism and Social Communication,* Cambridge: MIT Press, 1953.

A. Diskin, "Polarization and Volatility in the Election for the Tenth Knesset," *Government and International Relations,* No. 19-20, 1982, pp. 44-62 (Hebrew).

A. Diskin, "The Jewish Ethnic Vote: The Demographic Myth," *The Jerusalem Quarterly,* No. 35, Spring 1985, pp. 53-60.

A. Diskin, *Elections and Voters in Israel,* Tel Aviv: Am Oved, 1989 (Hebrew).

E. Don-Yehiya, "Stability and Change in a 'Camp Party': The NRP and the Youth Revolution," *State, Government and International Relations,* No. 14, 1980, pp. 34-43 (Hebrew).

E. Don-Yehiya, "The Politics of the Religious Parties in Israel," in S.V. Lehman-Wilzig and B. Susser (eds.), *Public Life in Israel and the Diaspora,* Ramat Gan: Bar Ilan University Press, 1981, pp. 110-137.

A. Doron, *The Struggle for Natonal Insurance 1948-1953,* Jerusalem: The Baerwald School of Social Work, The Hebrew University of Jerusalem, 1975 (Hebrew).

A. Doron, "National Insurance in Israel—Patterns of Structure and Change," *State and International Relations,* No. 13, Winter 1979, pp. 63-81 (Hebrew).

A. Doron, "The Welfare State: Issues of Rationing and Allocation of Resources," *Social Security,* No. 24, February 1983, pp. 5-15 (Hebrew).

A. Doron, N. Shamai, and Y. Tamir, "Income Maintenance, Policy from the Viewpoint of the Family—A Comparative Study of Eight Countries," *Bitachon Sociali,* No. 24, 1983, pp. 56-76.

Y. Drori, "Middle Class Political Organization in Eretz Israel," *Kathedra,* No. 44, June 1987, pp. 116-125.

S. Dubnow, *Letters on Old and New Judaism,* Tel Aviv: Dvir, 1937 (Hebrew).

D. Easton, *The Political System, An Inquiry into the State of Political Science,* New York: A. Knopf, 1953.

A. Eban, *Chapters of Life,* Tel Aviv: Sifriat Maariv, 1978 (Hebrew).

W. Eckhardt, "The Factor of Militarism," *Journal of Peace Research,* Vol. 2, 1969, pp. 123-132.

W. Eckhardt and A.G. Newcomb, "Militarism, Personality and Other Social Attitudes," *Journal of Conflict Resolutions,* Vol. 13, 1969, pp. 210-219.

S.N. Eisenstadt, *The Absorption of Immigrants,* London: Routledge and Kegan Paul, 1954.

S.N. Eisenstadt, "Traditional and Modern Social Values and Economic Development," *Annals of the American Academy of Political And Social Sciences,* No. 305, 1956, pp. 145-56.

S.N. Eisenstadt, *Israeli Society: Background, Development, Problems,* Jerusalem: The Magnes Press, 1966 (Hebrew).

S.N. Eisenstadt, *Israeli Society,* New York: Basic Books, 1967.

S.N. Eisenstadt, "Some New Looks at the Problem of Relations Between Traditional Societies and Modernization," *Economic Development and Cultural Change,* 16, No. 3, 1968, pp. 436-450.S.N. Eisenstadt, "Immigration

Absorption Integration of Immigrants from Different Countries of Origin and the Transformation of Israeli Society," in *The Integration of Immigrants from Different Countries of Origin in Israel,* Jerusalem: Magnes Press, 1969, pp. 6-13 (Hebrew).

S.N. Eisenstadt et al. (eds.), *Israel—A Society in the Making: A Sociological Analysis of Sources,* Jerusalem: Magnes Press, 1972 (Hebrew).

S.N. Eisenstadt and M. Curelaru, *The Forms of Society—Paradigms and Crises,* New York: John Wiley and Sons, 1976.

S.N. Eisenstadt, *Revolution and the Transformation of Societies, A Comparative Study of Civilizatons,* New York: The Free Press, 1978.

S.N. Eisenstadt, *The Transformation of Israeli Society,* London: Weidenfeld and Nicolson, 1985

A. Eliav, *Glory in the Land of The Living,* Tel Aviv: Am Oved, 1973 (Hebrew).

A. Eliav, *The Short Cut,* Tel Aviv: Am Oved, 1985 (Hebrew).

A. Elon, *The Israelis: Founders and Sons,* New York and London: Holt, Rinehart and Winston, 1971.

Y. Erez and A. Kfir, *Talk with Moshe Dayan,* Tel Aviv: Massada, 1981.

H. Eshed, *Who Gave the Order?,* Tel Aviv: Idanim, 1979 (Hebrew).

S. Ettinger, *History of the Jewish People,* Tel Aviv: Dvir, 1979 (Hebrew).

E. Etzioni-Halevy, "Patterns of Conflict, Generation and Conflict Absorption: The Case of Israeli Labor and Ethnic Conflicts," in E. Krausz (ed.), *Studies of Israeli Society,* Vol. 1, New Brunswick and London: Transaction Books, 1980, pp. 231-254.

Y. Evron, "Israel and the Atom: The Uses and Misuses of Ambiguity 1957-1967," *Orbis* 17, No. 4, 1974, pp. 1326-43.

Y. Evron, "The Relevance and Irrelevance of Nuclear Options in Conventional Wars: the 1973 October War," *The Jerusalem Journal of International Relations,* Vol. 7, No. 1-2, 1983.

M. O. Feld, "Military Self-Image in Technological Environment" in M. Janowitz (ed.), *The New Military,* New York: Russell Sage Foundation, 1964, pp. 159-194.

S. Feldman, *Israel Nuclear Deterrence: A Strategy for the 1980s,* New York: Columbia University Press, 1982.

G. field-Lowell and J. Higley, *Elitism,* London: Routledge and Kegan Paul, 1980.

S. E. Finer, *The Man on the Horseback: The Role of the Military in Politics,* London: Penguin, 1976.

B. Z. Fishler, "Language Instruction in the Period of Mass Immigration," in M. Naor (ed.), *Immigrants and Maabarot: 1948-1952,* Jerusalem: Yad Ben Zvi, 1987, pp. 145-156 (Hebrew).

J. Frankel, *Prophecy and Politics: Socialism, Nationalism and Russian Jews,* Cambridge: Cambridge University Press, 1981.

K. Frankenstein, *Poverty, Disturbedness, Primitiveness,* Jerusalem: The Szold Institute, 1957 (Hebrew).

M. Friedman, *Society and Religion, the Non-Zionist Orthodox in Eretz-Israel, 1918-1936.* Jerusalem: Yad Yitzak Ben Zvi, 1977 (Hebrew).

M. Friedman, "The National Religious Party in Crisis", in *State, Government and International Relations,* No. 19-20, Spring 1982, pp. 115-120 (Hebrew).

A. Gal, "Brandeis' View on the Upbuilding of Palestine," *Zionism,* Vol. 6, 1981, pp. 97-146.

M. Galnoor, "Transformation in the Israeli Political System Since the Yom Kippur War," in A. Arian (ed.), *The Elections in Israel 1977,* Jerusalem: Akademic Press, 1980, pp. 119-148.

I. Galnoor, *Steering the Polity: Communication and Politics in Israel,* Beverly Hills and London: Sage Publications, 1982.

I. Galnoor, D. Avnon and M. Biton, (eds.), *Government of Israel: Book of Sources,* Jerusalem: Akademon, 1984.

J. Galtung, "Rank and Social Integration: A Multidimensional Approach," in J. Berger, M. Zelditch, Jr. and B. Anderson, *Sociological Theories in Progress,* Boston: Houghton Mifflin Company, 1966, Vol. 1, pp. 145-198.

W. A. Gamson, "A Theory of Coalition Formation," *American Sociological Review,* Vol. 26, June 1961, pp. 373-383.

Y. Garber-Talmon, *The Individual and Society in the Kibbutz,* Jerusalem: The Magnes Press, 1970 (Hebrew).

R. Gavison, *Civil Rights and Democracy,* Jerusalem: The Israeli Association for Civil Rights, 1985 (Hebrew).

S. Gazit, *The Stick and the Carrot, The Israeli Administration of Judea and Samaria,* Tel Aviv: Zmora Bitan, 1985 (Hebrew).

C. Geertz, "The Integrative Revolution, Primordial Sentiments and Civil Politics in New Nations," in C. Geertz (ed.), *Old Societies and New States,* Glencoe Il: The Free Press, 1963, pp. 105-157.

C. Geertz, *The Interpretation of Culture,* New York: Basic Books, 1973.

N. Geertz, "The Few Against the Many: Rhetoric and Structure in Menachem Begin's Elections Speeches," *Simon Kria,* No. 16-17, April 1983, pp. 106-126 (Hebrew).

Y. Gleber, "Zionist Policy and the Transfer Agreement 1933," *Yalkut Moreshet,* No. 18, February 1974, pp. 97-151 (Hebrew).

Y. Gleber, *The Dissolution of the Palmach,* Jerusalem and Tel Aviv: Schocken, 1986 (Hebrew).

H. H. Gerth and C. Wright Mills (eds.), *From Max Weber: Essays in Sociology,* London: Kegan Paul, Trench Trubner and Co., 1947.

M. Geter, "The Immigration From Germany 1933-1939: Social-Economic Absorption Versus Social-Cultural Absorption," *Kathedra,* No. 12, July 1979, pp. 125-147 (Hebrew).

B. Gill, *30 Years of Immigration to Eretz Israel 1919-1949,* Jerusalem: The Jewish Agency, 1950 (Hebrew).

Z. Gil, *The House of Precious Stones: Case History of Israeli Television,* Tel Aviv: Sifriat Poalim, 1986 (Hebrew).

F. Ginor, *Socio-Economic Disparities in Israel,* Tel Aviv: Tel Aviv University and Transaction Books, 1979.

E. Goffman, *The Presentation of Self in Everyday Life,* Garden City, NY: Doubleday Anchor Books, 1959.

G. Goldberg, "The 'Mimona' Festivity in Morocco," in S. Deshen and M. Shokeid, (eds.), *Jews of the Middle East,* Jerusalem and Tel Aviv: Schocken, 1984, pp. 106-117 (Hebrew).

Z. Goldberg, "Democracy in Israel," in *From the Foundations: A Collection of Essays,* Tel Aviv: Amikam, 1962, pp. 220-229.

S. N. Goldthorpe, "Class, Status and Party in Modern Britain: Some Recent Interpretations, Marxist and Marxisant," in *Archives Europeennes de Sociologie,* Tame XIII, No. 2, 1972, p. 342-372.

D. Goren, *The Press in a Besieged Society,* Jerusalem: The Magnes Press, 1975 (Hebrew).

Y. Gorny, *Partnership and Conflict,* Tel Aviv: The Institute for the Study of Zionism, Tel Aviv University, 1976 (Hebrew).

Y. Gorny, *The Arab Question and The Jewish Problem,* Tel Aviv: Am Oved, 1986 (Hebrew).

U. Z. Greenberg, *The Book of Denunciation and Faith,* Jerusalem and Tel Aviv: Sadan, 1937 (Hebrew).

I. Greenberg, "The Sources for the financing of the War of Independence," in M. Naor (ed.), *The First Year of Independence 1948-1949,* Jerusalem: Yad Ben Zvi, 1988 (Hebrew), pp. 105-116.

N. T. Gross and J. Metzer, "Public Finance in the Jewish Economy in Interwar Palestine," in *Research in Economic History,* Vol. 3, 1978, pp. 87-160.

Y. Gutmann, *The Attorney General Versus the Government,* Jerusalem: Idanim, 1981 (Hebrew).

E. Gutmann, "Parties and Camps—Stability and Change," in M. Lissak and E. Gutmann (eds.), *The Israeli Political System,* Tel Aviv: Am Oved, 1977, pp. 155-170 (Hebrew).

C. Gvati, *A Century of Jewish Settlement,* Tel Aviv: Hakibbutz Hameuchad, 1981 (Hebrew).

E. Haber, *Today War Will Break Out,* Tel Aviv: Idanim Publishers, 1987 (Hebrew).

J. Habib, "Redistribution Through National Insurance in Israel by Income and Demographic Groups," *Bitachon Sociali,* No. 9-10, 1975, pp. 87-114 (Hebrew).

N. Halevi and R. Klinov, *The Economic Development of Israel,* New York: Praeger, 1968.

N. Halevi, *The Economic Development of the Jewish Community in Eretz Israel,* Jerusalem: The Falk Institute, 1979 (Hebrew).

J. Halper and H. Abramovitz, "The Saharana Festivity in Kurdistan and Israel," in S. Deshen and M. Shokeid (eds.), *The Jews of the Middle East,* Jerusalem and Tel Aviv: Schocken, 1984, pp. 260-270 (Hebrew).

J. Halper, "The Absorption of Ethiopian Immigrants: A Return to the Fifties," *Israel Social Science Research 3,* No. 1-2, pp. 112-39.

B. Halpern, *The Idea of the Jewish State,* Cambridge: Harvard University Press, 1969.

M. Handel, *Israel's Political-Military Doctrine,* Cambridge: Harvard University Center for International Affairs, Occasional Papers, 1973.

D. Handelman and L. Shamgar-Handelman, "Shaping Time: The Choice of the National Emblem in Israel," in E. Ohnuki-Tecracy (ed.), *Symbolism and History,* (forthcoming).

G. Hanoch, "Income Differentiation in Israel," in The Falk Institute, *5th Report 1959-1960,* Jerusalem: The Falk Institute, 1961.

Y. Harkabi, *Between Israel and the Arabs,* Tel Aviv: Maarachot, 1968 (Hebrew).

Y. Harkabi, *Fateful Decisions,* Tel Aviv: Am Oved, 1986 (Hebrew).

G. Harries-Jenkins (ed.), *Armed Forces and the Welfare Societies: The Challenge of the 1980s,* London: Macmillan, 1982.

N. Hassid and Y. Leser, "Defense and National Pie," in Z. Offer and A. Kober, *The Price of Power, op. cit.,* pp. 33-47.

E. Hassin and D. Horowitz, *The Affair,* Tel Aviv: Am Hassefer, 1961 (Hebrew).

S. Hasson, *The Protest of the Second Generation: Urban Social Movement in Jerusalem,* Jerusalem: The Jerusalem Institute for Israel Studies, 1987 (Hebrew).

S. N. Herman, *Israelis and Jews: The Continuity of Identity,* New York: Random House, 1970.

S. Hershkovitz, *Social-Diversity in Israel: The Spatial Pattern,* Jerusalem: The Jerusalem Institute for Israel Studies, 1984 (Hebrew).

A. Hertzberg, *The Zionist Idea,* Jerusalem: Keter Publications, 1970 (Hebrew).

A. Hertzberg, (ed.), *The Zionist Idea—A Historical Analysis and Reader,* New York: Atheneum, 1970.

H. Herzog, "Ethnic Political Identity: The Ethnic List to the Delegates' Assembly and the Knesset 1920-1977," Ph.D. thesis, submitted to Tel Aviv University, 1981.

H. Herzog, *Political Ethnicity: Image Versus Reality,* Yad Tabenkin, Hakibbutz Hameuchad, 1986 (Hebrew).

H. Herzog, "Ethnicity as a Negotiated Issue in the Israeli Political Order: The Ethnic Lists to the Delegates' Assembly and the Knesset (1920-1977)," in A. Weingrod (ed.), *Studies in Israeli Ethnicity After The Ingathering, op. cit.,* New York: Gordon and Breach, Science Publisher, pp. 159-78.

M. Hill and N. Karmon, *Project Renewal—an Israeli Experiment in Neighborhood Rehabilitation,* Haifa, The S. Neeman Institute, The Haifa Technion, June 1979, Publication No. 100/70/02.

K. Hope, "Models of Status Inconsistency and Social-Mobility Effects," *American Sociological Review,* Vol. 40, No. 3, June 1975, pp. 322-344.

D. Horowitz, *The Enigma of Economic Growth: A Case Study of Israel,* New York: Praeger, 1972.

D. Horowitz, *In the Heart of Events,* Ramat Gan: Massada, 1975 (Hebrew).

D. Horowitz, "Mapam Comes Back Home," *Molad,* No. 113-114, December 1957, pp. 571-580 (Hebrew).

D. Horowitz, "Between Pioneer Society and 'Like All Other Nations'," *Molad,* No. 146-147, October 1960, pp. 427-429.

D. Horowitz, "Flexible Responsiveness and Military Strategy: The Case of the Israeli Army," *Policy Sciences,* Vol. 1, 1970, pp. 191-205.

D. Horowitz and B. Kimmerling, "some Social Implications of Military Service and the Rserve System in Israel," *Archives Europeennes de Sociologie,* XV, 1974, pp. 262-276.

D. Horowitz, "More than a Change of Government," *The Jerusalem Quarterly,* No. 5, Fall 1975, pp. 3-20.

D. Horowitz, *Israel's Concept of Defensible Borders,* Jerusalem: The Leonard Davis Institute for International Relations, The Hebrew University of Jerusalem, 1975.

D. Horowitz and M. Lissak, *Origins of The Israeli Polity: Palestine Under the Mandate,* Chicago: The University of Chicago Press, 1978.

D. Horowitz, "The Control of Limited Military Operations: The Israeli Experience," in Y. Evron (ed.), *International Violence: Terrorism, Surprise and Control,* Jerusalem: The Hebrew University, The Leonard Davis Institute for International Relations, 1979, pp. 258-76.

D. Horowitz, "The Israeli Defense Forces: A Civilianized Military in A Partially Militarized Society," in R. Kolkowich and A. Korbonski (eds.), *Soldiers, Peasants and Bureaucrats,* London: G. Allen, 1982, pp. 77-105.

D. Horowitz, "The Yishuv and Israeli Society—Continuity and Change," in *State, Government and International Relations,* No. 21, Spring 1983, pp. 32-36 (Hebrew).

D. Horowitz, "Israeli War in Lebanon: New Patterns of Strategic Thinking and Civilian-Military Relations," in M. Lissak (ed., *Israeli Society and its Defense Establishment,* London: Frank Cass, 1984, pp. 83-102.

D. Horowitz, "Incomplete Association," in *Politica,* No. 17, October 1987, pp. 34-37 (Hebrew).

T. R. Horowitz, "An Awareness Without Legitimation: The Israeli Educational Response to Cultural Differences," *Journal of Educational Policy,* Vol. 3, No. 1, 1986, pp. 1-8.

M. C. Hudson, "Islam and Political Development," in J. L. Esposito (ed.), *Islam and Development: Religion and Socio-Political Change,* Syracuse: Syracuse University Press, 1980, pp. 1-24.

S. P. Huntington, *Political Order in Changing Societies,* New Haven and London: Yale University Press, 1968.

S. P. Huntington, *The Soldier and the State,* Cambridge: Vintage Books, 1975.

A. Inkeles, *Social Change in Soviet Russia,* Cambridge: MIT Press, 1968.

Z. Jabotinsky, *The Idea of Betar,* Tel Aviv: Betar Publications, 1934 (Hebrew).

Z. Jabotinsky, "On the Evacuation Plan," *Speeches 1927-1940,* Jerusalem: E. Jabotinsky, 1948, pp. 195-212 (Hebrew).

Z. Jabotinsky, *The Road to the State,* Jerusalem: E. Jabotinsky, 1953 (Hebrew).

M. Janowitz, *Military Institutions and Coercion in Developing Nations,* Chicago and London: The University of Chicago Press, 1977.

M. Janowitz, "Military Elites and the Study of War," *Journal of Conflict Resolution,* Vol. 1, March 1957, pp. 9-18.

M. Janowitz, "Armed Forces in Western Europe: Uniformity and Diversity," *Archives Europeennes de Sociologie,* Vol. 6, 1965, pp. 225-237.

R. Kahane, "Attitudes of the Dominant Ideology in the Yishuv Period Toward Science, Scientists and Professionals," in S. N. Eisenstadt et al. (eds.), *Strata in Israel,* Jerusalem: Akademon, 1968, pp. 181-236 (Hebrew).

R. Kahane and S. Kna'an, *The Behavior of the Press in Security Emergency Situations and its Influence on Public Support of Government,* Jerusalem: The Hebrew University, 1973 (Hebrew).

C. Kamen, "After the Disaster: The Arabs in Israel 1948-1952," in *Machbarot Lemechkar Velebikoret,* No. 10, December 1984, pp. 7-16 (Hebrew).

G. Kassaifi, "Demographic Characteristic of the Palestinian People," in K. Nakleh and E. Zureik (eds.), *The Sociology of the Palestinians,* London: Croom and Helm, 1980, pp. 13-46.

E. Katz and M. Gurevitch, *Leisure Culture in Israel,* Tel Aviv: Am Oved, 1973, pp. 101-103 (Hebrew).

J. Katz, *Between Jews and Gentiles,* Jerusalem: Bialik Institute, 1960 (Hebrew).

Y. Katz, *Out of the Ghetto,* New York: Schocken Books, 1978.

D. Kavanagh, "Political Behavior and Political Participation," in P. Geraint (ed.), *Participation in Politics, Manchester: Manchester University Press, 1973, pp. 102-123.*

A. Kedar, "The Views of Brit Shalom," in B. Z. Yehoshua and A. Kedar (eds.), Ideology and Zionist Policy, Jerusalem: The Zalman Shazar Center, 1978, pp. 97-114 (Hebrew).

B. Kimmerling, "The Israeli Civil Guard," in L. A. Zurcher and G. Harries-Jenkins (eds.), *Supplementary Military Forces, Reserves, Military, Auxilaries,* Beverly Hills and London: Sage Publications, 1978, pp. 107-125.

B. Kimmerling, "Determination of the Boundaries and Frameworks of Conscription: Two Dimensions of Civil-Military Relations in Israel," *Studies in Comparative International Development,* XIV, No. 1, 1979, pp. 22-41.

B. Kimmerling, *Zionism and Territory: The Socio-Territorial Dimension of Zionist Politics,* Berkeley: University of California, Institute for International Studies, 1983.

B. Kimmerling, *The Interrupted System: Israeli Civilians in War and Routine Times,* New Brunswick and Oxford: Transaction Books, 1985.

B. Kimmerling, "Between the Primordial and the Civil Definitions of the Collective Identity: Eretz Israel as the State of Israel," in E. Cohen, M. Lissak, and U. Almagor (eds.), *Comparative Social Dynamics, Essays in Honor of S. N. Eisenstadt,* Boulder and London: Westview Press, 1985, pp. 262-283.

B. Kimmerling, "A Paradigm for the Analysis of the Relationship Between the State of Israel and American Jewry," in *Yehadut Zemanenu—Contemporary Jewry,* No. 4, 1988, pp. 3-21 (Hebrew).

E. Kleiman, "From Cooperative to Industrial Empire: The Story of Solel Boneh," *Midstream,* March 1964, pp. 26-51.

E. Kleiman, "The Histadrut Economy in Israel in Search of Criteria," *The Jerusalem Quarterly,* No. 41, Winter 1987, pp. 84-89.

A. F. Kleinberger, *Society, Schools and Progress in Israel,* Oxford: Pergamon Press, 1969.

F. R. Kluckhon, "Dominant and Variant Value Orientation," in C. Kluckhon and H. A. Murray (eds.), *Personality in Nature, Society and Culture,* New York: A. Knopf, 1953, pp. 342-360.

D. Kochav, "Economy and Security," in Z. Offer and A. Kober (eds.), *The Cost of Power,* Tel Aviv: Maarachot, 1984, pp. 201-206, (Hebrew).

R. Kornhauser, *The Politics of Mass Society,* Glencoe Ill.: The Free Press, 1959.

V. Kraus and D. Weintraub, "Community Structure and the Status Attainment Process of the Jewish Population in Israel," *Zeitschrift fur Soziologie,* Vol. 10, No. 4, October 1981, pp. 364-378.

L. Kuper, *Plural Societies, Pespectives and Problems,* in L. Kuper and M. G. Smith (eds.), *Pluralism in Africa,* Berkeley: University of California Press, 1964.

N. Lamm, "The Ideology of Neturei Karta According to the Satmar Version," *Tradition,* Vol. 13, No. 1, Summer 1972, pp. 38-53.

J. M. Landau, *The Arabs in Israel: A Political Study,* London: Oxford University Press, 1970.

J. M. Landau, "The Israeli Political Elite: Features and Composition," in M. Lissak and E. Gutmann (eds.), *The Political System of Israel,* Tel Aviv: Am Oved, 1974, pp. 195-197, 212-219 (Hebrew).

K. Lang, "Technology and Career Management in the Military Establishment," in M. Janowitz (ed.), *The New Military,* New York: Russell Sage Foundation, 1964, pp. 39-82.

W. Laqueur, *A History of Zionism,* London: Weidenfeld and Nicolson, 1972.

H. Lasswell, "The Garrison State," *The American Journal of Sociology,* 46, No. 4, January 1941, pp. 455-462.

P. Lavon, "Beyond the Barriers," in *From the Foundations: A Collection of Essays,* Tel Aviv: Amikam, 1962, pp. 55-93 (Hebrew).

H. Lavski, "The First Days of Brit Shalom and the German Zionists," in *Yahadut Zemanenu: Contemporary Jewry,* No. 4, 1978, pp. 110-121.

G. E. Lenski, "Statue Crystalization, A Non-Vertical Dimension of Social Status," in *American Sociological Reviw,* Vol. 19, No. 4, August 1954, pp. 405-413.

N. Lewin-Epstein and M. Semyonov, "Ethnic Group Mobility in the Israel Labor Market," *American Sociological Review,* Vol. 51, June 1986, pp. 342-351.

C. S. Liebman and E. Don-Yehiya, *Relition and Politics in Israel,* Bloomington: Indiana University Press, 1984.

C. S. Liebman and E. Don-Yehiya, *Civil Religion in Israel,* Berkeley: University of California Press, 1983.

C. S. Liebman, "In Search of States: The Israeli Government and the Zionist Movement," *Forum,* 28-29, 1978, pp. 38-56.

A. Lijphart, "Consociational Democracy," *World Politics,* 21, No. 2, 1969, pp. 207-25.

A. Lijphart, "Cultural Diversity and Theories of Political Integration," *Canadian Journal of Political Science,* Vol. 4, No. 1, March 1971, pp. 3-6.

S. M. Lipset, *Political Man: The Social Bases of Politics,* Garden City, NY: Doubleday, 1960.

S. M. Lipset and S. Rokkan, "Cleavages, Structures, Party Systems and Voter Alignments: An Introduction," in S. M. Lipset and S. Rokkan (eds.), *Party Systems and Voter Alignments,* New York: The Free Press, 1967, pp. 1-64.

A. Liskovsky, "Resident Absentees in Israel," *Hamizrach Hachadash,* Vol. 10, No. 3, (39), 1960, pp. 186-192 (Hebrew).

M. Lissak, "Stratification Models and Mobility Aspirations: Sources of Mobility Aspirations," *Megamot,* Vol. 15, No. 1, January 1967, pp. 62-82 (Hebrew).

M. Lissak, *Social Mobility in Israel Society,* Jerusalem: Israel University Press, 1969.

M. Lissak, "Continuity and Change in the Voting Patterns of Oriental Jews," in A. Arian (ed.), *The 1969 Israeli Elections,* Jerusalem: Jerusalem Academic Press, 1972, pp. 264-277.

M. Lissak, *Military Roles in Modernization: Civil-Military Relations in Thailand and Burma,* Beverly Hills and London: Sage Publications, 1976.

M. Lissak, *The Elites of the Jewish Community in Palestine,* Tel Aviv: Am Oved, 1981 (Hebrew).

M. Lissak, "Immigration Policy in the Fifties: Organizational Aspects and Their Political Implications," in A. Shinan (ed.), *Emigration and Settlement in Jewish and General History,* Jerusalem: The Zalman Shazar Center, 1982, pp. 255-261 (Hebrew).

M. Lissak, "The Ethnic Problem and Ethnic Organizations in the Jewish Community in Palestine," *Meqamot,* Vol. 28, No. 2-3, 1984, pp. 295-315 (Hebrew).

M. Lissak, "Paradoxes of Israeli Civil-Military Relations," in M. Lissak (ed.), *Israeli Society and Its Defense Establishment,* London: Cass, 1984, pp. 1-12.

M. Lissak, "Convergence and Structural Linkages Between Armed Forces and Society," in M. L. Martin and E. Stern-McCrate (eds.), *The Military, Militarism and the Polity: Essays in Honor of Morris Janowitz,* New York: The Free Press, 1984, pp. 50-62.

M. Lissak, "Boundaries and Institutional Linkages Between Elites: Some Illustrations from Civil-Military Relations in Israel," in G. Moore (ed.), *Research in Politics and Society, Vol. I: Studies of the Structure of National Elite Groups,* 1985, pp. 129-48.

M. Lissak, "Political Social Map Overlap," *The Jerusalem Quarterly,* No. 38, 1986, pp. 28-42.

M. Lissak, "Immigrants' Images: Stereotypes and Stigmatization in the Period of Mass Immigration to Israel in the Fifties," in *Kathedra,* No. 43, March 1987, pp. 125-144 (Hebrew).

A. R. Luckham, "A Comparative Typology of Civil-Military Relations," in *Government and Opposition,* Vol. 6, Winter 1971, pp. 5-25.

D. Lockwood, "Some Remarks on the Social System," in N. J. Demerpath and R. A. Peterson (eds.), *System, Change and Conflict,* New York: The Free Press, 1967.

J. Lustick, *Arabs in a Jewish State: Israel's Control of a National Minority,* Austin, TX: University of Texas Press, 1980.

E. Luttwak and D. Horowitz, *The Israeli Army,* New York: Harper and Row, 1975.

A. Malamat, H. Tadmor, M. Stern, S. Safrai, H. H. Ben Sasson, and S. Etinger, (eds.), *History of the Jewish People,* Tel Aviv: Dvir Publishing, 1969 (Hebrew).

E. Margalit, *Hashomer Hatzair, From Youth Community to Revolutionary Marxism, 1913-1936,* Tel Aviv: Tel Aviv University and Hakibbutz Hameuchad, 1971 (Hebrew).

E. Margalit, *Anatomy of the Left,* Jerusalem: The Hebre University of Jerusalem and I. L. Peretz Press, 1976 (Hebrew).

E. Margalit, *Kibbutz, Society and Politics,* Tel Aviv: Am Oved, 1980 (Hebrew).

M. Maos, *Palestinian Leadership on the West Bank,* Tel Aviv: Reshafim, 1985 (Hebrew).

D. McCllelland, *The Achieving Society,* Princeton: Van Nostrand, 1961.

M. McLuhan and Q. Fiore, *War and Peace in the Global Village,* New York: Bantam Books, 1968.

P. Y. Medding, *Mapai in Israel,* Cambridge: Cambridge University Press, 1972.

P. Y. Medding, "Patterns of Elite Consensus and Elite Competitions: A Model and a Case Study," in H. D. Clarke and M. M. Czudnowski (eds.), *Political Elites in Anglo-American Democracies,* Northern Illinois University Press, 1987, pp. 17-43.

Y. D. Menuchin (ed.), *The Limits of Obedience,* Tel Aviv: The "Yesh Gvul" Movement and Siman Kria Books, 1985 (Hebrew).

P. H. Merkl, "The Sociology of European Countries, Member, Voter and Social Groups," in P. H. Merkl (ed.), *Western European Party Systems,* New York: The Free Press, 1980.

J. S. Migdal, *Palestinian Society and Politics,* Princeton: Princeton University Press, 1980.

A. Mintz, "The Military-Industrial Complex," in M. Lissak (ed.), *Israeli Society and its Defense Establishment,* London: Frank Cass, 1984, pp. 103-127.

A. Mintz, "Military-Industrial Linkage in Israel," *Armed Forces and Society,* Fall 1985, Vol. 12, No. 1, pp. 9-28.

D. Miron, "From Creators and Builders to Dwellers," *Igra: Almanac for Literature and Art,* No. 2, 1985-86, pp. 94-106 (Hebrew).

D. Miron, "An Israeli Document," *Politica,* a special appendix of the August 1987 issue, No. 16, pp. 31-44 (Hebrew).

C. Moskos, "Armed Forces and American Society: Convergence or Divergence?" in C. C. Moskos (ed.), *Public Opinion and the Military Establishment,* Beverly Hills and London: Sage Publications, 1971, pp. 271-294.

Y. Nahon, *Trends in Occupational Status—the Ethnic Dimension,* Jerusalem: The Jerusalem Institute for Israel Studies, 1981 (Hebrew).

Y. Nahon, *Patterns of Educational Expansion and the Structure of Occupational Opportunities—the Ethnic Dimension,* Jerusalem: The Jerusalem Institute for Israel Studies, 1987 (Hebrew).

A. Naor, *Cabinet at War: The Functioning of the Israeli Cabinet During the Lebanon War*

1982, Tel Aviv: Lahav, 1986 (Hebrew).

M. Negbi, *Chains of Injustice*, Jerusalem: Kana Publishers, 1982 (Hebrew).

M. Negbi, *Paper Tiger: The Struggle for Press Freedom in Israel*, Tel Aviv: Sifriat Poalim, 1985 (Hebrew).

M. Negbi, "The Boundaries of Disobedience," *Politica*, No. 7, April 1986, pp. 4-5 (Hebrew).

J. P. Nettle, "The State as a Conceptual Variable," *World Politics*, Vol. 20, No. 4, July 1968, pp. 559-592.

S. Newman, "Ethopian Jewish Absorption and Israeli Response: A Two-way Process," *Israel Social Science Research*, No. 1-2, pp. 104-111.

E. A. Nordlinger, *Conflict Regulation in Divided Societies*, Cambridge: Center for International Affairs, Harvard University, Occasional Papers, No. 290, January 1972.

A. Noybach, "The Burden of Security in the Economy of the State," in Z. Offer and A. Kober (eds.), *The Cost of Power*, Tel Aviv: Maarachot, 1984 (Hebrew).

Z. Offer and A. Kober, *The Price of Power*, Tel Aviv: Maarachot, 1984 (Hebrew).

S. Olzak, "Contemporary Ethnic Mobilization," *Annual Review of Sociology*, Vol. 9, 1983, pp. 355-374.

A. Oz, *Under this Blazing Light*, Tel Aviv: Sifriat Poalim, 1979.

A. Oz, *A Journey in Israel, Autumn, 1982*, Tel Aviv: Am Oved, 1983 (Hebrew).

M. Pail, *The Emergence of Zahal*, Tel Aviv: Zmora-Bitan-Modan, 1979 (Hebrew).

T. Parsons, *Structure and Process in Modern Societies*, Glencoe, Ill.: The Free Press, 1960.

D. Patinkin, "Israel's Economy in the First Decade," in *The Falk Institute for Economic Research, 4th Report, 1957-1958*, Jerusalem: The Falk Institute, 1959, pp. 73-82 (Hebrew).

S. Peres, "The Time Dimension," *Maarachot*, No. 146, September 1962, pp. 3-5.

Y. Peres, E. Yuchtman-Yaar and R. Shafat, "Predicting and Explaining Voters' Behavior in Israel," in A. Arian, (ed.), *The Elections in Israel—1973*, Jerusalem: Academic Press, 1975, pp. 189-303.

Y. Peres and S. Shemer, "The Ethnic Vote in the Elections to the Tenth Knesset," *Megamot*, Vol. 28, No. 2-3, March 1984, pp. 323-327 (Hebrew).

Y. Peres, "Horizontal Integration and Vertical Differentiation Among Jewish

Ethnicities in Israel," in A. Weingrod (ed.), *Studies in Israeli Ethnicity—After the Ingathering, op. cit.,* pp. 39-56.

Y. Peres, "The Stalemate," *Politica,* No. 18, December 1987, pp. 21-22 (Hebrew).

Y. Peri and M. Lissak, "Retired Officers in Israel and the Emergence of a New Elite," in G. Harries-Jenkins and J. Van Doorn (eds.), *The Military and the Problem of Legitimacy,* Beverly Hills and London: Sage Publications, 1976, pp. 175-192.

Y. Peri, "Political-Military Partnership in Israel," *International Political Science Review,* Vol. 2, No. 3, 1981, pp. 303-315.

Y. Peri, *Between Battles and Ballots, Israeli Military in Politics,* Cambridge: Cambridge University Press, 1983.

A. Perlmutter, *The Military and Politics in Modern Times,* New Haven and London: Yale University Press, 1977.

M. M. Polama, *Contemporary Socioilogical Theory,* New York: Macmillan Publishing Co., 1979.

Y. Porat, *The Emergence of the Palestinian-Arab National Movement 1918-1929,* London: Frank Cass, 1974.

Y. Porat, *The Palestinian-Arab National Movement 1929-1939—From Riots to Rebellion,* London: Frank Cass, 1977.

W. Preuss, "The Occupational Structure and Work Conditions of Jewish Oriental Workers," *Hameshek Hashitufi* (The Cooperative Economy), August 24, 1939, pp. 219-224 (Hebrew).

T. Raanan, *Gush Emunim,* Tel Aviv: Sifriat Hapoalim, 1980 (Hebrew).

Y. Rabin, *Service Book,* Tel Aviv: Maariv, 1979 (Hebrew).

D. Rapoport, "A Comparative Theory of Military and Political Tyupes," in S. Huntington (ed.), *Changing Patterns of Military Politics,* New York: The Free Press, 1962, pp. 79-101.

Y. Ratner, "The Military Government," *Mibefnim,* Vol. 19, August 1956, pp. 49-52 (Hebrew).

J. Rawls, "Distributive Justice," in P. Laslett and W. G. Runciman (eds.), *Philosophy, Politics and Society,* Oxford: Basil Blackwell, 1967.

E. Rekhes, "The Educated," in A. Layish (ed.), *The Arabs in Israel: Continuity and Change,* Jerusalem: The Magnes Press, 1981, pp. 180-196 (Hebrew).

S. Reshef, "Ben-Gurion and State Education," *Kathedra* No. 43, March 1987, pp. 103-114 (Hebrew).

Y. Reshef and M. Metzer, "The Forum of the thirteen Works Committees," *The Economic Quarterly*, No. 126, April 1983, pp. 532-541 (Hebrew).

W. Riker, *The Theory of Political Coalitions*, New Haven: Yale University Press, 1962.

R. Rose, "The Nature of the Challenge," in R. Rose (ed.), *The Challenge to Governance: Studies in Overloaded Politics*, Beverly Hills and London: Sage Publications, 1980, pp. 5-29.

E. Rosenstein, "Worker Participation in Management: Problematic Issues in the Israeli System," *Industrial Relations Journal*, Vol. 8, No. 2, pp. 55-69.

M. Rosner and J. R. Blasi, "Theories of Participatory Democracy and the Kibbutz", in E. Cohen, M. Lissak and U. Almagor (eds.), *Comparative Social Dynamics—Essays in Honor of S.N. Eisenstadt*, Boulder: Westview Press, 1984, pp. 295-314.

A. Rubinstein, *Constitutional Law of Israel*, Jerusalem and Tel Aviv: Schocken, 1979 (Hebrew).

A. Rubinstein, *From Herzl to "Gush Emunim,"* Jerusalem and Tel Aviv: Schocken, 1980, pp. 111-133 (Hebrew).

A. Rubinstein, *A Certain Political Experience*, Tel Aviv: Idanim, 1982 (Hebrew).

A. Rubinstein, "The Changing Status of the Territories," *Iyunei Mishpat*, Vol. 11, NO. 3, October 1986, (Hebrew).

D. Rudner, "On His Zionist Political Thought," in A. Pialkov and Y. Rabinowitz (eds.), *Yitzhak Tabenkin—His Life Story and Deeds*, Yad Tabenkin, Hakibbutz Hameuchad, 1982, pp. 320-324 (Hebrew).

S. Sager, *The Parliamentary System of Israel*, Syracuse: Syracuse University Press, 1985.

M. Samet, "Who is a Jew 1958-1977," *The Jerusalem Quarterly*, No. 36, Summer 1985, pp. 88-108.

S. Sandler, "The National Religious Party: Toward a New Role in Israel's Political System?" in S. L. Lehman-Wilzig and B. Susser (eds.), *Public Life in Israel and Diaspora, op. cit.*, pp. 158-170.

C. Sarkesian, "Military Professionalism and Civil-Military Relations in the West," *International Political Science Review*, Vol. 2, No. 3, 1981, pp. 283-198.

M. Sarnat, *Savings and Investment Through Retirement Funds in Israel*, Jerusalem: The Falk Institute, 1966 (Hebrew).

A. Sartori, "European Political Parties: The Case of Polarized Pluralism," in J.

Lapalombra and M. Weiner (eds.), *Political Parties and Political Development,* London: Princeton University Press, 1966, pp. 137-176.

Z. Schiff and E. Yaari, *A War of Deception,* Jerusalem and Tel Aviv: Schocken, 1984 (Hebrew).

U. Schmelz and S. Dellapergola, "World Jewish Population," *American Jewish Year Book,* 1982, pp. 277-290.

U. Schmelz, "Evolution and Projection of World Jewish Population," *Yahadut Zemanenu—Contemporary Jewry,* No. 1, 1984, pp. 301-318.

D. Schueftan, *A Jordanian Option,* Efal: Yad Tabenkin and Hakibbutz Hameuchad, 1986 (Hebrew).

S. Schweid, *The Word of A.D. Gordon,* Tel Aviv: Am Oved, 1970 (Hebrew).

H. Segal, *Dear Brothers,* Tel Aviv: Keter Publications, 1987 (Hebrew).

T. Segev, *1949—The First Israelis,* Tel Aviv and Jerusalem: Domino, 1984 (Hebrew).

M. Seliger, "Fundamental and Operative Ideology: The Two Principal Dimensions of Political Argumentation," *Policy Sciences,* Vol. 1, No. 3, 1970, pp. 325-338.

O. Seliktar, "Acquiring Partisan Preferences in a Plural Society: The Case of Israel," *Plural Society,* Vol. 11, No. 4, Winter 1980, pp. 3-20.

O. Seliktar, "Ethnic Stratification and Foreign Policy: The Attitudes of Oriental Jews Toward the Arab-Israeli Conflict," *Middle East Journal,* Vol. 38, No. 1, Winter 1984, pp. 34-60.

G. Shafir and Y. Peled, "Thorns in Your Eyes," the Socio-Economic Characteristics of the Sources of Electoral Support of Rabbi Kahane, *State, Government and International Relations,* No. 25, Spring 1986, pp. 115-130 (Hebrew).

G. Shaked, *Hebrew Narrative Fiction 1880-1980,* Jerusalem: Hakibbutz Hameuchad and Keter Publications, 1983 (Hebrew).

A. Shalev, *The West Bank: Line of Defense,* Tel Aviv: Hakibbutz Hameuchad, 1982 (Hebrew).

A. Shalev, "The Arms Race in the Middle East in the 1980s," in Z. Lanir, (ed.), *Israeli Security Planning in the 1980s—its Politics and Economics,* Tel Aviv: Misrad Habitahon and Tel Aviv University, 1985, pp. 15-30 (Hebrew).

M. Shalev, "The Political Economy of Labor Party Dominance and Decline," in J. J. Pempel (ed.), *Democratic Oddities: One-Party Dominance in Comparative Perspective,* Ithaca: Cornell University Press, 1988.

M. Shamgar, "On the Written Constitution," *Israel Law Review,* Vol. 4, No. 4, October 1974, pp. 467-476.

M. Shamgar, "Legislation, Judiciary and Civil Rights," *Hapraklit,* Vol. 37, No. 1-2, October 1986, pp. 5-12 (Hebrew).

M. Shamir and A. Arian, "The Ethnic Vote in Israel's 1981 Elections," *State Government, and International Relations,* No. 19-20, Spring 1982, pp. 88-104 (Hebrew).

A. Shapiro, "The Dream and Disillusion: The Political Development of the Labor Brigade," *Baderech,* No. 3, December 1968, pp. 34-63 and August 1969, No. 4, pp. 33-54 (Hebrew).

A. Shapira, *Futile Struggle: The Jewish Labor Controversy,* Tel Aviv: Hakibbutz Hameuchad and Tel Aviv University, 1977 (Hebrew).

A. Shapira, *Berl Katznelson: A Biography,* Tel Aviv: Am Oved, 1980 (Hebrew).

A. Shapira, *The Army Controversy 1948: Ben-Gurion's Struggle for Control,* Tel Aviv: Hakibbutz Hameuchad, 1985 (Hebrew).

Y. Shapiro, "The Weizman-Brandeis Conflict," *Zionism,* Vol. 3, 1974, pp. 258-272 (Hebrew).

Y. Shapiro, "The End of the Dominant Party System," in A. Arian (ed.), *The Electons in Israel 1977,* Jerusalem: Academic Press, 1980, pp. 23-38.

Y. Shapiro, *An Elite Without Successors: Generations of Political Leaders in Israel,* Tel Aviv: Sifriat Poalim, 1984 (Hebrew).

Z. Sharf, *Three Days,* Tel Aviv: Am Oved, 1959 (Hebrew).

Y. Shavit, *Revisionism in Zionism,* Tel Aviv: Yariv and Hadar, 1978 (Hebrew).

Y. Shavit, *From Hebrew to Canaanite: Aspects in the Hisgory, Ideology and Utopia of the "Hebrew Renaissance" from Radical Zionism to Anti-Zionism,* Jerusalem: Domino Press, 1984 (Hebrew).

G. Sheffer, "The Uncertain Future of American Jewry-Israel Relations," *The Jerusalem Quarterly,* No. 32, 1984, pp. 65-80.

G. Sheffer, "A New Field of Study: Modern Diasporas in International Politics," in G. Sheffer (ed.), *Modern Diasporas in International Politics,* London: St. Martin's Press, 1986, pp. 1-16.

I. Shelah, *Patterns of Cross-Community Marriages in Israel, 1952-1968,* Jerusalem: The Hebrew University of Jerusalem, The Center for Documentation and Research on Israeli Society, October 1973 (Hebrew).

S. Shetreet, "Israeli Democracy in a State of War," in *The Monthly Survey,* August-September, 1984, pp. 46-56.

S. Shiffer, *Snowball: The Story Behind the Lebanon War,* Tel Aviv: Yediot Aharonot-Idanim, 1984 (Hebrew).

J. Shilhav and M. Friedman, *Growth and Segregation—The ultra-Orthodox Community of Jerusalem,* Jerusalem: The Jerusalem Institute for Israel Studies, 1985, pp. 25-58 (Hebrew).

E. Shils, "comparative Study of the New Nations," in C. Geertz (ed.), *Old Societies and New States, op. cit.,* pp. 1-26.

E. Shils, "Tradition and Liberty: Antinomy and Interdependence," *Ethics,* Vol. XLVIII, No. 3, 1958, pp. 160-163.

E. Shils, *Center and Periphery—Essays in Macrosociology,* Chicago: The University of Chicago Press, 1975, pp. 3-16.

F. E. Shinar, *The Burden of Necessity and Emotions: Israel-Germany Relations, 1950-1966,* Jerusalem and Tel Aviv: Schocken, 1967 (Hebrew).

G. Shimoni, *Jews and Zionism: The South African Experience 1919-1967,* Capetown: Oxford University Press, 1980.

D. Shimhoni, *Israel Democracy: The Middle of the Journey,* New York: The Free Press, 1981.

M. Shoked and S. Deshen, *The Generation of Transition: Continuity and Change Among North African Immigrants to Israel,* Jerusalem: Yad Yitzhak Ben Zvi, 1977 (Hebrew).

M. Shokeid, "Precepts Versus Tradition: Religious Trends Among Middle Eastern Jews," *Megamot,* Vol. 28, No. 2-3, March 1984, pp. 250-264 (Hebrew).

E. Shprinzak, "Extreme Politics in Israel," *The Jerusalem Quarterly,* No. 5, Fall 1977, pp. 33-47.

E. Shprinzak, "Gush Emunim: The Iceberg Model of Political Extremism," *State, Government and International Relations,* No. 17, Spring 1981, pp. 37-42 (Hebrew).

E. Shprinzak, *Everyman Whatsoever is Right in His Own Eyes: Illegalism in Israeli Society,* Tel Aviv: Sifriat Poalim, 1986 (Hebrew).

A. Simon, "The Structure of Elementary Education in an Immigrants' Town," *Megamot,* Vol. 3, No. 3, July 1955, pp. 387-389 (Hebrew).

M. Sicron, *Immigration to Israel 1948-1953,* Jerusalem: The Falk Institute and the Central Bureau of Statistics, Special Series, No. 60, 1957.

E. Sivan, *Radical Islam: Medieval Theology and Modern Politics,* Tel Aviv: Am Oved, 1985 (Hebrew).

Y. Slutzky, *History of the Hagana,* Jerusalem: Maarachot and Am Oved, 1954 (Hebrew).

M. Smilansky, "The Educational System's Response to Problems of the Culturally Disadvantaged," in C. Ormian (ed.), *Education in Israel,* Jerusalem: Keter Publications, 1973 (Hebrew).

A. D. S. Smith, *Nationalism in the Twentieth Century,* Oxford: Martin Robertson, 1949.

M. G. Smith, "Some Developments in the Analytic Framework of Pluralism," in L. Kuper and M. G. Smith (eds.), *Pluralism in Africa,* Berkeley: University of California Press, 1964, pp. 415-448.

M. G. Smith, "Institutional and Political conditions of Pluralism," in L. Kuper and M. G. Smith (eds.), *Pluralism in Africa,* Berkeley: University of California Press, 1964, pp. 29-67.

M. G. Smith, *The Plural Society in the British West Indies,* Berkeley: University of California Press, 1965.

S. Smooha, *Israel: Pluralism and Conflict,* London: Routledge and Kegan Paul, 1972.

S. Smooha, "Arabs and Jews in Israel: Minority-Majority Group Relations," *Megamot,* Vol. 22, No. 4, September 1976, pp. 397-424 (Hebrew).

S. Smooha, "Existing and Alternative Policy Toward the Arabs in Israel," *Megamot,* Vol. 26, No. 1, September 1980, pp. 7-36 (Hebrew).

S. Smooha, "A Critique of an Updated Establishmentarian Formulation of the Cultural Perspective in Sociology of Ethnic Relations in Israel," *Megamot,* Vol. 29, No. 1, February 1985, pp. 57-72 (Hebrew).

J. Steiner, *Amicable Agreement Versus Majority Rule: Conflict Resolution in Switzerland,* Chapel Hill: University of North Carolina Press, 0000.

R. A. Stone, *Social Change in Israel: Attitudes and Events,* New York: Praeger, 1982.

P. Strum, *Louis D. Brandeis: Justice for the People,* Cambridge and London: Harvard University Press, 1984.

S. Swirski, *Orientals and Ashkenazim in Israel: The Ethnic Division of Labor,* Haifa: Machbarot Lemechkar Ulebikoret, 1981 (Hebrew).

N. Uriele and A. Barzilai, *The Rise and Fall of the Democratic Movement for Change,* Tel Aviv: Reshafim, 1982 (Hebrew).

J. Van Doorn, *The Soldier and Social Change,* Beverly Hills and London: Sage Publications, 1975.

D. Vital, *The Origins of Zionism,* Oxford: Oxford University Press, 1975.

E. Wald, *The Curse of the Broken Tools,* Jerusalem and Tel Aviv: Schocken, 1987, pp. 149-159 (Hebrew).

A. Weingrod, "Moroccan Jewry in Transition," *Megamot,* Vol. 10, No. 3, 1960, pp. 193-208 (Hebrew).

S. Weiss, "Results of Local Elections," in A. Arian (ed.), *The Elections in Israel 1969,* Jerusalem: Academic Press, 1972, pp. 96-108.

E. Weizman, *On Eagle's Wings,* Tel Aviv: Maariv, 1975 (Hebrew).

R. M. Williams, Jr., *The American Society,* New York: A. Knopf, 1952.

E. Yaar, "Differences in Ethnic Patterns of Socio-Economic Achievement in Israel: A Neglected Aspect of Structural Inquiry," *Megamot,* Vol. 29, No. 4, 1986, pp. 343-412 (Hebrew).

M. Yaari, *The Trials of Our Generation,* Tel Aviv: Sifriat Poalim, 1953, pp. 143-149 (Hebrew).

Y. Yagol, "The Strength of Socialism in Israel," in *Capitalism and Socialism,* Tel Aviv: Min Hayesod, 1963, p. 177-181 (Hebrew).

N. Yanai, *Split at the Top,* Tel Aviv: A. Levin Epstein, 1969 (Hebrew).

N. Yanai, *Political Crises in Israel,* Jerusalem: Keter Publications, 1982 (Hebrew).

G. Yatziv, *The Social Class Base of Political Party Affiliation,* Jerusalem: The Hebrew University of Jerusalem, Department of Sociology, 1979 (Hebrew).

G. Yatziv, *The Heart of the Matter: Essays on Socialism and Democracy in Israel,* Tel Aviv: Adam, 1986 (Hebrew).

A. B. Yehoshua, *Between Right and Right,* Jerusalem and Tel Aviv: Schocken, 1984 (Hebrew).

Y. Yishai, "Israel Right-Wing Jewish Proletariat," *The Jewish Journal of Sociology,* Vol. 24, No. 2, 1982, pp. 87-97.

Y. Yishai, *Interest Groups in Israel,* Tel Aviv and Jerusalem: Am Oved and the Eshkol Institute, The Hebrew University of Jerusalem, 1987 (Hebrew).

Y. Yoran, "An Economy in Structural Transition: The Israeli Economy after the Oil Crisis and Yom Kippur War," *The Economic Quarterly,* Vol. 37, No. 131, 1987, pp. 827-854 (Hebrew).

N. Yuval-Davis, *Matzpen—the Israel Socialist Organization,* Jerusalem: The Hebrew University of Jerusalem, Department of Sociology, 1977 (Hebrew).

M. Zemach, *Attitudes of the Jewish Majority in Israel Toward the Arab Minority,* Jerusalem: The Van Leer Institute, 1980 (Hebrew).

M. Zemach, *Through Israeli Eyes,* New York: The American Jewish Committee, 1987, pp. 20-37.

A. Zizling, "The State Education Law," *Mibefnim,* Vol. 17, No. 1-2, November 1953, pp. 29-33 (Hebrew).

P. Zuzman, "Why is the Burden of Seucrity So Heavy?," in Z. Offer and A. Kober (eds.), *The Cost of the Power,* Tel Aviv: Maarachot, 1984, pp. 17-26 (Hebrew).

Index